Tokyo
0 1000 m
0 1000 yds
Excursions page 198
page 188
page 112
page 140
SHIBUYA-KU
MINATO-KU
CHUO-KU
KOTO-KU
MEGURO-KU
SHINAGAWA-KU
OTA-KU
Tōkyō-kō
Yoyogi-Hachiman
Harajuku
KŌEN
Yoyogi-Kōen
Kokuritsu Yoyogi Kyogijo (National Yoyogi Stadium)
Omotesando Hills
Omotesando
Meiji-Jingumae
Aoyama-
Gaiemmae
AOYAMA REIEN
Nogizaka
Tokyo Midtown
Kokuritsu Shin Bijutsukan (National Art Centre)
Roppongi-dōri
Roppongi
Roppongi Hills
Akasaka
Tameike-Sannō
Toranomon
Kasumigaseki
Uchisaiwaichō
Shimbashi
Higashi-Ginza
Shintomichō
Tsukiji
Shiodome City Centre
Shiodome
HAMA RIKYŪ TEIEN
Tsukishima
Kiyosumi-dōri
Mitsume-dōri
Etchūjima
Monzen-nakachō
Kamiyachō
Onarimon
Sakurada-dōri
Daimon
Tokyo Tower
Zōjō-ji
Shiba-Kōen
Hamamatsuchō
Takeshiba
Hinode
Mita
Kaigan-dōri
Shibaura-Futō
Expressway No 3
Expressway No 2
Expressway No 9
Expressway No 11
Expressway No 1
Expressway Wangan Line
Rainbow Bridge
Komabatōdaimae
Shinsen
Shibuya
Daikan-yama
Ebisu
Nakameguro
Tokyo-to shashin Bijutsukan
SHIZENKYOIKŪEN (NATIONAL PARK FOR NATURE STUDY)
Yamate-dōri
Meguro
Meguro-dōri
Gakugeidaigaku
Meguro Fudo-son
RINSHINOMORI-KŌEN
Fudōmae
Takanawadai
Sengakuji
Daiichi-Keihin
Shinagawa
Gotanda
Ōsakihirokōji
Hara Bijutsukan
Kitashinagawa
Ōsaki
Musashikoyama
Togoshiginza
Togoshi
Nishikoyama
Kanpachi-dōri
Nakahara-kaidō
Ebara-Nakanobu
Senzoku
Ōokayama
Hatanodai
Nakanobu
Ebaramachi
Togoshikōen
Shimoshinmei
Ōimachi
Aomonoyokochō
Samezu
Shinbanba
Tennozu Isle
Nagahara
Senzokuike
Odaiba-Kaihin-kōen
Daiba
Aomi
Fune-no-Kagakukan
Fune-no-Kagakukan (Museum of Maritime Science)
Telecom Centre
Tatsumi

INSIGHT CITY GUIDE

TOKYO

Discovery Channel

APA PUBLICATIONS

Part of the Langenscheidt Publishing Group

INSIGHT GUIDES
TOKYO

Editorial

Editor
Francis Dorai
Series Editor
Dorothy Stannard
Picture Manager
Steven Lawrence
Cartography Editor
Zoë Goodwin

Distribution

UK & Ireland
GeoCenter International Ltd
Meridian House, Churchill Way West
Basingstoke, Hampshire RG21 6YR
Fax: 44-1256 817988

United States
Langenscheidt Publishers, Inc.
36–36 33rd Street, 4th Floor
Long Island City, NY 11106
Fax: 1-718 784 0640

Australia
Universal Publishers
1 Waterloo Road
Macquarie Park, NSW 2113
Fax: 61-2 9888 9074

New Zealand
Hema Maps New Zealand Ltd (HNZ)
Unit D, 24 Ra ORA Drive
East Tamaki, Auckland
Fax: 64-9 273 6479

Worldwide
Apa Publications GmbH & Co. Verlag KG (Singapore branch)
38 Joo Koon Road, Singapore 628990
Tel: 65-6865 1600. Fax: 65-6861 6438

Printing

Insight Print Services (Pte) Ltd
38 Joo Koon Road, Singapore 628990
Tel: 65-6865 1600. Fax: 65-6861 6438

First Edition 1991
Fourth Edition 2005 (Reprinted 2006)
Updated 2007 (Reprinted 2009)

About This Book

The first Insight Guide pioneered the use of creative full-colour photography in travel guides in 1970. Since then, the range has expanded to cater to our readers' need not only for reliable information about their chosen destination but also for a real understanding of that destination. Now, when the Internet can supply inexhaustible – but not always reliable – facts, our books marry text and pictures to provide that much more elusive quality: knowledge. To achieve this, they rely heavily on the authority of locally based writers and photographers.

How to use this book

The book is carefully structured both to convey an understanding of the city and its culture, and to guide readers through its sights and activities:

◆ The Best of Tokyo section at the front helps you to prioritise what you want to see: top family attractions, the best temples, gardens and parks, first-rate city views and shopping, as well as uniquely Tokyo attractions and money-saving tips.

◆ To understand Tokyo today, you need to know both about its past as well as what makes the city tick today. The first section covers the city's history and culture in lively, authoritative essays written by specialists who have lived in Tokyo for many years.

◆ The main Places section provides a full run-down of all the attractions worth seeing. The main places of interest are coordinated by number with full-colour maps.

◆ A list of recommended restaurants and cafés is included at the

end of each chapter in the Places section. The best of these are also described and plotted on the pull-out restaurant map that is provided with this guide.

◆ The Travel Tips section includes all the practical information you will need, divided into four key sections: transport, accommodation, activities (including nightlife, shopping and sports) and an A–Z listing of practical tips. Information may be located quickly by using the index printed on the back cover flap.

◆ Photographs throughout the book are chosen not only to illustrate geography and architecture but also to convey the different moods of the city and the pulse of its people.

◆ A detailed street atlas is included at the back of the book, complete with a full index.

The contributors

This new edition was edited by Insight's Singapore-based managing editor **Francis Dorai**, who restructured the book into its current practical and reader-friendly format. Assisting him in this task was British-born Tokyo resident **Stephen Mansfield**, who passionately chronicles this dynamic city in both his writing and photography. Apart from updating the work already contained in the previous edition, Mansfield was also responsible for writing the history and architecture chapters, updating the Places section and Travel Tips, and providing the brand-new restaurant listings.

The other Tokyo experts whose work features in this edition are: **Angela Jeffs** (Tokyoites); **Alexandra Waldman** (Fashion and Design); **Mark Schreiber** (Janglish and Pink Trade); **Dan Grunebaum** (Tokyo After Dark); and **Robbie Swinnerton** (Cuisine).

Among the prominent photographers whose images bring Tokyo to vivid life are **Richard Nowitz**, **Blaine Harrington** and the aforementioned **Stephen Mansfield**.

Past contributors whose work remains in condensed form in this edition include **Scott Rutherford**, **Miguel Rivas-Micoud**, **Joseph Zanghi**, **Stuart Atkin**, **John Carroll**, **Jim Bowers**, **Guy Fisher** and **Matsutani Yuko**.

In 2007 **Stephen Mansfield** updated all sections except the restaurant listings, which were covered by **Robbie Swinnerton**. The update was supervised by **Low Jat Leng**.

CONTACTING THE EDITORS

We would appreciate it if readers would alert us to errors or outdated information by writing to:

Insight Guides, P.O. Box 7910, London SE1 1WE, England.
Fax: (44) 20 7403 0290.
e-mail: insight@apaguide.co.uk

www.insightguides.com

Introduction

History

Features

Places

Photo Features

Information Panels

Travel Tips

TRANSPORT

ACCOMMODATION

ACTIVITIES

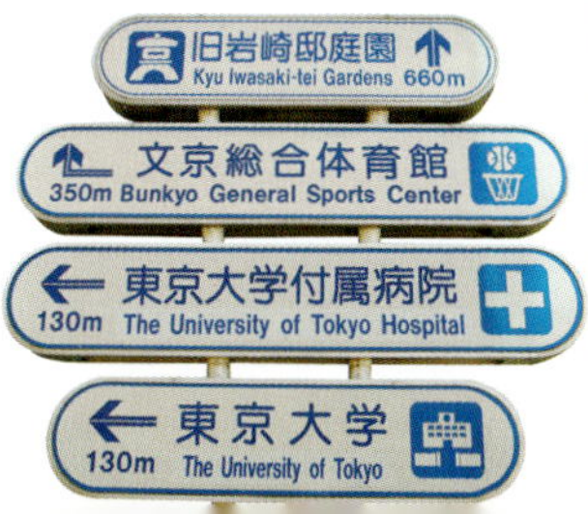

A–Z: PRACTICAL INFORMATION

LANGUAGE

FURTHER READING

Maps

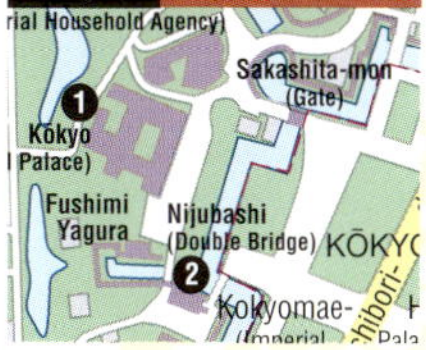

THE BEST OF TOKYO

Setting priorities, saving money, unique attractions... here, at a glance, are our recommendations, plus some tips and tricks even the locals won't always know

TOKYO FOR FAMILIES

These attractions are popular with children, though not all will suit every age group.

- **Tokyo Metropolitan Children's Hall**. Crammed with theme rooms, an art studio for origami and painting, jungle gyms, tubular mazes and miniature houses. *See page 114.*
- **Kiddyland**. Five floors stuffed with a mind-boggling array of toys and cute characters like Hello Kitty and Pokemon. *See pages 116 & 226.*
- **Kite Museum**. A colourful display of traditional Japanese kites. *See page 82.*
- **National Children's Castle**. Playhouses, a music room, a roof play port, and a huge jungle gym. Lots of rainy-day activities. *See page 114.*
- **DisneySea**. An addition to Tokyo Disneyland but requiring a separate ticket and a full day, the themes here are all connected to water. *See page 197.*
- **Tokyo Water Cruise**. Waterbuses ply the Sumida River and its bridges between Asakusa and the Tokyo Bay area. *See page 211.*
- **Ueno Zoo**. Children will enjoy the enclosure where they can pet small animals. *See page 151.*
- **Sony Building**. Older kids with a tech bent will want to check out the latest gadgets, especially the 6th floor devoted to Playstation. *See page 88.*
- **MegaWeb**. Part of Odaiba's unique Palette Town complex; enjoy a giant ferris wheel, the Toyota City Showcase, a virtual-reality arcade and a car museum. *See page 192.*

LEFT: kite making reaches new heights of creativity at the Kite Museum. Some 2,000 kites are on display here, in all shapes and sizes.

ABOVE: La Qua's amazing roller coaster climbs and plunges over tall buildings and then pierces through a ferris wheel.

ONLY IN TOKYO

- **Korakuen Amusement Park/La Qua**. The roller coaster here in space-starved Tokyo rises and plunges over actual buildings and pierces through a ferris wheel. *See page 170.*
- **Meguro Parasitological Museum**. A museum dedicated to those creepy body invaders; the highlight is a 8.8-metre (29-ft) tapeworm removed from a human intestine. Mites, lice and cockroaches add to the fun. *See page 143.*
- **Oedo Onsen**. Soak in authentic thermal springs in the middle of futuristic Odaiba. A theme park mood prevails. *See page 192.*
- **Department store terminals**. A fascinating consumer concept – train platforms feeding passengers straight into department stores – at Nihombashi, Ikebukuro, Shibuya and elsewhere.

BEST WALKS

- **Kyu Shibuya-gawa Promenade**. A river long since filled in provides a traffic-free amble from Omotesando across to Shibuya along a street of cafes, boutiques and a few old houses. *See page 116.*
- **Omotesando-dori**. If you are here for Christmas, this is Tokyo's most enchanting evening stroll. Two rows of zelkova trees are strung with twinkling lights. Expect heaving crowds, though. *See page 115.*
- **Yanaka's backstreets**. Start anywhere among the maze of narrow, winding streets that take you through one of the oldest surviving districts of Tokyo – speckled with a cemetery, temples and old houses. *See page 153.*

LEFT: Jizo statues are commonly found at cemeteries like Yanaka's. They supposedly save souls from hell, especially those of babies.

BEST ARCHITECTURE

- **Fuji TV Building**. Another Kenzo Tange masterpiece, this TV studio and its suspended dome of reinforced tungsten resembles the inside of a TV set. *See page 191.*
- **Prada Aoyoma**. Fluid and luminous, the tinted, diamond-shaped outer panels allow you to peer through the stylish interior. *See page 115.*
- **St Mary's Cathedral**. This early Kenzo Tange masterpiece is covered in dazzling stainless steel to symbolise the light of Christ. *See page 98.*
- **Tokyo Big Sight**. Do a double take when you see the inverted pyramids of a building that seems to defy gravity and common sense, but is still standing. *See page 192.*
- **Tokyo International Forum**. One of the most imaginative buildings in town. Raphael Vinoly's glass chrysalis seems to levitate off the ground. *See page 86.*

ABOVE: Shinjuku Park, in the midst of frenetic Shinjuku, is a delightful oasis to stroll in; take a peek at its domed greenhouse.

BEST PARKS AND GARDENS

- **Hama Rikyu Detached Garden**. An Edo-period stroll garden with a saltwater tidal pond and many ancient pine and cherry trees. *See page 190.*
- **Kiyosumi Garden**. Famous for its extraordinarily beautiful rocks from all over Japan. *See pages 62 & 182.*
- **Koishikawa Botanical Garden**. Although landscaped, the grounds of this Edo-period green haven have a natural and informal feel. *See page 168.*
- **National Park for Nature Study**.Parts of this lovely garden are preserved from the days when Tokyo was part of the Musashino Plain. *See page 143.*
- **Nezu Institute of Fine Arts**. The delighful garden and pond on the grounds of an art museum is light years away from central Tokyo. *See page 114.*
- **Rikugien**. This peaceful stroll garden dating from 1702 contains a teahouse, pond and wooded sections of zelkova, cherry and camphor. *See page 98.*
- **Shinjuku Imperial Garden**. A huge tree-filled garden divided into Japanese, French and English sections. *See page 106.*
- **Yoyogi Park**. A generous swathe of greenery popular with families and couples. *See page 122.*

ABOVE: garden at Nezu Institute of Fine Arts.
LEFT: Prada Aoyoma boutique.

ABOVE: you can expect heartstopping 360-degree views from the 54th floor of the Mori Tower.

Best Tokyo Views

- **Mori Tower**. Enjoy heartstopping 360-degree views of the city from the 54th floor, dubbed Tokyo City View. On a clear day, you can even see Mt. Fuji in the distance. *See page 133.*
- **Sunshine 60**. At 60-storeys, it's still the tallest view point in Tokyo. One of the fastest elevators too; the ride up takes 35-seconds. *See page 96.*
- **Tokyo Metropolitan Government Office**. The free observatory on the 45th floor has splendid views of sky-scrapers, gardens, city landmarks and the bay. *See page 102.*
- **Yebisu Garden Place**. The Restaurant Plaza on the 39th floor offers great views of the bay and westwards towards Shibuya and Shinjuku. *See page 144.*

ABOVE: Venus Fort, an indoor shopping street with an ever-changing artificial sky, has to be seen to be believed.

Most Original Stores

- **AsoBit City**. Stuffed with electronics, cartoon character goods, a shooting gallery and model train set. *See page 225.*
- **Don Quixote.** Crammed pell-mell with character goods, toys, kitchen ware, lifestyle goods and booze. *See page 226.*
- **Tsukumo Robocon Magazine Kan**. Expect cute human-friendly robot models of insects, dogs and turtles. *See page 226.*
- **Tsutsumo Factory**. Sheets of wrapping paper, including traditional *washi* paper. *See page 226.*
- **Hysteric Glamour**. Supercool, loud, body-clinging fashion from a leader in unique street clothing trends. *See page 226.*
- **Tokyu Hands**. A fun hardware store stocked with an endless, often surprising, array of goods. *See page 226.*
- **Venus Fort**. A Greco-Roman complex with an artificial sky that changes from sunrise to dazzling sunlight. *See page 192.*

Best Temples and Shrines

- **Asakusa Kannon Temple (Senso-ji)**. Tokyo's most visited temple hosts dozens of annual events and festivals. Naka-mise, the approach street, is full of craft and dry-food goods. *See page 161.*
- **Gokoku-ji Temple**. Miraculously surviving earthquakes and fires, this magnificent 17th-century temple strangely receives few visitors. *See page 98.*
- **Kanda Myojin Shrine**. One of Tokyo's liveliest shrines, especially on Saturdays when weddings, rituals and festivals are held. *See page 171.*
- **Meiji-jingu Shrine**. An amazing setting in the centre of a forest in the middle of Tokyo. Gravel paths lead to the shrine, an example of pure Shinto design. *See page 120.*
- **Tsukiji Hongan-ji Temple**. An architectural curiosity, this large and imposing temple is based on the ancient Buddhist monuments of South India. *See page 189.*
- **Yushima Seido Shrine**. Unusually dedicated to Confucius, this shrine, with its impressive black building, imparts a sense of kindly authority. *See page 172.*
- **Yushima Tenjin Shrine**. Associated with learning and wisdom; known for its plum and chrysanthemum festivals in Feb and Nov respectively. *See page 171.*

BELOW: paper lantern at the entrance of the Asakusa Kannon Temple.

RIGHT: a visit to a sumo stable to see these hefty wrestlers in action is an eye-opener.
FAR RIGHT: wooden *torii* gate entrance to the Meiju-jingu Shrine in Yoyogi Park.

FREE TOKYO

- **Amlux Toyota Auto Salon**. The largest car showroom in the world has five floors of cars, hands-on displays, a 3-D cinema and other exhibits. *See page 95.*
- **National Diet Building**. Free tour of the House of Councillors when it's not in session. Interesting interior details, like zelkova wood walls, stained glass ceiling and walls covered in gold-thread brocade. *See page 78.*
- **Department store basements**. Mind-boggling food selections, all beautifully presented. Try free samples of assorted food and drink: crackers, pickles, sweets and beer for instance. Isetan *(page 105)* in Shinjuku, and Matsuya *(page 89)* in Ginza are some of the best.
- **Street performers**. Spot weekend performers – musicians, magicians, dancers and others – along Shinjuku-dori, Jingu-bashi bridge at Harajuku, Yoyogi Park, and along Ginza.
- **Sumo stable visit**. Early morning practice sessions are open free to the public, but call the International Sumo Federation for permission to visit. Lower-ranked wrestlers start at 6am, the top players at 9pm. *See page 180.*
- **Temples and shrines**. All temples and shrines are open during daylight hours and, best of all, do not charge entrance fees.
- **Tokyo Stock Exchange**. Free one-hour tour in English. Visit the computer-assisted trading rooms and enjoy a life-size robot demonstrating the hand signals used on the trading floor. *See page 82.*
- **Tsujiki Fish Market**. The world's largest and most interesting fish market opens around 5am (get an extra early wake-up call), but continues throughout the morning. *See page 189.*
- **The Magazine House**. Just stroll in and enjoy over 900 magazines from around the world in a relaxing ambience. Grab a selection and take them with you to the in-house café. *See page 90.*

RIGHT: outdoor *butoh* performance at a Tokyo park.

MONEY-SAVING TIPS

Cheap Food & Drink Alcohol is not especially expensive in Tokyo, particularly when bought at supermarkets or from vending machines found all over the city. Many bars have a "happy hour" that in some cases lasts for as long as two hours. Set lunches and buffets in restaurants can be very cheap, often ¥1,000 or less. Many a thrifty foreign resident has found sustenance at *shishoku* (free food and drink samples) found in department store basements. The freebies range from skewered meats, tofu and slices of cake, to plastic cups of beer and wine.

Cinema Tickets These usually cost in the region of ¥1,800, but on the first Monday of every month in Tokyo, cinema entrance costs only half the usual price. Every Wednesday is also "women's day": tickets for women are reduced to ¥1,000.

Free Views Why pay over ¥1,000 at the Sunshine 60 Building when you can have great free views of the city at the Tokyo Metropolitan Government Office building in West Shinjuku *(see page 102)*, from the top of the Yebisu Garden Place *(see page 144)* in Ebisu, or from the Tokyo Big Sight building on Odaiba *(see page 192)*.

Shopping Refunds Some department stores offer a 5 percent discount (equivalent to the Japanese consumption tax) on purchases that cost over ¥10,000. Make sure to show your passport *(see page 224)*.

皇族下乗

TOKYO ENIGMAS

The world's largest city is crowded and chaotic, even ugly. Yet it pulsates with a youthful energy that stems from a tradition of constant change and reinvention. Drawn to these undercurrents, many visitors find the city strangely addictive

In submitting itself to repeated sessions of radical urban surgery and reconstruction, Tokyo's freshly remodelled surfaces always seem youthful, managing to escape the rigor mortis that envelops many European capitals. With their absolute faith in the new, Tokyoites are the ultimate early adaptors, their city a virtual petri dish for testing the latest in fashion, art and hi-tech. With its attention firmly on the here and now, Tokyo can seem like a city with a short-term memory. Tokyo novelist Masahiko Shimada expressed this preference for the present when he wrote: "Things that happened yesterday are already covered with shifting sand. And last month's events are completely hidden. The year before is twenty metres under, and things that happened five years ago are fossils."

Constantly mutating, Tokyo is a difficult animal to classify; a sense of artificiality and impermanence distinguishes it from all the other well-grounded, great cities of the world. Although Tokyo presents the visitor with glimpses of a mode of life that can seem both enigmatic and indecipherable, it need not be so.

Best experienced district-by-district, street-by-street and building-by-building, Tokyo is a city that should be walked. Seen from a train window or the upper floors of an office block, what appears to be a bland, glacial mass from afar will, on close-up, afford endless visual stimulation in the form of surprising oddities and sudden transitions.

In this ultra-modern mishmash, street and place names have survived intact from the ancient Edo era, sustaining history and nostalgia through their literary and narrative connections, long after their visible features on the cityscape have vanished. While Tokyo's streets, awash with the gizmos and gadgets of a portable, lightweight electronic culture, crackle with static and blink with neon, there is an older side to the city visible in quiet neighbourhoods of timeworn wooden houses and the leafy compounds of ancient temples and shrines.

Tokyo defies interpretation. The rapid changes of its urban landscape give it a vibrancy that seems at odds with the timelessness of its culture. And if that sounds like a contradiction, many more await the visitor. ❑

PRECEDING PAGES: a maze of elevated highways in the Shiodome area; doves in flight at the Yasukuni Shrine. **LEFT:** keeping in touch on the way to work.

主馬佐坂田金時

CREATING THE EASTERN CAPITAL

The rise of the great shogunates and their samurai warlords during the Edo period has instilled in the Japanese culture ways of thinking and behaviour that persist even in modern Tokyo

Travelling across the marshy Musashino Plain, site of present-day Tokyo, Lady Sarashina apparently failed to notice both the imposing riverside temple and the squalid fishermen's huts and nets nearby. The year was 1020 and the 12-year-old girl, her nurse and entourage were on their way to Kyoto after four years in the eastern provinces where her father had served as assistant governor. The journey, however, was not an easy one. The noblewoman recorded in her now-famous diary that the reeds growing across the plain were so high that "the tips of our horsemen's bows were invisible".

Four centuries later, the Musashino plain was still a wild and desolate place. The largest of Japan's three rice-growing plains, the area was blessed with an excellent river system and was the farthest removed from potential invasion from continental Asia. It also held the largest expanse of arable land for the grazing and exercising of warrior steeds.

Settlement of the plain

These auspicious natural features were among the considerations that led a minor member of the Taira clan in the 12th century to build a house and fortified compound on the central of five ridges that descended to the bay. He then renamed his family Edo, which means "Mouth of the River". After his death, the lands were split up and divided among his sons.

LEFT: woodblock print of Edo samurai at a board game.
RIGHT: illustration of courtier ladies from the 11th-century *The Tale of Genji*.

Little was heard of the area until Ota Dokan, a vassal of the Ashikaga shoguns, decided to build a castle above the Hibiya inlet in 1457. Dokan was taking advantage of a confused political climate in which two rival representatives of the shogun in Kyoto claimed dominion over the provinces. Dokan's creation of an efficient, well-drilled conscript army, his efforts to drain the marshes along the bay and create the area's first landfills, and his decision to charge levies on goods in transit at the mouth of the river aroused the suspicion and jealousy of his own lord, head of one of the branches of the Uesugi clan, who had his vassal murdered in 1486. In the century that followed, the powerful Hojo family occupied the site, but they in turn lost control over it after trying to resist the overwhelming forces of the warlord and future shogun Toyotomi Hideyoshi and his powerful ally, Tokugawa Ieyasu. The latter was awarded the eight provinces of the east that included the strategic site of Edo. Despite the insalubrious marshlands that formed the coastal areas and a lack of natural spring water, Ieyasu had the vision to see Edo. The area's position at the point where the Kosho Kaido, a road connecting Edo with the mountain province of Kai and the eastern route to Kyoto, promised a strategically positive placement.

CHADO: THE TEA CEREMONY

Chado – the way of tea – attained its fundamental character under Toyotomi Hideyoshi's tea master, Sen no Rikyu. Simply making tea is not the challenge. The objective is to make it in the right spirit. Years of training go to make the tea-making motions appear effortless. The implements and procedures of *chado* are valuable only towards achieving the aim of showing supreme hospitality.

The technique for making *matcha* (green tea) was brought from China in the 12th century and was first planted in Uji, near Kyoto. *Matcha* – loaded with caffeine – helped meditating Zen monks keep their concentration.

Building Edo

Ieyasu made his formal entry into the town on the first day of the eighth month of 1590. Wasting little time, he had his engineers working almost immediately on the construction of an impregnable castle on the site of Dokan's old fortifications. By the standards of the day, Edo Castle was massive, and when completed in 1638 it was the world's largest. Englishman Richard Cocks, visiting the city in 1616, seems to have been astonished by the scale of the fortress: "We went rowndabout the Kyngs castell or fortress, which I do hould to be much more in compass than the city of Coventry."

Moats, a canal reaching into the salt flats along the bay, and a conduit to transport the city's potable water were all added. Under Ieyasu's orders, earth was transported from the Kanda Hills to the north, and the Hibiya Inlet became the first of Edo's many landfills – a process of transformation that continues to this day. Further landfills were made to the east, forming the *shitamachi*, or "Low City", where the commoners, merchants, artisans, labourers, gardeners and others who worked for the shogun and his entourage lived. Ieyasu's trusted Dependent Lords – those who had supported him in his campaigns – were assigned villas between the outer and inner moats; the Outer Lords – those who had taken sides against Ieyasu at the decisive Battle of Sekigahara in 1600 – were consigned land beyond the outer moats in the vicinity of present-day Kasumigaseki and Hibiya. These estates were intended not only as living quarters but also as a first line of defence on the outer edge of the city.

To keep his lords militarily hobbled and in a constant shortage of funds, Ieyasu introduced the *sankin kotai* (alternate residence duty) system, whereby all lords – both Inner and Outer – were obliged to spend two years in Edo before returning to their provinces. Costly processions were also made compulsory for their exits and re-entrances. Financially bled, they were less likely to raise armies of resistance. The families of these lords were also expected to live permanently in Edo in a virtual state of hostage.

The security-obsessed Ieyasu took the added precaution of setting up barriers along the trunk roads into Edo, where a strict "no women out, no guns in" rule prevailed.

Although the castle was still unfinished, labourers, merchants and craftsmen trickled into the new settlement from the provinces, eventually forming the nucleus of Edo's townspeople. Conforming with the strictly enforced division of classes, the newcomers were accommodated on reclaimed land lying between the castle and the sea. The merchants clustered around the bridge named Nihombashi and the waterways flowing into the port, while the craftsmen inhabited Kanda and Kyobashi, areas to the north and south. The system required that each trade or craft should be identified with a specific quarter, plasterers in one area, dyers, smiths and carpenters in another. In practice, however, the system of strict zoning soon broke down as more people poured into the city.

The "Flowers of Edo"

The final blow to the original plan for segregation came in 1657 with the "Furisode-no-kaji" (Long-Sleeves Fire), which were a series of conflagrations that raged for three days. When the fires eventually abated, hapless residents were subjected to a fierce blizzard. With few buildings left in which to shelter, many froze to death. By the time of the fire, Edo had grown to a staggering 400,000 inhabitants, and a quarter of these died in the flames.

If the speed of destruction was astonishing, so too was the successive reconstruction. Firebreaks were created, and to relieve overcrowding, the city was enlarged and temples and shrines removed to less populous areas. More land was reclaimed from the sea, particularly in areas to the east of the Ginza, such as Fukagawa, Tsukiji and Honjo. A bridge, Ryogokubashi, was built to connect the new areas east of the Sumida River with the main city.

A half-century of sober consolidation followed the fire. Despite the improvements, fire – poetically called the "Flowers of Edo" – remained a scourge. Between 1603 and 1868, no less than 97 major conflagrations broke out. It became stoically accepted that the average inhabitant of Edo would have to vacate at least one home in a lifetime.

As the population grew, the good intentions of the town planners were soon disregarded. In the central districts of Kanda, Nihombashi and Kyobashi, open spaces disappeared as tenement huts were set up. These dwellings, occupied by labourers, tinkers, litter-bearers, itinerant entertainers and clerks from the large dry-goods stores of Nihombashi, were one-

LEFT: Tokugawa Ieyasu established Edo as capital.
ABOVE: typical street scene in Edo.

storey back-street slums fronting onto alleys often less than a yard wide. Toilets and drinking water were communal.

The growth of Edo city

While Edo continued its inexorable expansion, the older, more established cities of Kyoto and Osaka were enjoying a renewed flowering of culture that coincided with the Genroku era (1688–1704). Roughly contemporaneous with England's Restoration period, it bore some of the same flamboyance and florid style, reflected in the gorgeous costumes, oiled and scented wigs of the higher-class geisha, and in the artistic niceties and pretensions of its performing arts. Edo was also beginning to create its own distinctive counter culture. A more gritty, rambunctious affair, it was closer to entertainment and the life of the people than high art, although that would eventually follow.

Edo was an open-air city, all of its attractions on full display. Ryogoku Bridge was a good example of how ordinary people requisitioned space for their entertainment. Ryogoku Hirokoji, a broad firebreak leading to the bridge, was known for its outrageous concentration of freak shows, tricksters, erotic puppets, professional storytellers and models of Dutch galleons and giants, all packed into show tents or jammed behind tea stalls. This area was also the haunt of "silver and golden cats", as the unlicensed prostitutes who staked out this area were known.

Adding to the visible pleasures of Edo were festivals, a love of potted plant fairs, cherry blossom viewing in the spring and great annual summer firework displays along the river. By the early 1720s, Edo had become the most populous city in the world. It had developed its own ethos and style, marked by a love of comic verse, ribald and satirical, of haiku (a Japanese verse form) and of the *kabuki* theatre. This increasingly mercantile society, fixated on the here and now, found in *ukiyo-e*, woodblock prints of the "floating world", the perfect art form to express the transience, the delectable beauty and sadness of existence.

Although the shogunate was generally hostile to Edo's cultural *laissez-faire*, and periodic crackdowns took place, the cultural life of the irrepressible Edokko (Edo residents) proved too resilient. When the flamboyant *kabuki* theatre was banished to Asakusa, a district already boasting the important Senso-ji (or Asakusa Kannon) Temple and the pleasure quarter of Yoshiwara a short distance away in the rice fields to the north, the area's position as the foremost pleasure district was assured.

WEALTHY MERCHANTS

Many merchants amassed great wealth during the Edo period and built impressive homes made of thick, fire-resistant mud walls covered in tiles, then stucco finished in shiny black paint. At the same time, impoverished samurai were growing more dependent on the merchant class to provide them with loans.

Attemping to contain the merchants, the government introduced prohibitions that were cleverly evaded. Forbidden to wear quality fabrics, the merchants lined the inner sections of rough garments in the finest silk; prevented from building homes with more than two stories, they added extra interior levels to existing structures.

Calamities

A series of disasters took place in 1854 and the following year. Two powerful earthquakes, which killed over 9,000 people, were followed by torrential downpours that caused flooding to low-lying areas. There was also a cholera epidemic, famines and an unprecedented crime wave. These calamities were superstitiously blamed on the appearance of Commodore Perry's Black Ships.

Anchoring at the mouth of the bay, the American warships had arrived the year before, demanding that Japan restore imperial rule and open its doors to trade. Six months later, Perry returned and a treaty was signed, effectively ending over 250 years of isolation. The shoganate's inability to defend the country from the "Southern Barbarians" shattered its credibility and accelerated its demise. In 1859, the first US consul, Townsend Harris, arrived and set up a mission at Zenpuku-ji Temple in Azabu.

A coalition of powerful families from the western and southern provinces seized control of Edo in 1868. A formal procession led the young Emperor into Edo, and the Meiji Restoration thus began. The city was renamed Tokyo, or the "Eastern Capital", and the Meiji era, which was to last till 1912, saw a period of rapid industrialisation and prosperity.

Westernisation of Tokyo

In the flurry of excitement and activity at the creation of a new capital and the abolition of the old class system, many of the physical and mental trappings of the old feudal city were swept away. A shift in perception was even felt among the curious foreigners who arrived to see what it was all about. Isabella Bird, the intrepid Victorian travel writer, observed that "it would seem an incongruity to travel to Yedo [Edo] by railway, but quite proper when the destination is Tokiyo".

Other changes were taking place to the configuration of the city. The eastern bank of the Sumida River, the home of the poorer townspeople and impoverished samurai, was the first area of the city where factories and yards were built. Housing conditions along the river and further east were deplorable and exacerbated by flooding. The river could be expected to flood on average once every three years.

For the middle classes, on the other hand, things were very different. A faddish interest in everything Western, from food, clothing and hairstyles, to the new European-style brick buildings that were springing up, was accompanied by the introduction of telephones, beer halls, department stores and gas lighting. New roads were constructed, and tens of thousands of rickshaws, horse-drawn buses and bicycles crowded the streets. Many working people adopted Western clothing – a welcome convenience for the office, shop

LEFT: *ukiyo-e* woodblock print. **ABOVE:** the approach of the American "Black Ships" in 1853.

and factory workers. Men abandoned their topknots, and women, in imitation of the newly enlightened empress, stopped the tradition blackening of their teeth.

Rise of the Taisho period

Japan's military campaigns in China, its victory over Russia in 1904, and colonisation of Taiwan and Korea provided it with the raw materials, commodity markets and financial gains that assisted it in its last phase towards a full capitalist economy, with Tokyo as its engine of growth.

Japan's extraordinary Meiji era came to an end in 1912 with the death of the Meiji Emperor. In accordance with a tradition that stretched back over a millennia, the funeral was a Shinto rite. The hearse that passed through the hushed streets of Tokyo was drawn by five white oxen and escorted by an entourage of bowmen and banner-bearers. Sand was laid over the streets to muffle the sound of the wheels.

The Taisho era (1912–1926) provided a short respite from the dynamism of the preceeding era and the traumas of the next one. During the period, the authorities temporarily relaxed their hold on civil conduct, a reaction perhaps to the physically and morally corrupted state of its central symbol, the Taisho

TODAI: A LIFELONG TROPHY

Britain has its Oxbridge, the US its Harvard and Yale. But none comes close to the near-divine status given by Japanese to the University of Tokyo, or Todai. Its graduates are virtually guaranteed excellent career opportunities in the civil service and top Japanese corporations.

Because of the university's hallowed status – it dates back to 1877 – competition for entry to Todai and other top universities is very stiff; parents place relentless pressure on their children to study very early in life. The proliferation of *juku* (cram schools), which prepare students for compulsory school advancement tests, is testament to the extraordinary emphasis the nation places on education.

In 1992, then-prime minister Kiichi Miyazawa introducted measures to reduce Todai's over-representation in the civil service to less than half of all employees hired by government agencies. One of these measures prohibited graduates attending interviews from revealing their alma mater. Miyazawa's target was achieved in most ministries by 1996, and his efforts also resulted in a decision by several major companies not to consider the university background in hiring new graduates.

However, prejudices die hard, and today, students from University of Tokyo are still popularly portrayed as the brains behind the nation.

Emperor. Portrayed as a syphilitic lunatic, partial to bouts of drinking, womanising and eccentric behaviour, the new emperor was certainly a poor successor to his father.

Innovation in the arts, political dissidence and the so-called "new women" met with equal measures of admiration and opprobrium. The brevity of the Taisho experimentation did see the advance of the women's movement, however, as well as the growth of unions, and the brief flowering of the so-called "Taisho Democracy", but in terms of historical events and chronology, the Taisho era was less history than experience. The period did, however, represent a very real search for a modern cultural identity, an effort that to some extent is still going on today.

The Great Kanto Earthquake

By the 1920s Tokyo's population, many of them shoehorned into the more crowded quarters to the east, stood at over two million, a relevant statistic for what would be the most noteworthy event of the era. At precisely one minute before noon on 1 September 1923, as charcoal and wood fires and stoves were being lit for lunch, the Great Kanto Earthquake struck.

The firestorm that engulfed and destroyed three-quarters of the city and the adjacent area of Yokohama claimed 140,000 lives. Aftershocks rocked the city for days and the fires raged on, creating a hellish, charred landscape. The Sumida River was dense with the corpses of victims who had tried to escape the flames by jumping into the river, only to find its waters boiling. In his memoirs, film director Akira Kurosawa recalls walking through the old garment district near the Sumidagawa just hours after the earthquake had struck: "In some places the piles of corpses formed little mountains. On top of one of these mountains sat a blackened body in the lotus position of Zen."

Once again, Tokyo began to reconstruct itself, literally from the ashes. Parks and reinforced-concrete apartments were the most visible responses to the disaster. More people moved into the city, however, swelling its population and putting new demands on its transportation system. Buses and taxis began to appear, and in 1925, the Yamanote loop line was completed, enlarging the commuter belt and spurring the expansion of new urban subcentres like Shibuya and Shinjuku.

In the following year, the ailing Taisho Emperor passed away. As the shadows of militarism lengthened, the fashions and tastes of a more liberal and generous age were deemed subversive. With the military back at the helm and a highly acquiescent new Showa Emperor (1926–1989), generals and officers were the new arbiters of taste, and the "new women" went underground for a good decade before re-emerging from the rubble of defeat.

World War II

Japan's entry into the war made Tokyo the target of air raids whose intensity few could have imagined at the time. The sense of impending doom that hung over the city during the closing days and months of World War II was captured by Robert Guillain, a correspondent for *Le Monde*. Sensing the atmosphere of despair and doom in the city at the time, Guillain wrote, "The raids had still to begin, and yet, night after night, an obsession gripped the city plunged into darkness by the blackout, an obsession that debilitated and corroded it more than even the appearance overhead of the first enemy squadrons was

FAR LEFT: Meiji-era schoolboys posing for the camera.
LEFT: arched entrance, University of Tokyo.
RIGHT: Tokyo Station, circa 1920.

THE NEXT QUAKE?

Officials estimate that if a high-magnitude quake were to hit Tokyo today, half a million buildings may be destroyed, with casualties of up to 100,000.

able to do. Tokyo was a giant village of wooden boards, and it knew it."

Many of the firebombs fell on the civilian populations of Sumida-ku and other wards to the east during the 102 raids that were launched between January 1945 and Japan's surrender in August. Robert McNamara, then captain in the US Army Air Force – whose name would later be forever linked with the Vietnam War – took part in the planning of the raids, and he recalled later that "in a single night we burnt to death 100,000 civilians … men, women, and children."

Tens of thousands of residents of Fukagawa also perished that night beneath the fuselages of over 300 B-29s, which dropped lethal incendiary cylinders that the locals nicknamed "Molotov flower baskets". When asked how they spent the return flights after raining death and unimaginable grief on tens of thousands of unprotected Japanese civilians, the American crews routinely described listening to jazz on the radio or handing around pornographic photographs as diversions.

Post-war years

Reconstruction and economic growth took centrestage in the post-war years, but poverty and the US military presence continued for some years. The Tokyo Olympics in 1964 provided a much needed boost to the economy as well as national pride. Despite Japan's phenomenal economic progress over the following years, there were growing undercurrents of social unrest that came to a head in 1960 when hundreds of thousands of people took to the streets of Tokyo to protest the renewal of the Japan-US security treaty.

The economy, however, remained the main focus. Fixed exchange rates were dropped in 1971 and, after the Plaza Agreement in 1985, which saw the creation of the Group of Five (G5) countries (US, Japan, West Germany, UK and France) – a coordinated effort to make the US dollar fall in value – the rise of the yen seemed unstoppable. This led to artificially inflated asset values, speculation fuelling the so-called "bubble economy", and a construction frenzy the likes of which the city had never seen. The inevitable collapse in land and stock values came in 1990, leaving Japanese banks with mountains of bad debts. The 1995 sarin gas attack on the Tokyo subway by members of the doomsday cult Aum Shinrikyo added to the sense of unease that characterised Japan's "lost decade".

Present-day Japan

At the time of writing, Japan is experiencing its longest period of sustained economic growth since World War II. Much of this is dependent on a relatively weak yen facilitating healthy export levels and on the demand from a resource- and technology-hungry China. Tokyo is also presently in the grip of a building boom, with new housing complexes and mini shopping and leisure cities rising from newly razed land whose former function is quickly consigned to the past.

If the restless remodelling of the city seems to hint at a weak preservation ethic, one must remember that change itself *is* a tradition in Japan. And that renewal is second nature for Tokyo, where almost anything seems possible – even the recreation of history. ❑

LEFT: waving the flag for nationalism.

The Royal Family

Royal mania hit a high on 9 June 1993, when tens of thousands of well wishers turned out for a glimpse of the royal couple, Princess Masako and Crown Prince Naruhito, the heir to Japan's 2,600-old Chrysanthemum Throne.

The bubbly princess had given up a promising diplomatic career to marry Crown Prince Naruhito. Hopes, however, that she would become a "royal diplomat" who would give a human face in the manner of European princesses to the protocol-ridden Imperial Court were quickly dashed. The initial spontaneity was smartly squashed by the notoriously protocol-ridden Imperial Household Agency, and the princess was soon seen behaving in the self-effacing tradition of female royals.

A long-awaited pregnancy ended in miscarriage in 1999, but in December 2001 Masako gave birth to a girl, Princess Aiko. As the practice of crowning a female as Empress was terminated under the 1889 Meiji Constitution, which now limited the throne to male descendants, the pressure on a woman now in her 40s to produce a future Emperor has been intense.

Although the Agency preferred to keep imperial family problems under wraps, it had not been able to muzzle the reasons for Masako's long absence from public view. Hospitalised first in December 2003 with shingles, a stress-induced viral infection, she was also said to have suffered from a stress-induced adjustment disorder.

Masako's problems were not the first of its kind in the modern history of the court. In 1963, after a miscarriage, Empress Michiko, then Crown Princess, went into a three-month-long retreat at the Imperial villa. The first commoner to marry into the monarchy, she had to deal with hostility for the miscarriage from both the Agency and other royals. In a series of nervous disorders characteristic of royal females, the Empress lost her voice for several months in 1993 due to "strong feelings of distress".

The discontent built up inside the Crown Prince Naruhito over the years finally exploded at a press conference on 10 May 2004 during which he made surprisingly blunt comments in defence of his wife and hinted that members of the Agency were involved in repressing his wife's personality and denying her talents.

With the limitations placed on the Japanese press, virtually all royal "scoops" come from overseas. What some members of the Agency reportedly do is leak information to Japanese reporters, who then feed these facts to foreign newspapers. Once the stories have appeared overseas, the Japanese press then publishes these stories locally. Prince Naruhito thus bypassed the whole convoluted process by talking directly to the media.

RIGHT: Princess Masako with baby Aiko in 2002.

The succession crisis has now been temporarily resolved after Princess Kiko, the wife of the Crown Prince's younger brother Akishino, gave birth to a male heir, Prince Hisahito, in 2006.

It seems that what the Agency most fears is the common touch. The general public would certainly welcome a more relaxed, approachable style. Perhaps the Agency should, for once, give the people what they want. ❑

Decisive Dates

Chronicle of Tokyo

4000 BC: Geological activity causes Tokyo Bay to rise to the lower edges of the present Yamanote ridge.
AD 628: Senso-ji Temple founded in Asakusa district.
1180: First recorded use of the name Edo.
1457: Ota Dokan builds a fortified compound at Edo.
1590: Warlord Toyotomi Hideyoshi makes Edo his base.
1592: Hideyoshi attempts to invade Korea.

1600: Edo Period begins as Tokugawa Ieyasu takes control after defeating rivals in Battle of Sekigahara.
1603: Tokugawa returns capital to Edo.
1639: The system of national seclusion introduced.
1657: The notorious "Long-Sleeves Fire" devastates Edo.

Cultural Advances and Natural Calamities

1688–1704: The cultural flowering of Edo under the influence of the Genroku era.
1703: The 47 *ronin* incident occurs.
1707: Mount Fuji erupts, covering Edo in a shroud of ash.
1720s: Edo is proclaimed as the largest city in the world.
1742: Floods kill about 4,000 in Edo.
1804–29: The Bunka-Bunsei period marks the zenith of Edo merchant culture.
1853: Commodore Perry arrives with US naval ships. Japan forced to accept trade and diplomatic contact; shogunate weakened as a result.
1855: Earthquake kills over 4,000 in Edo. Floods and epidemics follow.

The Return of Imperial Rule

1868: Meiji Restoration returns the emperor to power. Last shogun Yoshinobu retires without resistance. The capital is renamed Tokyo.
1869: Yasukuni Shrine is established for Japan's war dead. Tokyo's first rickshaws appear on its streets.
1872: Samurai class abolished by imperial decree. First train service runs from Shimbashi to Yokohama.
1874: Tokyo's first gas lights start operations.
1882: The Bank of Japan established in Nihombashi district.
1883: The Rokumeikan, Tokyo's first Western-style building, is completed in Hibiya.
1889: New constitution promulgated.
1894: Marunouchi becomes the site of a European-style business quarter known as "London Town".
1895: Japan wins Sino-Japanese War.
1905: Japan wins Russo-Japanese War.
1910: Japan annexes Korea.
1912: Taisho emperor ascends throne.
1918: Japan hit hard by economic chaos; rice riots occur.
1922: The Imperial Hotel, designed by Frank Lloyd Wright, opens in Hibiya.
1923: Great Kanto Earthquake kills tens of thousands. Much of the city destroyed.
1925: Completion of Yamanote loop line.
1926: Taisho emperor dies. Hirohito ascends throne to begin Showa Period.
1927: Asia's first subway line opens in Tokyo, between Asakusa and Ueno.

War and Renewal

1931: Japanese occupy Manchuria. Japan leaves League of Nations.

1936: A bloody but unsuccessful military uprising in Tokyo; one of many in the 1930s.
1937: Japan begins military advances in China.
1941: Japan attacks Pacific and Asian targets. Within a year, Japan occupies most of East Asia and the western Pacific.
1945: American massive bombing raids on civilian targets. In August, atomic bombs dropped on Hiroshima and Nagasaki. Japan surrenders. General MacArthur sets up HQ in Tokyo. Start of US Occupation.
1946: New constitution under Allied occupation forces.
1952: San Francisco Peace Treaty settles all war-related issues; Japan returned to sovereignty, except for some Pacific islands, including Okinawa. Japan regains pre-war industrial output.
1955: Socialist factions merge to form the Japan Socialist Party; Liberals and Democrats create the Liberal Democratic Party (LDP).
1958: Building of Tokyo Tower completed.
1960: First demonstrations against renewal of the US-Japan security treaty.
1964: Summer Olympics held in Tokyo. Bullet train begins service between Tokyo and Osaka.
1968–9: Tokyo becomes focus of massive student unrest.
1970: Writer Mishima Yukio's spectacular ritual suicide at the HQ of the Self-Defense Forces in Ichigaya.
1972: US returns Okinawa to Japan, but establishes bases.
1980s: Japan's economy becomes world's second-most powerful. Banks extend loans to corporations and small companies based on inflated land values.
1989: Hirohito dies, son Akihito begins Heisei Period.

Perils of a New Era

1990: The so-called "economic bubble" of over-inflated land values and overextended banks begins to deflate, leading to economic slowdown.
1991: Opening of Kenzo Tange-designed Tokyo Municipal Government Office (Tocho).
1992: Japan's worst post-war recession begins.
1993: Series of scandals, including institutionalized bribes and collusion, creates backlash of voters. Members of LDP replaced with independents. New coalition government lasts seven months. Another coalition takes over, led by socialists.
1995: Aum Shinrikyo, a doomsday religious cult, releases sarin nerve gas in the Tokyo subway system, killing 12 people and sending Tokyo's citizens into a sheer panic.
1996: LDP returns to power.
1999: Efforts to revive economy continue. Nuclear accident at uranium processing plant near Tokyo.
2001: Junichiro Koizumi, a self-proclaimed reformist, is elected as prime minister.
2004: Japan sends troops to join the international coalition in Iraq, a move opposed by the majority of Japanese.
2006: Shinzo Abe takes over as prime minister, and almost immediately upsets Asian countries with revisionist comments about Japan's wartime activities.
2007: Elections are held for Tokyo governor; controversial right-winger Shintaro Ishihara is re-elected for a third consecutive term. ❑

LEFT: woodblock print of 17th-century Nihombashi Bridge. **RIGHT:** birthday celebration of the late Emperor Hirohito.

通常価格

TOKYOITES

Tokyo's inhabitants are a different breed, say Japanese from other parts of the country, but Tokyoites will admit only to being more cosmopolitan. They're certainly more reticent, more savvy, and more receptive toward change

Whether the economy is up or down, visitors to Tokyo are apt to receive the impression of a well-fed, stylishly dressed, decently behaved and well ordered society, a view corroborated by a new wave of hi-tech buildings, well-stocked shops and an exuberant street life.

All things being relative, Tokyo's standard of living remains high. It is reduced only from the giddy days of the late 1980s when gold leaf was sprinkled on rice and people bought new fridges instead of cleaning good ones.

Of course, every modern city has its problems. In Tokyo's case, the first of these is a matter of terminology. Ask its inhabitants what they call themselves and there may be puzzlement. The nearest equivalent term to a Parisian, New Yorker or Londoner is Edokko (a child of Edo). However, the old rules no longer apply; the only ties left are those bound by sentiment.

Since the days of Edo

For years after the Meiji Restoration, which took off in 1868 with the renaming of the city from Edo (Entrance to an Inlet) to Tokyo (Eastern Capital) and the associated move of the Imperial Court from Kyoto (Western Capital) to Kanto, anyone living in Edo who could claim at least three generations' allegiance to the city could call themselves Edokko.

Many families trace their roots back a dozen or more generations in the city. But what of

PRECEDING PAGES: flashy young Tokyoites.
LEFT: celebrating Adults Day in Ueno Park.
RIGHT: young Japanese couple relaxing in Yoyogi Park.

GERM PHOBIC

The Japanese obsession with cleanliness has reached new heights with recent products on the market.

Cosmetics maker Shiseido Company has isolated a substance called noneal as the source of body odour in older people. A line of shampoos, lotions and deodorants inhibits the breakdown of fatty acid in skin that creates noneal. Health drink Etiquette Water Fruit contains enzymes and minerals said to banish bad breath and underarm odour, while Elizabeth Arden Japan's Lip Lip Hooray neutralises compounds that cause bad breath. And SSK Corp promises that its deodorant T-shirts will eliminate odours on exposure to the sun's rays.

those immigrants who have lived in Tokyo only 50 years? Would they describe themselves as Tokyo-*jin* (Tokyo people)? No, they say. In English, the term could be Tokyoite; but in Japanese, really, there is no translation.

Culture of convenience

The city's culture of convenience is impressive. Tokyo still operates as the collection of independent communities it once was, each insular and self-reliant. There is no need to cross the city to make a purchase as facilities are generally just around the corner: the butcher, the baker, the *tatami* maker and, more recently, the all-purpose convenience store, or *konbini* as it's known. Stocking everything from hot take-out meals, magazines, deodorants and stationary to socks and prophylactics, there is said to be a store every 500 metres in Tokyo. The city's random style of development obviously works. One can only marvel that an organism so complex can run so smoothly, day after day.

Well before dawn, frozen tuna rank in their hundreds at Tsukiji fish market. By 7am, hundreds of thousands of children are on their way to school. Not long after, the city swells with 12 million commuters (the average journey is over an hour in each direction) and then empties through the evening, like an ever-elastic, ever-accommodating balloon.

The statistics for keeping this well-oiled machine ticking are frightening. Remember, this is a country with no natural resources whatsoever. Tokyo relies on a steady stream of imported raw materials – to create manufactured items for export and to cosset the population in the manner to which it is accustomed.

Tokyo Metropolis (part of the Greater Tokyo Megapolis that is home to 26 percent of Japan's total population) is located near the centre of the Japanese archipelago, on the Pacific coast of its largest island, Honshu. A vast self-governing unit, Tokyo Metropolis consists of 23 special inner wards (*ku*), 27 cities, five towns and eight villages. As of February 2000, the declining population of the Tokyo metropolitan area stood at 12 million. This is due in part to the lowest-ever national birthrate (about one child per family); many young women in the capital are loathe to give up their independence to become a mere wife and mother.

There is also the phenomenon of "urban flight". A severe residential drain from the wards of Chiyoda, Chuo, Minato and Shinjuku began in 1980, as property developers broke up established communities with offers people simply could not refuse. Some people moved upmarket to, say, Setagaya-ku; the majority escaped altogether to adjoining prefectures.

ROOM FOR RUDENESS

Paul Theroux comments in *The Great Railway Bazaar*: "The Japanese have perfected good manners and made them indistinguishable from rudeness."

One segment of the population that has grown in recent years is the homeless. Many of them are elderly, others are victims of the recession, while more than a few have chosen to be vagrants in preference to mainstream responsibilities. They congregate largely in major rail stations, parks, along riverbanks and in Senroku's Sanya district in downtown Bunkyo-ku, where itinerant labourers are picked up each morning for work in the construction industry and in the nuclear plants.

Little elbow room

If Tokyoites have one common grumble, it is that their city is too crowded. This is particularly true of train stations at peak periods and popular sightseeing spots at holiday time. The high level of safety has fostered an environment in which, when push literally comes to shove, commuters who have little hesitation in retaliating likewise. Late middle-aged women are the most aggressive, perhaps getting their own back after years of repression. Such behaviour may trigger strong reactions in the West, but ironically, the lack of fear here allows for isolated incidents of amazing rudeness.

Overcrowding in the city has tested Japan's pride in a cultural homogeny that includes consideration for others, making many Tokyoites appear self-centred on occasion. Crowds invariably step over a hobo in the gutter without concern as to whether the person is dead or alive. It has been observed that, apart from family and close friends, most Tokyoites are not concerned about the rest of humanity.

But yet crime figures are low. Tokyo is one of the few cities in the world where a salaried worker can pass out drunk on the street and wake up to find his wallet intact. Temples and shrines stay open day and night without incident or loss. The only places graffiti tends to be seen is where young Westerners hang out.

LEFT: packing commuters like sardines in Shinjuku.
RIGHT: film poster depicting pressures of subway travel.

By contrast, homicides and robberies are on the increase. And the incidence of rape in Tokyo is high, especially in summer when windows and doors are left open. Statistics are hard to cite as assaults tend to go unreported.

Newcomers speak of intolerable noise levels, especially in major shopping areas and railway stations. Sounds are seemingly layered one upon another, jostling for attention. The only way to maintain sanity is to do as the locals do: edit out or switch off completely.

All this allows one to view cultural phenomena such as *pachinko* (pinball machines) and *manga* (comics) as psychological safety valves. In the world of *pachinko,* the deliber-

ately induced sensory overload is hypnotic and gridlocks players into a mindless world focused purely on gambling. In the same way, *manga* *(see text box on page 35)* is perhaps an escape route for repressed desires – just another price for maintaining a largely docile society. While Japan's pornography is largely produced in Osaka, *manga* is from Tokyo.

The city's population is made up of Edokko, more recent Tokyoites, transients such as the homeless, street-traders (largely Israelis, who find work as language teachers), tourists – and small pockets of immigrants (who work in industries and services shunned by locals). They are as likely to live in private apartments as in state-subsidised estates or wooden houses without baths, in which case people resort to that wonderful institution, the *sento*, or bathhouse. The more wealthy may also live in luxurious homes or period houses of wood and paper.

While many people continue to rent homes, a growing number, especially in the inner and outer suburban areas, are buying property, grabbing the opportunity to secure loans while interest rates remain low and land prices in all but the most chic areas of Tokyo continue their long, seemingly endless decline.

Land ownership rules in Tokyo. Forget about town planning or green belt conservation. As a result, small farms operate along-

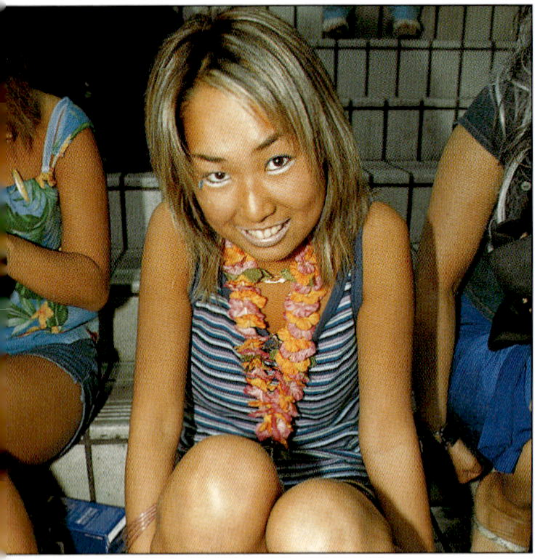

side factories; a neon-lit *pachinko* parlour may stand amid paddy fields. A family can go away on holiday and return to find a new building just inches from their own. The result is a startling mish-mash of the good, the bad and the ugly which, while never broadly pleasing to the eye, is full of interest and always immensely human.

Young people are attracted to the city's unrestricted lifestyles and abundance of part-time jobs. Farmers from distant rural areas converge for the winter and return for spring planting. Foreign students come to study; expats to fulfil contracts. Japanophiles dig deep into the culture; travellers make money (by teaching English, selling on the streets, or working in bars and clubs) and have fun.

The economic downturn of the early 1990s resulted in a crackdown on illegal immigrants, which the city has so covertly welcomed when employment was high and menial jobs that no local wanted abounded. But today, overall figures of foreigners have risen, with large numbers of Koreans, Chinese, Japanese-Brazilians and Filipinos settling in Tokyo.

About 270,000 foreigners were registered in Tokyo as of 1999. Many are third- or fourth-generation residents. Some are relocated company executives, more than a few are students, while a number are married to Japanese. Illegal immigrants – many from Southeast Asia – keep a low profile which, especially in the exploitative sex industry, works against their interests.

The indigenous population is ageing fast, giving rise to concern as to how welfare services will manage in the future. One local study forecasts a "Silver Society" of 2½ million aged 65 and above by the year 2010. For now, the youth market keeps Tokyo's domestic economy afloat. It is an intensely spoiled generation, with high disposable incomes due to over-indulgent parents and easily available jobs. More than 80 percent of the Japanese have mobile phones; the most frequent users are those under 20. Oddly enough, signs and announcements on the subways and trains exhort commuters not to use their phones onboard.

As the corporate strategy of lifetime employment breaks down, the educational system shows signs of strain. With more and more young people rejecting the system, the Education Ministry is pressured to make changes. But the wheels of progress grind slowly. In the meantime, truancy is rising, as is the number of youths who refuse to attend school at all.

Tokyo small talk

When meeting a stranger, a Tokyoite asks: Where are you from? How old are you? Are you married? What is your hobby? The answers will enable them to address and treat the other party in a manner appropriate to their own situation. The custom of giving *meishi* (name cards) is a ritualised extension of this.

Ask a woman her hobby and she is as likely to say shopping as the study of tea ceremony.

Ask her husband and he will (wistfully) say golf – realistically, he watches baseball or *sumo* wrestling, or goes fishing. Many Tokyoites spend most of their money and time on alcohol (used without discretion as a social tool for loosening up), eating and karaoke.

Every Tokyoite considers himself or herself middle-class, egalitarian and politically disenchanted, from *kitamachi-jocho* (downtown folk) and *yamanote-fu* (uptown snobs) to all the people in between. They are certainly savvy and more *ekakoshi* (politely reticent) than their country cousins, who think Tokyoites are from another planet altogether. There is a certain aloofness about the Tokyoite that is obvious to other Japanese. Tokyo people are not like the rest of us, they say. Tokyoites see themselves as cosmopolitan (meaning there are more signs in English and they make an effort to notice that not all Westerners are American).

Hungry for change

What keeps Tokyo vibrant and alive is the way in which it so richly and confidently reinterprets its own age-old norms and practices as well as imported Western ones. Nothing ever stands still. Fads and fashions come and go, as do buildings, businesses and people. The city is a living organism, hungry for change and renewal, and eternally in a state of flux.

The catastrophic effects of a possible major earthquake hitting Tokyo are a concern and there is talk of relocating political functions. Such a project is seen as "wasteful" by Governor Shintaro Ishihara, who believes the city's very concentration is "the essence of civilisation". He envisions its transformation as "an international exchange city thronged with millions of visitors".

If the prospect of tourist hordes on the loose is unpalatable, enjoy the already limited breathing space now – while you can. ❑

FAR LEFT: Shibuya trendite with tinted hair and a tan.
ABOVE: *manga* comics; and *pachinko* machines.

MANGA MANIA

For centuries, *manga* simply meant "sketch". The idea of satirising the human condition originated in the Heian Period with a drawing of birds and animals mimicking people at play. The 1950s bred a new type of *manga* – *gekiga* – aimed at young people and bearing increasingly realistic titles. The first weekly, *Shonen Magazine*, was published in 1960. Since then, growing demand has seen subjects extend from children's fantasy and romance to sadistic pornography and even business management. Today's top seller is *Shonen Jump*, a thickly bound weekly for men with a circulation of nearly 4 million. The women's version, *Ribon*, sells 1.5 million copies.

FESTIVALS

Exuberant *mikoshi* (shrine) fights indicate the Japanese willingness to embrace frivolity within the solemn. In the same way, cherry blossom picnics, though not religiously significant, are adhered to as a yearly spring ritual

One of the great thrills of travelling in Japan – for first-time visitor, foreign resident and Japanese alike – is running across a local festival. Almost every day of spring, summer and autumn, a festival takes place in Japan. Seasonal differences are the basis for almost the whole system of festivals; exceptions are observances of historic events, foundings, birthdays and the like.

Yet even the way in which events are feted may take the nature of a seasonal observance, especially if the festival is an old one. Culture Day (November 3), the birthday of the Meiji Emperor, is an example. If the seasons are seen in terms of the emotional effects they produce, then the soft melancholy of autumn and early winter puts one in the mood to read and sop up culture. Thus, the Meiji Emperor's birthday did not become Family Day but, with great psychological precision, Culture Day.

Like the Koreans, the Japanese sensitivity to the character and changes of the seasons is reflected in their festivals.

A kind of holy madness

One basic element in a typical Japanese festival is the *mikoshi*, or portable shrine. The god-presence embodied in the *mikoshi* is carried about the village or urban neighbourhood on the shoulders of the young men of the community, although women are increasingly permitted to join, with ritual purification beforehand and much drinking of *sake*.

A common practice is to jounce the *mikoshi* to express the exuberance of the god; the amount of *sake* drunk, too, is a manifestation of the god in a kind of holy madness. In communities where nearby shrines have festivals on the same day, *mikoshi* fights are a custom. The youths carrying one *mikoshi* may try to jostle their way through and "win" over other *mikoshi* on the same road.

Japanese festivals often bear strong sexual symbolism, whether implicit or explicit. The god of a number of shrines scattered about the country is manifested as a huge phallus, which is carried about the streets at festival time.

The two major observances of the year are Oshogatsu (New Year) and Obon, similar to "All Souls" day. Occurring in mid-winter and late summer, respectively, both are celebratory occasions that bring the extended family together. Oshogatsu is a series of rituals and observances that lasts many days. There are, in fact, two New Years – a Greater New Year and a Lesser one. The Greater New Year starts with the new moon and the Lesser New Year, 15 days later with the full moon.

The ending of one year and the beginning of the next is a time of purification and an occasion to start afresh. Although a religious festival, the event is centred on the individual and the family, not the temple. The mood is calm, optimistic and joyful.

The New Year starts with a thorough cleaning of the house at the end of December – *shoji* screens are repapered and worn things replaced – and ends either on January 3, 5 or 7. There are different things to do at set times during the festival – special decorations to put up and special food to prepare. The symbolism behind them hinges on the values of longevity, prosperity and happiness.

Purification is also a major theme of the Lesser New Year, which involves religious ancient practices associated with agriculture and rice. To urbanised Japanese, however, it is a nostalgic occasion to dress up.

FAR LEFT: having a bawl during a temple festival.
ABOVE: *mikoshi* shrine; Shinto priest headgear.

January, February

New Year's Day (Shogatsu) is a national holiday. People don traditional attire and visit Buddhist temples and Shinto shrines to make wishes for the new year. *Sake* is drunk during the first few days of the year.
Water Purification Rites: January 10–12 at Kanda Myojin Shrine. Young people coming of age this year use buckets to pour freezing water over themselves and undergo other cleansing rituals.
Coming-of-Age Day: Second Monday of January is Seijin no Hi. Girls aged 20 put on their best kimono for an "adulthood" ceremony at a shrine.

SHINTO IN DAILY LIFE

The indigenous Shinto religion, which forms the basis of many of Japan's festivals, also plays a role in the professional and daily lives of Tokyoites.

One of the most common rites is *oharai*, at which the priest waves a wand with strips of paper attached. With this a new car is blessed for accident-free driving and purification rites are held at a construction site or at the completed building. Amulets are popular purchases at shrines. *Omamori*, special talismans, are purchased to ensure good luck, or to ward off evil. Taxi drivers often have a "traffic safety" talisman dangling from the rearview mirror of their vehicle.

Hatsubasho: the first sumo tournament of the year goes on for two weeks in January.
Setsubun: On February 3, this bean-throwing ceremony is held to purify the home. Beans are thrown out the windows and doors to shouts of "*Oni wa soto*" (Devils, go out), followed by, "*Fuku wa uchi*" (Good luck, come in). Ceremonies are held at various temples and shrines.
Plum Viewing: The most famous spot for this mid-February event is Yushima Tenjin Shrine, with its floral displays and tea ceremonies.

March, April

Girls' Day: On March 3 is Hina Matsuri, when *hina* dolls representing imperial court figures are displayed at home and elsewhere.

Golden Dragon Dance: March 18 in the precincts of Asakusa's Senso-ji (or Asakusa Kannon) Temple. A lively event that is repeated at 11am, 2pm and 3pm.
Cherry Blossom Viewing: From early to mid-April is Ohanami, an important spring rite. Japanese picnic, drink *sake* and sing under the pink cherry blossoms. Some famous spots are Aoyama cemetery, Chidorigafuchi Park, Sumida Park, Ueno Park and Yasukuni-jinja Shrine.
Birthday of Buddha: On April 8 is Hana Matsuri with commemorative services at temples such as Senso-ji, Zojo-ji and Hommon-ji.
Azalea Festival: April 10–May 5 at the Nezu-jinja Shrine. Hundreds of the colourful bushes planted here are in dazzling bloom. *Koto* (Japanese harp) music is played at this time.
Horseback Archery Event: April 19 is when *yabusame*, mounted archers in samurai costumes, storm through Sumida Park.
Golden Week: April 29 also marks the first day of the Golden Week holiday period.
Meiji Shrine Spring Festival: From April 2 to May 3, this colourful celebration features *yabusame* (horseback archery) and other traditional displays.

May

Children's Day: On May 5th is Kodomo no Hi. Though supposedly for all children, its focus is on little boys. Carp banners are flown from homes where boys reside and it is hoped they will grow up big and strong like the carp – a symbol of strength and manhood in Japan.
Summer sumo tournament: In mid-May, catch the 15-day Natsubasho at Kokugikan.
Sanja Matsuri: On the third Saturday and Sunday, Tokyo honours the two brothers who found the image of Kannon in the river. There are shrine processions, traditional dancing and music at Senso-ji Temple in Asakusa.
Kanda Matsuri: This important festival is one of Tokyo's "Big Three" traditional events. It takes place in mid-May during an odd-numbered year. Costume parades and rites start from the Kanda Myojin Shrine.

June, July

Torigoe-jinja Taisai: This night-time festival based at the Torigoe-jinja Shrine falls on the second Sunday in June, when the biggest *mikoshi* is carried through the streets of Tokyo.
Tsukiji Festival: Held in the precincts of the fish market, this June 7–8 event is wonderfully boisterous. Drum performances, portable shrines, sushi-cutting displays and more.
Sanno Matsuri: During June 10–16, this big Edo festival has people parading in traditional garb at the Hie-jinja Shrine on Saturday.
Iris Viewing: See the irises on the grounds of Meiji-jingu Shrine in full bloom during June.
Morning Glory Fair: July 6–8 is Asagao Ichi, when over 100 merchants set up stalls selling the flowers at Iriya Kishibojin.
Tanabata Matsuri: July 7 is the only day in

Chocolates for the Men

On Valentine's Day (February 14), it is the custom for women to give men gifts of chocolate. The men get a chance to return the favour on White Day (March 14).

the year when two legendary lovers are able to cross the Milky Way to meet. People write wishes on coloured paper and hang them on bamboo branches before floating them down a river the next day.

Ground Cherry Fair: During July 9–10, Hozuki Ichi takes place at Senso-ji Temple from early morning to midnight.

graves and offer prayers to departed ancestors.

Autumnal Equinox Day: Shubun no Hi is on September 23, a national holiday.

October, November

Sports Day: Taiiku no Hi falls on October 10.

Chrysanthemum Viewing: Mid- to late-October is the time to head for Shinjuku Imperial Garden, Meiji-jingu and Asakusa-jinja shrines and Yushima Tenjin and Daien-ji temples, which are some of the best viewing places.

Shichi-Go-San: On November 15, this ceremony (literally, "Seven-Five-Three") has five-year-old boys and three- and seven-year-old girls taken round to visit local shrines.

Sumida River Fireworks: On the last Saturday in July is Sumidagawa Hanabi Taikai – the biggest fireworks display in Tokyo. The best spots are the Komagata Bridge and between the Kototoi and Shirahige bridges.

August, September

Fuji Rock Festival: In late July–early August, international and local acts gather for this three-day fest.

Obon: August 13–16 is a time when people return to their hometowns to clean up ancestral

LEFT: women in kimono at cherry blosson viewing time.
ABOVE: priests conducting a ritual at Senso-ji Temple.

December

Gishi Sai: On the 14th, a service at Sengaku-ji Temple recalls the famous 47 *ronin* (masterless *samurai)* who, on this day in 1702, avenged the death of their master and later committed suicide. They are buried at Sengaku-ji.

Hagoita Ichi: A "battledore" fair is held at Senso-ji Temple from the 17th to 19th.

Joya no Kane: At midnight on December 31, every temple bell throughout the country begins to toll. The bells toll 108 times to represent the 108 evil human passions. The public is allowed to join in and strike the bells at two places in Tokyo: the Zojo-ji Temple in Shiba Park and the Kan'ei-ji Temple in Ueno. ❑

FESTIVALS AND STREET PERFORMANCES

Tokyo's streets are lively at any time of the year, be it an elaborate temple street procession or an impromptu street jazz performance

Something extraordinary happens to the usually decorous Japanese when they attend festivals, as the customary *pro forma* manners and inhibitions vanish. *Matsuri* (festivals) have always been integral to the life of Tokyo, and hardly a week goes by without one. Linked to Shinto religious beliefs and to the honouring of local gods, they often seem more like community street parties, with plenty of food and drink to confirm the impression. If their function is to give thanks, petition the gods for favours and protection, and promote the solidarity of the community, they are also about celebrating the sheer joy of life.

The range of festivals is staggering, from the tolling of bells (108 times to atone for the year's sins) to a more earthy event celebrating how, with the intercession of an iron phallus, a young maiden was saved from the attentions of a razor-toothed demon. The synergetic Japanese have even made Christmas, stripped of any religious meaning, their own. Watch out for Santas in shop windows, fairy lights strung along main streets, and muzak arrangements of *White Christmas* belting out from cafés.

ABOVE: Geisha making a rare public appearance in a temple procession; they are known for their social skills and are adept at singing, dancing and playing traditional music. "Geisha", in fact, literally translates as "art person".

LEFT: The graceful and highly stylised movements of the *bugaku*, an ancient court dance, performed in front of the main sanctuary of Tokyo's Meiji-jingu Shrine during the spring Golden Week holiday *(see page 120)*.

TOP: *Mikoshi* shrine being paraded along the streets near Senso-ji Temple (or Asakusa Kannon Temple) during the Sanja Matsuri *(see pages 38 and 161)*. Portable shrines are still made by hand.
ABOVE: A spring Gyoki (Buddhist Devotional) at Zojo-ji Temple *(see page 134)*, in celebration of Honen, the founder of the Jodo sect of Buddhism. The priests wear sumptuous silk brocade stoles.

LIFE ON THE STREETS

If a healthy street life means a healthy city, then Tokyo is brimming with vitality. The Japanese may not be exhibitionists, but they can be just as expressive as anyone else. Tokyo street life is a lively spectacle, with a varied repertoire of acrobats, magicians, parading brass bands, even fire-eaters. On weekends, Yoyogi Park hosts rock bands, stand-up comics and buskers singing their hearts out on everything from Dylan to J-Pop. You might even come across the curiosities of *butoh (see photo above)*, a modern dance form that, depending on your point of view, is either art, or life reduced to tortured gestures and grimaces.

How to explain, though, the man playing the bagpipes every morning in Hibiya Park, dressed in full Highland clan costume, right down to the kilt and leather brogues? Or the couple who sometimes pop up in the Ginza, performing a spirited tango from the cafés of Buenos Aires. Maybe it's a love of performance and dressing up, or *cosplay*, as the Japanese call it. If all the world's a stage, Tokyo wants to be on it.

RIGHT: saxophonist at a Shibuya street corner.

CUISINE

Japanese cuisine is as much a sensation for the eyes as for the taste buds. Seasoning is minimal and every chef bows to the bible of freshness. Meals are easy to handle as food is served in delicate portions and bite-sized morsels

When it comes to number and variety of restaurants, Tokyo has no rival anywhere else on the planet – especially when it comes to Japanese food. Even in simple eateries, the quality is remarkable; in the best places, it is exceptional. The degree of specialisation is impressive. A sushi shop serves only that. If you want *tempura*, go to a *tempura* restaurant. A place serving only beef *shabu-shabu* may sit next door to another devoted to grilled eel.

Tokyo claims many dishes as its own, from Edomae sushi to the clam-based pilaf known as Fukagawa *meshi*, but it is also a microcosm of the entire country. It is possible to sample the local specialities of any region of Japan, from Hokkaido to Okinawa, without straying past the confines of the Yamanote loop line.

Creative, cosmopolitan tastes

At the same time, Tokyo's sophisticated and cosmopolitan tastes encompass not only other Asian cuisines but also those of Europe, Africa and the Americas. Explore the traditional by all means, but sample the contemporary as well when you eat your way around Tokyo.

Eating out is not as expensive as one would expect it to be, especially the budget-priced lunch sets under ¥1,500. Dinner is more expensive; expect to pay about ¥3,000 per head. Some of the top places are pricier and can go up to ¥10,000 per person; if there is no menu posted at the entrance, look elsewhere.

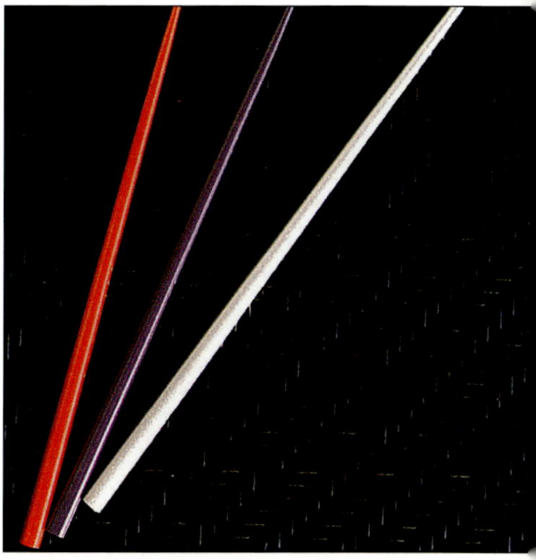

LEFT: a delectable selection of sushi.
RIGHT: chopsticks are common eating utensils in Japan.

MEAL ETIQUETTE

Good table manners – Japanese-style – go a long way. It is bad manners to wave your chopsticks around, use them to point at someone, to spear food or to pull dishes forward. Do not pass food from your chopsticks to someone else's or even into their mouths.

Japanese soups and noodles in broth (except *ramen*) are sipped straight from the bowl. Vigorous slurping is acceptable when eating noodles. Pour soy sauce into the dipping saucer provided, not onto your food (especially rice). It is polite to say *itadakimasu* ("I accept") before starting to eat and *gochisosama deshita* ("it was a banquet") after every meal.

It is quite possible to eat well in Tokyo without resorting to the ubiquitous fast-food burger chains. Neighbourhood Japanese diners may have little ambience but prices are low. Noodle shops are found everywhere. Conveyor-belt sushi is good value and *okonomiyaki* pancakes are fun dining. If all else fails, follow the example of local students and head for convenience stores. They offer good, fresh, ready-to-eat snacks and light meals, such as *bento* (lunch boxes) and instant noodles.

If Tokyo lacks anything, it is in choices for vegetarians. A small but increasing number of restaurants, however, are catering to visitors who cannot afford the vegetarian delights of *shojin ryori* (traditional but expensive temple cuisine). Menus may not always match expectations, though. A "vegetarian salad" may be green, but topped with diced ham. Essentially, there are no food taboos in Japan, only preferences. People with diet restrictions may have some difficulty. Tofu and bean dishes are usually a safe bet. Check the plastic samples in restaurant windows for content as they are generally accurate indicators.

Fresh, naked flavours

The building blocks of any Japanese meal are rice, a bowl of savoury *miso* soup, a small plate of pickles and a cup of green tea. Even on their own, these are enough for a square meal. Usually, however, the staple grain is accompanied or preceded by side dishes.

Unlike Western cuisines, Japanese cooking focuses on accentuating the inherent flavours rather than enhancing them with sauces or seasonings. Meals are based on fish, vegetables, seaweed and tofu. Eggs, meat and fowl are used in limited quantities, while dairy foods play no part in the traditional diet. Portions are small and served in bite-sized morsels that are easy to handle.

Ingredients always reflect the seasons. Every self-respecting chef tailors his menu to what is at its peak of freshness. Seafood and produce are generally at their best in spring and autumn, while local gourmets look forward to hearty hotpots in winter and the aroma of broiled eel in midsummer.

Presentation is equally important. Plates, bowls and utensils are made of ceramic, glass, stone, wood or lacquer. Like the ingredients, they are changed to fit the season for maximum rapport with the food.

This celebration of the seasons finds its ultimate expression in the formal cuisine known as *kaiseki ryori*. If time and budget permit, do not pass up an opportunity to sample the exquisite and refined pleasures of a traditional multi-course banquet. Far more than just pleasing the taste buds and filling the stomach, it is a total aesthetic experience. *Kaiseki ryori* is derived from the formal banquets served as part of the tea ceremony. The taste and visual appeal of the dishes are heightened in a setting created to ensure perfect harmony. At the most exclusive restaurants, the dining room is decorated with calligraphy, a seasonal flower arrangement and perhaps a view of a Zen garden with ancient rocks or a pool.

Kaiseki ryori is composed of numerous small courses, some little larger than a mouthful, and each prepared using a different cooking style. They follow a prescribed order. First, a selection of appetisers (*zensai*); next, some sashimi (*nama mono*) and a clear soup (*suimono*). Then follows dishes that have been grilled (*yakimono*); seasoned with a thick dressing (*aemono*); simmered (*nimono*); steamed (*mushimono*); deep-fried (*agemono*); and dressed with vinegar (*su-no-mono*).

Sake is served alongside the dishes but never with the final course, which consists of rice, a bowl of *miso* soup and a few pickles. Hot green tea is served alongside, and dessert is usually a small portion of fresh fruit.

Sushi, sashimi and other staples

The Japanese love seafood and are enthusiastic about eating it as close as possible to its natural state – either as *sashimi,* served with a dip of soy sauce, usually seasoned *wasabi* (horseradish) or on vinegared rice, as sushi.

There are various kinds of sushi, but the best known both in Japan and abroad is the Tokyo style, known as *nigiri-sushi*. The concept of eating small patties of rice topped with cuts of raw seafood originated in the days of Edo. This variety is still called *Edomae sushi,* because the seafood was all caught in the waters of the bay right in front of the city (and some still is, in spite of water pollution fears). Some of the best *sushiya* (*sushi* shops) are found near the central fish market in Tsukiji.

There are two approaches at a *sushiya*: either sit at the counter and choose each serving from the seafood arrayed in front of you; or sit at a table and order a mixed selection of sushi (most places offer a variety of set courses). Most people like to start with a little *sashimi,* washed down with *sake,* before embarking on the main part of the meal.

Good sushi demands that ingredients are of good quality and absolutely fresh. That may mean a dauntingly expensive experience. The alternative is a *kaiten-sushi* shop, where small dishes of sushi pass by on a conveyor belt along the counter, often for as little as ¥10 per plate. These are easier to find in areas of Tokyo where young Japanese congregate (especially Shibuya, Harajuku and Shinjuku). The atmosphere may lack sophistication and the fish is not from a premium cut (indeed, often it is unfrozen), but the outlay will not be excessive.

LEFT: set lunch options on display at a restaurant.
RIGHT: grilled octopus is a local delicacy.

One of the pleasures of visiting Japan in the cold season is the variety of hearty hotpots served throughout the winter. Known as *nabe-ryori* (casserole cuisine), every area has its own distinctive variations, many of which can be found in Tokyo's speciality restaurants.

Originating from Hokkaido is *ishikari-nabe*, based on salmon and vegetables. *Hoto*, from Yamanashi Prefecture, includes handmade *udon* noodles. In Ibaraki Prefecture, the specialty is *anko-nabe*, made with angler fish. *Fugu-chiri*, from Yamaguchi, in western Japan, features the white meat of the puffer fish. Tokyo's best-known homegrown *nabe* is *Yanagawa-nabe*, made with *dojo* (an eel-like loach) cooked in a savoury omelet.

A favourite among locals – and an acquired taste for visitors – is *oden*. Made with *daikon*, potatoes, whole hard-boiled eggs, tofu and other ingredients, this hotpot is one of the standard dishes served at *yatai* street stalls and is now available at convenience stores.

The classic dish of summer is *unagi*, broiled eel served on a bed of rice. Since Edo times, this has enjoyed a reputation for imparting energy during the hot and humid days of summer. This belief has some nutritional basis since *unagi* contains more protein than beef.

Another summer food is *yakitori*, skewers of chicken, often grilled over charcoal, much like the *satay* of Thailand and Indonesia. Almost every part of the bird is eaten, from the breast to the gizzard and heart. Gourmet versions can be had in upscale restaurants but most people prefer the ambience of the smoky street stalls (check out those under the railway tracks near Yurakucho Station).

If you like a frisson of fear with your food, you will enjoy the dangerous delicacy known as *fugu*. Although the flesh of the puffer fish is safe for eating, its internal organs are so poisonous that it can only be prepared at licensed restaurants. If ingested, the toxin paralyses the nervous system, eventually leading to heart failure. Once a skilled chef has removed all the dangerous parts, along with the spiny skin, *fugu* is served as *sashimi*, sliced so thinly the pattern of the plate shows through the translucent slices. *Fugu-sashi* is a great delicacy with a subtle flavour. The rest of the fish goes into a casserole that is served with a spicy dip.

Oodles of noodles

Noodles are the original Japanese fast food. Wholesome, filling, quick to prepare and even quicker to eat, they make a good light lunch or dinner. Just as often, they are eaten as a simple snack to keep energy levels up.

There are three main types: thin, grayish-brown *soba* noodles made with buckwheat flour; chunky *udon*, made from white wheat flour; and *somen*, a delicate vermicelli also made from wheat flour. While *udon* is usually served with a hot savoury broth, *somen* is invariable eaten chilled as a summer dish. *Soba* is equally popular either hot or cold.

GOOD SPOTS FOR FOOD HOUNDS

Whether you fancy Japanese, Chinese, French or Italian, there is never a shortage of eating options anywhere. Generally speaking, Ginza is for upscale eating; Shimbashi for raucous salarymen; Shibuya for young people; and Aoyama, Azabu and Roppongi for chic, contemporary cuisine. Akasaka has a good cross-section of choices, while Shinjuku has it all, from designer bars to insalubrious dives.

Apart from noodle shops, most restaurants close between lunch and dinner. English-language menus are not common, but many eateries, especially in tourist areas, have plastic food displays in their windows. The top floors of department stores offer a good selection of local and foreign fare. The Japanese restaurants here offer more diverse menus, rather than just one speciality.

In the evening, *izakaya* (restaurant-pubs) are a reliable source for reasonably priced local food and alcohol, and plenty of ambience. They identify themselves with a string of red lanterns hanging over the door. *Izakaya* don't do full-course meals and there is no pressure to eat quickly. Order beer or *sake*, and sample a few dishes such as *sashimi*, grilled fish, *yakitori* or tofu. End with rice or noodles.

Noodle shops range from venerable establishments that have been in business for generations (Kanda Yabu Soba is the prime example) to cheap and cheerful stand-and-slurp counters on the platforms of railway stations.

The best *soba* is *te-uchi*, freshly prepared and chopped by hand to order. This typically has a buckwheat content of 80 percent, with just 20 percent wheat flour to add bulk (in cheaper, mass-produced noodles, the proportions are reversed). Buckwheat is not just a nutritious source of vitamins, but also contains plenty of dietary fibre. Top-quality *soba* needs little seasoning. It is cooked, chilled and served on a bamboo tray, accompanied by a dip made from soy sauce, *mirin* (sweet sake) and *katsuobushi* (shaved flakes of dried bonito), together with *wasabi* (horseradish) and thinly sliced scallions. Prepared like this, it is known as *zaru-soba*. The same noodles may also be served with lightly battered and fried *tempura*-style shrimp and grated *daikon*.

In colder weather, *soba* is more often eaten with a hot broth, topped with *tempura*, *sansai* herbs, *wakame* seaweed, deep-fried tofu (*kitsune*) or with a raw egg cracked into it (*tsukimi*). The classic dish, however, is *kamo-nanban*, in which the hot broth contains slices of rich duck meat and sliced leeks.

While *soba* is favoured more in northeast Japan, the central mountains and around Tokyo, the heartland for *udon* is Nagoya, Osaka and the western region. The wheat-flour noodles are a cold-weather favourite, served in a hot soy-base broth with scallions and a variety of toppings. A thinner *udon*, known as *hiyamugi*, is eaten chilled in summer.

The classic hot-weather noodle is the fine vermicelli known as *somen*, served in iced water, with strips of omelette, shrimp and green vegetables and a sesame-flavoured dip. It is a light, refreshing treat on a hot summer day.

FAR LEFT: serving up cupfuls of hot green tea.
ABOVE: fresh *udon* noodles; kneading *udon* dough.

One other type of noodle is more popular than all the others. Despite its Chinese roots, *ramen* has become an honorary part of the Japanese diet, especially at late-night diners. It is served in a very hot, soy-flavoured broth, typically with pickled bamboo, chopped scallion and slices of *cha-shu* (roast pork).

No meal is complete without a serving of *tsukemono* (pickles) to add nutrition and texture, cleanse the palate and assist the digestive process. A wide variety of produce goes into it, including cucumber, turnip, cabbage, eggplant, burdock, lotus root and ginger. ❑

● *Individual restaurant recommendations are listed at the end of each chapter in the Places section.*

TOKYO AFTER DARK

Evenings are when the neon-clad capital comes alive. There is much to see, hear and do, whether your taste tends toward the traditional or the new. You can catch a rousing *kabuki* play or dance the night away at an ultra-mod club

Tokyo's neon-spangled streets, as night descends, are an irresistible invitation to come out and play. While the older generation are enjoying a *kabuki* performance, their children may be catching the latest Leonardo di Caprio flick or honing their break dance moves at a Shibuya hip hop club. The variety can be bewildering so here is a brief introduction.

Traditional music

Gagaku: Meaning elegant, authorised music, *gagaku*, is the same today as it was at least 1,500 years ago. It incorporates not only orchestral music played on wind instruments such as the *shakuhachi* (bamboo flute), string instruments, and gongs and drums, but also singing and dancing, when it becomes known as *bugaku*. Most *gagaku*, barely distinguishable to the untrained ear, are based on music imported centuries ago from Korea, India, China and Southeast Asia . Performances are staged at the Imperial Palace in spring and autumn, but one needs a connection to gain entrance. There are, however, occasional outdoor performances at some shrines, or at the National Theatre.

Hogaku: This refers to popular Japanese music in its entirety, from *minyo* (folk songs) accompanied on the *shamisen* (a banjo-like instrument) to contemporary *enka* (ballads) and J-pop – exuberant and youthful Japanese pop music. In 1999, the first *hogaku* live house, Waon, opened its doors in Nishi-Nippori. It is an ideal starting point for *hogaku* enthusiasts.

LEFT: poster depicting a *kabuki* actor.
RIGHT: *bugaku* combines *gagaku* music with action.

Japanese theatre and dance

Noh: This minimalist theatre form has origins in religion. Aristocratic patronage led to the development of its characteristic form from earlier temple plays. The aristocrats demanded esoteric poetry, sophisticated language and a refined simplicity of movement, precisely what you see now six centuries later. It is difficult to describe *noh* – words like ethereal, inaccessible and subtle spring to mind. Fortunately, English translations are available. Catch *noh* performances at the Ginza Noh-gakudo, the National Noh Theatre and the new Cerulean Tower Noh Theatre.

Kyogen: Many people much prefer *kyogen*,

comic interludes designed to provide light relief between *noh* performances. Some last only 10 minutes and present amusing situations based on folk tales and Buddhist parables. Universal human foibles are represented, much like in Shakespeare. There are *kyogen* performances in English, which is not as bizarre as it sounds.

Bunraku: These puppeteers trace their art to the 7th century, when itinerant Chinese and Korean performers presented semi-religious puppet plays. *Bunraku* is adult theatre and deals with themes such as revenge and sacrifice, love and rejection, reincarnation and futility.

Each major puppet is manipulated by three operators, a logistic marvel in itself. In theory,

THE ART OF THE GEISHA

Geisha are a vanishing breed of performers who sing, dance, play silly games and serve *sake* with finesse. There are very few true geisha left, and that's why one has to pay a lot – cash, no credit cards – for their company. Few foreigners really derive much pleasure from a geisha evening as the entertainment is designed for Japan's middle-aged businessmen and politicians.

There are, however, occasional chances for lesser mortals to see the geisha in their finery: at parades, such as the Sanja Matsuri in May, and at special performances of Japanese dancing, or *buyo*, at theatres such as the Shimbashi Embujo and the Meiji-za.

the audience doesn't notice all the shuffling around of these silent professionals, concentrating instead on the puppets themselves, which are roughly one-third human size. The real tour de force, though, is perhaps the narrators, the *gidayu* performers, who speak, gesture and weep from a kneeling position at stage left. Tokyo's National Theatre is the best venue for *bunraku*.

Kabuki: Japan's most splendid theatre form is *kabuki*. Difficult to categorise, *kabuki* resembles opera and ballet. In Japanese, *kabuki* translates as "song-dance skill", with no mention of theatre. The word *kabuki,* as used in the early 16th century, meant "avant-garde" and referred to all-female performances, often of a licentious nature. The Tokugawa shogunate took exception to this and, in 1629, banned female performers. This started the all-male tradition that continues today, actresses being allowed only for certain special events.

Kabuki developed into its present form during the 17th and 18th centuries when it was theatre for the Edo masses. The actors were the rock stars of feudal Japan. The older plays, still performed today, began as puppet plays that contained social comment and satire. English programmes are sometimes available.

The main *kabuki* theatres are the National Theatre, the Kabuki-za and the Shimbashi Embujo. Most programmes span 10 hours, with generous intervals for tea-drinking and socialising. The Kabuki-za allows the choice of seeing only one act or part of an act.

Butoh: This avant-garde dance form whose shows abroad are always sold out is almost unknown in Japan. With the closing of the legendary Asbestoskan, the best places for viewing *butoh* are the Setagaya Public Theatre, the Die Pratze theatre, and *butoh* company Dairakudakan's Studio Kochuten in Kichijoji. Its basic message stresses inhumanity, desperation and nihilism – a devotion not to physical beauty and harmony but ugliness and discord.

Western influences

Western theatre: Translations of foreign plays and musicals are very popular, ranging from Chekhov to Cats. Musicals are imported from London or New York, though most are performed in Japanese by Japanese dancers and singers. Lyrics, however, are sung in English. These performances are sometimes disastrous, and occasionally an improvement. The group Yumeno Yuminsha has a large and devoted following. Watch out for performances at the Setagaya Public Theatre in Sangenjaya and Theatre Tram.

A handful of amateur drama and comedy groups performing in English call Tokyo their home. The Tokyo International Players' season runs from late September till late May; most performances take place at the American Club. The Tokyo Comedy Store performs at Oh! God Cinema Play Café in Harajuku for free.

Takarazuka: The *takarazuka* revue, an all-female song and dance extravaganza, lies somewhere between Las Vegas and the London Palladium. Not a male actor in sight, but expect lots of mustachioed and thigh-slapping singers falling in love with each other, and largely misty-eyed young girls making up the audience. Catch it at Yurakucho's Takarazuka Theatre.

Classical concerts: Fine concert halls include Suntory Hall, Casals Hall in the university district of Ochanomizu and Bunkamura complex in Shibuya. Tokyo Opera City, a mammoth skyscraper and arts complex near Shinjuku is the home of the superb New National Theatre, which plays Mozart as well as Puccini. Smaller adjoining theatres offer ballet and drama, while the Takamitsu Memorial Concert Hall premieres works by contemporary Japanese and foreign composers.

Pop and rock: Tokyo has always been the home of a fevered pop and rock music scene. It has offered to the world innovative acts – from the electro-pop of Ryuichi Sakamoto's Yellow Magic Orchestra and the avant-garde noise rock of the Boredoms to new Japanese-Western hybrid acts like rock group Love Psychedelico and R&B queen Crystal Kay, as well as the unchallenged *aidoru* (idols) of J-Pop, Hikaru Utada and Ayumi Hamazaki.

Concerts take place most nights at vast venues like Tokyo Dome and the Budokan; medium-sized places like Club Quattro and Liquid Room; and at tiny "live houses" which sprinkle Tokyo's trendy youth districts.

The annual Fuji Rock Festival is a three-day event that, along with Japanese artists, attracts international acts of the calibre of the Chemical Brothers, Lou Reed and Elvis Costello.

Jazz: There are hundreds of small jazz clubs and coffee shops featuring all styles from swing to free jazz. Many performers have had great success abroad, notably saxophonist Sadao Watanabe and trumpeter Terumasa Hino. Likewise, many American jazz

LEFT: a geisha tea ceremony in progress.
ABOVE: rock band at Space Lab Yellow in Roppongi.

greats visit Japan regularly, performing at nightclubs such as the world-class Blue Note Tokyo in Aoyama, the Pit Inn in Shinjuku and B-Flat in Akasaka. Another highlight are the jazz festivals that liven up torrid Tokyo summers, such as the Tokyo Jazz festival.

Karaoke: In the 1970s, Japan gave karaoke to the world. Even if not all the world is thankful, singing along to music videos is here to stay. Karaoke, meaning "empty orchestra", is either masochistic or sadistic, depending on your tolerance level and which side of the microphone you are at. It is a popular stress reliever and a bonding platform for co-workers or friends. Karaoke bars in Roppongi offer English titles targeted at English-speaking foreigners and Japanese who wish to bone up on their English.

Bars and clubs

With its liberal alcohol laws and tolerance of drunkenness, Japan is a barfly's paradise. Innocents entering the wilds of nightlife hubs Roppongi and Shinjuku will be dazzled by the dizzying array of watering holes. The city's constantly morphing mass of bars and clubs range from the tiniest hole-in-the-wall bar to flashy see-and-be-seen mega discos such as Roppongi's Velfarre. Since the 1990s dance culture explosion, Tokyo has incubated a sophisticated club culture on par with New York and London.

Japan's answer to the corner bar is the *izakaya*, the small roll-up-your shirtsleeves restaurant-bars where Japan's army of *salariman* go to unwind after work. *Izakaya* are found near train stations and range from mom-and-pop affairs to chains such as Tsubohachi.

The 1990s saw a surge in English-Irish pubs, with the Japanese broadening their drinking tastes into British-style beers. These establishments allow homesick tourists to quaff a pint of Bass or Guinness – but at US $8 a pop, it doesn't come cheap. In addition to Japanese chains such as Dubliners in Shinjuku and Ikebukuro, What the Dickens in Ebisu and The Fiddler in Takadanobaba are favoured by expats and often feature live bands.

Dozens of miniature DJ bars devoted to rock, reggae, hip hop, techno, house, garage and other styles provide Tokyo's DJs the chance to hone their technique and students a venue for that most ancient of youthful preoccupations – dating and mating.

Tokyo's clubs are similar in nature to its DJ bars with one difference – size. Bigger venues such as Velfarre in Roppongi, Space Lab Yellow in Nishi-Azabu, Maniac Love in Aoyama, Code in Shinjuku, Milk in Ebisu, Womb, La Fabrique and Air in Shibuya, and Ageha in Shin-Kiba play host to top touring DJs spinning the latest sounds from Europe and the US. Ruby Room in Shibuya, model hangout Lexington Queen in Roppongi and the meat market Gas Panic chain are also popular hotspots. For hardcore clubbers, there are after-hours parties that often stretch past noon on weekends.

Taking the lead from Europe, Japan has developed a rave culture that regularly sees thousands of Ecstasy-fuelled dance fanatics turning out for parties both in Tokyo and in the countryside. This is not surprising as the electronic music technology behind modern dance music was invented in Japan.

Fans of techno, house, trance, drum 'n' bass and other styles are not left out either. Huge CD shops in Shibuya and Shinjuku publicise upcoming events and the free magazine *Metropolis* (www.metropolis.co.jp) has up-to-date information in English. ❑

● *Individual nightlife spots are listed in the Travel Tips* section *(see pages 220–224)*

LEFT: Tokyo girls letting their hair down.

The "Pink" Trade

Commercial sex in Tokyo spells big bucks and many "pink" businesses flaunt their trade openly – if you know where to go. Sex industry magazines and guidebooks provide detailed information from phone numbers and prices to the names and photos of the women.

For short-term visitors looking for this sort of titillation and who are unable to converse in Japanese, the situation is not encouraging. Over the past 10 years or so, two barriers have been responsible. The first is price: while foreigners are not necessarily gouged, Japanese definitely are. Generally, compared with other Asian countries, customers pay much more in US dollar terms for such services. The second is the spread of AIDS, which has led many establishments to close their doors to non-Japanese patrons. However, many women now dispensing sexual services in Tokyo are foreigners and they may be more inclined to take on foreigners, albeit at Japanese rates.

Although Tokyo's nightlife is generally safe, its sex trade is never completely respectable. If you choose to partake, common sense dictates you go with a local (or at least someone conversant in Japanese) who knows the ropes.

Where it's happening

The largest of Tokyo's adult entertainment zones are in Shinjuku, Ikebukuro, Ueno, Shibuya, Roppongi and Kinshicho.

At hostess bars, female employees sit beside male customers, pour their drinks and make idle conversation. The higher-end establishments might feature live music or a floor show. Prices are usually based on an hourly or flat rate, with the former around ¥8,000 and up and the latter, ¥12,000 and up. Some places may pad the bill with taxes or service charges, so it is prudent to determine all charges in advance. (Beware of amateurs; under new regulations, the penalties for sex with underaged females are severe.)

"Pink salons" are cabarets where hostesses wear skimpy costumes. The room is dim, leaving customers' hands free to roam. Prices start from ¥8,000 and up, depending on options.

At strip clubs, women performers strip to music; some places feature live sex shows while others invite audience participation. Admission fees start at ¥3,000. Image clubs, or *ime-kura*, allow customers to act out their sexual fantasies. In some establishments, attendants even dress male clients, if they are so inclined, in diapers and "baby" them for the session. Prices are at ¥12,000 and up.

RIGHT: erotica shop in Roppongi.

At so-called "fashion health clubs" customers are given a sexually stimulating shower and rubdown. Variations are "aesthetic" salons (*esute*) and "delivery health" (*deri-heru*), which service outcalls. Prices go from ¥8,000. Then there are "soaplands" that provide a sudsy, arousing shower and massage which can go further, depending on the price. Prices go from ¥25,000.

Tokyo's largest clusters of love hotels – where rooms are rented by the hour or overnight for sexual trysts – are in Kabukicho in Shinjuku, Maruyamacho in Shibuya and the area adjacent to Uguisudani Station near Ueno. Rates start from ¥3,500. ❑

FASHION AND DESIGN

A coat with no armholes? An ironing board encrusted with plastic jewels? The ceaseless innovations coming out of Tokyo are firmly grounded in the chaotic diversity of the city, and the world's attention has been caught by their potent mix of simplicity, asymmetry and irreverence

The easy co-existence of the traditional and the contemporary in Tokyo is a refreshing feature of a modern city. The Japanese have long demonstrated a rare syncretic genius in borrowing and adapting from their own culture and elsewhere, and then retooling and recodifying these materials into something uniquely Japanese.

The willingness to accommodate any number of seemingly conflicting ideas, beliefs and styles – drawing strength, in fact, from polarities – partly explains why it is so easy for Japanese consumers to move on to a new development in fashion and design so quickly, without apparent regret or sentimental attachment to older models. A willing collusion exists between consumer and designer, with both sides understanding that new models are only provisional and soon to be superseded. Durability is not the virtue being marketed; of-the-moment perfection is.

Deconstruction in fashion

It is no accident that the concept of deconstruction in fashion – the idea of effecting asymmetry while maintaining balance – was born in Japan. Examples are seen in a coat with no armholes; sleeves of different lengths sewn tightly to the body; dresses with sewn-in humps. These attempts to transcend the logic of symmetry are echoed in other art forms: *ikebana* (floral arrangement), which rejects symmetry as unnatural, and *shodo* (calligraphy), in which the young are taught to pay attention to the empty spaces of a page just as readily as the inked ones.

When Rei Kawakubo's controversial catwalk creations debuted in front of an entrenched and sceptical European fashion establishment nearly 30 years ago, it marked more than the birth of a new star. Faced with her success, the Western fashion scene was forced to accept the unusual beauty of distortion in shape and cut, and the world grudgingly began to admire this new concept of beauty. Asymmetry as a viable fashion movement was born, and Tokyo gained the reputation of an innovative fashion trailblazer.

Ask style-conscious dressers about Japanese fashion today and they will throw out the names of Japanese couture pioneers: Comme des Garçons, Yohji Yamamoto and Issey Miyake. But Japan's burgeoning fashion industry boasts new names, many of whom have long captured the attention of the fashion capitals of Paris, Milan, London and New York. Among these are Tsumori Chisato, Kosuke Tsumura, Arakawa Shinichiro and Maruyama Keita. Outside this new fashion establishment, more daring and ever-younger designers, shops and labels are springing up.

Tokyo's grassroots designers, like those of any other fashion capital, are firmly grounded in the chaotic diversity of the metropolis. Young and streetwise brands like Beast, National Standard, Under Cover, Vandalize,

Acide and Mixed-Up Confusion are names every Tokyo trendsetter knows.

Tokyo as fashion centre

The post-war generation approached fashion from a position of cultural insecurity. For them, "made in Japan" labels at the time bore the stigma of poor quality and lack of style and status, while the opposite was true of American and European products. Today's fashion conscious are more knowing and multifaceted. At one end of the spectrum are trendy Tokyoites who think nothing of blowing an entire month's salary on high-end designer goods and international labels. Among these imports, brands such as Prada, Gucci, Fendi and Paul Smith reign supreme. At the other end of the scale, "groupthink" continues to be the dominant mindset among teenagers. Young people identify strongly with various fashion tribes defined by distinct looks and influences – such as Harajuku's walking-doll "cuties" or the super-chic Ginza girl – each with its own favourite shopping district and hangout territory.

Regardless of which side of the coin they fall under, Japan's young consumers are becoming ever more discerning about quality,

FAR LEFT: Issey Miyake – Japanese fashion icon.
ABOVE: from kimono to designer classics.

THE KIMONO

The kimono as we know it today originated in the Edo Period (1600–1868), although descriptions of various versions of the garment can be found in classical Japanese literature that dates back more than 1,000 years. Sewn from a single piece of material, most kimono are made of silk, although they also come in cotton, wool and linen. The one-size-fits-all kimono is relatively easy to make and is simply adjusted to fit a customer's measurements.

A woman cannot put on a kimono without assistance and must enlist the help of a professional dresser or a knowledgeable member of the family.

and this is helped by relatively high disposable incomes and extensive media coverage. At least twice a year, Tokyo plays host to the fashion world. As domestic and international fashion cognoscenti turn out to see some of the biggest names in design, the Tokyo Collections, organised by the Council of Fashion Designers (CFD), provides an opportunity for fashion's movers and shakers to showcase their newest creations.

Viewings are not easy for the general public to gain access to, and strong connections are required for those who want to peek at Tokyo's fashion czars. Standing room is available at certain shows which are worth attending for their glamorous atmosphere as well as the designs themselves. The collections are shown all over the city and locations are decided just before each season.

Those who enjoy the trappings of the fashion world – streets teeming with models, cafés catering to sophisticated purveyors of style and a nightlife brimming with attractive, well-groomed people – will not be disappointed.

Hi-tech, hi-culture designs

Tokyo is unquestionably Japan's design mecca. While London has its 100 Percent Design and Milan its Furniture Fair, the Tokyo Contemporary Design Exhibition, entitled Happening, has given both established and rising stars of the furniture design stage a venue to showcase their talents. For 10 days in October, innovative local as well as international designs are showcased at hip shops and cafés all over the city. This event not only allows interior and industrial designers exposure to local and international talent, but is also carnival time for admirers of good design.

The need to meet ever-increasing demands for new and avant-garde styles by the Tokyo dweller has led manufacturers and designers to pool their creative efforts together to create all-encompassing labels. One of the newest brainchilds of the Tokyo design-marketing machine is WiLL: behind this name are five unrelated manufacturers who create products especially for design-conscious 20- and 30-somethings. One popular product is Toyota's contribution: the WiLL car, targeted at the single, young woman about town. The design, loosely based on Cinderella's pumpkin carriage, aims to induce a feeling of security.

Insatiable quest for the new

The average Tokyo home stocks a continuous series of replaceable products. "Big Garbage"

ABOVE: WiLL, a popular designer car by Toyota.
RIGHT: getting an instant tattoo in Omotesando.

day, a pre-arranged time for the disposal of furniture and appliances, is a veritable treasure trove of electronics and interior goods. Everybody wants the latest design, be it a plasma television screen or a rubber sofa.

Industrial design in Tokyo can be shoeboxed into four categories: miniaturisation, the element of fun, disposability and minimalism. Miniaturisation is most evident in the world of technology. Japan has long been praised for its ability to make Western ideas better, faster and ever smaller. One glance around Tokyo's bustling Shibuya area will reveal countless mobile phones, electronic organisers and portable video games, any of which can be hidden in one's palm.

Fun with products can be seen in store windows that display shocking pink vacuum cleaners and ironing boards encrusted with plastic jewels and glitter; mundane household products transformed by urban fantasy.

Minimalism versus clutter

Perhaps one of the biggest paradoxes in Japanese design is its association, in the Western mind, with minimalism. The austere sparseness of the *tatami* room exists increasingly in the confines of temples and the imaginations of tourists. In their daily lives, most Japanese cannot afford the luxury of empty space.

In Tokyo, where rent is often astronomical, homes are filled to bursting with clothes, toys and collections of *mono* (objects) that reflect a hectic and fast-paced city life. In his highly recommended photo book, *Tokyo Style,* Kyoichi Tsuzuki brilliantly demonstrates the character of the modern Tokyo dwelling.

The must-visit locations for any design-curious visitor include Tokyu Hands, which showcases everything from jewellery to furniture; Daikanyama, the chic youth fashion district, Shimokitazawa with its trendy trinket shops; and Odaiba, a futuristic island in the bay that hosts design fairs and some of Tokyo's most innovative architecture.

One often gets the feeling that whether stripped down to the elemental beauty of its ancient aesthetics or dressed up in the gaudy glow of its crowded entertainment districts, Japan's capital city is searching and finding, then searching again, for the design ideal. ❑

MECHANICAL FRIENDS

Gimmicks, gadgets and gizmos, objects that are both innovative and fun, have been around for a long time. Where Westerners tend to anthropomorphise animals, the Japanese have the habit of personalising objects, superimposing human qualities on them that promote a comfortable, almost intimate co-existence in both the workplace and at home. This fondness is evident in Japan's early spring-operated dolls. *Karakuri ningyo* (mechanical dolls), first appearing in the 18th century, were made for both pleasure and amusement as well as a design spectacle. Testifying to the excellence of Japan's mechanical technology in the 17th century was the intricate *chahakobi ningyo*, a tea-serving doll. Besides its novelty value, the fact that the model was required to carry a bowl of green tea without spilling a drop, hints at the exacting mechanics involved in the doll's conception. A happy symbiosis with tools, machines and gadgets has made the transition from dolls to life-like robots a relatively small conceptual step. The basic ideas, aesthetics and skills required to develop today's humanoid robots – creations that embody bipedal ambulation technologies unrivalled in the world – were already in place long before Honda's Asimo "mechanical assistant", or Sony's wildly popular Aibo robot pet took to the stage.

ARCHITECTURE

The capital, with its mishmash of architectural styles, has an astonishing penchant for rebuilding. The city's skyline is like a drawing on an immense whiteboard that can suddenly be erased and replaced by something completely different

If Tokyo ever possessed a blueprint showing everything in its ordained place, it has vanished without a trace in the face of countless natural disasters that have been visited upon the city with an almost Old Testament wrath.

There are historical antecedents, though, to suggest that the erasing of the past is not altogether involuntary. Long before Nara, Kyoto and, finally, Tokyo became permanent seats of power, it was the custom to demolish entire capitals with the enthronement of a new emperor. Today, economic imperatives rather than ritual purity are the catalysts for pulling down buildings. Japanese architecture has always – and to a far greater extent than elsewhere in the world – been linked to the fluctuations of the economy and the progress of technology. This has led to intense periods of creative activity followed by the abrupt shelving, in some cases, of entire projects.

An urban laboratory

Tokyo is a permanently unfinished cityscape driven as much by pragmatism as human needs. Deprived of the cosy illusion that anything could ever be permanent, Tokyoites have voiced little objection to seeing their city transformed into the world's foremost urban laboratory. With Tokyo's sights firmly set on the future, there is little compulsion to dwell on the past: a condition ideal for aspiring architects eager to make their mark.

"These extremely contemporary-looking structures," commented Donald Richie on Tokyo in his book, *A Lateral View*, "are like the tents of the nomads – with the difference that the Japanese move not in space but in time." Built for reasons of economy, convenience and sometimes symbolism, buildings – like the sets found in the back lots of corporate movie studios – are allowed to remain standing only for as long as they serve a purpose, after which they are remorselessly torn down.

The problem of how futuristic buildings can be adapted to an existing, older urban landscape is resolved by simply ignoring altogether the aesthetics of coordination. New structures are inserted into the body of the city in the same manner as a surgeon would replace body parts.

The organic labyrinth

Tokyo's original structure comprised a series of concentric rings radiating from Edo castle, which combined the interests and needs of defence, commerce and geomancy. This grid has long since disappeared under the modern mire of spontaneous urban expansion.

Organic growth has replaced the civic model in a city where plots of land take precedence over streets. Any infrastructure of public roads linking these sites had to be superimposed on the existing mass, in the form of elevated expressways and train lines. The result is a layered complexity that seems to go its own way, obeying organic rather than structural codes.

Japanese architects

Tokyo's early Meiji and Taisho period architects were strongly influenced by Western models and by the European architects and teachers such as Josiah Conder, who worked here, and his former student Tatsuno Kingo, who designed the Queen Anne-style Tokyo Station (*see page 80*). The Showa Period saw more experimentation: Watanabe Hitoshi's 1932 Wako Building (*see page 89*) is a good example. Architect Ito Chuta turned to Asian culture for the inspiration for his Tsukiji Hongan-ji Temple (*see page 189*) in Tsukiji, and to ancient Shinto forms for the now-reconstructed Meiji-jingu Shrine (*see page 120*) in Harajuku. Contemporary architects, such as the world-famous master Tadao Ando, have their own unfettered vision. Ando's Collezione building in Omotesando (*see page 115*) is a prime example.

Beyond their obvious functional purposes, the more experimental of Tokyo's buildings are design catalysts that can also be read as discourses on aesthetics and the role of modern architecture. The Aoyama Technical College in Shibuya, designed by Makoto Sei Watanabe, is, for example, a bizarre yet com-

LEFT: bird's eye view of the city from Tokyo Tower.
ABOVE: Queen Anne-style Tokyo Station.

NEW MILLENNIUM DESIGNS

Tokyo embraced the new millennium and its architectural possibilities without so much as a moment's hesitation. Highlights from the first decade of the century include: **National Art Centre**, Kisho Kurokawa's glass façade inspired by cliffs and seashores (*see page 133*); **Prada Aoyama**, which dazzles like a greenish yellow space craft at night (*see page 115*); **Mikimoto Ginza 2**, Toyo Ito's design inspired by jewel boxes, which glitters through randomly positioned, cell-like windows (*see page 89*); and Tadao Ando's **21_21 Design Sight**, whose plunging triangular rooftops look like wing tips balanced on sheets of glass (*see page 133*).

pelling construction of a sci-fi-like montage of poles, lightning rods, water tanks and posts that creep almost organically over the building's surfaces. Other Shibuya constructions, such as the Bunkamura, Shibuya Beam and the Humax Pavilion, seem tame by comparison.

Kenzo Tange's newest addition to the Tokyo skyline is the headquarters for the Fuji-Sankei Communications Group, better known as Fuji TV Building, in Odaiba. Its "corridors in the sky" – connecting walkways that link the two main towers – and a titanium-panelled silver sphere positioned in between, give the impression of a building resembling a widescreen TV. This is no coincidence, as the building houses both Nippon Broadcasting and Fuji Television.

Foreign architects

Flexible building regulations have encouraged many foreign architects to work in Japan. Raphael Vinoly's majestic Tokyo International Forum (*see page 86*), for example, is a premier culture convention centre in Yurakucho. Comprising four graduated cubes, encased in granite, abutting a high, tapering trajectory of glass and steel, it is aptly named "Glass Hall".

The striking Prada fashion boutique in Aoyama (*see page 115*) also generates a new

architectural experience. Origami-like surfaces and vertical planes form an exoskeleton where there is no separation between the structure itself, its surface and the interior space. The drama of the building is most evident at night, when the glass skin, latticed frame and interior lighting turn the whole building transparent.

Architecture meets shopping, leisure and entertainment in the new and somewhat controversial Roppongi Hills complex (*see page 132*). Whether you like the design and concept or not is purely instinctive. The outdoor sculpture of a giant spider by French artist Louise Bourgeois certainly gets a lot of attention.

KENZO TANGE'S VISION

No other architect has left his mark on Tokyo more than Kenzo Tange (1913–2005). His style is to write large across the city, not only in his signature Yoyogi National Stadium, where the 1964 Olympic Games were held, or the controversial Tocho building in Shinjuku, but also in such projects as St Mary's Cathedral in Mejirodai, the Aoyama's United Nations University, the 1996 Fuji TV Building in Odaiba, and other post-modernist eruptions.

Tange's ambitious 1960 proposal to impose a vast grid system similar to ancient Chinese cities on Tokyo, a web of roads and new zones that would stretch out into the bay, however, was never implemented.

A sci-fi city

Contrasting with Tokyo's techno-aided verticality is a counter-tendency to burrow deeper into the earth's surface. Tokyo already has a considerable underground life. In addition to the world's largest subway system which is still vigorously expanding, miles of subterranean corridors connect train lines and concourses with countless underground shopping malls. Tokyo Electric Co. has operated a power station under a Buddhist temple for almost two decades now; and an Asahi television studio, built 20 metres below ground in Roppongi, operates a simulated downpour behind the announcers when it rains above ground.

In William Gibson's sci-fi novel, *Idoru*, skyscrapers in Shinjuku are hatched from an organic building substance that seems "to ripple, to crawl slightly... a movement like osmosis or the sequential contraction of some sea creature's palps." This may not be as far-fetched as it sounds. Tokyo, with its natural propensity to shed old skins, would no doubt be the ideal place to test such a material.

As if to prove the point, the designers of Kajima Corporation's aptly-named 220-storey Dynamic Intelligence Building, or DIB-220, have proposed installing seismic sensors to detect movement and vibration. The transmitted data would then be analysed by a computer system designed to adjust the building's centre of gravity, thereby maintaining its equilibrium.

There are other plans afoot to create newer structures that incorporate hi-tech ventilating systems to heat and reuse air, install roof-mounted solar collectors, erect wind walls to direct breeze flows to aerial courtyards and internal spaces, and to use photo-voltaic glass to effectively turn buildings into power stations.

The penetration of media and information technologies into urban settings has replaced intellectual engagement with an increasing concern with image in architecture. This is evident in the use of strong primary colours and pastels. Materials such as glass tubing, gleaming metallic adjuncts, raw concrete, oxidized aluminium plates, translucent screens and fibre canopies are the order of the day – representing, perhaps, a new form of deconstructivism, or at least a disposition towards exterior surfaces that can be dismantled and replaced at will.

FAR LEFT: Kenzo Tange's Fuji TV Building in Odaiba.
LEFT: futuristic Tokyo International Forum.
RIGHT: Roppongi Hills and its giant spider sculpture.

Perpetual change

Japanese contractors, particularly the big five – Kajima, Takenaka, Taisei, Obayashi and Shimizu – have played a key role in transforming the appearance of these cities. The design and construction management within these companies work closely with their own cutting-edge research laboratories. With their immense financial resources, these companies have been called "the richest powerhouses of advanced technology in the world".

Where building values are only one-tenth the asset value of the land, it is hardly surprising that the urban building stock undergoes constant change. The downside, of course, is a city with no memory, or at best, an inaccuracy-prone collective memory.

As with the structures in Italo Calvino's novel, *Invisible Cities* – a spider-web of "ropes and chains and catwalks suspended in the air" – Tokyo knows that its edifices are not built to last. As a highly corporeal, perpetually embryonic city, it is ideally suited, however, to a transition in which, from its monuments to its lean-to shacks, the mortality of its structures is keenly sensed. ❑

THE ART OF LANDSCAPING

Compact, organised and highly introspective: words which stereotypically describe the Japanese might just as well be applied to their gardens

As a fully developed art, gardening can be traced to its introduction from China and Korea during the 6th century. The balance between nature and man-made beauty, with water and mountain as prototypical images, are the principles that form the basis for the traditional Japanese garden.

Artfully blended with ponds, gurgling brooks, banks of irises and moss-covered rocks, carefully contrived Japanese gardens are objects of quiet contemplation. "In order to comprehend the beauty of a Japanese garden," the 19th-century writer Lafcadio Hearn wrote, "it is necessary to understand – or at least to learn to understand – the beauty of stones." This is especially true of Japanese Zen gardens. Essentially, there are three types: stroll, pond, and so-called flat gardens. The dry-landscape garden, the *karesansui*, is the best example of the latter Zen-style garden.

The idea of confined space combined with the Zen idea of discovering limitless dimensions in the infinitely small saw the creation of the *kansho-niwa*, or "contemplation garden", created as both tools for meditation and works of art. Carefully framed like a scroll, they are intended to be appreciated like a painting that changes with the seasons and the quality of light.

LEFT: originally used to light the way to temples and shrines, stone lanterns are now a popular and characteristic feature of Japanese gardens.

ABOVE: in a dry landscape garden, rocks which represent islands and mountains in an "ocean" of sand are carefully incorporated into the garden design. Some of the rocks may represent auspicious crane and turtle islands.

LEFT: bridges, usually painted vermilion, suggest a link between heaven and earth. Some are known fancifully as "rainbow bridges".

LEFT: naturally sculptured stones of great distinction like these, were brought from all over Japan to help create the Kiyosumi Garden *(see page 182)*. Stones are said to represent the "bones" of a garden, water its "veins".

BELOW: a stone basin filled with water is used by tea ceremony guests to cleanse themselves before entering through the garden to the teahouse.

BLUE-BLOODED BLOOMS

In Japan, the cultivation of exhibition chrysanthemums is considered an art form. *Kiku* (Japanese for chrysanthemums) were first introduced from China in the late 7th century, though legend has it that the first flowers materialised from the necklace of Izanagi, the legendary father of the gods. Heian courtiers were known to drink *sake* tinted with the flower petals in the 9th century.

In the 13th century, the 16-petal chrysanthemum was adopted as a symbol of the Imperial household, and used as design motifs for clothing, on sword blades, banners and on official documents.

Blooming late in the year, the flower is a symbol of longevity. In November, many of Tokyo's gardens and temple grounds become venues for the Kiku Matsuri (Chrysanthemum Festival). *Kiku-ningyo*, life-size dolls representing court ladies and historical figures, are fashioned out of the chrysanthemums. Connoisseurs of the flower look for uniformity, enhanced by subtle differences; colours should be lively but not vulgar.

LEFT: paths are an integral component of Japanese stroll gardens. They suggest order and direction, contributing to the overall sense of a journey unfolding.

SUNTORY WHISKY
響
HIBIKI
KYOCERA
京セラ
TASAKI
Papawash
NINA'S
スタッフサービス
0120-022-022
504iS
英会話
ジオス

PLACES

A detailed guide to the city with the principal sites clearly cross-referenced by number to the maps

For all its modernity, Tokyo is a city impregnated with the past. In its backstreets and in the crevices between its post-modernist architecture and elevated expressways lie hundreds of temples, shrines, stone steles, Buddha images, and statues of Jizo and Kannon, the beloved Goddess of Mercy. Parts of Tokyo – its formal gardens, remnants of old Edo Period estates, teahouses, restaurants and craft shops run by generations of the same family, and schools dedicated to the traditional arts – are easily sought-out time capsules. At first glance, the world's largest city resembles a formless, oversized suburb, a hydra-headed experiment in urban living in danger of spinning hopelessly out of control. Closer examination, however, reveals concentrated patterns and order to the mass and sprawl of Tokyo.

For administration purposes, the city is made up of 23 wards, or *ku*, which are segmented into districts that are sub-divided into numbered sections called *chome*. Individual buildings, blocks and mini-zones that fall within their parameters are numbered separately. An address given as 3-7-2 Minami-Azabu, for example, indicates that it can be found in the third *chome* of Minami-Azabu, on block seven, within building number two *(see also page 230)*.

Good maps are an essential part of Tokyo life. Only important streets, the city's main thoroughfares, have names. Addresses are seldom written in English. Adding to the confusion is the fact that buildings are usually assigned numbers according to when they are built. Numbers are therefore often unsequenced. Every neighbourhood has a local police box called a *koban*, which is invaluable if you are lost or in doubt about an address. Police officers have detailed maps of the area and are usually very helpful.

Tokyo has an extensive bus network, but its routes are often convoluted or plagued by traffic congestion. By far the easiest way around the city is to use the underground Tokyo subway (officially re-named Tokyo Metro in April 2004, although people continue to use the term "subway") and the overground Japan Railways (JR) Yamanote Line. The latter egg-shaped track takes roughly an hour to complete a full loop around the inner city. Almost all the main sights, as well as Tokyo's major hotels and nightlife spots, are located inside or near one of the 29 stops of the loop. Tokyo's 13 subway lines intersect at all but a few of the stations on the Yamanote Line. Helpful maps can be found inside stations or at their exits. ❑

PRECEDING PAGES: the 54th-floor observation deck at Mori Tower in Roppongi; sculpture at the courtyard of the Tokyo Municipal Government Building. **LEFT:** neon-lit Ginza.

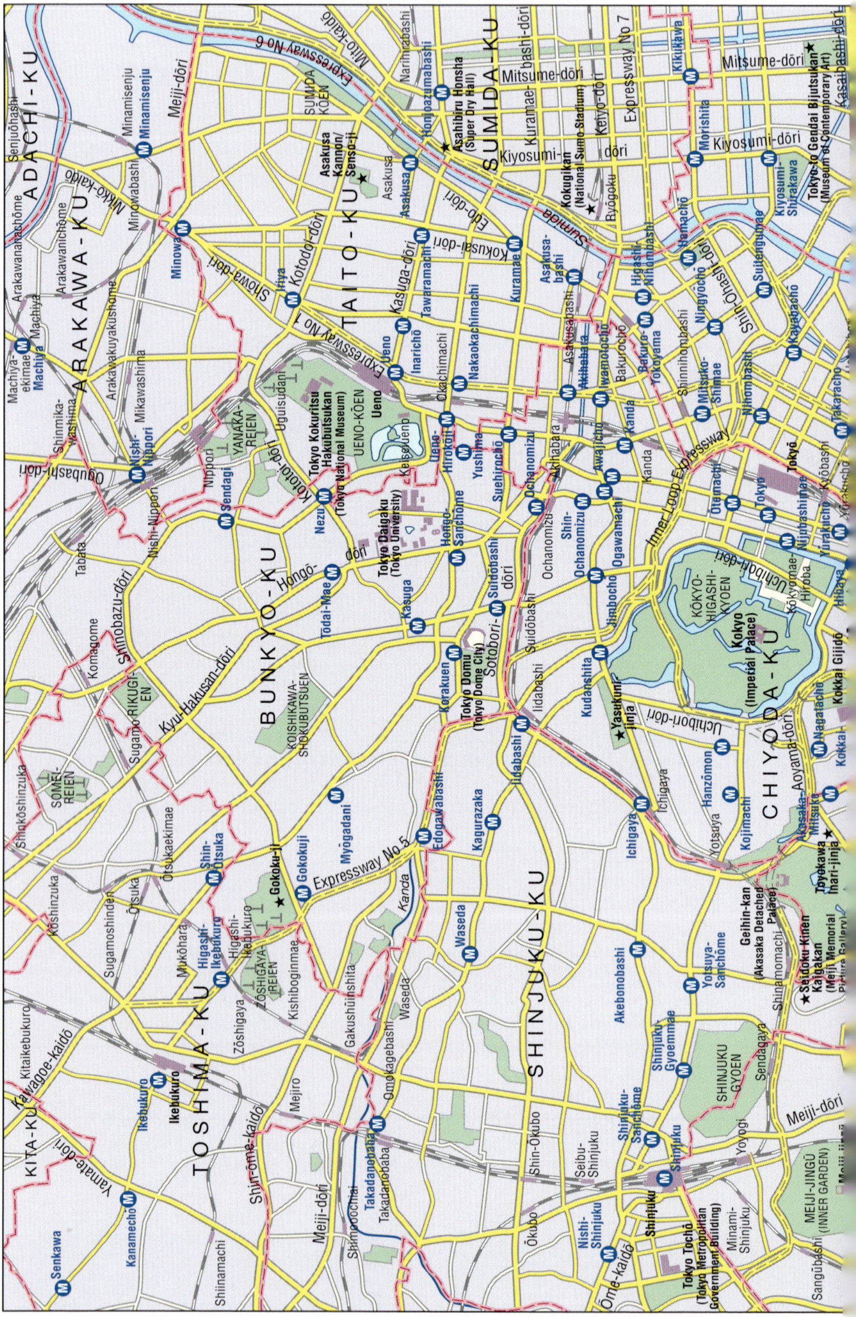
ADACHI-KU
ARAKAWA-KU
TAITO-KU
SUMIDA-KU
BUNKYO-KU
TOSHIMA-KU
KITA-KU
SHINJUKU-KU
CHIYODA-KU
Expressway No 6
Expressway No 1
Expressway No 5
Expressway No 7
Inner Loop Expressway
Sumida
Kanda
Meiji-dōri
Shōwa-dōri
Kototoi-dōri
Kasuga-dōri
Kokusai-dōri
Edo-dōri
Kiyosumi-dōri
Mitsume-dōri
Hongō-dōri
Shinobazu-dōri
Kyu-Hakusan-dōri
Sotobori-dōri
Uchibori-dōri
Yamate-dōri
Kawagoe-kaidō
Shin-ōme-kaidō
Ōme-kaidō
Nikkō-kaidō
Mito-kaidō
Asakusa Kannon (Sensō-ji)
Asahibiru Honsha (Super Dry Hall)
Kokugikan (National Sumo Stadium)
Tokyo-to Gendai Bijutsukan (Museum of Contemporary Art)
UENO-KŌEN
Tokyo Kokuritsu Hakubutsukan (Tokyo National Museum)
Tokyo Daigaku (Tokyo University)
Tokyo Domu (Tokyo Dome City)
KOISHIKAWA-SHOKUBUTSUEN
RIKUGI-EN
SOMEI-REIEN
YANAKA-REIEN
ZŌSHIGAYA-REIEN
Gokoku-ji
Yasukuni-jinja
KŌKYO-HIGASHI-GYOEN
Kokyo (Imperial Palace)
Kokkai Gijidō
Toyokawa Inari-jinja
Geihin-kan (Akasaka Detached Palace)
Seitoku Kinen Kaigakan (Meiji Memorial Picture Gallery)
SHINJUKU GYOEN
MEIJI-JINGŪ (INNER GARDEN)
Tokyo Tochō (Tokyo Metropolitan Government Building)
Ueno
Akihabara
Ochanomizu
Iidabashi
Ikebukuro
Shinjuku
Tokyo

Tokyo
0 1000 m
0 1000 yds
N
Tōkyō-kō
KOTO-KU
CHUO-KU
MINATO-KU
SHIBUYA-KU
MEGURO-KU
SHINAGAWA-KU
OTA-KU
Expressway No 9
Expressway No 11
Expressway No 1
Expressway No 2
Expressway No 3
Expressway Wangan Line
Rainbow Bridge
Harumi-Unga
Tatsumi
Shinonome
Toyosu
TOYOSU KŌEN
Etchūjima
Eitai-dōri
Tsukishima
Shintomichō
Tsukiji
Higashi-Ginza
Shimbashi
Shiodome
Shiodome City Centre
HAMA RIKYŪ TEIEN
Takeshiba
Hinode
Shibaura-Futō
Hamamatsuchō
Kiyosumi-dōri
Mitsume-dōri
Ariake
ARIAKE TENNIS-NO-MORI KŌEN
Kokusai-tenjijo
Kokusai-Tenjijō-Seimon
Tokyo Big Sight-Tokyo Kokusai Tenjijō (Tokyo International Exhibition Hall)
Tokyoteleport
Aomi
Telecom Centre
Fune-no-Kagakukan
Fune-no-Kagakukan (Museum of Maritime Science)
Odaiba-Kaihin-kōen
Daiba
Tennōzu Isle
Kaigan-dōri
Keihin
Daiichi-
Toranomon
Uchisaiwaichō
Kamiyachō
Onarimon
Daimon
Zōjō-ji
Tokyo Tower
Shiba-Kōen
Mita
Sakurada-dōri
Roppongi
Roppongi Hills
Tokyo Midtown
Roppongi-dōri
Akasaka
Nogizaka
Kokuritsu Shin Bijutsukan (National Art Centre)
AOYAMA REIEN
Gaiemmae
Aoyama-dōri
Omotesandō
Omotesandō Hills
Meiji-Jingumae
Harajuku
Yoyogi-Kōen
YOYOGI KŌEN
Kokuritsu Yoyogi Kyogijo (National Yoyogi Stadium)
Shibuya
Shinsen
Daikan-yama
Ebisu
Nakameguro
Meguro
Meguro-dōri
Yamate-dōri
Tokyo-to shashin Bijutsukan
SHIZENKYOIKUEN (NATIONAL PARK FOR NATURE STUDY)
Sengakuji
Shinagawa
Takanawadai
Gotanda
Ōsaki
Ōsakihirokōji
Hara Bijutsukan
Kitashinagawa
Shinbanba
Aomonoyokochō
Samezu
Ōimachi
Shimoshinmei
Togoshikōen
Togoshi
Togoshiginza
Nakanobu
Ebara-Nakanobu
Ebaramachi
Musashikoyama
Nishikoyama
Fudōmae
Meguro Fudō-son
RINSHINOMORI-KŌEN
Nakahara-kaidō
Hatanodai
Senzoku
Kanpachi-dōri

IMPERIAL PALACE AND SURROUNDINGS

Little is left of the once formidable imperial compound, but its grounds offer leisurely exploration in the heart of Tokyo. Here too is the city's main business districts of Marunouchi and Nihombashi, interspersed with fine museums and glitzy shopping malls

Map on page 74

At the historic and topographic core of a city struggling to accommodate over 12 million people, lies, quite unexpectedly, a sublimely empty space – the grounds of the **Imperial Palace** ❶ or Kokyo (inner grounds only opened two days of the year – 2 January and 23 December 9.30am–3pm; free). The palace is home to the Japanese Emperor and his family, the world's longest unbroken line of monarchs. This impregnable embryo of moats and stone walls occupy a 110-hectare (280-acre) expanse of green – its innermost folds the habitat of rabbits and pheasants, its outer ring of moats and bridges the home of turtles, carp and gliding swans.

This idyll of meticulously controlled ecology is deceptive. The palace, sitting at the centre of a district which also includes the Diet building, a number of key ministries, the Supreme Court and the Metropolitan Police Quarters, remains a fortified citadel at the core of establishment Japan, nourishing as it has always done the centers of power.

Palace history

The palace grounds mark the spot where Ota Dokan *(see page 17)* built a fortified mansion in 1457 on a bluff rising from an inlet overlooking present-day Tokyo Bay. Edo's elevation to the world's largest city began when Ieyasu Tokugawa, the future shogun, chose the site as his new headquarters in 1590. Ieyasu's purpose was to create an unassailable stronghold, a military capital that would also reflect his own position as Japan's de facto ruler.

In the construction of Edo Castle, nothing was left to chance. The first line of defence involved the construction of a complex system of moats and canals integrating existing bodies of water to form a web that

LEFT: the elegant Nijubashi stone bridge at the Imperial Palace.
BELOW: policemen on palace grounds.

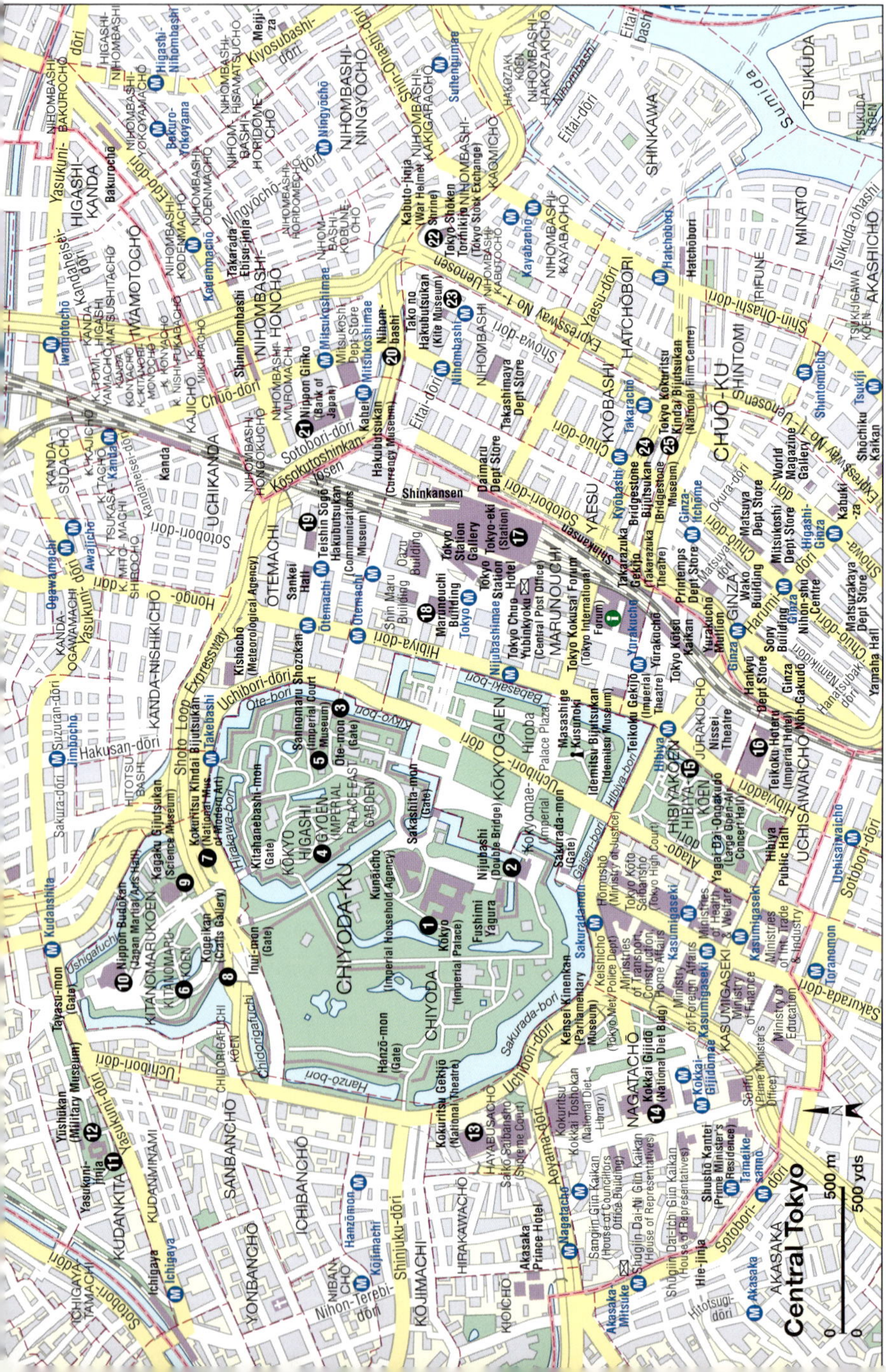
Central Tokyo
0 500 m
0 500 yds
N
CHIYODA-KU
CHŪŌ-KU
CHIYODA
Kōkyo (Imperial Palace)
Kōkyo Higashi Gyoen (Imperial Palace East Garden)
Kōkyogaien
Kōkyomae-Hiroba (Imperial Palace Plaza)
Kitanomaru-Kōen
Hibiya-Kōen
Nijubashi (Double Bridge)
Fushimi Yagura
Kunaichō (Imperial Household Agency)
Sakuradamon (Gate)
Sakashita-mon (Gate)
Ōte-mon (Gate)
Kitahanebashi-mon (Gate)
Inui-mon (Gate)
Hanzō-mon (Gate)
Tayasu-mon (Gate)
Sannomaru Shōzōkan (Imperial Court Museum)
Kokuritsu Kindai Bijutsukan (National Mus. of Modern Art)
Kōgeikan (Crafts Gallery)
Kagaku Gijutsukan (Science Museum)
Nippon Budōkan (Japan Martial Arts Hall)
Yūshūkan (Military Museum)
Yasukuni-jinja
Kokuritsu Gekijō (National Theatre)
Saikō Saibansho (Supreme Court)
Kokkai Gijidō (National Diet Bldg)
Kensei Kinenkan (Parliamentary Museum)
Kokuritsu Kokkai Toshokan (National Diet Library)
Shushō Kantei (Prime Minister's Residence)
Hie-jinja
Akasaka Prince Hotel
Idemitsu Bijutsukan (Idemitsu Museum)
Teikoku Gekijō (Imperial Theatre)
Teikoku Hoteru (Imperial Hotel)
Tokyo Kokusai Forum (Tokyo International Forum)
Tokyo Station
Tokyo Station Gallery
Marunouchi Building
Shin Maru Building
Kishōchō (Meteorological Agency)
Teishin Sōgō Hakubutsukan (Communications Museum)
Nippon Ginkō (Bank of Japan)
Mitsukoshi Dept Store
Takashimaya Dept Store
Daimaru Dept Store
Kabuto-jinja
Tokyo Shōken Torihikijo (Tokyo Stock Exchange)
Tako no Hakubutsukan (Kite Museum)
Bridgestone Bijutsukan (Bridgestone Museum)
Tokyo Kokuritsu Kindai Bijutsukan (National Film Centre)
Kabuki-za
Sony Building
Wako Building
Matsuya Dept Store
Printemps Dept Store
Hankyū Dept Store
Nissei Theatre
Yamaha Hall
Hibiya Public Hall
Yagai-Dai-Ongakudo (Large Open-Air Concert Hall)
Ministries of Health & Welfare
Ministry of Finance
Ministry of Foreign Affairs
Ministry of Education
Ministries of Int. Trade & Industry
MARUNOUCHI
ŌTEMACHI
YAESU
KYŌBASHI
GINZA
NIHOMBASHI
HATCHŌBORI
SHINKAWA
SHINTOMI
TSUKUDA
MINATO
IRIFUNE
AKASHICHŌ
UCHISAIWAICHŌ
KASUMIGASEKI
NAGATACHŌ
AKASAKA
KŌJIMACHI
HIRAKAWACHŌ
HAYABUSACHŌ
YONBANCHŌ
ICHIBANCHŌ
SANBANCHŌ
KUDANMINAMI
KUDANKITA
KANDA-NISHIKICHŌ
UCHIKANDA
HIGASHI KANDA
IWAMOTOCHŌ
KANDA
YŪRAKUCHŌ
Uchibori-dōri
Hibiya-dōri
Sotobori-dōri
Chūō-dōri
Yasukuni-dōri
Eitai-dōri
Shōwa-dōri
Harumi-dōri
Yaesu-dōri
Hakusan-dōri
Shinjuku-dōri
Aoyama-dōri
Sakurada-dōri
Shuto Expressway
Shinkansen
Sumida
Tokyo
Ōtemachi
Nijūbashimae
Hibiya
Yūrakuchō
Ginza
Kasumigaseki
Sakuradamon
Nagatachō
Kudanshita
Takebashi
Jimbōchō
Awajichō
Kanda
Mitsukoshimae
Nihombashi
Kayabachō
Hatchōbori
Takarachō
Kyōbashi
Shintomichō
Tsukiji
Higashi-Ginza
Toranomon
Uchisaiwaichō
Hanzōmon
Kōjimachi
Ichigaya
Akasaka-Mitsuke
Tameike-sannō
Suitengūmae
Ningyōchō

would entrap, or at least delay, the enemy. The water spirals were spanned by bridges guarded by fortified gates. By the time the castle was completed in 1640, it was the largest fort in the world comprising an astonishing 110 entry gates, 30 bridges, 21 watchtowers and 28 armouries.

Fires, engagingly referred to by the townspeople as "the flowers of Edo", were a far greater problem to the city than armed rebellion. One of the most devastating, the infamous so-called "Long-Sleeves Fire", occurred in 1657. The intensity of the heat not only destroyed most of the castle buildings, but also melted the shogun's gold reserves.

Although very little remains of the original, skeletal impressions of Ieyasu's medina-like ground plan for his castle and the city that grew around it remain, together with a concourse of moats, interconnecting canals and defensive gates.

Nijubashi Bridge

It is possible to visit the outer grounds of the Imperial Palace throughout the year. There are several approaches: most visitors cross the section of the inner defensive canal known as the **Babasaki Moat**, which leads to the gravel paths of the **Imperial Palace Plaza** (Kokyomae Hiroba).

Fine stands of pine and a well-manicured lawn lead to **Nijubashi Bridge ❷**, a two-tiered construction referred to as the "Double Bridge". The elegant arches of the bridge connect across the moat into the inner domain of the palace grounds, open only twice a year – on December 23, the Emperor's birthday, and January 2 – when the Imperial family traditionally assemble on a balcony to greet well wishers. This takes place seven times from 9.30am–3pm.

Niju Bridge, framed by willow trees, and the water that flows beneath it, stocked with orange carp and gliding swans, is one of the most photographed corners of Tokyo. The image is completed by massive stone ramparts and the graceful outline of the 17th-century **Fushimi Tower** (Fushimi Yagura), one of the few remaining original buildings in the complex.

Map on page 74

In the 17th century, Edo was the world's largest city with over one million people. By 1970, the figure had reached nine million. Today, including the 23 inner wards and the metropolitan area, it is said to be 26 million, making Tokyo again the most densely inhabited capital worldwide.

BELOW: a protective moat surrounds the grounds of the Imperial Palace.

Volcanic rocks from quarries on the Izu Peninsula were used to build the Imperial Palace walls. So precise was the work of the stone-masons that, it was said, not even a knife blade could be inserted between the blocks.

Imperial Household Agency

Close to the Imperial Palace, a 1968 ferro-concrete structure that embodies several traditional Japanese design elements houses the offices of the **Imperial Household Agency** (Kunaicho), a body which exercises a very strict (some might say sinister) hand over everything from the personal conduct of the royal family and their highly scripted public appearances, to press releases.

Imperial Palace East Garden

In its heyday, the main entrance to Edo Castle was via the **Otemon Gate ❸**. The present gate is a 1967 replica of the original, which was destroyed by a bomb towards the end of World War II. It is one of three entrances to the **Imperial Palace East Garden ❹** (Kokyo Higashi Gyoen), an immaculately kept ornamental Japanese garden replete with a pond, stone lanterns, a miniature waterfall, bridges and an authentic tea pavilion (Tues–Thur, Sat–Sun 9am–4pm; free).

Just inside the Otemon Gate is the **Imperial Court Museum ❺** (Sannomaru Shozokan), which displays a tiny fraction of the vast collection of Japanese art owned by the Imperial family (daily 9am–4pm; free). Sections of the original impregnable castle walls remain. The **Shiomizaka** (or "Tide-Viewing Slope") is another original feature that once offered views of Tokyo Bay and Mount Fuji. Today's main prospect looks onto the business districts of Nihombashi and Otemachi.

Kitahanebashi Gate (Kitahanebashi-mon), which forms the northern passageway out of the Imperial Palace East Garden, leads into a central, stone-walled square and yet another gate, wickedly angled to ensnare any assailant who might be foolish enough to approach the castle. The lush and extensive grounds of **Kitanomaru Park ❻** (Kitanomaru Koen), with trails and dense woodland, is home to several important cultural institutions (daily 24 hours; free).

Nat Museum of Modern Art

Located in the park is the **National Museum of Modern Art ❼**

BELOW: manicured grounds of the Imperial Palace East Garden.

(Kokuritsu Kindai Bijutsukan), which displays contemporary Japanese art from the Meiji Period to the present day (Tues–Sun 10am–5pm; admission charge; tel: 03-5777 8600). The 3,000 or more pieces in the collection, which also includes work by Western artists, are exhibited in rotation.

The museum's superb annexe, the **Crafts Gallery** ❽ (Kogeikan), is housed in a 1910 government-listed building, one of only five Meiji-era brick structures left in Tokyo (Tues–Sun 10am–5pm; admission charge; tel: 03-5777 8600). The gallery exhibits a fine collection of lacquerware, bamboo, ceramics and textiles, and has occasional demonstrations by craftsmen.

Science Museum

A short walk north under a section of the Shoto Expressway, sticking to the paths of Kitanomaru Park, leads you to the **Science Museum** ❾ (Kagaku Gijutsukan). Despite its unpromisingly austere exterior, the museum is both instructive and fun, especially for children (daily 9.30am–4.50pm; tel: 03-3212 8544; www.jsf.or.jp/index_e.html). Its two floors include space-age exhibits, working models, interactive displays and even a robot that gives lectures on electricity.

Martial Arts Museum

The octagonal **Japan Martial Arts Hall** ❿ (Nippon Budokan), which lies just northwest of the Science Museum along the same main pathway, was built in 1964 to stage the Olympic judo events (irregular opening times; tel: 03-3216 5100). To watch martial arts matches for free, call the above number. Until the Tokyo Dome was built in 1986, the Nippon Budokan was the city's main rock venue. The Beatles performed at the Budokan in 1966 to scenes of mass hysteria.

Chidorigafuchi Park

As you exit the park through **Tayasu Gate** (Tayasu-mon), one of the castle's finest gates, turn left and follow the moat with its dazzling line of cherry trees to the aquatic **Chidorigafuchi Park** (Chidorigafuchi Koen; daily 9am–5pm; free). The boathouse rents out skiffs for rowing along the moat. Front rooms at the **Fairmont Hotel**, a quiet retreat facing the moat, have views of the cherry blossoms in spring.

Yasukuni Shrine

One of Tokyo's most popular cherry blossom viewing venues are the grounds of the **Yasukuni-jinja Shrine** ⓫, accessed by walking back to the Tayasu Gate and crossing to its entrance just beyond Yasukuni-dori (Yasukuni Street). Founded in 1869 as a resting place for the souls of those who died in the conflicts leading up to the Meiji Restoration, the names of 2½ million soldiers and other personnel, including war criminals, have been added to those honoured at the shrine.

The shrine is now a focus for right-

Map on page 74

TIP

The Tokyo rush hour is not confined to a single hour in the morning and evening. On subway lines and routes like the Yamanote Line, which has one of the highest passenger capacities of any urban railway in the world, the evening crush can easily last from 5pm until 8–9pm.

BELOW: the Kogeikan (Crafts Gallery) annexe of the National Museum of Modern Art.

The exhibits at the Military Museum (Yushukan) in Yasukuni should be taken with a pinch of salt: one of the exhibits implies that British and American foreign policy forced Japan to attack Pearl Harbor in 1941.

wing elements who view Japan's activities during the war as crusades to liberate Asia from Western imperialism. The shrine's controversial **Military Museum ⓬** (Yushukan) displays torn uniforms, fading photos, letters from soldiers, a curious human torpedo and a suicide glider (daily 9am–5pm; admission charge; tel: 03-3261 0998; www.yasukuni.or.jp). Given the deliberate absence of data on the horrors perpetrated by the Japanese military in Asia, it conveys the disturbing impression of a monument to heroism. Exhibits in the newer glass annexe next to the museum include a real Zero fighter plane used in World War II.

The shrine is entered by passing under a grand *torii* gate and walking along a path lined with cherry and gingko trees. Behind the main hall is a garden with a pond, a teahouse and a ring for *sumo* wrestling and performances of court music and dance, *noh* dramas and *kendo* martial art.

National Theatre

Moving south along Uchibori-dori, the avenue which skirts the western side of the Imperial Palace, is the **National Theatre ⓭** (Kokuritsu Gekijo), a centre for traditional Japanese performing arts (box office 10am–5pm; tel: 03-3230 3000). The larger of its two auditoriums stages *kabuki* plays and *gagaku* recitals. Performances of *bunraku* puppet dramas and *kyogen* farces take place in the smaller hall *(see pages 49–50)*.

National Diet Building

Just two blocks south of the National Theatre is the **National Diet Building ⓮** (Kokkai Gijido) in the area known as Nagatacho (tel: 03-3581 3111 for tours). A plaza with fountains and gardens stands in front of the main edifice, which dates from 1937. The Diet is surrounded by an assortment of government offices and the **Prime Minister's Residence** (Shusho Kantei).

The **Parliamentary Museum** (Kensei Kinenkan), a short walk northeast from here in the direction of Uchibori-dori, has exhibitions as well as guided tours (Tues–Fri 9.30am–5pm; admission charge).

BELOW: votive tablets on display at the Yasukuni-jinja Shrine.

Map on page 74

Hibiya Park/Imperial Hotel

Continuing along Uchibori-dori, past **Sakurada Gate** (Sakurada-mon) – another gate leading to the Imperial Plaza – turn right into **Hibiya Park** ⓯ (Hibiya Koen). Ieyasu's less favoured Outer Lords had their homes here before the Meiji government confiscated the land and turned it into Tokyo's first Western-style park (open 24 hours; free).

Across the park on the corner of Hibiya-dori (Hibiya Street) and Miyuki-dori (Miyuki Street) stands the site of a former city landmark: the **Imperial Hotel** ⓰ (Teikoku Hoteru). The present hotel is built on the site of Frank Lloyd Wright's original design, which was completed in 1923. Wright's masterpiece, a curious Mayan-style design with Western interior features, survived earthquakes and World War II, but not the attentions of Tokyo's busy, postwar construction boom – it was torn down in 1967 and replaced with the much larger current version.

Marunouchi District

The Marunouchi business district, an area extending from the Imperial Plaza, down to Yurakucho and over to the western façade of Tokyo Station, has long been identified with power and prestige. Marunouchi was where Tokugawa Ieyasu instructed his senior retainers to build their mansions in the early 1600s. Its name means "Within the Castle Walls". Concealed from view behind steep walls of their own, the defining features of the area's sprawling feudal villas were their gates, plain or ostentatious according to wealth and rank. With the fall of the shogunate in 1868, the walls and gates were torn down. Once the figurative walls came down, so did other barriers.

By the end of the century, the government, in an attempt to drum up much needed funds to feed its growing military machine, persuaded a rich merchant clan, the Iwasaki, to purchase a large section of land in front of the palace grounds for purposes of commercial development.

The Iwasaki hired Josiah Conder, an English architect in Tokyo, to realise their vision of a Western-style business complex. Doubts about earthquakes and Tokyo's subtropical summers were put aside as Conder's blueprint for Marunouchi and his client, the Mitsubishi group, materialised with the block of three-storey, red-brick neo classical buildings known as Itcho Rondon, or "London Town", and its first building, the Mitsubishi No.1 Hall.

Although the European architecture eventually overcame the problems of its transplant, Paul Waley in his superb collection of narratives, *Tokyo: City of Stories*, said it revealed "a pronounced sense of unease. The buildings need carriages and trolleys and the bustle of late-Victorian and Edwardian London. Instead, all they have to look out on is a few rickshaws and the occasional disoriented passer-by."

Most of Conder's buildings were

Even after over a decade of recession, and a still beleaguered economy, one sq. metre of land in the Marunouchi business district costs a hefty ¥14 million.

BELOW: Marunouchi business district.

Aside from being one of the main gateways into the city centre, Tokyo Station also has the dubious distinction of being the place where two prime ministers were assassinated in the 20th century.

replaced in the 1930s by larger, more imposing structures. The last of the original Mitsubishi blocks was demolished in 1967, a victim of the post-war construction boom. In the scramble for economic growth, traditions as well as landmarks were set aside. The old prohibition, which disallowed buildings of over eight floors out of deference to the nearby Imperial Palace, was ignored and the practice of placing a Buddha image beneath the roof as a safeguard against lightning, forgotten.

Tokyo Station

An outstanding survivor of Marunouchi's flirtation with European architecture is the **Tokyo Station** ⓱ (Tokyo-eki). With the extension of the railway from Shimbashi into the centre of the city and the completion of Tokyo Station in 1914, Marunouchi's future was assured. The station's red-brick, Queen Anne-style design, based on the Amsterdam Central Station, was the work of Tatsuno Kingo, a former student of Josiah Conder. It is one of the main gateways into Tokyo, a staggering 3,000 trains passing through each day. The main focus within the concourse is the **Tokyo Station Gallery** (Tues–Sun 10am–5pm; admission charge; tel: 03-3212 2485). Built in the same year as the station and offering fine views through Georgian windows is the venerable **Tokyo Station Hotel**, currently closed for renovations.

Marunouchi Building

The old redbrick façade of the station is a surprisingly snug design match to the surrounding grove of skyscrapers completed in 2004. Of foremost interest to the visitor is the reconstructed and expanded **Marunouchi Building** ⓲. One of Tokyo's new mini-city complexes, the structure has superb gourmet food stores, a shopping zone, and all manner of restaurants. The upper levels offer sweeping views of the Imperial Palace grounds and beyond.

Across the street on the same side, the **Shin Maru Building**, a 38-floor structure designed by the British architect Sir Michael Hopkins, offers a similar mix of shopping and dining.

BELOW: artists at work outside the Tokyo Station.

Located in the next block along, the **Oazu Building**, is **Maruzen**, one of Tokyo's best book shops. Check in advance, as it is due to return to its old Nihombashi location in the near future (tel: 03-5288 8881).

Communications Museum

Walking north across Eitai-dori towards the A5 exit of Otemachi Station, you will come to the massive **Communications Museum** ⑲ (Teishin Sogo Hakubutsukan). Occupying four floors of the Teishin Building (Tues–Sun 10am–4pm; admission charge), it traces the history, present operations and future of communications networks. Philatelists especially will like the collection of 200,000 postal stamps.

Shopping options

Immediately in front of Tokyo Station's east side is **Daimaru**, a good all-round store. Three blocks directly east along Chuo-dori (Chuo Street), **Takashimaya** is one of Japan's oldest department stores. In addition to its fine kimono department, the store has an interesting roof area with a bonsai garden and a small Shinto shrine.

A brisk 10-minute walk north of Takashimaya, a giant statue of a female deity, Tennyo Magiokoro, the Buddhist Goddess of Sincerity, greets customers to **Mitsukoshi**, Tokyo's most luxurious store. Mitsukoshi began life as a dry goods store in 1673 and was the first store to display goods in glass cabinets, to employ women sales assistants, sell imported wares and, in later years, to install an escalator.

Nihombashi Bridge

At the centre of Marunouchi district lies the **Nihombashi Bridge** ⑳, Tokyo's "Bridge of Japan". Ieyasu had a wooden, arched structure built here as a starting point and distance post for the five main roads that led out of the city. These included the Tokaido, the great "Eastern Road" connecting Edo and Kyoto.

The present bridge, a solid but elegant structure made of stone and metal, was completed in 1911. A bronze pole called the **Zero Kilometre Marker** (Tokyo-to Dorogenpyo) continues to serve as a distance post for the city's national highways.

Nihombashi District

At the heart of the financial district of **Nihombashi** is the imposing **Bank of Japan** ㉑ (Nippon Ginko), a single block northwest of Mitsukoshi along Nichigin-dori (Nichigin Street). Built in 1898 on the former site of the shogun's gold, silver and copper mints, the bank represents the city's first Western-style construction designed by a Japanese architect. Guided tours in English take in the bank's history and present operations.

An annexe houses the **Currency Museum** (Kahei Hakubutsukan), displaying coinage from the Roman Period to the introduction of Chinese currency during the late Heian Period, as well as all the Japanese

Map on page 74

At major department stores such as Daimaru and Takashimaya, staff greet the first customers of the day with a polite bow.

BELOW: Takashimaya department store.

Map on page 74

A film poster at the National Film Centre showing a heavily tattooed woman.

coins ever circulated (Tues–Sun 9.30am–4.30pm; tel: 03-3277 3037).

Tokyo Stock Exchange

The last behemoth in the district is the **Tokyo Stock Exchange** 22 (Tokyo Shoken Torihikijo). It faces the Nihombashi River (Nihombashi-gawa), a few minutes' walk north of Kayabacho Station on the Tozai Line. When the exchange opened in Kabuto-cho in 1878, trading hours were determined by burning a length of rope. Business was conducted in a kneeling position above *tatami* mats, and messages were relayed by young boys positioned at street corners. When the rope burned down, the day's trading came to an end. A touch of the arcane survives in the fascinating hand signals used by clerks on the trading floor, which can be observed from a glass-walled mezzanine level (Mon–Fri 9–11am and 12.30–3pm; free; tel: 03-3665 1881; www.tse.or.jp).

Kite Museum

Below: waxwork tableau at the Kite Museum.

West of the Tokyo Stock Exchange, just out from the A4 Exit of Nihombashi station – on the fifth floor above the Taimei Ken restaurant – is the **Kite Museum** 23 (Tako no Hakubutsukan), a splash of colour in this business district (Mon–Sat 11am–5pm; free; tel: 03-3275 2704; www.tako.gr.jp/eng/museums_e/tokyo_html). Kite flying has a long tradition in Japan among children and adults, who stage jousting contests.

The museum's collection exceeds 2,000 kites from around the world. Among the Japanese displays are kites shaped to resemble birds, squid and Mount Fuji. Others are like canvases, with paintings of samurai warriors, *manga* characters and *ukiyo-e* style woodblock images.

Bridgestone Museum

A few blocks south from Nihombashi Station, at the corner of Chuo-dori and Yaesu-dori, is the Bridgestone Building, with the **Bridgestone Museum** 24 (Bridgestone Bijutsukan) on its second floor (Tues–Sat 10am–8pm, Sun and holidays 10am–6pm; admission charge; tel: 03-3563 0241; www.bridgestone-museum.gr.jp). The museum's collection comprises mainly the works of the Impressionists, but there are some works of early 20th-century painters and post-Meiji-era Japanese artists, as well as Greek and modern sculptures.

National Film Centre

South of the museum and close to Takaracho Station is the **National Film Centre** 25 (Tokyo Kokuritsu Kindai Bijutsukan), Japan's only state-sponsored film institute (Tues–Fri 10.30am–6pm; tel: 03-3561 0823). The centre was set up to research and preserve Japanese archival footage and foreign films. There are almost 20,000 films in its collection. Two cinemas hold screenings throughout the year. Film buffs enjoy its gallery of photos and posters and film-related design, as well as its library. ❑

RESTAURANTS

Australian

Salt

Shin-Marunouchi Bldg, 5F, 1-5-1, Marunouchi, Chiyoda-ku. Tel: 03-5288 7828. Open: daily L and D. ¥¥¥ www.pjgroup.jp/salt

Aussie celebrity-chef Lujk Mangan prepares superb modern fusion cuisine in his first overseas venture located in the newly rebuilt Shin-Marunouchi Building, opposite Tokyo Station. Lots of great seafood matched with an excellent selection of wines from Down Under. Highly recommended.

Italian

De Niro

2F, 1-8 Nihombashi Hakozakicho, Chuo-ku. Tel: 03-3639 1475. Open: Mon–Sat L and D. ¥¥

No connection to the Hollywood actor, De Niro the restaurant offers affordable dishes for white-collar folk, despite its central location. Very decent quantities of everything, from pizzas and spaghettis to inventive pasta dishes and salads, are served. Especially popular deals here are the lunch plates. Decent wine list to pick from.

Locanda Elio

2-5-2 Kojimachi, Chiyoda-ku. Tel: 03-3239 6771. Open: Mon–Sat L and D. ¥¥

Elio Orsara is a European restaurateur of the old school. He serves great focaccia, freshly rolled pasta, Calabrian country-style soups and some of the best southern Italian food in Tokyo.

Japanese

Breeze of Tokyo

Marunouchi Bldg, 36F, 2-4-1 Marunouchi, Chiyoda-ku. Tel: 03-5220 5551. Open: Mon–Sat 11am–midnight, Sun 11am–11pm. ¥¥¥

A skilful blend of Japanese and French cuisine in a setting with sweeping views of the Imperial Palace grounds. There are over 30 types of champagne, sparkling wines and cocktails. Very refined ambience.

Hayashi

1-12-10 Nihombashi-Muromachi, Chuo-ku. Tel: 03-3241 5367. Open: Mon–Sat L and D. ¥¥¥¥

Expensive but sublime; the *tempura* (deep-fried battered seafood and vegetables) is in a league of its own. The seafood and vegetable morsels here are closer to the light, non-fatty variety of the elegant restaurants and inns of Kyoto. The décor also hints at the graciousness of the old imperial city. The prices are, regretfully, commensurate with this world of good taste.

Kizushi

2-7-13 Nihombashi Ningyocho, Chuo-ku. Tel: 03-3666 1682. Open: Mon–Sat L and D. ¥¥¥

Blending perfectly into an old neighbourhood, Kizushi strives to be individualistic in the competitive world of sushi, offering some of the best *nigiri* sushi to be found in Tokyo. Comparable to the best sushi establishments in the rough-and-ready Tsukiji Fish Market district.

Kurosawa

2-7-9 Nagatacho, Chiyoda-ku. Tel: 03-3580 9638. Open: Mon–Sat L and D. ¥¥¥

A great place for fans of the great filmmaker Akira Kurosawa (*The Seven Samurai*). Supervised by the master's daughter, Kazuko, the *soba* (buckwheat noodles), *shabu-shabu* beef and other dishes are those favoured by the late director. The exterior is actually modelled on a building used in his *Samurai* film set; the interior features movie posters and paintings by the director himself.

Muromachi Sunaba

4-1-13 Nihombashi Muromachi, Chiyoda-ku. Tel: 03-3241 4038. Open: Mon–Sat 11.30am–8pm. ¥

Meaning something like "sand pit", Sunaba is more of a pit stop for office workers on a tight budget. The *tenzaru soba* (cold soba with shrimp *tempura* dipping sauce) is the most popular dish, but the sticks of *yakitori* (charcoal-grilled chicken) are good value.

Ten-mo

4-1-3 Nihombashi-Motomachi, Chuo-ku. Tel: 03-3241 7035. Open: Mon–Sat L and D. ¥¥¥

This tiny old-style tempura shop is a hidden gem. Ten-mo's third-generation owner prepares the morsels of seafood and vegetables in the traditional Edo way, using rich sesame oil. There are only half a dozen seats at the modest counter, so reservations are essential.

Yukari

3-2-14 Nihombashi, Chuo-ku. Tel: 03-3271 3436. Open: Mon–Sat L and D. ¥¥¥

Superb fish dishes are aesthetically presented with all the seasonal ingredients and garnishings. Specialities include snapper, ark shell, conger eel sashimi and *sanpoukan* (Japanese citrus stuffed with crab, shrimp, ginger and milt). Try a glass of Koshu Nouveau Dry with your food: it's the perfect complement to Yukari's wonderful cuisine.

PRICE CATEGORIES

Prices for three-course dinner per person without drinks and taxes:

¥ = under ¥2,000
¥¥ = ¥2,000–¥3,000
¥¥¥ = ¥3,000–¥5,000
¥¥¥¥ = over ¥5,000

GINZA TANAKA
GINZA TANAKA
GINZA TANAKA
GINZA TANAKA
GINZA TANAKA

YURAKUCHO AND GINZA

Both elegance and exclusivity mark Ginza as a world-famous shopping destination. But there is also an old theatre devoted to *kabuki* performances, a traditional bathhouse and lots of tiny art galleries

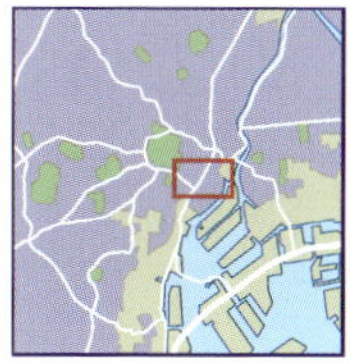

During the Edo Period there was little to suggest the sartorial elegance and good taste the name Ginza now conjures up. Contiguous with the southern ribbon of the teeming, plebeian quarters of the townspeople, it occupied a rather undefined area between the feudal mansions of the Outer Lords and the newly reclaimed land of Tsukiji.

Tokugawa Ieyasu *(see page 18)*, established a silver mint (*gin-za*) here in 1612. The mint moved on to Nihombashi in 1800, but the name stuck. Fire and steam rather than coinage were the two main elements in Ginza's rise. In 1872, Ginza and Tsukiji suffered the second of two almost consecutive fires. Nearly 3,000 homes were destroyed and the area virtually reduced to cinder. The governor of Tokyo decided to build a European-style quarter in Ginza, consisting of hundreds of fire-proof red-brick buildings, arcades and tree-lined avenues.

The plan coincided nicely with the opening the same year of a train line from Yokohama to Shimbashi, a district adjacent to Ginza. The rail terminus at Shimbashi brought new life to Ginza, which suddenly found itself in the enviable position of being the main gateway into Tokyo.

The remodeling of Ginza took 10 years. By the time it was completed, its streets could boast a horse-drawn tram (soon replaced by an electric tram system), shops selling Western goods, theatres, European-style cafés, bakeries, beer halls, tearooms and the offices of several newspaper companies. By 1894, the district's most famous landmark, the Hattori Clock Tower (later rebuilt as Wako Building), was already in place. The city's keen instinct for merchandising had found a new home. Many of the best known businesses and shops that line Ginza today date from this time.

Map on page 86

LEFT: Ginza shopping. **BELOW:** a Jackie Chan movie poster along Ginza.

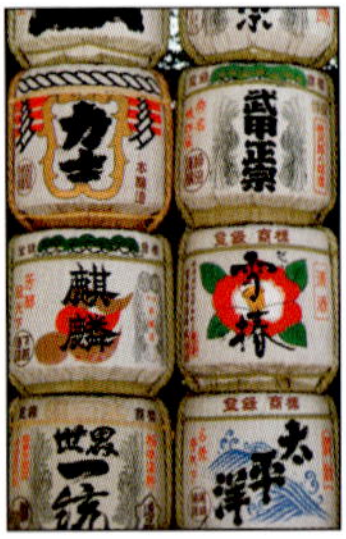

An excellent place to sample different brands of sake and learn about the brewing process is the Sake Plaza. Located at Nishi-Shimbashi (tel: 03-3519 2091), it is open from Mon to Fri 10am–6pm.

Despite its new reinforced buildings, Ginza was not immune to disaster – its brick buildings were laid to waste in the Great Kanto Earthquake of 1923. Undeterred, larger, more fortified buildings sprang up in the 1930s. Most, however, suffered a similar fate during the air raids of 1945. The 1932 Hattori Building, now called Wako, is virtually all that remains of an older Ginza, with the exception of a few smaller pre-war buildings in some of the backstreets.

Idemitsu Museum

There are several possible starting points from which to explore Ginza and its environs. One of the easiest is from the JR Yurakucho Station or the Yurakucho Line subway.

Located at the borders of Hibiya and Ginza is the outstanding **Idemitsu Museum** ❶ (Idemitsu Bijutsukan), on the ninth floor of the Teigeiki Building (Tues–Sun 10am–5pm; admission charge; tel: 03-3213 9402; www.idemitsu.co.jp/museum). Its collection, one of the finest showcases for Asian art in the city, reflects the eclectic but discerning tastes of its wealthy founder, petroleum industrialist Idemitsu Sazo.

Its main room features an impressive collection of Chinese ceramics. There are fine Japanese pieces here too, including examples of Kakiemon, Imari, Kutani and Seto wares. Ancient pottery shards from all over the world crowd the show-cases of a room with a magnificent view of the Imperial Palace. There are also gold-painted screens, Zen calligraphy and *ukiyo-e* prints.

Tokyo International Forum

Two blocks east of Idemitsu Museum, pressed against the tracks of the Yamanote Line, an architectural vision unlike any other you are likely to have seen rises in the spectacular form of the **Tokyo International Forum** ❷ (Tokyo

BELOW: interior of Tokyo International Forum.

Kokusai Forum, tel: 03-5221 9000). In the face of stiff competition, New York-based architect Raphael Vinoly was given the contract to design this exhibition space divided into two enormous, interconnecting buildings. Whether intentionally or not, the right side contours of the east building, the forum's Glass Hall, follow the curving tracks of the elevated JR train lines.

This post-modernist masterpiece has provided the capital with a new conference, concert, dance and theatre space. The complex's Cultural Information Lobby has an excellent audio-visual library focusing on Tokyo attractions and sights. Its futuristic 60-metre (196-ft) high glass atrium, with its sweeping skywalks, curved walls and immense roof, is the visual highlight of the complex, a sense of which can be had by taking the lift up to the seventh floor and then descending by stairs.

Yakitori restaurants

In one of those abrupt changes of time and mood that this most spatial of cities is known for, an older, very different Yurakucho materialises south of the station with a number of cubbyhole restaurants and stalls located directly under the raised tracks of the Yamanote Line. These are the last remnants of the American Occupation years when the area played host to a lively, downtown throng of street markets, small workshops, and pavement beer and *sake* stalls lit up with roadside lanterns.

A glimmer of those days remains in Yurakucho's *yakitori* (charcoal-broiled skewers of chicken slathered with a sweet sauce) joints under the tracks. There are few more appetising and atmospheric places to eat *yakitori* than here, among the lively, alcohol-stimulated babble of salarymen and office ladies.

Shopping diversions

Continuing along Harumi-dori (Harumi Street), under the railway bridge that bullet trains constantly pass, the next building of note is the 14-storey **Yurakucho Mullion**, a cinema and theatre complex that also includes the **Hankyu** and **Seibu** department stores.

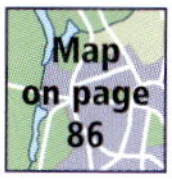
Map on page 86

"Ginza Street, Tokyo's 'Broadway', is completely fabulous in the size and vulgarity of its neon signs. At the top of one high building, a motor-car revolves, floodlit, on a silver pillar. Starlight and moonlight haven't a chance in this bedlam."

Extract from "The Flowery Sword" by Ethell Manning.

BELOW: a late-night *yakitori* eatery in Yurakucho.

All-women casts dominate the stage performances at the Takarazuka Theatre.

Running all the way from the Imperial Hotel, under the tracks of the Yamanote Line, to just behind the Mullion Building, are the tourist-oriented shops of the slightly tacky **International Arcade**. Japanese tourists from the provinces come here for souvenirs. The excellent store **Hayashi Kimono** has sizes for foreigners, as well as antique kimono.

Takarazuka Theatre

Just three blocks north of the Mullion Building is the **Takarazuka Theatre** ❸ (Takarazuka Gekijo; box office 03-5251 2001). Exacting a little revenge perhaps on *kabuki* dramas with their all-male casts, all the parts in the spectacular musicals *(see page 51)* put on by the Takarazuka are played by young women. Loyally supported by an audience of mostly middle-aged housewives and adoring adolescents, the unashamedly romantic, highly entertaining shows employ flamboyant settings and gorgeous costumes.

The adulation of its fans has been known to reach delirious levels. When it was announced in 1944 that the company would be closed, the crowd that gathered outside the building, according to writer John H. Martin in his *Tokyo: A Cultural Guide to Japan's Capital City*, "was so large and in danger of becoming unruly that the police unsheathed their swords to maintain order."

BELOW: Wako Building is a landmark feature at the Ginza 4-chome intersection.

Along Harumi-dori

Return to Harumi-dori, the road that runs all the way to Tokyo Bay before intersecting Yurakucho and Ginza, turn left and almost immediately on your right, you will see the **Fuji Photo Salon**, one of 300 or so small photo and art galleries in the area (daily 10am–8pm; free; tel: 03-3571 9411). Many are private and do not charge entrance. Harumi-dori and its side streets also have many competitively priced camera shops.

On the next corner down the street is the **Sony Building** ❹, its several floors crammed with the newest tech gadgetry and plenty of hands-on and interactive equipment to play with (daily 11am–7pm). The PlayStation showroom on the sixth floor gets especially crowded on weekends. Two exclusive restaurants, Sabatini's and Maxim's, are located in the same building.

The **Kyocera Contax Salon**, with regular photo exhibitions, is a short stroll from here, at the corner of Harumi-dori and Chuo-dori, near a black glass obelisk that is actually a police box (Thur–Tues 10.30am–6.30pm; free; tel: 03-3574 1921).

Along Chuo-dori

Chuo-dori ❺ (Chuo Street) is the Ginza's main shopping drag, a showcase for some of the city's finest stores. Here, in the area known as **Ginza 4-chome**, people enjoy the pleasures of *Gin-bura*, or "strolling in the Ginza", a tradition that goes back to the district's early days as an experiment in continental shopping and leisure. Strolling in the Ginza is especially pleasant on weekends when the street is turned into a pedestrian zone, a European-style boulevard with café tables and umbrellas placed along its stretch.

Two stores dominate the Ginza 4-chome intersection. The first is the old Hattori, or **Wako Building ❻**, an elegant seven-storey edifice owned by Seiko, the watch company. Seiko's name means "precision" in Japanese, a reputation its clock tower, an exacting rendezvous site, has upheld since it was built in 1932. To enter Wako, which is said to attract women shoppers from Tokyo's older, well-connected families, is to pass into a world of refined taste with prices to match. Its window displays alone are a huge draw.

Facing Wako is the no less august **Mitsukoshi**, a branch of the Nihombashi store. The building has an interesting roof garden where miniature bonsai trees are displayed, along with a small Shinto shrine. There is also a statue of Jizo here, patron deity of travellers and children, who also obligingly serves the interests of the business community.

Mikomoto and Matsuya

With branches in Paris, London and New York, **Mikimoto Pearls**, a little further on the left after Wako Building, have truly arrived. The shop's founder, Mikimoto Kokichi, discovered that by inserting an irritant into the shell of the oyster, it was possible to create a cultured pearl. Mikimoto's first Ginza showroom opened in 1899 on the site of the present premises, which contain in addition to the shop, a pearl museum upstairs.

Also in the area, on a backstreet between Matsuya-dori and Okura-dori, is a second, newer store, the 10-storey **Mikimoto Ginza 2**, designed by the renowned architect Toyo Ito. Its jewel-box-inspired architecture features a pinkish façade perforated by irregular-shaped windows. Besides pearls, the store sells cosmetics and high-quality sweets.

Walking in a northeasterly direction up fashionable Chuo-dori takes you to the next block where the main building of note is the classy **Matsuya** department store, with a good selection of traditional Japanese souvenirs on the fifth floor. Its

Map on page 86

TIP

Japanese department stores generally open their doors at 10am and close between 7–9pm. Sunday, without any religious restraints, is a normal shopping day, the busiest of the week.

LEFT: a department store elevator attendant. **BELOW:** expect high fashion with prices to match at Ginza.

Itoya, which dates back to 1904, produces beautifully crafted stationery items as well as art and office supplies. Be sure to stop by its large store in Ginza.

clothing department has items by renowned designers like Issey Miyake. The **Matsuya Gallery**, which features temporary exhibitions is on the seventh floor (daily 10am–5pm; admission charge),

Paper and stationery

Just further up from Matsuya is **Itoya**, a seven-storey shop that sells Japanese handmade paper called *washi* and stationery items – including calligraphy items such as ink stones – which make excellent gifts.

Back at the Ginza 4-chome intersection, next door to the San-ai Building, **Kyukyudo**, a store with a history of over 300 years, sells both traditional paper goods, tea ceremony utensils and beautiful crafted lacquer letterboxes. Its speciality is incense, which was first brought to Japan in the 6th century when Buddhism was first introduced from China. Apart from religious purposes, and the pleasures of incense parties in which guests would compete to identify specific wood chips as they were burnt, incense was also incorporated into the Japanese tea ceremony.

BELOW: ornate exterior of the Kabuki Theatre.

Kabuki Theatre

Just a few steps beyond the crossing to the left, overseas visitors are always delighted to see the **Kabuki Theatre** ❼ (Kabuki-za), a building that, amid the Fifth Avenue pretensions of the Ginza, finally looks as if it belongs in Japan (box office tel: 03-5565 6000). Founded in 1899, the theatre has been rebuilt on two occasions. The present cream building, with a traditional roof and a grand entrance, dates from 1949. Highly stylised *kabuki* melodramas *(see page 50)*, very different in spirit from the transcendentally calm performances associated with *noh* drama, combine art and high jinks in a programme of dance, sword fighting, romantic episodes and tragedy.

The all-male actors, swathed in ostentatious costumes, perform for an audience who frequently bring their own box lunches, chat during performances and shout out the names of their favourite actors or heroes. This lively scene evokes the mood of an art that had great appeal for the common townspeople of Edo. Afternoon and evening matinees are staged twice a day. If a whole play seems too daunting, buy tickets for a single act alone.

More galleries and stores

Magazine House, a well-known publishing company, has its office directly behind the Kabuki Theatre. **The Magazine House**, its excellent reference library located on the mezzanine floor, stocks over 800 international titles, any of which can be removed and read at one of the tables there or in the café upstairs (Mon–Fri 11am–7pm; free; tel: 03-3545 7227).

Walking in the opposite direction along Chuo-dori from the Ginza 4-chome crossing, past the car showrooms of the **Nissan Gallery** (Tues–Sun 10am–5pm; free), you will come to the venerable **Matsuzakaya** department store. This 300-

year-old establishment appeals to more traditional, female shoppers.

One block up on the same side is the **Yamaha Hall**. Crammed with keyboards, guitars and other instruments, this is a musician's dream.

Traditional Japanese confectionery can be sampled at **Toraya**, across the road from the Yamaha Hall (Mon–Fri 8.30am–8pm, Sat–Sun 8.30am–6pm). These beautiful cakes, made from sweet bean paste called *wagashi*, were served during the Azuchi-Momoyama Period as accompaniments to the tea ceremony. The sweetness of *wagashi* was intended to complement the strong, slightly acerbic taste of green tea.

Just along from Toraya along Chuo-dori is the **Ginza Art Space**, a venue for occasionally contentious art shows (daily 10am–6pm; free). Behind it is the **Shiseido Gallery**, located in the basement of Shiseido Parlour, the famous cosmetics boutique. The gallery features experimental art by mainly young Japanese and foreign artists (Tues–Sat 11am–7pm, Sun 11am–6pm; free; tel: 03-3572 3901).

One street east of the gallery, **Shiseido Art House** has interesting exhibitions (Tues–Sun 11am–7pm; free; tel: 03-3571 0401). The advertising work for the company, past and present, is especially arresting.

Konparu-yu Baths

A traditional communal bath at the **Konparu-yu Bathhouse** ❽, a pre-Meiji-era bathhouse, on the small street behind Shiseido, should not be missed (Tues–Thur 11am–11pm, Fri–Sun 11am–1am; admission charge; tel: 03-3571 5469). Most Tokyo neighbourhoods had *sento* (public baths) until the 1970s, but these institutions, no longer necessary as most families have private baths, are fast disappearing. A Shinto altar sits in the rafters above the men's and women's sections, which have two baths apiece, one marked "tepid", the other "very hot".

The surrounding area is a former geisha quarter. A few Meiji-era buildings remain, evoking the atmosphere of a time when geishas came in the early hours to wash off their make-up and soak in the steaming pools.❑

Map on page 86

TIP

Bathhouse etiquette dictates that everyone should thoroughly soap and rinse themselves before entering the shared bath, which is for soaking only. Stories of bath owners having to drain entire pools and then refill them after an uninitiated bather (read foreigner) has plunged in covered in suds, are not uncommon.

BELOW: modern-day geishas near Konparu-yu Bathhouse.

Japanese Bathhouses

In the 8th century, some of the larger temples in Nara had baths built for monks and local residents. The connection between cleanliness and godliness may explain why many traditional public baths resemble temples. Edo's first public bath was built in 1591. An entrance fee of one *sen*, a modest copper coin, was charged. Public baths were henceforth called *sento*, meaning "money water". Mixed bathing was common and baths were not only centres for social intercourse but also sexual license.

Although the number of public baths is dwindling, there are still roughly 1,500 left in the Tokyo area.

RESTAURANTS

Café-Patisserie

Café Paulista

Nagasaki Centre, 1F, 8-9-16 Ginza, Chuo-ku. Tel: 03-3572 6160. Open: daily 8.30am–10.30pm. ¥

This venerable Ginza coffee shop only uses the best imported Brazilian coffee beans for its aromatic brews. Perfect place to linger over a cuppa and a slice of cake. This was one of the first pre-war coffee shops to set up in the Ginza. A bit faded but atmospheric and very affordable.

French

Aux Amis des Vins

2-5-6 Ginza, Chuo-ku. Tel: 03-3567 4120. Open: Mon–Fri 5.30pm–2am, Sat noon–midnight. ¥¥¥

Standing rib roast is the speciality of the house. The meat comes from Yoshida-buta, a species of pig raised in the Kawagoe area in Saitama. Also tasty fish of the day dishes. As the name suggests, this restaurant is renowned for its wine list. Several hundred to choose from, 40 of which can be sampled by the glass. Reservations required for Fridays and Saturdays.

Fusion

Cardenas Ginza

Ginza Kanematsu Bldg, 7F, 6-9-9 Ginza, Chuo-ku. Tel: 03-5537 5011. Open: daily L and D. ¥¥¥
www.cardenas.co.jp

California fusion cuisine with a large selection of West Coast wines. Special house dishes include grilled chops with Thai sauce, linguine with prawns and tomato cream sauce, crab cakes in sweet chilli sauce, as well as plain old grilled snapper. The sashimi appetisers are recommended.

Indian

Dhaba India

2-7-9 Yaesu, Chuo-ku. Tel: 03-3272 7160. Open: Mon–Sat L and D. ¥¥

The best South Indian cuisine in the city is here. Fragrant, coconut milk-rich curries, generous *thali* meals and superb *marsala dhosas*, prepared by chefs from the subcontinent. There are plenty of choices for vegetarians too.

Nair's

4-10-7 Ginza, Chuo-ku. Tel: 03-3541 8246. Open: daily except Thurs 11.30am–9.30pm, Sun 11.30am–8pm. ¥¥

Long-serving, ever-dependable Indian diner in the heart of the city. Nothing fancy, but good all-round choice of dishes from the subcontinent. Nair's often gets media coverage on TV, drawing the odd celebrity through its doors.

Italian

Enoteca Pinchiorri

Core Bldg, 7F, 5-8-20 Ginza, Chuo-ku. Tel: 03-3289 8081. Open: daily L and D. ¥¥¥¥

Tokyo's best Florentine restaurant is reputed for its extensive cellar of premium Italian and French wines. The food, equally impressive, has won many accolades. The atmosphere is refined, and prices reflect the upmarket Ginza locale. The lunch set meals start from ¥5,000; dinner from ¥17,000.

Japanese

Bird Land

Tsukamoto Sozan Bldg, B1F, 4-2-15 Ginza, Chuo-ku. Tel: 03-5250 1081. Open: daily except Sun and Mon 6–10pm. ¥¥¥

Yakitori (grilled skewers of chicken) is basically blue-collar fare, but Bird Land presents it in upmarket form, using morsels of free-range chicken carefully prepared over premium charcoal. The set meal includes chicken liver pâte and the delectable *sansai-yaki* (chicken breast grilled with Japanese pepper). Wash it down with Belgian beer or Chablis.

Ginza Hokake

4-7-13 Ginza, Chuo-ku. Tel: 03-3564 2491. Open: Mon–Sat L and D. ¥¥¥

Old style décor in the heart of modern Ginza, there is much charm to this well-known sushi restaurant where, despite the uncompromising quality of its sashimi, seaweed rolls and *nigiri* sushi, the head chef's motto is "Relax and enjoy. No need to take it too seriously."

Hashizen

1-7-11 Shimbashi, Minato-ku. Tel: 03-3571 2700. Open: Mon–Sat 11.30am–9pm, Sun 12–8pm. ¥¥

The city's oldest *tempura* shop (founded 1831), the building has been reconstructed and renovated several times, like most Tokyo restaurants that claim a long heritage. Sparkling modern décor, kimono-clad waitresses and traditional food. Great value.

Little Okinawa

8-7-10 Ginza, Chuo-ku. Tel: 03-3572 2930. Open: Mon–Sat 5pm–3am. ¥¥

The exotic cuisine of Japan's southernmost prefecture is strong on pork (from the ears to the trotters), stir-fries featuring gourd and bitter melon, and Chinese-style noodles, to be washed down with *awamori*, a potent rice-based liquor unique to Okinawa. At this intimate bar-restaurant, the ambience, food, music and décor all evoke the laid-back vibe of those subtropical islands.

Ohmatsuya
2F, 6-5-8 Ginza, Chuo-ku. Tel: 03-3571 7053. Open: Mon–Fri 5–10pm, Sat 4.30–9pm. ¥¥¥¥
Gourmet fare from the mountains and fishing villages of far-off Yamagata, by the Sea of Japan. Ancient farmhouse setting with wooden beams and smoky charcoal grills where fresh seafood and mountain herbs are cooked right in front of you. Also known for its excellent *sake*.

Otako Honten
5-4-16 Ginza, Chuo-ku. Tel: 03-3571 0057. Open: Mon–Sat 11.30am–10pm. ¥
Oden (fish, tofu, eggs and vegetables simmered in a rich broth) is snack food, to be nibbled while sipping *sake*. Otako serves this plain and simple fare in this upmarket district of Tokyo. Sit at the counter where you can see the bubbling pots of stew.

Rangetsu
3-5-8 Ginza, Chuo-ku. Tel: 03-3567 1021. Open: daily L and D. ¥¥¥
This long-established restaurant offers refined Japanese cuisine based around *shabu-shabu* (hot pot) and *sukiyaki* (one-pot meal), cooked at your table for you by kimono-clad waitresses. Only the finest cuts of beef from premium Wagyu steer are used. A range of seafood dishes are also served. The set lunches are good value.

Robata
1-3 Yurakucho, Chiyoda-ku. Tel: 03-3591 1905. Open: Mon–Sat 5pm–midnight. ¥¥
The down-home interior of this old-style restaurant evokes a rustic farmhouse, but the menu blends Western dishes with Japanese country fare. Choose from the large platters of cooked food arrayed on the wooden counter, or order simple grilled foods and salads from the kitchen out back.

Sakyo Higashiyama
Oak Ginza, B1F, 3-7-2 Ginza, Chuo-ku. Tel: 03-3535 3577. Open: daily L and D. ¥¥¥
A chance to sample Kyoto cuisine – the most sophisticated in Japan – if you can't go there. Fish and meat dishes are prepared with charcoal using a traditional sand pot. All ingredients are from Kyoto, including the water from the city's Higashiyama district, said to have a soft taste.

Shabusen
2F, 5-8-20 Ginza, Chuo-ku, Tokyo. Tel: 03-3571 1717. Open: daily 11am–10pm. ¥¥
Good-value restaurant at prices well below the norm for this part of town, and for this generally quite expensive dish. The house speciality is *shabu-shabu*, gossamer-thin slices of prime beef dipped in a bubbling cauldron of water. The more common *sukiyaki* (one-pot meal) barbecue options are also available.

Shin Hinomoto
2-4-4 Yurakucho, Chiyoda-ku. Tel: 03-3214 8021. Open: Mon–Sat 5pm–midnight. ¥
Noisy, friendly no-nonsense *izakaya* (tavern) built under the railway tracks, serving good fresh seafood at very reasonable prices. English-speaking and foreign visitors welcomed. The aromas drift out to the street, luring customers with the promise of hearty *yakitori* (grilled skewers of chicken), fish and ice-cold draught lager.

Ten-Ichi Deux
4-1 Ginza, Chuo-ku. Tel: 03-3566 4188. Open: daily 11.30am–10pm. ¥¥
Budget offshoot of Tokyo's best known *tempura* house serves simple meals of deep-fried battered seafood and vegetables in a stylish café ambience. While the *tempura* sets are delectable, simpler lunchtime fare is available in the form of *tendon:* tempura prawns on rice served with miso (fermented soybean) soup.

Tonton Honten
2-1-10 Yurakucho, Chuo-ku. Tel: 03-3508 9454. Open: daily 11.30am–11pm. ¥¥
Noisy and full of life, this casual *yakitori* chicken place is not for the squeamish. Located in the east-west tunnel section, bullet trains rumble overhead every few minutes, though some tables outside on the pavement can be pleasant with good company and ice-cold beer.

Yukun Sakagura
1-16-14 Shinbashi, Minato-ku. Tel: 03-3508 9296. Open: Mon–Sat L and D. ¥¥
The boisterous atmosphere in this eatery, which specialises in dishes from the island of Kyushu, replicates the supposed feisty character of the good folk there. The dishes are displayed on a 10-metre long (33-ft) counter. *Mutsugoro*, a grilled fish from Ariake Bay, is a popular choice.

Thai

Bangkok Kitchen
Ginza Corridor, 8-2-saki Ginza, Chuo-ku. Tel: 03-5537 3886. Open: daily L and D. ¥¥
Full-flavoured Thai food in a smart yet casual setting along the "restaurant row" under the Ginza Expressway. The dishes are all authentically spicy, especially the *tom yam goong* (hot and sour soup) and the *laab* salads of Thailand's rural northeast.

PRICE CATEGORIES

Prices for three-course dinner per person without drinks and taxes:
¥ = under ¥2,000
¥¥ = ¥2,000–¥3,000
¥¥¥ = ¥3,000–¥5,000
¥¥¥¥ = over ¥5,000

IKEBUKURO AND MEIJIRODAI

Leisure choices of a more eclectic nature can be found in this shopping and entertainment area, including a massive Toyota car showroom, a huge mall dubbed "a city within a city" and a stainless steel covered church

Map on page 96

One of the premier shopping and entertainment centres along the Yamanote Line, Ikebukuro was a relative latecomer to the Tokyo scene. The district only began to expand after the arrival of the railways in the early 20th century.

The final phase in Ikebukuro's transformation from agricultural hamlet to one of Tokyo's main sub-cities, came about through the sibling rivalry of two half-brothers, Yasujiro Tsutsumi and Kaichiro Nezu, respective heads of the Seibu and Tobu commercial groups. Their first incisions into the area, the Seibu and Tobu train lines, were crowned with two opulent department stores of the same name. Seibu now dominates the east side, with a building that runs like a fire-wall along the edge of the station, while Tobu defends its interests along the western portion of the tracks.

Seibu, Parco & Mitsukoshi

Constructed over the site of a post-war black market that existed up to the early 1960s, the **Seibu** ❶ department store is known for its innovative clothing and designs. Its two basement food halls offer a vast selection of Japanese and imported food; its sports floor has the novelty of an indoor running track, and its rooftop, a tennis court.

In this mash of stores, another arbiter of fashion, **Parco**, stands cheek-to-jowl with Seibu, while the **Mitsukoshi** department store, an altogether more classy enterprise, occupies a corner of Sunshine-dori (Sunshine Street) a block away.

Amlux Toyota Salon

Walking east along Sunshine 60-dori, past **Tokyu Hands**, Tokyo's largest and most novel hardware and leisure goods store, will take you to **Amlux Toyota Auto Salon** ❷ (Tues–Sun

LEFT: creative outdoor advertising near the Ikebukuro Station. **BELOW:** an early evening crowd at Ikebukuro.

Car buffs will be thrilled by the displays at the Amlux Toyoto Auto Salon , some of which are prototype models not seen elsewhere.

11am–7pm; free). This massive five-floor showroom features several different car designs. Other attractions include a 3-D cinema, a virtual driving simulator and a design studio where you can create your own car.

Sunshine City

Just adjacent is **Sunshine City** ❸, a complex of four buildings. This self-styled "city within a city" could fill up a whole day. The first building in the set is **Sunshine 60**. One of the world's fastest elevators will carry you up to the 60th floor of the tower where there is an observation gallery with a sweeping view of Tokyo: suburbs vanishing into infinity, the neon towers of Shinjuku and, on a clear day, the distant outline of Mount Fuji.

The massive **Sunshine City Prince Hotel** occupies the second building, and the **World Import Mart**, the third. On the 10th floor of the latter is a large **planetarium** (daily 11am–7pm; admission charge) and an **aquarium** (daily 10am–6pm; admission charge).

The **Culture Hall** (Bunka Kaikan) is the final highlight of the complex (daily 10am–9pm; admission charge). The **Sunshine Theatre** is here and, on the seventh floor, the **Ancient Orient Museum** ❹ (Kodai Oriento Hakubutsukan) has a fine collection of pre-Islamic Middle Eastern art objects, including pottery, glass, jewellery and mosaics (Mon–Fri 10am–8pm, Sat–Sun 10am–6pm; admission charge).

One half of Sunshine City's **Namco Namja Town** is an indoor amusement park based on the concept of food, known as **Gyoza Stadium**. *Gyoza* are Japanese fried dumplings with meat and vegetable fillings. At last count, there were 25 varieties to choose from (*see page 99*).

Tobu Department Store

West of Ikebukuro station is **Tobu** department store ❺, selling every-

thing from international *haute couture* to hardware and traditional Japanese products. Some 20 percent of Tobu's revenue comes from edibles – it has a gigantic food basement and six floors of restaurants.

Japan Traditional Craft Centre

One block south of Tobu, the **Japan Traditional Craft Centre ❻** has selections from over 130 different arts and crafts, and demonstrations by potters, textile workers, lacquerware specialists and many other craftspeople (daily 11am–7pm; tel: 03-5954 6066; www.kougei.or.jp/english/center.html).

Metropolitan Art Space

Two blocks west of Tobu's Metropolitan Plaza is **Metropolitan Art Space ❼** (Tokyo Geijutsu Gekijo), a cultural complex housing concert halls, theatres, exhibition centres and a green area of trees, shrubs and artificial waterfalls under a 30-metre (100-ft) high atrium. The interior is a beacon of tranquillity among the crowds of shoppers and pleasure seekers that swarm Ikebukuro.

Ikebukuro Bosai-Kan

The **Ikebukuro Bosai-Kan ❽**, a short distance south, is an earthquake simulation centre run by the Tokyo Fire Department. It is not the most obvious sight that springs to mind on a trip, but in a city like Tokyo, earthquakes are an ever-present possibility (Wed–Mon 9am–5pm; tel: 03-3590 6565; free). The experience of being in a room during an earthquake of magnitude six is decidedly weird.

Jiyu Gakuen School

Fans of architecture will want to visit the former **Jiyu Gakuen ❾** girls' school (Tues–Sun 10am–4pm; admission charge; tel: 03-3971 7535; www.jiyu.jp), located further south. Designed by Frank Lloyd Wright in 1921, the building, whose original name means "School of Freedom", was renamed Myonichikan, the "House of Tomorrow". The interior of this unique building features flowing lines, a light-filled interior and some of the original furniture.

Rikkyo Daigaku University

Crossing Gekijo-dori behind the Art Space takes you into a quieter, older section. Heading west past restaurants, bars and the edge of Nishi Ikebukuro Park will bring you to **Rikkyo Daigaku University ❿** and its decidedly academic, redbrick gate. Also known as St Paul's, it was founded in 1918 by America missionary C.M. Williams. The leafy campus, with its well-weathered wood and brick buildings and masses of ivy, is a nice contrast to the downtown glitter of Ikebukuro.

Zoshigaya Cemetery

At Higashi-Ikebukuro, just one stop from here on the Yurakucho Line metro, **Zoshigaya Cemetery ⓫** (Zoshigaya Reien) is an even quieter spot. The cemetery's tree-lined

Map on page 96

TIP

Ikebukuro Station is a veritable labyrinth with five overhead train tracks and subway lines feeding into it. To add to the confusion, there are over 40 exits. Most arrivals find the first exit at hand and then use the department stores and other cardinal buildings to orient themselves.

BELOW: Ikebukuro's Sunshine City.

Map on page 96

A prayer rattle used by priests for invoking the spirits.

paths and avenues of cherry blossoms are the resting grounds of several well-known literary figures, including Tokyo's finest chronicler, Nagai Kafu. The inscription on the headstone of this self-effacing novelist modestly reads: "The Grave of Kafu the Scribbler".

Gokoku-ji Temple

Exit from the east side of the cemetery to the grounds of **Gokoku-ji Temple** ⓬, an important but surprisingly underrated site, one that sees few visitors. The main hall of this incredibly well-preserved and maintained temple dates from 1681. The buildings are approached by climbing a series of steps lined with zelkova trees, up to the main compound. Make sure to leave by the **Nio-mon Gate**, flanked by a pair of beautifully carved Nio statues.

Zoshigaya Museum

Another little-visited spot in this older part of the city is **Zoshigaya Missionary Museum** ⓭ (Zoshigaya Kyu-senkyoshikan), a lovingly preserved American colonial-style house (daily 10am–5pm; free). It was built in 1907 by an American missionary, John Moody McCaleb, who spent 50 years in Japan.

BELOW: old-world Zoshigaya Missionary Museum.

St Mary's Cathedral

About 10 minutes on foot from here, through the prosperous residential back streets of Mejirodai, is the **St Mary's Cathedral** ⓮ (Tokyo Katedoraru Sei Maria Daiseido), an early work by Tokyo's pre-eminent architect Kenzo Tange. The spacious structure is completely covered in stainless steel, an effect intended to symbolise the light of Christ.

The design of the cathedral, with a spire as sharp and narrow as a rooster's talon, resembles hands outstretched in prayer. Less successful, however, is a replica of the St Bernadette's grotto at Lourdes.

Four Seasons' garden

Across the road from the cathedral is one of Tokyo's premier hotels, the **Chinzan-so Four Seasons Hotel** ⓯. Wedding banquets are frequently held here. More interesting is the garden, with pagodas, *rakan* stones, an Inari shrine and sacred trees brought together and arranged in a neat cultural digest. A stone basin, carved for thirsty pilgrims by the wandering monk Mokujiki-shonin, flows with sparkling clear water.

Komagome's gardens

East of Ikebukuro on the Yamanote Line takes you to **Komagome** ⓰, which has two excellent gardens. The **Rikugien Garden** is the closest to the station, created in 1702 by feudal lord Yoshiyasu Yanagisawa. The other sight of note is **Kyu Furukawa Garden** (Kyu Furukawa Teien), a 10-minute walk north of the station. The garden and its main building, a charcoal-grey stone residence resembling a Scottish manor house and completed in 1917, are the work of British architect Josiah Conder. ❑

RESTAURANTS

Chinese

Chion Shokudo

Miyakawa Bldg, B1F, 1-24-1 Ikebukuro, Toshima-ku. Tel: 03-5951 8288. Open: daily 11–3am. ¥

Sichuan cuisine as spicy and authentic (and almost as cheap) as you'll find anywhere in China. Most of the customers are from the Mainland too. The *mabo-dofu* (ground pork and tofu) is recommended, and so are the fiery Sichuan hot pots. Wash it down with Tsingtao beer at just ¥280 per bottle.

Japanese

Akiyoshi

3-30-4 Nishi-Ikebukuro, Toshima-ku. Tel: 03-3982 0644. Open: daily 5–11pm. ¥¥

Tasty *yakitori* (charcoal-grilled skewers of chicken) restaurant that is visible from the street with its long counter and the flames that spit appetisingly over the grills. The basic skewered chicken dishes on offer here are popular with after-hour office workers and locals, and they go down well with icy-cold draught beer.

Goemon

1-1-26 Hon-Komagome, Toshima-ku. Tel: 03-3811 2015. Open: Mon–Sat L and D. ¥¥

The healthful properties of tofu need little introduction these days. Goemon serves multi-course meals featuring tofu in numerous guises, in a traditional setting overlooking a tranquil garden. It also has a couple of rustic bowers outside that are popular in warm weather.

Mawaru Sushi Hana-kan

3-13-10 Minami-Ikebukuro, Toshima-ku. Tel: 03-3988 6124. Open: daily 11am–11pm. ¥

A moderately priced *kaiten-sushi* joint where the plates chug around on a conveyor-belt circuit. Stools and family tables are set beside the belt. You pick the plates off as you like. Plates from ¥120–500 each. They also offer *sushi bento* (boxed set) take-aways.

Namja Town Ikebukuro Gyoza Stadium

Sunshine City, 2F, 3 Higashi-Ikebukuro, Toshima-ku. Tel: 03-5950 0765. Open: daily 10am–10pm. ¥

Of Chinese origin, but changed almost beyond recognition by the Japanese, *gyoza* are meat-and-vegetable-filled dumplings fried and served with rice, pickles and other trimmings. The Namja Town theme park boasts over a dozen stalls selling various types of *gyoza*.

Sasashu

2-2-6 Ikebukuro, Toshima-ku. Tel: 03-3971 6796. Open: Mon–Sat 5–10pm. ¥¥

Premium *sake* brews from all round the country. The spectrum of *sake* here is impressive, ranging from new varieties of carbonated new *sake* that are becoming fashionable, to *daiginjo*, the premier cru of *sake*. A good selection of appetising food, including grilled salmon, is served in the traditional *izakaya* (tavern) ambience. Most people like to finish their meal with duck noodles.

300B ONE

3-30-11 Nishi-Ikebukuro, Toshima-ku. Tel: 03-3986 6612. Open: daily 4pm–midnight. ¥¥

Its name pronounced "Sambyaku B One", this is a lively *izakaya* (tavern)-style restaurant with an eclectic choice of dishes from grilled fish to skewered meats. The all-you-can-drink deals (from ¥2,500 for two hours) are hugely popular.

Southeast Asian

Malaychan

3-22-6 Nishi-Ikebukuro, Toshima-ku. Tel: 03-5391 7638. Open: daily L and D. ¥¥

Chinese and Malay dishes mainly, with a few Thai treats thrown in. It's a bit eclectic but fun. Chinese shark's fin soup, Thai green curries, Malay *nasi lemak* (rice cooked with coconut milk and spicy toppings) and grilled fish are some offerings that go well with Tiger beer or a Singapore Sling.

Mekong

3-26-5 Nishi-Ikebukuro, Toshima-ku. Tel: 03-3988 5688. Open: Wed-Mon L and D. ¥¥

Authentic Thai curries and other spicy delicacies in a simple setting. Quench the heat with Thai and Singaporean beers. The weekend buffet lunches are great value.

Saigon

Torikoma Dai-ichi Bldg, 3F, 1-7-10 Higashi-Ikebukuro, Toshima-ku. Tel: 03-3989 0255. Open: daily L and D. ¥¥

This is a down-to-earth and moderately priced Vietnamese eatery. Hot pancakes in spicy sauce, beef noodle soup and spring rolls are the order of the day, while mouth-watering desserts made from fresh fruits, taro flour and jelly are well worth sampling. The lunchtime sets are under ¥1000.

PRICE CATEGORIES

Prices for three-course dinner per person without drinks and taxes:

¥ = under ¥2,000
¥¥ = ¥2,000–¥3,000
¥¥¥ = ¥3,000–¥5,000
¥¥¥¥ = over ¥5,000

小田急
ODAKYU
カードは
JCB
ファンケル
化粧品
さくらや
TAKANO

SHINJUKU

Some two million people pass through Shinjuku each day. This unrivalled density makes it a microcosm of all that is Tokyo: soaring highrises, massive malls, tiny shops, classy boutiques and a maze of entertainment venues

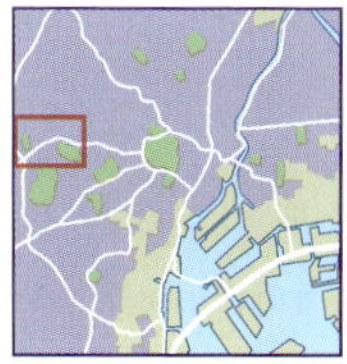

With no castle, river or temple to found itself on, Shinjuku came into existence because of its position at the junction of two key arteries leading into the city from the west. It even had to invent its own name. Shinjuku simply means "New Lodgings", a reference to the post station that was built on the more important of the two routes, the Kosho Kaido Avenue, to allow weary horses and travellers to rest overnight before completing the last leg of their journey in Edo.

The facility, proposed by five brothel owners from Edo's thriving pleasure quarters, was little more than a pretense to tap the captive market of travellers. Inns and stores soon lined the streets of Naito Shinjuku, as it was called. Its main attractions were the teahouses employing dozens of "rice-serving girls", whose function was more carnal than culinary. The district was closed down after an incident at one teahouse involving a relative of the shogun, but reopened in 1772. Within a decade, over 50 inns and teahouses had sprung up.

Freight trains started to roll into Shinjuku Station in 1885, followed by passenger trains and a tram system. The major factor in Shinjuku's rise to urban pre-eminence, however, occurred with the Great Kanto Earthquake of 1923. While most of the old city centre was laid to waste, Shinjuku emerged unscathed. Huge numbers of residents moved in and, soon, department stores like Mitsukoshi and Isetan opened new branches here, followed by theatres, cafés and artists' studios. By the early 1930s, with writers, painters and students *in situ*, Shinjuku had become Tokyo's bohemian quarter.

The area's commercial importance and high civilian population made it an inevitable target for

Map on page 102

LEFT: Shinjuku is so busy it seems all of Tokyo converges here.
BELOW: bustling Shinjuku shopping area.

Vending machines are a ubiquitous feature of Tokyo life. They sell everything from food and beverages to flowers and film tickets. There are an estimated 20 million nationwide. The first vending machines appeared at Tokyo and Ueno stations in 1926 and have remained a fixture since then.

American bombing missions, the most terrifying of which occurred on 25 May 1945, when air raids leveled the entire district, leaving only one building standing, the Isetan department store. The area quickly resurrected itself, and by the early 1970s, with a growing reputation as a business centre and with the district's first skyscrapers in place, its property values had become the highest in the country, even topping Ginza.

Seven railway lines and two subways feed over 2 million passengers through Shinjuku station every day, making it the city's most densely populated commercial centre. Shinjuku today likes to style itself as "the city of the future". Like so many other self-designations in Tokyo, this is only half-true, applicable in this case to just one side of the mini-city – its western interface, Nishi Shinjuku, where the Keio and Odakyu department stores face the locus of skyscrapers that define this area.

West Shinjuku skyscrapers

The first skyscraper to go up in this part of Tokyo was the Keio Plaza Hotel in 1971. Since then many have followed, the most conspicuous being the **Tokyo Metropolitan Government Office** ❶ (Tocho), the capital's City Hall. Its twin 48-storey towers are the work of Kenzo Tange, who designed the original metropolitan offices in Yurakucho in 1957. The observation galleries (daily 9.30am–11pm; free) on the 45th floors of both towers afford superlative views across the city and, on fine days, even Mount Fuji.

South of the Tocho, along Tocho-dori (Tocho Avenue), the highlight of the 30-storey **NS Building** ❷ is its hollowed-out interior and a roof made from 6,000 pieces of glass. With a glass elevator to match, the views as you ascend along the exterior of the building are spectacular. An observatory at the top, and restaurants there, afford good views.

Map on page 102

Central Park

West Shinjuku has tended to develop vertically, leaving plenty of intermittent space between tower blocks in which to stroll. Adding to that sense of space is **Shinjuku Central Park** (Shinjuku Chuo Koen), with its pleasant pathways, trees and hillocks (daily 24 hours; free).

Tucked into the northwest corner of the park is **Kumano-jinja Shrine**, a small building founded in the 15th century. The shrine, which had a pond and several teahouses until the 1960s, and once stood at the centre of a geisha district, seems cowed by the wall of skyscrapers that rise on its eastern flank.

Bunka Costume Museum

Walking southeast and crossing the old Kosho Kaido Avenue that brought Shinjuku into existence brings you to the **Bunka Women's University**, with its prestigious fashion school, and the **Bunka Gakuen Costume Museum** ❸ (Bunka Gakuen Fukushoku Hakubutsukan) The complete collection is too large to show at one time, but its partial displays are always interesting, particularly its Edo Period clothing. Exhibits range from *kosade* dresses and *noh* drama costumes to the hippy trends of the 1960s (Mon–Sat 10am–4pm; admission charge).

Park Hyatt and Opera City

A little west of the museum, back on the other side of Kosho Kaido Avenue, the hand of Kenzo Tange surfaces again in the 52-storey **Shinjuku Park Tower** ❹. Five floors are set aside for the shops and showrooms of the **Ozone Living Design Centre**.

Occupying the top 14 floors of the Shinjuku Park Tower is the luxury **Park Hyatt Tokyo**. The bamboo garden on the 41st floor that forms the centrepiece of Peak Lounge, with its superb views, is one of the most sophisticated spots in the city to take high tea. Park Hyatt Tokyo was where Sofia Coppola's award-winning film *Lost in Translation* was set.

Southwest of Shinjuku Park Tower, the 54-storey **Tokyo Opera City** ❺, just beyond the striking NTT East HQ building, is one of Tokyo's newest

The Bunka Gakuen Costume Museum has clothing displays that go back to the Edo Period. This particular one dates from 1928.

LEFT: Tokyo Metropolitan Government Office building, or Tocho. **BELOW:** a security officer in the Tocho Assembly Hall.

Yakitori, or skewered chicken dipped into barbecued sauce and grilled over hot charcoal, goes down well with cold beer.

office and cultural complexes. The **New National Theatre** (Shin Kokuritsu Gekijo), consisting of an opera house, playhouse and a smaller, more Shakespearean-scale theatre, is housed here (tel: 03-5352 9999, www.operacity.jp). Also worth a visit are the multimedia art displays in the **NTT InterCommunication Centre** on the fourth floor of Opera City (Tues–Sun 10am–6pm; admission charge). Innovative exhibitions and interactive displays show how technology can promote creativity.

More skyscrapers

Back on Chuo-dori, the street that runs from Shinjuku's west exit to the Tokyo Metropolitan Government Office, is a cluster of older buildings, many of them with observation floors that allow free entry. The six-sided 52-storey **Shinjuku Sumitomo Building** ❻ is constructed around an open well. Light floods down to the lobby through a massive glass roof.

The 55-storey **Mitsui Building**, built in 1974 and recognisable for its blue reflective glass, occupies most of the next block east. Exhibitions on space can be viewed at the **Museum of Future Science and Technology** (Mirai Kagaku Gijutsu Joho-kan) in Mitsui building (Tues–Sun 10am–5pm; admission charge). The **Pentax Gallery** is also housed on the same premises (daily 10am–5pm; free). The restaurants on the 54th and 55th floors have observation decks.

The adjacent **Shinjuku Centre Building** and **Nomura Building**, have equally fine views from their respective 53rd and 50th floors.

BELOW: Van Gogh's *Sunflowers* on display at the Seiji Togo Art Museum.

Sompo Japan Art Museum

The final building of note in this area is **Sompo Japan Building**. The **Sompo Japan Museum of Art** ❼ (Sompo Bijutsukan) on the 42nd storey displays works by several Japanese artists (Tues–Sun 10am–5.30pm; free; tel: 03-3349 3081). The core of the exhibition are works by Seiji Togo (1897–1978), a skillful but unremarkable painter who specialised in portraits of young women. The highlight of the museum, however, is Van Gogh's controversy-ridden *Sunflowers*, which was bought for a whopping ¥6 billion (US$40 million) during the free-spending bubble economy years. There is also one work apiece by Cezanne, Gauguin and Renoir.

Old-style eateries

An old-fashioned, highly atmospheric row of tiny bars, *yakitori*, noodle and other cheap restaurants vie for space along **Shomben Yokocho**, a narrow passage whose name translates unappealingly as "Piss Alley", apparently on account of its establishments having to share their toilet facilities. The alleys are just to the left of the underpass that connects East and West Shinjuku. You will meet a friendly, if rather offbeat, set of customers here. Go soon, though. The location, sitting as it is on a prime piece of real estate, has "condemned" written all over it.

East Shinjuku shopping

The east exit of the station, incorporating the fashion shopping complex called **My City**, comes out onto a small plaza in front of the landmark **Studio Alta** ❽, several floors of youthful designer clothing with a huge, signature video screen, one of Tokyo's best known rendezvous points. The Alta sits at the head of **Shinjuku-dori**, a busy shopping street which becomes a traffic-free zone with buskers on Sundays.

The **Kinokuniya Book Store** ❾, with part of its sixth floor devoted to English titles, is on the left just past the Mitsui Bank as you walk east along the street. Kinokuniya started business as a charcoal dealer supplying railway yards and residences before turning to the book trade. A theatre and art gallery are also found here. Another branch of the well-regarded **Mitsukoshi** department store is just up the road on the other side. Its south annexe has the **Mitsukoshi Museum** (Mitsukoshi Bijutsukan) with shows on themes like fashion and jewellery (daily 10am–6pm; admission charge).

Marui, one of Tokyo's so-called "fashion buildings", is easily spotted on the next block. Popular with young people, the store houses over 50 boutiques and design labels.

One of Japan's top department stores, **Isetan**, stands across the road from here. The store is divided into two sections: the old store, the only pre-war building in the area, and a newer section which has the highly regarded **Isetan Museum** ❿ (Isetan Bijutsukan), a gallery featuring first-rate touring exhibitions (Tues–Sun 9.30am–4.30pm; free).

Two small blocks east of Isetan, rows of coloured lanterns decorate the outside of **Suehiro-tei**, a small theatre, one of the few stages left in Shinjuku for *rakugo*, a form of traditional storytelling in which the narrator addresses the audience in a seated position.

Facing the station's south exit is **Takashimaya Times Square** ⓫. Apart from a Takashimaya department store, the futuristic complex includes a branch of **Tokyu Hands**, a Sega virtual reality arcade called **Joypolis**, and an **IMAX theatre**.

Map on page 102

TIP

Japanese trains during rush hour can be plagued by *chikan*, or female-groping men. Cultural and social norms, though slowly changing, keep Japanese women from publicly castigating the *chikan*. Instead, they will endure the indignity until the next stop). Some foreign women have been targets as well.

LEFT: Studio Alta, a landmark store on Shinjuku-dori. **BELOW:** a typical eatery in the Shinjuku area.

TIP

If you find yourself on the subway during an earthquake, remember that underground tremors are generally smaller than those felt above ground. Unless there are gas or fire leaks, stay there until the emergency lights come on.

Shinjuku Imperial Garden

Like its district, the **Shinjuku Imperial Garden ⓬** (Shinjuku Gyoen), a short stroll directly east from Times Square, excels at variety (Tues–Sun 9am–4.30pm; daily during April cherry blossom season; admission charge). The former estate of the Naito feudal lords, the grounds later passed into the hands of the Imperial Household Agency, which used it for receptions and cherry blossom viewing parties before giving it to the state.

Today, the garden is still a popular spot for viewing cherry trees when they are in bloom, but what strikes most people is the park's sheer size and the sense of space it imparts here in the centre of downtown Tokyo. The garden is divided into French, English and Japanese sections and also has a large botanical garden full of tropical plants housed in an old, domed greenhouse.

Shinjuku Historical Museum

A fair distance northeast of the garden, signposted from the Yotsuya-Sanchome station, is the small but stimulating **Shinjuku Historical Museum ⓭** (Shinjuku Rekishi Haku-butsukan), which provides insights into what the district must have looked like in its days as a post town (Tues–Sun 9am–5pm; admission charge).

A little north of Shinjuku Garden is the apparently unexceptional **Jokaku-ji Temple ⓮**. Closer scrutiny reveals a tombstone, placed here in 1860 by innkeepers from the brothel district, marking the spot of a communal grave where prostitutes who died were unceremoniously disposed of without the usual burial rites. The place is a sober reminder of the unglamorous existence of Shinjuku's "rice serving girls".

Hanazono Shrine

Returning to Isetan Museum, the **Hanazono-jinja Shrine ⓯**, set back from busy Yasukuni-dori, is best approached by entering under a *torii* gate and walking along a stone path lined with red and white paper lanterns that are lit at night. Although the structure, with its vermilion walls and wood rails, is a post-war creation, the site itself has a long history. The shrine's principal deity is Yamatotaeru-no-Mikoto, a 4th-century prince and hero of campaigns against the aboriginal tribes.

Golden Gai

Taking the exit behind the shrine will lead almost immediately into the **Golden Gai ⓰** area. Shomben Nakacho, as it is properly known, provides a glimpse of Shinjuku in former times. Confined to a few small blocks, its cinder-block tiny bars, dim lantern-lit pedestrian alleys and importuning women evoke a more intimate 1950s scene popular with Japanese working classes. Already, the spectre of urbanisation is evident: recently, several bars have been turned into rock clubs and trendy bars.

BELOW: the dome-shaped greenhouse at the Shinjuku Imperial Gardens.

Kabuki-cho

Golden Gai provides a rather gentle transition into **Kabuki-cho**, a more lively, provocative nightlife experience. In the early post-war years, it was decided to rebuild the Kabuki Theatre here and turn the district into a high-class entertainment centre. The plan was dropped, but the name remained. Apart from the remaining one or two traditional halls like **Koma Theatre** ⑰ (Koma Gekijo), which puts on musicals and samurai dramas, the aspirations of today's Kabuki-cho, the capital's, and country's, foremost sex quarter, are unabashedly lowbrow – porn cinemas, "pink" salons, no-panties cafés, telephone clubs, peep-show joints, "soaplands" (read brothels) and extortionate hostess bars. Kabuki-cho is pretty much a local scene, but it's safe for foreigners to stroll.

Those who are so inclined may seek out Tokyo's vibrant underground gay scene, which has its epicentre at the nearby **Shinjuku ni-chome**, near Shinjuku San-chome Station. Over 300 gay bars and clubs are located around its central street, **Naka-dori**.

Tokyo's "Little Asia"

Take almost any of the narrow roads or alleys that run directly north from Kabuki-cho, away from Yasukuni-dori, and you will soon hit lively **Okubo-dori**. The main strip of this avenue is an extraordinary place even by Tokyo standards. The area might have been gentrified by now but for the influx of foreigners – Koreans, Thai, Filipinos, Chinese, Russians among them – and old-time neighbourhood shopkeepers who have made **Shin-Okubo** ⑱, dubbed as "Little Asia", their home. Once a semi-rural residential district on the periphery of Shinjuku, it has now acquired a distinctly urban, working class cosmopolitan character of its own.

At night, the neon strip of Okubo-dori and the pedestrian alleys that feed into it, are vibrant with conversations and importunings in a dozen different languages. Its Burmese, Thai, Malaysian and Korean restaurants release pungent smells into the atmosphere, giving the impression that one is on an island detached from mainland Tokyo. ❑

Map on page 102

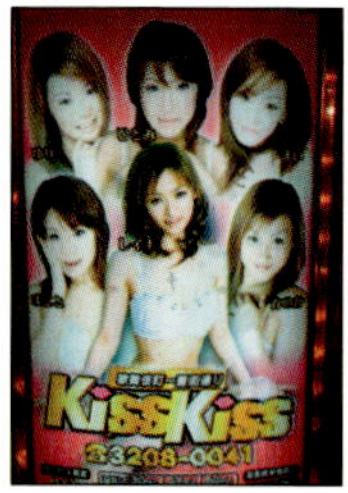

A poster in Kabuki-cho advertising erotic services by young women.

BELOW: a tongue-studded waitress welcomes all and sundry to Kabuki-cho.

RESTAURANTS

American

New York Grill
Park Hyatt Hotel, 52F, 3-7-1-2 Nishi-Shinjuku, Shinjuku-ku. Tel: 03-5322 1234. Open: daily L and D. ¥¥¥¥
Power dining with North American bravado in a spectacular skyview setting in the glass-fronted apex of Shinjuku's Park Hyatt Hotel (as featured in the award-winning film *Lost in Translation*). The massive Sunday brunches, with sirloin steaks and lobster ceviche topping most diners' favourite choices, and also the cocktails at the New York Bar, are an institution for the expat community.

Café-Patisserie

Ben's Café
1-29-21 Takadanobaba, Shinjuku-ku. Tel: 03-3202 2445. Open: daily 11.30am–11.30pm. ¥
www.benscafe.com
This is an artsy and laid-back Seattle-style coffee house with a selection of very tasty cakes and homemade bagels and a good range of Japanese, German and other imported beers. The coffee is also very good and the staff speak English. Refer to the walls of the café for information on the occasional events that are held here; these include poetry readings, ensemble music as well as art displays.

French

Restaurant Le Coupe Chou
1-15-7 Nishi-Shinjuku, Shinjuku-ku. Tel: 03-3348 1610. Open: daily L and D, closed 3rd Monday of the month. ¥
In the unlikely heart of Shinjuku's discount camera and electronic district, Le Coupe has a ¥1,500 four-course lunch that is one of the best French deals in town. Go early as it's popular with housewives and the local office crowd, and the dining room fills up quickly.

Tete à Tete
2-3-9 Yotsuya, Shinjuku-ku. Tel: 03-3356 1048. Open: Mon–Sat L and D. ¥
One of the best and most consistent of the many no-frills French bistros that Tokyo is blessed with. Serving a wide range of dishes from all regions of France, and a good choice of well-priced wines, and three-course dinners that are just ¥2,500. It's no wonder it's a hit with Tokyo's French community.

Italian

Carmine Edochiano
9-13 Arakicho, Shinjuku-ku. Tel: 03-3225 6767. Open: daily L and D. ¥¥¥
Upscale Italian fare in the most remarkable setting: a beautiful old Japanese house in an old-style neighbourhood that is like a time slip in this modern city. Upstairs you can dine on Tuscan-accented cuisine; downstairs is more casual, serving authentic Neapolitan pizzas from a wood-fired oven.

Japanese

Daikokuya
Nakadai Bldg, 4F, 1-27-5 Kabuki-cho, Shinjuku-ku. Tel: 03-3202 7272. Open: daily 5–11pm. ¥¥
A *shabu-shabu* (quick-boiled beef) restaurant that also offers other meat dishes in the form of *sukiyaki* (one-pot dish) and Korean *yakiniku* (grilled meat). A popular spot with students and young office workers who come here for some serious drinking as well as eating. Friendly and unpretentious.

Donjaca
3-6-12 Shinjuku, Shinjuku-ku. Tel: 03-3357 8090. Open: Mon–Sat 5pm–2am. ¥
This cheerful, sometimes boisterous specialist *sake* pub stocks numerous brews from around the country, with many rarely found in Tokyo. There's a selection of tasty tavern fare, including good sashimi and grilled fish. The staff speak little English, but the welcome is always friendly.

Hayashi
2-22-5 Kabuki-cho, Shinjuku-ku. Tel: 03-3209 5672. Open: Mon–Sat 5–11pm. ¥¥
Here you sit around the sand hearth, nibbling on meat, fish tidbits and seasonal vegetables grilled over charcoal in a traditional rustic setting that seems light years away from Kabuki-cho's carefully cultivated image as sin city.

Kurumaya
2-37-1 Kabuki-cho, Shinjuku-ku. Tel: 03-3232 0301. Open: daily L and D. ¥¥
Across the street from the Kirin City Beer Hall, this restaurant represents good value in smart surroundings. The steak and seafood sets are tasty and plentiful. A popular choice for Japanese customers is the *ise ebi* (Japanese lobster), a succulent monster that is served straight or slightly garnished.

Kuu
Shinjuku Sumitomo Bldg, 50F, 2-6-1 Nishi-Shinjuku, Shinjuku-ku. Tel: 03-3344 6457. Open: daily 5–11.30pm. ¥¥
Located atop one of Shinjuku's skyscrapers, this casual *izakaya* (tavern) proves that you don't have to pay sky-high prices to get panoramic views over the city. The core of the

menu here is charcoal-grilled seafood, chicken and seasonal vegetables. It is also an affordable place to explore premium *sake* from all around Japan.

Tenkaippin
1-14-3 Kabuki-cho, Shinjuku-ku. Tel: 03-3232 7454. Open: daily 11am–6am. ¥
Calorie-rich noodles served in the thickest broth you'll find anywhere. Look out for the red lanterns and red-and-white décor. *Kotteri* is the thick soup; *assari* is the thin one, but they are both dense and savoury. Popular with clubbers and night owls.

Tsunahachi
3-31-8 Shinjuku, Shinjuku-ku. Tel: 03-3352 1012. Open: daily 11am–10pm. ¥¥¥
Great value, with huge portions of satisfying no-frills tempura (deep-fried battered seafood and vegetables) in a lively downtown atmosphere. The building itself, a decrepit-looking pre-war wooden affair, is a remarkable holdover from older times – and so are the prices. That's why it's always busy.

Korean

Kankoku Shokudo
1-12-3 Okubo, Shinjuku-ku. Tel: 03-3208 0209. Open: daily 9am–4am. ¥
Kankoku is Japan's name for South Korea; *shokudo* means "canteen". Expect cheap and savoury home cooking at this restaurant located in Tokyo's Little Seoul district. Glasses of cold beer go down well with the lashings of *kimchi* (pickles), spicy seaweed, savoury side dishes and assorted barbecue dishes grilled on individual hot-plates at this lively eatery.

Matsuya
1-1-17 Okubo, Shinjuku-ku. Tel: 03-3200 5733. Open: daily 11am–5am. ¥
Another favourite Korean restaurant in the heart of Little Seoul. Fiery meat-laden stews, sizzling hot *bibimba* rice bowls (meat mixed with a spicy sauce and served in a sizzling, super-hot stoneware bowl), savoury *chijimi* (pancakes) and plenty of *kimchi* (pickled vegetables), of course.

Tokaien
1-6-3 Kabuki-cho, Shinjuku-ku. Tel: 03-3200 2934. Open: daily 11–3.30am. ¥¥
For *yakiniku* (Korean barbecue) lovers, this is the final portal. Located right on the edge of the raunchy sex industry district of Kabuki-cho, Tokaien boasts no less than nine floors devoted to this and other Korean meat dishes. An all-you-can-eat blowout is offered on the sixth floor for those who can manage it.

Southeast Asian

Angkor Wat
1-38-13 Yoyogi, Shibuya-ku. Tel: 03-3370 3019. Open: Mon–Sat L and D, Sun D only. ¥
Cheap, crowded and as consistently authentic, right down to the spices, as any Cambodian street market stall. Perky Cambodian waitresses serve chicken and green mango salads, rice and pork dishes, plus fiery side dishes in a plain dining room full of ambience. The extensive menu also includes Thai, Chinese and Vietnamese dishes.

Ban-Thai
1-23-14 Kabuki-cho, Shinjuku-ku. Tel: 03-3207 0068. Open: Mon–Fri L and D, Sat–Sun 11.30am–11pm. ¥¥
One of Tokyo's best venues for authentic street-side Thai food and one of the first to open in the city. Always cheerful, always crowded. Well situated just at the entrance to Kabuki-cho, the curries and soups here are first rate, which explains why it always draws plenty of Thai customers.

Hyakunincho Yataimura
2-20-25 Hyakunin-cho, Shinjuku-ku. Tel: 03-5386 3320. Open: Mon–Sat L and D. ¥
Street food from half a dozen Asian countries under one very low-budget roof is the nearest thing Tokyo has to an indoor hawker centre. Wander from stall to stall, making up a combination meal from the Indonesian, Thai, Korean and other cuisines represented here. Cheap, great fun and open till the wee hours.

Rendevous Café
Yanagiya Bldg, B1, 2-18-6 Takadanobaba, Shinjuku-ku. Tel: 03-5285 0128. Open: daily 1–11pm, closed 1st & 3rd Wed of the month. ¥¥
This tiny hole-in-the-wall eatery is located in a basement in the Little Myanmar district. Its menu is surprisingly authentic, featuring pungent dishes like *mohinga*, a savoury stew with fermented fish sauce; *tofu-joh*, or yellow lentil curd; and *lape-toh*, which is green-tea salad. An interesting drinks list includes tamarind fizz and grain spirits from Myanmar's northeastern Shan states.

Restaurant Mahathir Malaysia
1-17-10 Hyakunin-cho, ST Bldg, Shinjuku-ku. Tel: 03-3367 3125. Open: daily 11am–2pm. ¥
Great for budget travellers, this restaurant offers one of the cheapest lunch sets in town for just ¥750, including a cold drink and coffee to top it off. The dishes, combinations of rice, chicken, crackers and dried fruits are loosely based on the classic Malay-style *nasi goreng* (fried rice) plate.

PRICE CATEGORIES

Prices for three-course dinner per person without drinks and taxes:
¥ = under ¥2,000
¥¥ = ¥2,000–¥3,000
¥¥¥ = ¥3,000–¥5,000
¥¥¥¥ = over ¥5,000

AOYAMA AND OMOTESANDO

Prepare for a change of appearance as you approach Tokyo's Paris quarter. Sip coffee in a French-style pavement café amid elm trees and boutiques where *haute couture* has pride of place

Although there is little to remind you of the past in Aoyama or Omotesando, where designer quarters, cosmopolitan tastes and sophistication reign today, these were once home to lush rice-paddies, hunting grounds and sprawling feudal estates. A close advisor of the shogun Tokugawa Ieyasu, Aoyama Tadanari, was given land here in 1590, the year Edo became the nation's martial capital.

Aoyama Cemetery

In the years after the Meiji Restoration, these estates were turned into parade grounds and cemeteries. **Aoyama Cemetery ❶** (Aoyama Reien) was one of Tokyo's four largest burial grounds, created by the government after it had abandoned a rather quirky scheme to plant the area with mulberry trees in the hope of cultivating raw silk to export in exchange for foreign currency.

The area's arboreal dreams resurfaced, however, when hundreds of attractive cherry trees were planted later. The plaintive setting of Aoyama Cemetery is perfect for the evanescence the cherry blossoms symbolise. Well over 100,000 people are buried here, including many of Tokyo's eminent political and military leaders, writers and even a few notable foreigners.

Nogi-jinja Shrine

The remains of General Nogi Maresuke, a hero of several military campaigns in China and Russia during the Meiji Period, are interred in Aoyama Cemetery along with those of his wife. Such was the devotion of the couple to the Meiji Emperor that, on 13 September 1912, on the occasion of the emperor's body being removed from the Imperial Palace for burial in Kyoto, the general – in the manner of ancient samurai following their lord into

Map on page 112

LEFT: Aoyama has a vibrant café culture. **BELOW:** statue of Kannon, Goddess of Mercy, at Aoyama Cemetery

Japanese textiles and paper (pictured here) are found at the Traditional Crafts Centre.

death – performed the art of *seppuku* (ritual disembowelment) while his wife slit her own throat.

The posthumously dedicated shrine, **Nogi-jinja Shrine** ❷, along with a park, hall and the general's house, are near to Nogizaka Station, along Gaien Higashi-dori, east of Aoyama Cemetery. The house and its bloodstained death clothes can be viewed twice a year, on the eve and day of the Nogi suicides. On a more upbeat note, there is a very fine Sunday flea market here, with some quality items.

Aoyama Avenue

A sensation of space and formal planning is apparent along **Aoyama-dori** (Aoyama Avenue), the district's main conduit for traffic as well as culture. Aoyama-dori is synonymous with the refined pursuits of shopping, gallery visits and sipping coffee – activities which sometimes converge. At the intersection of Aoyama-dori and Gaien Nishi-dori is **Bell Commons** ❸, a "fashion house" popular for its designer labels, cafés and restaurants.

Watari-um Museum

On the left side, north along Gaien Nishi-dori, also rather disconcertingly known as "Killer-dori" on account of the huge number of traffic accidents that occur there, is the **Watari-um Museum** ❹ (Watari-um Bijutsukan), an ultra modern art space designed by Swiss architect Mario Botta in 1990. It features the work of some of today's best Japanese and international avant garde artists (Tues–Sun 11am–7pm, Wed 11am–9pm; admission charge; tel: 03-3402 3001).

The coffee shop in this building contains unusual interactive art displays and games.

Meiji Memorial Gallery

Continuing northeast from Bell Commons along Aoyama-dori, Icho

Namiki, better known as **Gingko Tree Avenue**, is on the left, equidistant between Gaienmae and Aoyama-Itchome metro stations on the Hanozomon Line. The trees are at their best in October when their leaves turn gold and yellow.

The avenue leads straight to the **Meiji Shrine Outer Gardens** (Meiji-Jingu Gaien) and **Meiji Memorial Picture Gallery** ❺ (Seitoku Kinen Kaigakan), built in 1926 to commemorate the life and achievements of the Meiji Emperor (Tues–Sun 10am–5pm; admission charge). Solemn looking on the outside, its interior is more impressive, with a domed ceiling and an imposing stairwell made of marble from Gifu Prefecture. Its 80 Japanese and Western style works have detailed explanations in English.

Spiral Building

Returning south and continuing past Omotesando Station along, the contemporary lines of the striking **Spiral Building** ❻ stand out among the façades of Aoyama-dori. Owned by the lingerie company Wacoal, the building incorporates a gallery, theatre, gift shop and café. The building is the work of leading architect Fumihiko Maki. The centrepiece of the building is its spiral ramp, a structure that floats and curves upwards to the next floor around the exhibition space below.

The **Kinokuniya Supermarket**, with its own delicatessen and wine shop, stands across the street, and is a favourite hunting ground for Tokyo's expatriates in search of imported food items.

United Nations University

Just along from the Kinokuniya Supermarket is yet another building designed by the famous Kenzo Tange. Despite its name, the **United Nations University** ❼ (Kokuren Daigaku), a development and coordination centre for the world organisation, has no student body. Tange, who won the Pritzker prize in 1987 – the equivalent of the Oscar in the architectural world – designed this UN facility, a symmetrical building with a solid main axis, said to represent well-intended authority.

Map on page 112

The leaf of the gingko is the symbol of Tokyo. At the Meiji Shrine Outer Gardens, gingko trees were planted to commemorate the lives of the Meiji Emperor and the Empress Dowager Shoken.

LEFT: installation art display at the Watari-um Museum. **BELOW:** Dior store along Omotesando Street.

National Children's Castle

Built to commemorate the UN Year of the Child in 1979, the **National Children's Castle ❽** (Kodomo no Shiro), next to the university, strikes a fun note (Tues–Fri 12.30– 5.30pm, Sat–Sun 10am–5.30pm; admission charge; tel: 03-3797 5666; www.kodomono-shiro.or.jp). Several floors here are set aside for music and computer rooms, art space, jungle gyms and a rooftop playground.

This delicate screen painting of purple irises by Ogata Korin (1658-1716) – on display at the Nezu Institute of Fine Arts – is regarded as one of the artist's finest works.

Tokyo Metropolitan Children's Hall

A few minutes' walk from the National Children's Castle is the **Tokyo Metropolitan Children's Hall ❾** (Tokyo-to Jido Kaikan), with lots of hands-on activities from art to skating and unicycling, games and models (daily 9am–5pm, till 6.30pm July–August; free; tel: 03-3409 6361; www.fukushihoken.metro.tokyo.jp/jidou/English/index.html).

Nezu Institute of Fine Arts

Back at the intersection straddled by Omotesando Station, turn right for the **Nezu Institute of Fine Arts ❿** (Nezu Bijutsukan), a few minutes away (Tues–Sun 9.30am–4.30pm; admission fee; tel: 03-3400 2536; www .nezu-muse.or.jp). Concealed behind a sandstone wall, the art museum houses the collection of Meiji-era politician and railway tycoon Kaichiro Nezu.

The permanent displays in the main building and a more recent annexe feature fine examples of Chinese bronzes, ceramic and lacquerware, calligraphy, textiles and Chinese and Japanese paintings. Its fine art pieces include exceedingly rare objects registered as National Treasures. Among these are a screen painting by Ogata Korin called *Irises*, and a Kamakura Period scroll painting called the *Nanchi Waterfall*. The museum's collection exceeds 7,000 pieces. Its lovely garden is a densely wooded and hilly landscape with a small iris pond and a number of teahouses, one of which is open to the public.

BELOW: a pond framed by irises at the gardens of the Nezu Institute.

Antique Street

Four streets southwest of Nezu Institute, **Kotto-dori ⓫**, better known as "Antique Street", makes for an apt stroll after the treasures of the Nezu Institute. The avenue is dense with antiques shops, showrooms and art dealers, and the quality of the items on display here is exceedingly high. Even if you don't buy anything, the street is great for window shopping.

Return to the same street that you exited into Kotto-dori, turn first left and a little along on the right is the **Taro Okamoto Memorial Hall ⓬** (Wed–Mon 10am–6pm; admission charge; tel: 03-3406 0801). On display are sculptures by one of Japan's most prolific and zaniest artists.

Collezione and Prada

Returning to the Nezu Institute, turn left into Omotesando-dori. The first building of note here on the left is the striking mass of concrete, glass

Map on page 112

and aluminum panels that make up **Collezione** ⓭. This is the work of well-known architect Tadao Ando. Completely self-taught, Ando was a boxer before turning to buildings. The inspiration for this "strata architecture", as Ando calls it, came from a visit to an Indian well where, descending to the water's edge, "the eyes perceive gradations of light and the skin experiences a reduction in temperature." There are couture shops, a gallery and a gym within.

Even more arresting is the **Prada Aoyama** ⓮ store, completed in 2004 and just further along on the same side. A diamond-shaped, steel latticework wraps around the building, creating the effect of a three-sided column of bubblewrap. The design is the work of Swiss architecture firm Herzog & de Meuron, who are reported to have said, "We could only do this building here in Japan."

Tokyo's Champs Elysées

Tokyoites like to think of gently sloping **Omotesando-dori** as the capital's Champs Elysées, a boulevard whose chic establishments carry a hallmark of quality. Certainly the **Hanae Mori Building** ⓯, a little up from the Prada store on the same side, does. Yet another design by Kenzo Tange, this shrine to *haute couture*, the flagship of one of Japan's former fashion giants, also houses **Le Papillon de Paris** *(see page 117)*, one of Tokyo's best French restaurants and known for its Sunday brunches. The French theme is sustained farther along the street in places with names like Chez Toi, the Café de Flore, Chat Noir and Gallerie de Pop. Just across from Le Papillon de Paris, the **Gallery Asahi**, renowned for its second-floor collection of painted screens, is an antiques shop with an eclectic range of objects for sale.

Omotesando Hills

Continue up the slope to a vermilion and green East Asian-style building on the left aptly named the **Oriental Bazaar** ⓰. Its large interior, run by English-speaking staff, stocks a good collection of reasonably priced new and original Japanese arts and crafts. Just a few doors

The striking and almost surreal glass façade of the Prada Aoyama store is a landmark icon in ever-so-chic Omotesando.

BELOW: window display at the Hanae Mori Building.

Map on page 112

up, **Fuji Tori** has a superb collection of antique ceramics, hanging scrolls, screens and paper goods for sale.

Cross the zelkova-lined road and you will be facing Tokyo's latest all-purpose fashion and lifestyle complex, the much feted **Omotesando Hills** ⓱. For those who were fond of the old, ivy-covered Dojunkai Apartments it replaced, Omotesando Hills signals the death of the area; others praise its original design, the work of Tadao Ando, one of the world's foremost architects. Cafés, specialist shops, boutiques and restaurants are ranged along a central atrium bordered by spiralling walkways. Yves Saint Laurent, Jimmy Choo, Dolce & Gabbana, the extraordinary Tokyo jewellery e.m. and many other top-end brand names have outlets here.

Kiddyland, one of Tokyo's largest toy shops, is close by, a popular store not only with children, but also with teenagers and young adults afflicted with Japan's Peter Pan syndrome, the obsession with *kawai* (cuteness) that seems to grip many of the young and not-so-young Japanese.

Banners directing visitors' attention to the L'Anniversaire café in Omotesando.

Just across the street from the toy shop, the **Shiseido Cosmetics Garden** does not actually sell anything, but you are welcome to try out the samples and check out the range offered by Shiseido, one of Japan's leading cosmetics companies (Tues–Sun 11am–7.30pm, closed 2nd Tues of the month; tel: 03-5474 1534).

L' Anniversaire café

The ever so chic **L'Anniversaire** (tel: 03-5411 5988), one of Tokyo's trendiest French-style coffee shops and patisseries, is found just across the street. Favoured tables are those out on the terrace where good-looking svelte waiters in white shirts and black aprons ply a mostly young, well-dressed Japanese clientele with espresso, Pernod and fresh croissants.

Walk through the arch at the side of the café where you will see an extraordinary cream-coloured stucco European-style wedding chapel and hall run by the same management.

Omotesando to Shibuya

Now take a walk along the **Kyu Shibuya-gawa Promenade** ⓲, a section of the now cemented over Shibuya River. A pleasant place to stroll, the promenade provides space for more designer names like Anna Sui and Todd Oldham, and several chic cafés and art spaces. The south-west flow of this traffic-free promenade provides a quiet, scenic short cut to Meiji-dori, a major street running north of Shibuya Station.

Where the districts of Omotesando and Aoyama end and Harajuku, the next fashion town, begins is not clear. But the transition from the European pretensions of Aoyama to the younger, more crowded streets of Harajuku, signals a mood shift. Pavement cafés, chocolatiers and elm trees still prevail in this quarter, but must contend with hamburger joints, jewellery peddlers, strip lighting and small eruptions of neon. ❑

BELOW: shoppers outside the Prada store in Omotesando.

RESTAURANTS

Chinese

Fumin
Aoyama Ohara Bldg, B1, 5-7-17 Minami-Aoyama, Minato-ku, Tel: 03-3498 4466. Open: daily L and D. ¥¥
Chinese home cooking that's reasonably priced for this fashionable part of town. Fumin's popularity means queues can be long, but the food is worth the wait – especially the house specialities, such as scallion wontons.

French

Benoit
La Port Aoyama, 10F, 5-51-8 Jingumae, Shibuya-ku. Tel: 03-5468 0881. Open: daily L and D. ¥¥¥
Compared to Beige in Ginza, the other restaurant opened by Michelin-starred master chef Alain Ducasse, Benoit is more informal and affordable, and concentrates on Mediterranean flavours. It's still worth getting dressed up for food of this high calibre.

Le Papillon de Paris
Hanae Mori Bldg, 5F, 3-6-1 Kita-Aoyama, Shibuya-ku. Tel: 03-3407 7461. Open: Mon–Sat L and D, Sun L only. ¥¥¥¥
Haute cuisine served in an upmarket ambience – just as you'd expect at the headquarters of the Hanae Mori fashion house. The surroundings are elegant and service is impeccable. The Sunday buffet brunch is highly recommended.

Indian

Nataraj
Sanwa-Aoyama Bldg, B1F, 2-22-19 Minami-Aoyama, Minato-ku. Tel: 03-5474 0510. Open: Mon–Fri L and D, Sat–Sun 11.30am–11pm. ¥¥
www.nataraj.co.jp/en
Tokyo's foremost Indian vegetarian restaurant serves a range of curries and grills from the tandoor oven. Spice levels are generally mild but can be toned up on request. Branches in Ginza (tel: 03-5537 1515) and Ogikubo in western Tokyo (tel: 03-3398 5108).

Japanese

Maisen
4-8-5 Jingumae, Shibuya-ku. Tel: 03-3470 0071. Open: daily 11am–10pm. ¥¥
The main branch of a large chain serving reliable *tonkatsu* (deep-fried breaded pork cutlets). Part of the dining room is situated in a converted traditional bathhouse. Besides pork, the menu also includes deep-fried chicken and oysters. English menu available.

Senba
4-4-7 Jingumae, Shibuya-ku. Tel: 03-5474 5977. Open: daily 11am–10.30pm. ¥
A well-established little restaurant specialising in *udon* (thick wheat-flour noodles) and handmade *soba* (buckwheat noodles) with a few innovative twists. Three to five different types of noodles may be served with an equal choice of sauces. Pickles and mountain vegetables are served as side dishes. Branches in Kanda (tel: 03-3251 8007) and Akihabara (tel: 03-3251 8645).

Korean

Jap Cho Ok
Alteka Belte Plaza, B1F, 4-1-15 Minami-Aoyama, Minato-ku. Tel: 03-5410 3408. Open: Mon–Sat 11.30am–2pm, 5.30pm–3am, Sun and holidays 5.30–11pm. ¥¥
This sophisticated yet casual restaurant proves that there's much more to Korean cuisine than just barbecue beef and *kimchi* (pickled vegetables). The menu includes seafood dishes and even Zen Buddhist vegetarian temple cooking. The stylish, modern décor evokes the calm of a mountain monastery.

Pub Grub

Helmsdale
Minami-Aoyama Mori Bldg, 2F, 7-13-12 Minami-Aoyama, Minato-ku. Tel: 03-3486 4220. Open: daily L and D. ¥
Alongside a good range of ales, this Scottish pub-bar-restaurant boasts a remarkable whisky list, with over 300 single-malts, including many very rare bottles. The food menu is extensive, offering smoked salmon, Scotch eggs, herb sausages, kippers and even homemade haggis.

Vegetarian

Crayon House
3-8-15 Kita-Aoyama, Minato-ku. Tel: 03-3406 6409. Open: daily 11am–10pm. ¥¥
The basement of this children's bookstore features two separate organic (but not entirely vegetarian) restaurants. **Hiroba** serves brown rice, veggie main dishes and healthy desserts, as well as a nicely priced buffet lunch. **Home** serves more upscale European food.

Pure Café
5-5-21 Minami-Aoyama, Minato-ku. Tel: 03-5466 2611. Open: daily 8.30am–10.30pm. ¥
Housed inside a modern, glass-fronted building, this self-service all-day café serves light meals that are entirely vegan and additive-free. The early opening time is welcome for those looking for a healthy breakfast with organic coffee.

PRICE CATEGORIES

Prices for three-course dinner per person without drinks and taxes:
¥ = under ¥2,000
¥¥ = ¥2,000–¥3,000
¥¥¥ = ¥3,000–¥5,000
¥¥¥¥ = over ¥5,000

HARAJUKU AND SHIBUYA

While Harajuku, home of the stately Meiji Shrine, has a few time-honoured reminders of the past, Shibuya is firmly wedged in the present, partying (and shopping) with youthful vigour

Harajuku may seem like a section of Tokyo that lives in the ever present, but closer scrutiny reveals both a past and a co-existence with the traditional. In the 11th century, Harajuku was a well-known post station on the Kamakura Kaido, the road to the wild northern provinces. *Hara*, in fact, means "field", *shuku*, a "place of lodging".

Among Harajuku's swirl of boutiques and fashion houses and other contemporary implants with names like Harajuku Quest, Touch Your All, Octopus Army and Candy Stripper, are reminders of an older city in the roadside shrines, teahouses and cultural museums.

Ota Museum of Art

A short stroll from the intersection of Meiji-dori and Omotesando-dori, just behind Laforet, with its trendy boutiques for the young, is the **Ukiyo-e Ota Memorial Museum of Art ❶** (Ukiyo-e Ota Kinen Bijutsukan) with what is arguably the city's finest collection of Edo Period *ukiyo-e* woodblock prints, over 12,000 works in all, including ex–tremely rare prints by artists such as Utamaru, Sharaku and Hiroshige (Tues–Sun 10.30am–5pm; admission fee; tel: 03-3403 0880). Visitors have to remove their shoes before entering the museum.

Takeshita Street/Togo Shrine

The pedestrian currents grow stronger as you follow the alleys that gravitate towards **Takeshita-dori ❷** (Takeshita Street). Cheap fashion, accessories, cuddly toys, hair salons, fast food restaurants and noodle shops lure teenagers for a taste of distilled subcultural kitsch.

Immediately behind Takeshita-dori, but light years away in spirit are the peaceful grounds of the **Togo-jinja Shrine ❸**, dedicated to Admiral Heihachiro Togo, whose ships

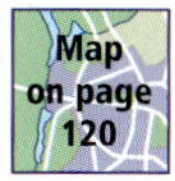

LEFT: Harajuku's colourful subculture.
BELOW: the Togo-jinja Shrine.

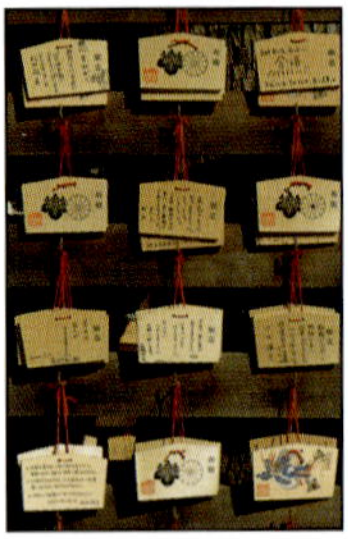

Wooden votive tablets outside the Meiji-jingu Shrine in Harajuku.

defeated the Russian fleet in the Tsushima Straits during the 1904–05 Russo-Japanese War. The original building had been lost in an air raid, but was rebuilt along with the Togo Memorial Hall and a treasury. One of Tokyo's best flea markets is held here at its grounds on the first and fourth Sunday of every month.

Meiji Shrine and Gardens

Exiting west out of Takeshita-dori, the mock-Tudor façade of Harajuku Station (Harajuku-eki) comes into view as you climb the hill toward another station, **Meiji-Jingumae**. Designed in 1924, it is one of the few Japan Rail stations to have survived intact. The station abuts one of Tokyo's major sights, the **Meiji-jingu Shrine** ❹. Before reaching the shrine, you have to pass across an open plaza above the railway tracks, a popular spot on weekends for Tokyo's fashion tribes, buskers and other street performers, and then through the **Ichi-no-torii**, a massive gate made from 1,700-year-old cypress trees taken from Mount Alishan in Taiwan.

The shrine, dedicated to the memory of the Meiji Emperor and his

wife, Empress Shoken, is tucked in the centre of **Meiji Shrine Inner Gardens** (Meiji-Jingu Gyoen), an expanse of dense forest of over 125,000 trees and shrubs brought from all over Japan. The park's famous **Iris Garden** (Jingu Naien), where over 100 varieties come into bloom in mid-June, was designed by the Meiji Emperor for his wife.

The shrine itself, a sublimely beautiful example of Shinto architecture, with its plain cypress pillars, sweeping copper roof and a white gravel forecourt, was completed in 1920. The original shrine burnt down in an air raid and the present building is a perfect 1958 reconstruction. The compound, with its shrine maidens in white kimono and orange tunics, plays host to lively events including formal Japanese weddings.

As many as 3 million people come here to pray during the days following the New Year. And on the second Monday in January, young women dressed in their best kimono come here to celebrate Coming-of-Age Day. The advent of spring in late April and early May is marked with horseback archery, traditional dances and court music.

Located in the northern section of the park, the **Imperial Treasure House** ❺ (Meiji-jingu Hakubutsukan) displays a rather modest collection of sacred objects, garments and personal effects of the Imperial family (Mar–Oct daily 9am–4.30pm, Nov–Feb daily 9am–4pm; admission charge; tel: 03-3261 8326).

Sword Museum

A few streets northwest of the Imperial Treasure House, following the tracks of the expressway that looms above Koen-dori (Park Avenue) is the **Japanese Sword Museum** ❻ (Token Hakubutsukan; Tues–Sun 9am–4pm; admission charge; tel: 03-3379 1386). Swords were banned during the years of the American Occupation, along with mixed bathing in public bathhouses. (In the bewildering double standards of the day, *kabuki* theatres were temporarily closed down at the same time the city's first strip clubs opened.)

The museum, run by the Society for the Preservation of Japanese Art

Map on page 120

Crowds of 20-year-olds, many of the women dressed in kimono, descend on the Meiji-jingu Shrine on the second Monday of January to celebrate the Coming-of-Age Day.

BELOW: *torri* gate at the entrance to Meiji-jingu Shrine.

Swords, has an astounding collection of 6,000 swords, over 30 of which are registered National Treasures.

Yoyogi Park and stadium

Fringing the southwestern borders of the Meiji Shrine Inner Gardens is another generous swath of green, **Yoyogi Park** ❼ (Yoyogi-koen). American military personnel and their families were billeted here for several years after the war when the area was known as Washington Heights.

The land was handed back to the Japanese government and turned into a village for athletes attending the Tokyo Olympics in 1964. Kenzo Tange's highly original design for the **Yoyogi National Stadium** ❽ (Kokuritsu Yoyogi Kyogijo), built for the event, looks remarkably contemporary even today.

Also erected in 1964 and located to the southwest along Inokashira-dori is **NHK Hoso** (NHK Broadcasting Centre), the national television and radio headquarters. Free tours (only in Japanese) of its adjacent **Studio Park** offer the chance to see programmes as they are filmed.

Tobacco and Salt Museum

A 10-minute walk directly south of the NHK complex, along Koen-dori (Koen Avenue), is the **Tobacco and Salt Museum** ❾ (Tabako to Shio no Hakubutsukan). The museum is less of an abnormality than you might think, in a country where tobacco consumption is distressingly high and talk of political correctness in such matters has yet to be aired (Tues–Sun 10am–5.30pm; admission charge; tel: 03-3476 2041).

Salt and tobacco were a government monopoly until the early 20th century. Even after sales were liberalised, it remained under strict state control until 1985. The museum, built from the lucrative profits of the present Japan Tobacco and Salt Public Corporation, traces the history of salt and tobacco production in Japan and overseas through fascinating displays that include smoking implements and salt sculptures. The highlight is the fourth-floor special exhibition of *ukiyo-e* woodblock prints of courtesans and other Edo-Period figures in relaxed poses as they prepare their pipes.

In the post-war era, Shibuya's thriving black market was run by traders from Taiwan. Today, many Taiwanese continue to live in Shibuya, making it home to some of Tokyo's best Taiwanese restaurants.

BELOW: Yoyogi Park skateboarders communicate.

Map on page 120

Energy Museum

Located along Fire-dori, two blocks east of the Tobacco and Salt Museum is the **TEPCO Electric Energy Museum** ❿ or Denryokukan (Thur–Tues 10am–6pm; admission charge; tel: 03-3477 1191). The eight-storey museum can be recognised from its distinctive silver dome. Run by the Tokyo Electric Power Company, its exhibits and interactive displays on every aspect of electricity are especially popular with children.

Shibuya

From the Tobacco and Salt Museum, all avenues and alleys slope gently towards the human congestion of **Shibuya Station** (Shibuya-eki). During the late Edo Period, Shibuya sat on the western outskirts of the city, marking the transition from urban to rural. It is difficult to imagine that, only a century ago, this stridently trendy district, with its love hotels and consumer implants, was a place of tea plantations and rice mills.

Along with the exodus of people who moved into the western suburbs after the 1923 Kanto Earthquake, Shibuya-eki played a significant role in the growth of the area. What really put the district on the map was the choice of Shibuya as the site for the terminals for the Inokashira and Toyoko lines and the incorporation of the Ginza Line. Six railway lines converge on different floors, with stores, shops and restaurants forming a seamless part of the same complex.

The plaza in front of the station's north exit, dominated by huge video screens, is the site of one of the city's most otherworldly concentrations of neon advertisements and illuminated glass. The streets behind the screens continue the commercial theme with some of Tokyo's premier fashion and design buildings.

Shibuya shopping sprees

Connected by walkway to the JR Shibuya Station, **Mark City** ⓫, a major complex of lifestyle stores, boutiques, restaurants and the Shibuya Excel Tokyu Hotel, is the newest building to spring up on the west side of the tracks.

Directly facing the north exits of the station, the **Seibu** department

An interactive display at the TEPCO Electric Energy Museum.

BELOW: the Hachiko wall mural outside Shibuya Station. The bronze statue of Hachiko is found just opposite.

Hachiko the Faithful

A popular rendezvous spot for the youths who throng Shibuya is a small bronze statue of a dog named Hachiko, which stands in front of the Hachiko exit at Shibuya Station. Hachiko accompanied his owner Ueda Eisaburo, a university professor, to the station each day and waited for his return in the evening, a pattern that continued until a spring day in 1925, when his master died while teaching a class. Undaunted, Hachiko returned each day to the same spot to wait, even after the professor's relatives had moved the dog to Asakusa, a distance away. In order to shorten the tireless dog's daily treks to the station, a new home was found for him in nearby Yoyogi.

Commuters grew fond of the dog and, after newspaper *Asahi Shimbun* ran the story in 1932, Hachiko's fame as a symbol of almost *samurai*-like loyalty was assured. A bronze statue was unveiled in 1935, and a special ceremony is held every year on April 8 to honour Hachiko's memory. When Hachiko died at age 13, the responsibility for his immortalisation passed into the hands of taxidermists. The very life-like Hachiko can be seen encased in Tokyo's National Science Museum *(see page 152)*.

Tokyo's Fashion Tribes

In his essay titled *The Tongue of Fashion*, one of Japan's foremost expatriate writers, Donald Richie writes: "In Japan, a land where the emblematic is most visible and where signs and signals are more openly displayed, the language of dress is more codified than in many countries in the West." Even the national costume, the kimono, categorises those who wear it into clearly defined groups, conforming wearers to certain unwritten rules and conventions of dress.

The Japanese are fond of characterising themselves as a homogeneous family, a *minzoku*, or tribe. The closest most Japanese youth get to making a truly radical fashion statement is by electing to be part of a fashion tribe, one that offers the benefits of individualism within the security of a group.

Youths move through Tokyo's fashion towns in packs that often reflect styles strongly identified with specific boutiques or fashion chains. It is not difficult to pick out followers of Laforet, Candy Stripper, or the highly distinctive wardrobe of those who shop at cult store Hysteric Glamour.

"Din Alley", a pedestrian strip beside Harajuku's Yoyogi Park, was once a venue for Rockabilly dancers, punks with strawberry pelts and high priests of ska and mod. Fashion cults like the *Takenokozoku* (Bamboo Tribe), groups of mostly teenaged girls decked out in flouncy 1950s skirts, Minnie Mouse hair ribbons and headbands inscribed with the name of the town or district they come from, had their street headquarters here in the early 1980s. The city elders had the event squashed, but irrepressible youth groups are staging a comeback, occupying the fringes of the park.

Interestingly enough, Yoyogi Park was the birthplace of Japan's *bosozoku* ("Speed Tribes"), groups of discontented youth who cruise suburban Tokyo at night on motorbikes with silencers removed. The riders, belonging to different "tribes" and their affiliated chapters, typically sport kamikaze suits and dark glasses and fly Rising Sun flags from their bikes. With names like Black Emperor, Midnight Angels and Medusa, they may not be arbiters of fashion, but their tribal credentials are unassailable.

Less threatening but equally conspicuous are the so-called *Cos-play-zoku*, mostly female gangs from Saitama and Chiba, who can be found adjusting their *manga*-like costumes and blue lipstick to reflect the styles of the *visual-ke*, or "visual-type", trend they follow.

If Harajuku prioritises fashion cults for teens, Shibuya moves the process up a gear for the early-20s crowd. Style-conscious Tokyo fashion magazines have given the area saturation coverage. One recent Shibuya look combines lightened hair, tanned skin, blue and green contact lenses, micro-miniskirts and vertigo-inducing platform shoes, creating an effect not unlike Edo Period *oiran*, high-class prostitutes fond of bright layers of fabric and towering clogs.

The city may be plastered with the logos of globalisation, but youths ahead of the curve find their sartorial inspiration in sci-fi fantasy and *manga*, and elements from traditional arts like *kabuki* and *geisha*, all effortlessly mixed with the new pop-culture themes. You may have to use your imagination though to visualise what recent trends like "cute conservative" and "used touch" are. ❑

LEFT: teen New Age rockers in Yoyogi Park.

store is popular for its affordable collections by up-to-the-minute fashion designers. Seibu offshoots include **Loft Building**, a store selling funky household goods, and **SEED**, whose bold, contemporary fashions, art gallery and performance hall attract a more arty, avant-garde crowd.

Parco Part I and Part II are nearby, offering designs by some world famous names. **Tokyu Hands** is next door, a huge store specialising in hobby and leisure goods.

109 Building & Love Hotel Hill

Immediately west of the station, the **109 Building** ⓬ forms a wedge between Bunkamura and Dogenzaka-dori. The structure, a striking silver capsule resembling a silo, houses an array of stylish boutiques, restaurants and speciality stores. **Dogenzaka** ⓭, the slope that splits off to the left of the 109 Building, gets its name from a 13th-century highwayman, Owada Dogen, who attacked travellers here as they passed up the slope towards the mountains. The narrow backstreets that snake around the slope, offering short-stay rooms in dozens of whimsically designed buildings, have given rise to a nickname "Love Hotel Hill".

Dogenzaka's nightlife does not revolve exclusively around discreet carnality. This tiny but enthralling area, its cosy restaurants (offering dishes regarded as sexually fortifying – such as grilled eel), corner shrines and even one or two old wooden residences squeezed in between the hotels, has a lively music night scene with rock venues like On Air East and its counterpart On Air West, and discos like Dr Jeenans and Club Asia, with live ethnic and crossover sounds.

Bunkamura

Back at the 109 Building, take the right fork, and directly in front of the Tokyu department store, you will see **Book 1st**, an excellent store with a wide selection of English titles on its fourth floor and the city's largest collection of magazines on the first floor.

Farther up the slope, behind the Tokyu, the **Bunkamura** ⓮ is

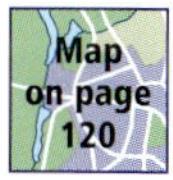

Shibuya's landmark 109 Building with its distinctive column.

LEFT: the Bunkamura is a centre devoted to the arts.
BELOW: Gas Panic Bar in Shibuya.

The fortress-like and almost unwelcoming facade of the Shoto Museum of Art. Thankfully, its interior is more pleasant.

Shibuya's premier culture centre – its 2,150-seat **Orchard Hall** is home to the Tokyo Philharmonic. The name of this multi-complex art centre means "Culture Village" in Japanese.

Owned by the Tokyu Corporation, it is the company's last advance in an intensely fought battle with its main rival Seibu. At the last count, Tokyu controlled nine building plots, Seibu eight. The centre houses galleries, shops, boutiques, a cinema and the **Bunkamura Museum of Art** (Bunkamura Bijutsukan), well regarded for its displays of modern art by Japanese and foreign artists (Mon–Thur 10am–7pm, Fri–Sun 10am–9pm; admission charge; tel: 03-3477 9111; www.bunkamura.co.jp).

No admission is charged to the **Bunkamura Gallery** to the left of the main lobby, where exhibitions of photography, painting and contemporary art installations are regularly held.

More arts venues

The Bunkamura is located on the edge of an expensive residential district called **Shoto**, the site of tea plantations in the 19th century. A pleasant stroll at any time of the year, this leafy district has a number of interesting small museums and galleries. The **Shoto Museum of Art** ⓯ (Shoto Bijutsukan) – a short walk from the Shisen Station on the Inokashira Line – features local artists in a cosy setting with a tearoom where pictures can be viewed from the comfort of armchairs (Tues–Sun 9am–5pm; admission charge; tel: 03-3465 9421).

Anyone with even a passing interest in ceramics will appreciate the exquisite collection at **Toguri Museum of Art** ⓰ (Toguri Bijutsukan), north of the Shoto Museum (Tues–Sun 9.30am–5pm; admission charge; tel: 03-3465 0070). Housed in a yellow brick building, only a small selection from the Toguri's 3,000-strong collection is shown at any one time. Its Imari, Nabeshima and Hagi pieces, captioned in both Japanese and English, are outstanding.

The nearby **Gallery TOM** ⓱ provides a very different experience (Tues–Sun 10am–5.30pm; admission charge; tel: 03-3467 8102).

BELOW: the always-packed Shibuya road crossing.

Owned by a constructivist sculptor, the concept gallery (the acronym stands for "Touch Our Museum") is designed for the blind. Broad stairs and handrails lead you to sculptures, which are set at waist level. Visitors are encouraged to touch the forms and let their hands lead them around.

Folk Craft Museum

Two stops on the Inokashira Line at **Komaba Todaimae**, the station's west exit faces another Tokyo University campus, but the real interest lies a few minutes walk west. Many consider the **Japan Folk Craft Museum** ⓲ (Mingei-kan) to be one of the best among Tokyo's several hundred museums (Tues–Sun 10am–5pm; admission charge; tel: 03-3467 4527). The lovely old wood and stone building, once owned by master potter Soetsu Yanagi, is a shrine to *mingei*, Japan's folk craft movement. A variety of ceramics, furniture and textiles are exhibited here.

Komaba Park

Nearby **Komaba Park** (Komaba-koen) has two buildings of interest. The **Tokyo Metropolitan Museum of Modern Japanese Literature** ⓳ (Toritsu Kindai Bungaku Hakubutsukan) is housed in a Western-style building dating from 1929 (daily 9am–4.30pm; free; tel: 03-3466 5150). Literature aside, the sumptuous interiors provide insights into how the well-to-do lived at that time.

Adjacent to the museum is the **Former Maeda Residence**, the 1930s home of the Marquis Maeda (Tues–Sun 10.30am–4pm; free; tel: 03-5271 7287). The appealing simplicity of this Japanese-style dwelling is matched by views from its verandah, which looks out into the exquisite gardens and carp pond.

Shimokitazawa

Shimokitazawa ⓴, located two stops farther west from Komaba Todaimae Station could hardly be more different. The word that best describes the shabby but vibrant Shimokitazawa is eclectic. Its carefully cultivated collegiate ambience, the assorted bric-a-brac and clothing shops, market stalls, used record stores and offbeat bookstores suggest a kind of Ivy League junk shop.

Shimokitazawa also has one of the densest concentrations of tiny live music houses in the city, playing a blistering mix of hip-hop, ambient, drum'n'bass, jazz, cyber and Japanese indie punk. The idiosyncrasies of the district are evident in its lively mix of restaurants and bars too.

Daikanyama

One stop southwest of Shibuya on the Tokyu Toyoko Line is one of the city's most fashionable quarters, **Daikanyama** ㉑. Look out for *couture* brands like Viviene Westwood and Tsumori Chisato, squeezed between trendy teen stores like Love Girls Market, and chic French restaurants, cafés and wine bars. More options abound at **La Fuente**, a complex of stores and eateries. ❑

Map on page 120

TIP

The newest starlet among Tokyo's mini-fashion towns and "oshare" (stylish) venues is Nakameguro, one stop down the Tokyu Toyoko Line after Daikanyama. Young entrepreneurs have set up their innovative boutiques, ateliers, al fresco bars and thrift shops which somehow combine cost-effective shopping with cool.

BELOW: interior, Japan Folk Craft Museum.

RESTAURANTS

American

Beacon

1-2-5 Shibuya, Shibuya-ku. Tel: 03-6418 0077. Open: daily L and D. ¥¥¥¥

This sleek, upmarket "urban chop house" serves some of the best steaks in the city – sirloin, fillet and rib eye, from Aussie grain-fed cattle, grilled to perfection over charcoal. There's also good seafood and free-range chicken, plus a huge cellar of Californian wines. A great place to entertain, especially for those who are in Tokyo on business.

Brazilian

Barbacoa Grill

Omotesando Square Tokyo Reit, B1, 4-3-24 Jingumae, Shibuya-ku. Tel: 03-3796 0571. Open: daily L and D. ¥¥¥

Popular with Tokyo's Brazilian community, this authentic churrasco restaurant is a meat lover's Mecca, though the salad bar offers some healthy relief. Brazilian beers and strong caipirinha cocktails are the proper accompaniment; mango ice cream makes the perfect dessert.

French

Chez Matsuo

1-23-15 Shoto, Shibuya-ku. Tel: 03-3485 0566. Open: daily L and D. ¥¥¥¥

Top-end French cooking in one of the most elite residential areas of Tokyo. Soak up the atmosphere of privilege in an exclusive 1920s ivy-covered villa with leafy garden views. A daunting wine list to go with the rich sauces and classic dishes, such as Matsuo's supreme of duck.

L'Artemis

2-31-7 Jingumae, Shibuya-ku. Tel: 03-5786 0220. Open: Thur–Tues L and D, closed 2nd Tues of the month. ¥¥¥

Excellent and affordable French cuisine worthy of far grander surroundings. Chef Nakada has studied with some of the best in France, and his ¥3,990 three-course dinner menu is a steal. The wine list is less of a bargain but it's worth splurging a bit with cooking this fine.

Fusion

Fujimamas

6-3-2 Jingumae, Shibuya-ku. Tel: 03-5485 2262. Open: daily 11am–11pm. ¥¥¥

www.fujimamas.com

The menu covers a spectrum of eclectic American-Asian influences, with a few Latin flavours added for good measure. But it's the architecture – a converted wooden workshop – and overall ambience that have made this casual restaurant-bar such a hit with locals and visitors alike.

Indian

Oh' Calcutta

Ota Bldg, B1, 26-9 Shibuya-ku. Tel: 03-3780 2315. Open: daily 11am–11pm. ¥¥

Located in a basement along Shibuya's main youth street, Center-gai, Oh' Calcutta features mouth-watering northern and southern Indian food, including vegetarian and mutton *biryani* dishes. Run by Indians, this is the real thing. Best of all is the eat-as-much-as-you-can lunch buffet, which costs just ¥1,050. Lovely yogurt and lassi drinks.

Japanese

Gesshinkyo

4-24-12 Jingumae, Shibuya-ku. Tel: 03-3796 6575. Open: Mon–Sat 6–10pm. ¥¥¥¥

Owner-chef Tanahashi studied traditional Zen vegetarian cuisine at a Buddhist nunnery in Kyoto, then created his own approach, using up to 40 different kinds of vegetables in each meal. Appreciate the artistry of his multi-course meals in this traditional, no-smoking setting. By reservation only.

Gonpachi

E.Space Tower, 14F, 3-6 Maruyamacho, Shibuya-ku. Tel: 03-5784 2011. Open: daily L and D. ¥¥¥

The main Gonpachi (in Nishi-Azabu) may be grander and more atmospheric, but it cannot match this branch in terms of location. The main dining room serves a range of Japanese dishes, including *yakitori* (gilled skewers of chicken) and *soba* (buckwheat noodles). But it is the separate sushi shop that has the spectacular panoramic view.

Kanetanaka-so

Cerulean Tower, Tokyu Hotel, 2F, 26-1 Sakuragaoka-cho, Shibuya-ku. Tel: 03-3476 3420. Open daily L and D. ¥¥¥¥

Kaiseki ryori, Japan's traditional *haute* cuisine, can be hard to approach, but here it is presented in a modern dining room with chairs (not tatami mats). The exquisite multi-course banquets follow the traditional format, but with stylish, contemporary arrangements.

Sasagin

1-32-15 Yoyogi-Uehara, Shibuya-ku. Tel: 03-5454 3715. Open: Mon–Sat 5–11pm. ¥¥¥

Roughly 80 brands of premium *sake*, personally selected by Narita-san, the master of the establishment, are available along with an interesting selection of modern Japanese cuisine. The décor is simple and casual, and prices are moderate, given the quality. Narita-san speaks good English, so you can ask him for recommendations.

Soranoniwa
4-17 Sakuragaoka-cho, Shibuya-ku. Tel: 03-5728 5191. Open: daily 5–11.30pm. ¥¥
Tofu cuisine doesn't have to be stuffy, formal and expensive. This casual diner close to the JR railway tracks in Shibuya is affordable and approachable. Highlights include tofu *shumai* dumplings and *yuba* (soymilk "skin") prepared at the table. English menu available.

Sushi-dokoro Sawa
2-9-19 Kitazawa, Setagaya-ku. Tel: 03-6407 2555. Open: Thur–Tues 5pm–midnight. ¥¥¥
A short walk from Shimokitazawa Station, near the Honda Theatre (Honda Gekijo), expect top-quality sushi at reasonable prices. Don't look for a menu, there isn't one. Let the fish pictures on the walls be your guide. A relaxed atmosphere, popular with the young folk who have made this area their own.

Sushi Ko
2-18-14 Jiyugaoka, Meguro-ku. Tel: 03-3717 1720. Open: Mon–Sat 5pm–midnight. ¥¥¥¥
25 types of sushi are available at all times, including traditional Edo-mae *nigiri* sushi. Some innovative additions include California influenced sushi and a number of vegetarian sushi made from eggplant and leek, all of which add interest. Spotlessly clean and absolutely no-smoking.

Sushi Ouchi
2-8-4 Shibuya, Shibuya-ku. Tel: 03-3407 3543. Open: Mon–Sat L and D. ¥¥¥
Maverick sushi chef Ouchi does everything a bit differently, from the restful dark-wood décor and classical music on the sound system to his insistence on all-natural ingredients. That means no artificially reared fish and absolutely no MSG or other chemicals.

Mexican

Fonda de la Madrugada
Villa Bianca, B1F, 2-33-12 Jingumae, Shibuya-ku. Tel: 03-5410 6288. Open: daily 5.30pm–5am. ¥¥¥
Located in an interior courtyard reminiscent of a village plaza, two floors below street level and complete with wandering mariachi musicians. As well as the usual burritos, enchiladas and other Mexican favourites, there are high-quality fish dishes and steaks. These go down well with Dos Equis beer or shots of tequila.

La Casita
Selsa Daikanyama, 2F, 13-4 Daikanyama-cho, Shibuya-ku. Tel: 03-3496 1850. Open: daily noon–11pm. ¥¥¥
Passably authentic Mexican cantina in one of Tokyo's newest fashion towns. Mouth-watering burritos, tortillas, enchiladas and avocado salads in a lively, fun ambience. Plenty of Mexican beers with lime, and also a good bar for ordering those salt-encrusted glasses of margaritas.

Pub Grub

The Aldgate
Shiniwasaki Bldg, 3F, 30-4 Udagawa-cho, Shibuya-ku. Tel: 03-3462 2983. Open: daily 6pm–2am. ¥
www.the-aldgate.com
A home away from home for expats and Anglophiles. Besides the usual fish n' chips, sausages, shepherd's pie, and other solid, no-frills pub nosh, the Aldgate also has surprisingly good vegetarian dishes. It also claims to have Japan's best collection of British rock CDs, and it features all the big soccer matches on television.

Hiki Café
R. Bldg, 1F, 32-8 Udagawa-cho, Shibuya-ku. Tel: 03-3770 1345. Open: Sun–Thur 11.45–12.30am, Fri–Sat 11.45–4.30am. ¥¥
This popular café attracts a lively mix of locals and expatriates. Reasonably priced food, including tasty hamburgers and pasta lunches, and at night there's an extensive cocktail bar. This is a good place to people watch, especially if you can get a table on the open terrace.

Turkish

Ankara
Social Dogenzaka, B1F, 1-14-9 Dogenzaka, Shibuya-ku. Tel: 03-3780 1366. Open 5–11.30pm daily. ¥¥¥
www.ankara.jp
This popular restaurant can be hard to find, up the hill behind the Mark City mall, but it's worth the effort. The cooking is excellent, especially the selection of meze appetisers, the juicy kebabs, and the pide (Turkish "pizza") topped with meat or cheese. Friendly and casual, and there's an English menu.

Vegetarian

Alicia
Dai-ni Suzuki Bldg, 2F, 2-9-23 Kitazawa, Setagaya-ku. Tel: 03-3485 3681. Open: Fri–Tues L and D; Sat–Sun 11.30am–7.30pm. ¥¥
A small whole-food café serving simple macrobiotic meals. The set menus feature dishes like sesame tofu, curried chickpea croquettes and salads, together with miso soup, rice and light, sugar-free desserts. Some seafood dishes are available but definitely no meat. The log-cabin surroundings are a bit gloomy.

PRICE CATEGORIES

Prices for three-course dinner per person without drinks and taxes:
¥ = under ¥2,000
¥¥ = ¥2,000–¥3,000
¥¥¥ = ¥3,000–¥5,000
¥¥¥¥ = over ¥5,000

MORI ART MUSEUM
TOKYO CITY VIEW
美術館
展望台

ROPPONGI AND AKASAKA

Tokyo's nightlife centres on Roppongi, but these days it faces competition from the slick Roppongi Hills enclave of upmarket shops and restaurants. Nearby Akasaka has an important shrine that draws pregnant women

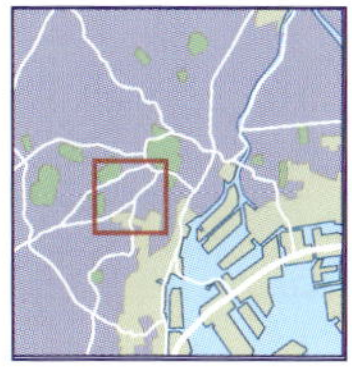

In the lower middle of the oval defined by the Yamanote Line, just to the southwest of the Imperial Palace, is an area favoured by Tokyo's expatriate community: Minato-ku, a Tokyo ward made up of Aoyama, Akasaka, Roppongi and Azabu. The area is peppered with embassies and high-priced expat housing, and liberally spiced with nightclubs, British pubs, live music houses and restaurants. The recent development of lifestyle complexes such as Roppongi Hills and Tokyo Midtown has drawn a fresh new crowd to the area.

Up on a hill served by the Hibiya Line, Roppongi, meaning "six trees", was once a garrison town for the Meiji government, and later, after World War II, the Americans established barracks here. It is today the heart of Minato-ku's nightlife.

Most people begin exploring Roppongi and adjacent Akasaka at the Roppongi Crossing, the intersection between Gaien-Higashi-dori and Roppongi-dori (Roppongi Avenue), where the **Almond Coffee Shop**, a popular meeting place, is found.

Ark Hills

Following this stretch of raised motorway northeast leads to **Ark Hills** ❶, a modern complex of two twin towers, shops, restaurants, cafés, offices and highly exclusive apartments. The **Japan Foundation Library** (Kokusaikoryu Kikin Toshokan), with thousands of books on Japan in English, the Asahi TV Studios, the **Suntory Hall** concert venue and the **ANA Hotel** are all within the complex. There are also Japanese and fast food restaurants, and a Starbucks coffee shop.

Okura Shukokan Museum

Behind Ark Hills, nestled amid a number of embassies and exclusive

Map on page 132

LEFT: entrance to the Mori Art Museum and Tokyo City View at Roppongi Hills.
BELOW: cheerful sales assistant.

An erotica shop in Roppongi peddling sex paraphernalia.

residential backstreets, just beyond the American Embassy, the **Okura Shukokan Museum of Fine Art** ❷ (Okura Shukokan Bijutsukan) was set up by Baron Okura Tsuruhiko in 1917 (Tues–Sun 10am–4.30pm; admission charge; tel: 03-3583 0781). A Chinese-style anomaly in a city of architectural anomalies, the museum houses a small but intriguing collection of Asian antiquities and Buddhist sculptures.

Musée Tomo

A few steps away, behind the Hotel Okura, is the extraordinary **Musée Tomo** ❸ (Tues–Sun 11am–6pm; tel: 03-5733 5311). With a broad collection of the very best ceramics, from Imari vases to Raku tea bowls, the gallery also features the work of modern pottery masters.

Roppongi Hills

Heading west along Roppongi-dori and a short walk from the Roppongi metro is the massive **Roppongi Hills** ❹ complex (www.roppongihills.com). Like Shiodome *(see page 190)* and the Marunouchi Building *(see page 80)*, this much-trumpeted complex is among the brashest of

Map on page 132

Tokyo's mini-cities. The 16-hectare (40-acre) site is impressive; its towering office blocks, luxe Grand Hyatt Tokyo, nine-screen cinema, apartments, and over 200 shops and interconnecting walkways make up one of the largest upmarket shopping and entertainment developments in Japan. The array of restaurants and cafés alone is stunning, including eateries by star chefs like Todd English, Joel Robuchon and Wolfgang Puck.

The **Mori Art Museum** on the 54th floor of **Mori Tower** is a first-rate contemporary gallery (Wed–Mon 10am–10pm, Tues 10am–5pm; admission charge; tel: 03-6406 6100; www.mori.art.museum). The adjacent **Tokyo City View** is an observation deck with a heart-stopping 360-degree view of the city and its bright lights (daily 9am–midnight; admission charge).

Tokyo Midtown

Tokyo Midtown ❺, about 500 metres (550 yds) north of Roppongi Hills, poses a stern challenge to the latter (www.tokyo-midtown.com). It has high-end fashion, luxury dining, concert spaces, the city's first Ritz Carlton hotel, extensive gardens and observation gallery, all of which are capturing the city's imagination. In a city where superlatives count, the Midtown Tower stands out as Tokyo's current tallest building.

Within Tokyo Midtown is the **Suntory Museum of Art** ❻. Its collection of lacquerware, ceramics and paintings from the 17th century to the present is housed in a very sleek and light-filled design featuring high ceilings and louvred windows (Wed–Mon 10am–8pm; admission charge; tel: 03-3479 8600; www.suntory.co.jp/sma). **21_21 Design Sight** ❼, designed by Tadao Ando, sits in a green corner of the 10-hectare (25-acre) grounds (Wed–Mon 11am–8pm; admission charge; tel: 03-3475 2121; www.2121designsight.jp). This space, with fashion leader Issey Miyake among its directors, has progressive theme-based design exhibitions.

National Art Centre

Within walking distance of these two museums is the **National Art Centre** ❽. It completes the Art Triangle Roppongi concept, an attempt to create an art precinct as an alternative to the district's nightlife (Wed–Mon 10am–6pm; tel: 03-5777 8600; www.nact.jp). Designed by renowned architect Kisho Kurokawa, the centre, the largest art space in Japan, is unique for having no private collection of its own, giving it complete freedom over the exhibitions it mounts.

Tokyo Tower

South of the Roppongi Crossing towards the district of Shiba on the fringes of Azabu is a fashionable residential quarter favoured by diplomats, bankers and media people. **Tokyo Tower** ❾, reminiscent of a red-and-white barber's pole,

The much maligned Tokyo Tower sheds its shabby daytime image at night, when it is illuminated to startling effect – a sight to silence its most vocal critics.

BELOW: Tokyo Tower is spectacular when lit up at night.

Stone lanterns, such as this in Shiba Park, provide an important focal point in Japanese gardens; they were originally used to light the way in gardens and at temple entrances.

dominates the skyline here. Taller than the Eiffel Tower, to which it is optimistically compared by the Japanese, the 333-metre (1,090-ft) structure, completed in 1958, was designed as a transmitting tower. Compensating for its lacklustre aquarium and wax museum is its Special Observatory with exceptional views of the city, and on a clear day, of Mount Fuji; its lower Main Observatory has less stunning views (both observatories daily 9am–10pm; admission charge).

Zojo-ji Temple

Just behind the tower, and almost as visible in the spacious grounds of Shiba Park (Shiba Koen), stands one of Tokyo's grandest temples, the **Zojo-ji Temple ⓾**. Founded in 1393, the site was chosen by the Tokugawa clan in the late 1600s as their ancestral temple, as part of a scheme to protect Edo from evil spirits. Close to the bay and the Tokaido Road, it also served as a post station for travellers and pilgrims. Most of the temple buildings, once numbering over 100, were destroyed by fires and air raids, but its main entrance, the 1612 red-lacquered **Sanmon Gate**, an Important Cultural Treasure, is original.

Pass through the gate, with its large bell made from melted down hairpins donated by the ladies of the shogun's court, to the **Main Hall** (Taiden). It contains many important sacred objects, including ancient sutras and statuary. The new leaders of the Meiji government showed their contempt for the outgoing Tokugawa by confiscating the temple, turning the grounds into a park and removing six of the mummified shogun to a less prestigious resting place at the rear of the Main Hall, near a row of cheerful Jizo statues, each with a windmill in its hand.

Hie-jinja Shrine

Back to Ark Hills, following the Roppongi-dori north, a sharp left along Sotobori-dori takes you to **Hie-jinja Shrine ⓫**, on the borders of Akasaka and Nagatacho districts. Transplanted here in the 17th century in the belief that it would help to deflect evil from Edo Castle, a

BELOW: Sanmon, the main entrance to the Zojo-ji Temple in Shiba Park.

massive stone *torri* gate leads uphill through an avenue of smaller, red-lacquered gates to the current buildings, put up in 1967. The shrine's role as protector is still evident today; look carefully at a carving to the left of the main shrine and you will see a monkey cradling its baby. Pregnant women come here to pay wishful homage to the image.

Every two years in June, the shrine is the stage for a great Tokyo festival, the **Sanno Matsuri**. Hundreds of participants in period costumes take part in an impressive parade, which includes the carrying of heavy *mikoshi* (portable shrines) on the shoulders of local residents.

Long established hotels

North from the shrine, past Akasaka-Mitsuke subway, will take you to Benkei-bori moat (Benkei-bashi). Crossing the Benkei Bridge leads you into the requisitioned estates of former aristocrats. The 40-storey **Akasaka Prince Hotel ⓬** is named after one of those nobles. The building, a creation of Kenzo Tange, is worth a short detour. Made of reflective white glass and aluminum, the structure is shaped like a folding fan. Sections of an older wing, built in 1928 as a guest residence for Prince Yi of Korea, are used as a ballroom and restaurant.

Another 40-storey structure, the **Hotel New Otani ⓭** also lies within the castle's outer moat near Benkei Bridge. The hotel's **New Otani Art Museum** (Wed–Mon 10am–6pm; free) on the sixth-floor of the Garden Court wing, has a small but notable collection of works by Japanese and European painters, including Modigliani and Chagall. In keeping with most of Tokyo's deluxe hotels, the gallery has a tea ceremony room serving high-grade green tea at an equally refined price. Entry to its delightful Japanese garden, however, is free.

Akasaka Detached Palace

The museum is close to the extensive grounds of the **Akasaka Detached Palace ⓮** or Geihin-kan (only the grounds are open to public). Completed in 1909, the palace does not quite succeed in emulating the homes of European royalty. Part Versailles, part Buckingham Palace, its exterior may have inspired the intended awe but the poorly designed interior, once inhabited by the Meiji Emperor, his wife and staff, is a cavernous and drafty place. The palace is currently the Guest House for visiting heads of state and dignitaries.

Toyokawa Inari Shrine

Wedged between Aoyama-dori and the borders of the palace grounds, is the **Toyokawa Inari-jinja Shrine ⓯**, also called Myogon-ji. A Zen temple with Shinto trappings, it has a chaotic clutter of images lining the approach to the main sanctuary: orange banners and lanterns, statues of the goddess Kannon and the child-protector deity Jizo, and figures of red-bibbed foxes. ❑

Map on page 132

TIP

Every last Thursday and Friday of the month, the Roppongi Flea Market, a cornucopia of old bric a brac, used kimono, old aquatint postcards as well as junk, is set up in front of the Roi Building, south of the Roppongi Crossing.

BELOW: young drummers participating in the Sanno Matsuri festival at the Hie-jinja Shrine.

RESTAURANTS

American

Roti Brasserie
Tokyo Midtown, Garden Terrace, 1F, 9-7-4 Akasaka, Minato-ku. Tel: 03-5413 3655. Open: daily 11am–10.30pm. ¥¥¥
This modern wine bar-diner offers modern North American cooking in a stylish brasserie setting. The cellar is extensive, with 20 different wines available by the glass, and there is plenty of good food to go with it – oysters on the half shell, rotisserie chicken, pasta dishes and even spicy Cajun catfish burgers.

Chinese

Chinese Café Eight
Court Annex, 2F, 3-2-13 Nishi-Azabu, Minato-ku. Tel 03-5414 5708. Open: daily 24 hours. ¥¥
It's remarkable to find Chinese food at these budget prices so close to Roppongi Hills, and even more amazing that this place stays open around the clock. Peking duck (for 3–4 people) is a bargain at ¥3,680; the *gyoza* dumplings are three for just ¥105. Not surprisingly, this place is always crowded. Be warned, though: the staff tend to be brusque – and the décor is rather risqué.

Toh-Ka-Lin
Hotel Okura, 6F, 2-10-4 Toranomon, Minato-ku. Tel: 03-3505 6068. Open: daily L and D.
Great general Chinese cuisine and access to the Hotel Okura's seemingly bottomless wine cellar. Many beloved customers of Toh-Ka-Lin would support its claim to be the number one Chinese restaurant in Tokyo.

French

L'Atelier de Joël Robuchon
Roppongi Hills Hillside, 2F, 6-10-1 Roppongi, Minato-ku. Tel: 03-5772 7500. Open: daily L and D. ¥¥¥¥
Master chef Joël Robuchon presents his impeccable cuisine in a sophisticated but informal setting, less complex than his top-end restaurants. Diners sit not at tables but at the counter running along the open kitchen. Robuchon adds tapas flavours to signature dishes such as the *chaud-froid* ("hot-cold") starter of clams, and quail with balsamico. Reservations are taken only for the first sitting at lunchtime; otherwise it's first come first served.

The French Kitchen
Grand Hyatt Tokyo, 2F, 6-10-3 Roppongi, Minato-ku. Tel: 0120-588 288. Open: daily 7am–10pm. ¥¥¥
The Grand Hyatt's main restaurant is a large, upmarket brasserie and bar serving superior regional French cuisine, backed up with an outstanding wine cellar. Sit inside in view of the busy open kitchen, or outside on the terrace. The attached bar is a popular watering hole for visiting businessmen, while expats tend to prefer the extensive cellar at the **Oak Door** grill, on the hotel's 6th floor.

Fusion

Roy's
West Walk Roppongi Hills, 5F, 6-10-1 Roppongi, Minato-ku. Tel: 03-5413 9571. Open: daily L and D. ¥¥¥¥
Roy Yamaguchi, one of Hawaii's top chefs, creates delicious Asian-American fusion cuisine that's as impressive on the eyes as on the palate. The setting is stunning too, especially at night, with a panoramic view of Tokyo Tower on the horizon.

The Tokyo Restaurant
2-4-1 Minami-Azabu, Minato-ku. Tel: 03-5418 7555. Open: daily L and D. ¥¥¥
Stylish contemporary dining in a converted bank. With high ceilings and the luxury of plenty of elbow room, the decor here is New York loft style. The cooking is an eclectic mix of Californian and nouvelle cuisines, while the attention to detail is pure Japanese. English menu and a first-rate wine list are available.

Japanese

Butagumi
2-24-9 Nishi-Azabu, Minato-ku. Tel: 03-5466 6775. Open: Wed–Mon L and D. ¥¥
The finest *tonkatsu* (deep-fried breaded pork cutlets) in the city, served in a traditional setting. The cutlets are prepared from premium free-range pork, making it pricier than at other places. Choose between fatty *rosu* and lean *filet* meat. Or, if you want the best, order the superb Iberico cutlets. No English menu, but a little English is spoken.

Fukuzushi
5-7-8 Roppongi, Minato-ku. Tel: 03-3402 4116. Open: Mon–Sat 5.30–11pm. ¥¥¥
Upmarket surroundings and well-heeled clientele define this place, but there is none of the snotty attitude found at many of the traditional sushi shops. The English menu helps you to negotiate the familiar tastes of tuna, mackerel and cod, as well as the unfamiliar delights of conger eel, shad and grouper. Like the best sushi restaurants, this one is an educational experience.

Hassan
Denki Bldg, B1, 6-1-20 Roppongi, Minato-ku.

Tel: 03-3403 8333. Open: daily L and D. ¥¥¥
The main attraction here is the ¥5,040 all-you-can-eat menu of *shabu-shabu* (thin slices of Japanese Wagyu beef dipped in broth) with side dishes of other traditional Japanese favourites in a lovely traditional setting. Lunch is a bargain, with courses from ¥1,050.

Inakaya East
5-3-4 Roppongi, Minato-ku. Tel: 03-3408 5040. Open: daily 5–11pm. ¥¥¥
Inakaya East – together with its nearby sister restaurant, Inakaya West – is a long-time favourite in Roppongi. Chefs in traditional *happi* coats grill fish, meat and vegetables to order, then pass them on long wooden paddles across to where you're sitting. It's theatrical and fun – but not cheap.

Ninja
Akasaka Tokyu Plaza, 1F, 2-14-3 Nagatacho, Chiyoda-ku. Tel: 03-5157 3936. Open: Mon–Sat 5.30pm–2am, Sun 5–11pm. ¥¥¥
In a rambling space designed to resemble the basement of a feudal castle, black-clad waiters dressed like ninjas show you to your private room, then entertain you as you nibble on simple Japanese food. Lots of fun for all in the family.

Nodaiwa
1-5-4 Higashi-Azabu, Minato-ku. Tel: 03-3583 7852. Open: Mon–Sat L and D. ¥¥¥
The speciality here is *unagi* (eel) – one of the great under-appreciated delicacies of Japanese gastronomy. Fillets of wild eel are carefully grilled over charcoal, daubed with a savoury sauce and served with rice. Besides serving the best *unagi* in Tokyo, Nodaiwa also boasts a refined and unique setting – an old storehouse building transported from the mountains.

Pintokona
Metrohat, B2F, 6-4-1 Roppongi, Minato-ku. Tel: 03-5771 1133. Open: daily 11am–11pm. ¥¥–¥¥¥
Unlike most conveyor-belt sushi restaurants, this one emphasises quality, not quantity. You can also order from a menu, which includes some light *izakaya* (tavern)-style dishes, rather than choosing from whatever passes in front of you. This is a stylish place where you can linger for a while. Definitely worth the extra yen.

Poisson Rokusaburo
Plaza Mikado, 1F, 2-14-5 Akasaka, Minato-ku. Tel: 03-5570 6317. Open: daily except Mon, L and D. ¥¥¥
www.rokusaburo.com
Delicious fish dishes that blend global touches like Italian balsamic vinegars and Korean flavours with traditional Japanese preparations. The lunches are light and healthy (and easier on the wallet); the dinners are more ponderous gourmet affairs. Try the evening "Poisson Course" or the extensive nine-course special "Par Excellence" set.

Tofuya Ukai
4-4-13 Shiba Koen, Minato-ku. Tel: 03-3436 1028. Open: daily 11am–10pm. ¥¥¥–¥¥¥¥
Sitting in the shadow of Tokyo Tower, this remarkable restaurant boasts traditional architecture and a beautiful rambling garden with carp ponds. The refined multi-course meals, served in private rooms, revolve around numerous variations of tofu. If you want fully vegetarian food, let them know when you reserve.

Korean

Kusa no Ie
Mita Bldg, 3F, 2-14-33 Akasaka, Minato-ku. Tel: 03-3589 0779. Open: daily 11.30–3.30am, Sat–Sun 5–10pm. ¥¥¥
A popular Korean restaurant with branches in Shinbashi and Azabu-Juban; the speciality here is *yakiniku*, thin slices of marinated beef, grilled at your table barbecue-style and served with side dishes of rice and *kimchi* (pickled vegetables). You may have to wait for a table.

Mugyodon
Sangyo Bldg, 2F, 2-17-74 Akasaka, Minato-ku. Tel: 03-3586 6478. Open: Mon–Sat 5pm–12.30am. ¥¥
Authentic Korean cuisine with no softening or realigning of the food for Japanese palates. All the usual options such as Korean barbecue, *kalbi* (ribs) stews and fiery *kimchi* (pickled vegetables). A very friendly, informal place, which means it's very popular.

Vegetarian

Akasaka Tofuya
3-5-2 Akasaka, Minato-ku. Tel: 03-3582 1028. Open: Mon–Fri L and D. ¥¥
Tofu in its many forms is featured throughout the meals served here, but the soup stocks are made from fish, so it is not strictly vegetarian. But even confirmed carnivores will be impressed by the freshness and flavour of both the regular tofu and the *goma-dofu* (sesame tofu).

Daigo
Forest Tower, 2F, 2-3-1 Atago, Minato-ku. Tel: 03-3431 0811. Open: daily L and D. ¥¥¥¥
Buddhist temple cooking elevated to the finest level of *kaiseki* cuisine. Extended vegetarian banquets feature 10–15 courses of amazing delicacy and complexity, all served in private rooms. Budget plenty of time (and expense). Reservations are essential.

PRICE CATEGORIES

Prices for three-course dinner per person without drinks and taxes:
¥ = under ¥2,000
¥¥ = ¥2,000–¥3,000
¥¥¥ = ¥3,000–¥5,000
¥¥¥¥ = over ¥5,000

SHINAGAWA, MEGURO AND EBISU

You can visit the burial grounds of the 47 samurai, a legendary tale every Japanese knows, picnic among trees that were around when Edo was a fishing village, or shop in Ebisu's massive all-in-one mall

A key checkpoint and post station at the start of the great Tokaido (East Sea Road) that connected Edo with Kyoto, Shinagawa once stood on a stretch of dismal tidal flats at the edge of the city. Founded on fishing and the cultivation of seaweed, the area's main trade soon gave way to services catering to travellers, and inns and teahouses flourished. Along with these arose the inevitable facilities catering for pleasures of the flesh. When the feudal system collapsed with the advent of the Meiji era however, railways and industry moved in.

Shinagawa and its much sought after residential districts of Higashi-Gotanda, Takanawa and Shirokanedai have come up in the world since then. Close to Shinagawa Station's west exit are the Keihin Hotel and Shinagawa Prince Hotel, while a block north is a cluster of first-class hotels like the Takanawa Prince Hotel, New Takanawa Prince and Meridien Pacific Tokyo, all arranged around a lovely garden, once the private grounds of a member of the Imperial family.

Hara Museum

There are several cultural features to what at first appears to be a rather drab district of offices, embassies and hotels. Modern art finds an interesting home in the **Hara Museum of Contemporary Art ❶** (Hara Bijutsukan), a 15-minute walk south of Shinagawa Station along Dai-ichi Keihin, a broad road running beside the railway tracks. (Tues–Sun 11am–5pm, Wed till 8pm; admission charge; tel: 03-3445 0651; www.haramuseum.or.jp).

Five rooms with connecting corridors are used to display the museum's changing exhibitions, which have included works by international

Map on page 140

LEFT: a Buddhist monk at Shinagawa's Sengaku-ji temple. **BELOW:** installation art at Hara Museum of Contemporary Art.

Auspicious red prayer banners at the Daien-ji Temple.

BELOW: tombstones of the legendary 47 *ronin* at Sengaku-ji Temple.

artists such as Christo and Andy Warhol. The grandfather of the museum's founder, Hara Toshio, had the Bauhaus-style home built in 1938. One of Japan's leading architects, Isozaki Arata, was brought in more recently to add an annexe, the **Café d'Art**, where you can enjoy drinks while overlooking a sculpture garden.

Sengaku-ji Temple

North of the Hara Museum and a short walk west of the Sengakuji Station is the **Sengaku-ji Temple** ❷. This temple, known to almost every Japanese, was the setting for part of one of Edo's best known true stories. Reproduced countless times in *kabuki* and *bunraku* plays, the 18th-century tale concerns the tragic fate of 47 *ronin* (or "masterless samurai"). Their master, Lord Asano, taunted and scorned by his teacher Lord Kira, caused grave offence by drawing his sword in anger. Because the offence occurred within the castle grounds, Asano was obliged to perform *seppuku* (ritual suicide). On 1 December 1702, Asano's 47 retainers, in an act of revenge, decapitated Kira in his mansion on the banks of the Sumida River and carried the head through the streets of Edo to their lord's grave at Sengaku-ji. Thereafter, as retribution, the 47 *ronin* were ordered to commit *seppuku*.

Much admired by the Japanese as a morality tale demonstrating the code of duty and self-sacrifice that was the highest samurai ideal, incense is placed every day on the graves of the 47 retainers and their Lord Asano, who are buried together at Sengaku-ji. The temple was rebuilt after the war, but its entrance gate, a beautifully carved and decorated work with a dragon motif dating from 1836, remains intact. A small side building, the **Gishiken** (Hall of Loyal Retainers), contains some of the personal effects of the 47 *ronin*.

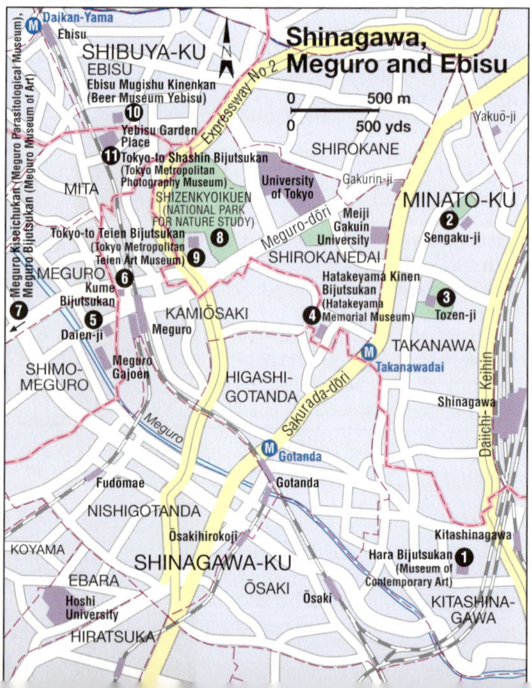

Tozen-ji Temple

Directly south of Sengaku-ji is a small Zen temple with an air of purity and simplicity that is worth a short detour. **Tozen-ji Temple ❸** was the British Legation between 1859 and 1873, a reflection of the housing problems that existed even back then. The temple was not quite the shelter the British had envisaged. When retainers from the influential Mito clan burst in one day, Britain's first representative, Sir Rutherford Alcock, barely managed to escape death by hiding in the temple's bathtub. The minister's crime? He was spotted defiling sacred Mount Fuji by climbing to its summit.

Hatakeyama Museum

A second exhibition venue that is worth visiting in neighbouring Shirokanedai is the **Hatakeyama Memorial Museum ❹** (Hatakeyama Kinen Bijutsukan). This can be reached by walking due west of Shinagawa Station, or five minutes on foot from Takanawadai Station on the Toei Asakusa Line (Tues–Sun 10am–4.30pm; admission charge; tel: 03-3447 5787).

The museum is located on a wooded hill at the heart of an estate once owned by the Lord of Satsuma in Kyushu. A section of the old garden still remains. The museum reflects the interests of its founder, the industrialist and tea ceremony master, Hatakeyama Issei. Galleries display tea utensils and bowls, hand scrolls and other tea ceremony objects, but also lacquerware and *noh* costumes. There are three tea ceremony rooms as well.

Meguro Club Seitei

The JR Yamanote tracks, underscored by the Hibiya Line subway, mark the border between Shinagawa and Meguro wards. Exiting Meguro Station, the fairytale turrets of a medieval European castle loom above the traffic. This is the **Meguro Club Seitei**, one of Tokyo's most flamboyant love hotels. One room is reputed to have a bed that revolves in a cylinder lined with mirrors; another has a ceiling that emits lightning flashes and cloud bursts.

Daien-ji Temple and Meguro Gajoen Hotel

Five minutes southwest of the station, down a rather steep slope, **Daien-ji Temple ❺** is home to a no less fabulous creation: 500 lifelike *rakan* (Buddha disciple) images. Made as an offering to the spirits of those who died in a disastrous fire that destroyed the original temple in 1772, the stone figures stand row upon row against one of the temple's walls. Highly individualised, each pose and face is different.

Right behind the temple is the **Meguro Gajoen Hotel**. This exquisite old-world Japanese-style inn has lovely gardens, original art works on the walls and ceilings, and a refined atmosphere. It is very popular as a venue for weddings.

Map on page 140

Capsule hotels are an ingenious solution to limited space. A pigeonhole sleeping chamber includes bedding, a TV and an alarm clock.

BELOW: a Shinto wedding ceremony at the Meguro Gajoen hotel.

Encounters with "Janglish"

While riding on a bus, a visitor once spotted a restaurant sign with the name "Cheese Doll". What an odd name for an eatery, he thought, and filed it away for future reference. Not long afterwards, the bus passed a second establishment with the same appellation, and at this point, he noted that both of them had been housed in matte yellow buildings.Then suddenly it all made sense: the owner had tried to emulate the name "Chez d'Or", but unaware that it meant "house of gold" in French, and unable to find either of these words in his English dictionary, settled for the closest equivalents he could find. This flair for mangling the English language is one of Japan's most endearing characteristics. They chop it up and reassemble it in imaginative ways that resemble the linguistic equivalent of abstract art.

When English is packaged solely for domestic consumption, Japanese seem indifferent to the rules of correct usage; and when informed of this fact, they seldom care. English exists, not as a medium of international communication, but rather as decorative icing on the cake of commercialism.

In addition to names of businesses, this fractured English, which goes by such unflattering names as "Janglish" and "Japlish", can be encountered in building signs, on T-shirts, on shopping bags, in product instruction manuals, advertising slogans, subway posters, product names and publications of all sorts. More recently, the Internet has vastly multiplied the opportunities to disseminate this strange mutant of English around the globe.

Janglish manifests itself in a number of forms, including confusion between the letters "r" and "l" (JAL flight attendant: "We hope you enjoy your fright."), or "b" and "v" (Sign in Osaka hotel: "Tooth Brush Bending Machine".) Translations, moreover, are often rendered straight out of the dictionary, leading to expressions that are, to be kind, less than idiomatic.

Japanese themselves refer to this linguistic phenomenon as "Wasei Eigo", or Made-in-Japan English. Indeed, rather than adopt English words as they are, they have been known to create their own unique forms. A car's windscreen is "front glass". A rear-view mirror is a "back mirror". The steering wheel is a "handle", a hubcap is a "wheel cover", and so on.

Some of the greatest mirth is created when these spill over into oddball product names, such as "Creap" for a powdered coffee creamer, "Flavour My Drip" for individual pre-mixed coffee servings and "Pocket Wetty" for premoistened hand wipes. An all-time favourite is a now-defunct line of individual servings of microwave-ready dishes that its maker named "Dish of Quickie", blissfully unaware of any sexual overtones.

Some foreign residents find it irritating that word borrowings seem most likely to be adopted when the subject is negative. When the 3 percent consumption tax was introduced in 1989, government posters identified it as *nyuu takusu*. Another highly unpopular subject, *risutora* – restructuring – generally implies laying off workers. And although a perfectly good Japanese word exists for sexual harassment – *seiteki iyagarase* – the media invariably refers to such acts as *seku-hara*. ❑

LEFT: Janglish manifests itself everywhere.

Kume and Meguro Museums

Just opposite Meguro Station's west exit on the left corner, the **Kume Museum** ❻ (Kume Bijutsukan) houses a collection of paintings by Kume Kuchiro, the first Japanese painter to practice Impressionism (Thur–Tues 10am–5pm; admission charge; tel: 03-3491 1510).

Continue west and cross Shimbashi Bridge to one of the city's strangest institutions, the **Meguro Parasitological Museum** ❼ (Meguro Kiseichukan), on the right of a small turning that runs left off the main road (Tues–Sun 10am–5pm; admission charge; tel: 03-3716 1264). Unless you have a morbid interest in playing host to one of 45,000 parasites collected by the museum, or would like to see the remains of an 8.8-metre (29-ft) tapeworm removed from the body of a 40-year-old man, you could safely give this museum a miss.

North towards the Meguro-gawa River is the **Meguro Museum of Art Tokyo**, a spacious space by city gallery standards, in pleasant surroundings (Tues–Sun 10am–6pm; admission charge; tel: 03-3714 1201). It houses a collection of international and local craft and fine-art works.

Nature Study Park

A short distance east of the station, passing under Tokyo's own giant tapeworm, the monstrous Shuto Expressway, is a sight you would least expect in a city like Tokyo: an expanse of deliberately undeveloped land. The **National Park for Nature Study** ❽ (Shizenkyoikuen), an effort to preserve in its original form a section of the Musashino Plain that once covered much of the area Edo was built on, covers 20 hectares (49 acres) (Tues–Sun 9am–4pm, till 5pm during summer; admission charge; tel: 03-3441 7176; www.ins.kahaku.go.jp).

Among the 8,000 or more trees (160 species in all) in the park, moss-covered ones that were here when Edo was a mere fishing village still stand. In a city deprived of greenery, this reserve provides an invaluable space to breathe in, not only for humans but also the aquatic flora that flourish in its ponds and

Map on page 140

TIP

The Happo-en along Meguro-dori, a popular wedding hall, offers a patch of green in crowded Tokyo. Its beautiful Edo Period stroll garden was once part of an estate owned by retainers of Tokugawa shogun.

BELOW: irises at the National Park for Nature Study.

Map on page 140

wetlands, and the large variety of birds that stop by. Only 300 people are allowed into the park at a time. You will be issued with a returnable ribbon as you go in.

Tokyo Metropolitan Teien Art Museum

At the entrance to the park are signs to the **Tokyo Metropolitan Teien Art Museum** ❾ (Tokyo-to Teien Bijutsukan), housed in the former villa of Prince Yasuhiko Asaka (daily 10am–5.30pm, closed 2nd and 4th Wed every month; admission charge; tel: 03-3443 0201). This member of the Imperial family has the dubious reputation of being the general in charge of Japanese troops during the Nanking massacre in China. The residence was converted into a museum in 1983, but of more interest is the fact that the villa may well be the city's only surviving art deco building. The house, surrounded by lovely French and Japanese-style landscaped gardens, reflects tastes acquired during the prince's three-year sojourn in Paris in the 1920s.

A poster exhibit at Beer Museum Yebisu.

BELOW: Ebisu Gardens Place at twilight.

Yebisu Garden Place

One stop up the line from Meguro Station is **Ebisu**, an old district that has become chic only in the last few years. Ebisu is the name given to one of the seven gods of good fortune, but the name of the district derives from the popular Yebisu beer. Ebisu Station, connected by the JR Yamanote and Hibiya subway lines, was built as a freight depot to transport beer from factories and breweries lining the Meguro and Shibuya rivers.

Redesigned in the late 1990s, the south side of Ebisu Station has a long horizontal escalator that takes visitors to the **Yebisu Garden Place**, a massive shopping, hotel, office and entertainment complex. Built on the site of the old Yebisu brewery, it is filled on weekends with young people and couples. The name is a misnomer though as there is hardly any greenery here. Around the plaza are shops and boutiques, bars, cafés, a concert hall, the Westin Hotel, and French restaurant Taillevent Robuchon, housed in a florid Disneyesque French chateau.

Beer and Photo Museums

Befitting its location on the site of the old Yebisu Beer Brewery, the **Beer Museum Yebisu** ❿ (Ebisu Mugishu Kinenkan) traces the history and brewing methods of beer around the world (Tues–Sun 10am–5pm; admission charge; tel: 03-5423 7255). Video displays include a virtual reality trip through a brewery. The entrance fee includes the sampling of Sapporo beers.

On the eastern side of the plaza is the superb **Tokyo Metropolitan Photography Museum** ⓫ (Tokyo-to Shashin Bijutsukan), the premier exhibition space for notable photography and video art (Tues–Sun 10am–6pm, Thur–Fri till 8pm; admission charge; tel: 03-3280 0031). Major Japanese and Western photographers are featured here. ❑

RESTAURANTS

Fusion

Fummy's Grill
2-1-5 Ebisu, Shibuya-ku. Tel: 03-3473 9629. Open: daily 11.30am–2am. ¥¥
Fumihiro Nakamura was the first to serve Californian inspired cuisine in Tokyo at affordable bistro prices, a brilliant formula that ensures he's always busy with a varied crowd of local business people, artsy types and the foreign community. Bring your own wine or try something from his New World selection. English menu.

T.Y. Harbor Brewery
2-1-3 Higashi-Shinagawa, Shingawa-ku. Tel: 03-5479 4555. Open: daily L and D. ¥¥
www.tyharborbrewing.co.jp
A refreshing range of microbrewed ales and a peaceful canal-side location. Stand and nurse your drink at the high-tech bar, or sit down in the spacious restaurant next door to a menu of steaks, burgers and pizzas. English menu.

Stellato
3F, 4-19-17 Shiroganedai, Minato-ku. Tel: 03-3442 5588. Open: daily 5.30pm–2am. ¥¥¥¥
www.global-dining.com
Theatrical décor – chandeliers, log fire and brash, ersatz Moroccan architecture – but serious contemporary cuisine with creative Asian flourishes. This is one of the well-regarded Global Dining chain outlets in Tokyo. The rooftop lounge provides views of Tokyo Tower. English menu.

Japanese

Buri
1-14-1 Ebisu-Nishi, Shibuya-ku. Tel: 03-3496 7744. Open: daily 5pm–3am. ¥¥
There's a great list of *sake* from around the country; the food is tasty and affordable; and the place stays open till late. What's the catch? There are no seats: Buri is a standing-only bar. The *sake* is served chilled in small individual jars; just choose from the array decorating the wall. Or ask another customer – everyone's friendly.

Chibo
Yebisu Garden Place Tower, 38F, 4-20-3 Ebisu, Shibuya-ku. Tel: 03-5424 1011. Open: daily 11.30am–3pm, 5–10pm. ¥¥
The speciality here is *okonomiyaki* – savoury pancake-like creations. They are made before your eyes on a grill set into the table. It's fun and affordable anywhere, but here you also get a great view from the top of the high-rise Yebisu Garden Place mall.

Ebisu Imaiya Sohonten
1-7-11 Ebisu-Nishi, Shibuya-ku. Tel: 03-5456 0255. Open: Sat–Thur 5pm–1am, Fri 5pm–3am
www.imaiya.co.jp
This cosy diner specialises in delectable free-range Hinai chickens from the Akita prefecture, which are served either as *yakitori* skewers, grilled over charcoal, or in warming *nabe* hot pots, cooked on the table before you. The place is spotless and efficient, and everything is explained in English.

Ippudo
1-3-13 Hiroo, Shibuya-ku. Tel: 03-5420 2225. Open: daily 11am–4am. ¥
Ebisu is famous for its *ramen* noodle shops, and this Kyushu-style hole-in-the-wall is one of the best. You specify how well cooked you want your noodles, and what kind of broth (red or white, both pork based). Add seasonings to taste (garlic, sesame seeds or spicy bean sprouts). Then just slurp it down. Cash only.

Tonki
1-1-2 Shimo-Meguro, Meguro-ku. Tel: 03-3491 9928. Open: Wed–Mon 11.30am–9pm. ¥¥
Classic *tonkatsu* (deep-fried crumbed pork cutlets) served at a spotless counter. Dishes come with Bulldog sauce (similar to Britain's HP sauce), rice and shredded cabbage. Popular, especially at lunchtime.

Pub Grub

The Dubliners' Irish Pub
Shinagawa Mitsubishi Bldg, Grand Passage, B1F, 2-16-3 Kounan, Minato-ku. Tel: 03-6718 2834. Open: daily 11.30am–11pm. ¥
Authentic British pub grub in the form of fish n' chips, Irish stew and cottage pie. Guinness, Kilkenny and other stouts and ales are on tap. Also a decent cocktail bar with live music. Branches in Nishi-Azabu, Shinjuku and Shibuya.

Southeast Asian

Keawjai
B1, 2-14-9 Kami-Osaki, Shinagawa-ku. Tel: 03-5420 7727. Open: daily 11.30am–9.30pm, closed 2nd and 3rd Mon of the month. ¥¥
The cuisine here is well spiced, carefully prepared and attractively presented. Apart from the use of short-grain Japanese rice, which does not suit Southeast Asian curries, the cooking is as authentic in terms of taste and ingredients as it can get in Tokyo. Staff are mostly from Thailand, and so are many diners, since the Thai embassy is nearby.

PRICE CATEGORIES

Prices for three-course dinner per person without drinks and taxes:
¥ = under ¥2,000
¥¥ = ¥2,000–¥3,000
¥¥¥ = ¥3,000–¥5,000
¥¥¥¥ = over ¥5,000

ゴミ箱

UENO AND YANAKA

At cherry blossom time, Tokyoites descend on Ueno-koen park in droves to celebrate the season. Yanaka, by contrast, is the dignified preserve of reclusive artists and literati

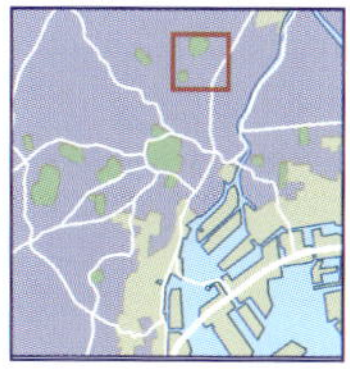

Map on page 148

North of Tokyo Station, eight minutes on the Yamanote train, is Ueno Station (Ueno-eki). It is a subtle impression, but the area around the station seems more down to earth, if not grittier, than other parts of Tokyo. This was once the commoner's part of town, the Shitamachi. In the post-war years, many of Tokyo's orphaned children, lived in the park.

Ameyoko Market

Tucked under the JR railway tracks and parallel with Ueno's main street of Chuo-dori is **Ameyoko ❶**, one of Tokyo's liveliest street markets. The name is a composite of *ame* (sweets) and *yoko* (alley). "Confectioner's Alley" did a roaring trade in sweets, mostly made from sweet potato and beans, in the immediate post-war years. During the Korean War, it was a thriving black market for American goods. Over 500 shops and stalls cram into the 400-metre (1,300-ft) strip. Most of the goods, like dried fish, kelp, fruit, rice crackers and pickles are edible, though the market is branching out into selling clothing and electronics.

Ueno Park

The centrepiece of Ueno, a meeting place for the capital's old merchant culture, is its **Ueno Park** (Ueno-koen), a fine place for people watching, especially on weekends. In spring, the park is cherished among Japanese for its cherry blossom trees (*see page 150*).

If you enter the park at the south end, near **Keisei-Ueno Station** (Keisei-eki), it is a short walk up a slight incline to the modest 1892 **statue of Saigo Takamori ❷**. Leading the Imperial forces to Edo in 1868, Takamori, a former supporter of the Meiji government, succeeded in taking the Tokugawa castle with-

LEFT: celebrating the bloom of cherry blossoms at Ueno Park.
BELOW: seafood vendor at Ameyoko market.

Koban (police boxes) are a highly visible feature of Tokyo. Ranging from the tiny to the very small, the designs of these posts often mirror the mood of an area. Apart from crime prevention, its main function is to answer queries about directions.

out battle. The statue shows him walking his dog, wearing a summer kimono, his sword safely sheathed.

To the left is the **Shogitai Tomb**, the resting place of loyal Tokugawa samurai who refused to accept the shogunate's collapse in 1868 and retreated to Ueno.

Kiyomizu Kannon Hall and Benten Hall

Ahead to the left, on the edge of a small bluff, is **Kiyomizu Kannon Hall** ❸ (Kiyomizu Kannon-do). Built in 1631 and moved to its present site in 1698, it is a dwarfish imitation of the far grander Kiyomizudera Temple in Kyoto. The main image of worship is the Senju Kannon (Thousand-Armed Goddess of Mercy), but another image, the Kosodate Kannon, believed to answer the prayers of childless women, is more popular. Those who subsequently give birth return and leave a small doll as an offering of their gratitude.

The temple's location was partly chosen for its fine view of the **Shinobazu Pond** ❹ (Shinobazu-no-ike) and its tiny island, home to the **Benten Hall** ❺ (Benten-do), built in 1958 although its history

dates back to the early 17th century. The abbot Tenkai dedicated the temple to Benten, patron of the arts and goddess of beauty. Now a freshwater pond, Shinobazu was once a salty inlet of Tokyo Bay. It is at its best in July and August when lotus plants bloom each morning. It is also a sanctuary for many species of birds and waterfowl, including egrets, grebes and cormorants.

Yokoyama Taikan Memorial Hall

Two interesting diversions lay just to the west of the pond, across Shinobazu-dori. The **Yokoyama Taikan Memorial Hall** ❻ was home to one of Japan's foremost painters of *nihonga* (traditional Japanese painting in a modern vein), Yokoyama Taikan, born in 1868 (Thur–Sun 10am–4pm; admission charge; tel: 03-3821 1017). If his paintings don't move you, his beautifully designed gardens will.

Kyu Iwasaki-tei Gardens

A couple of minutes south, the **Kyu Iwasaki-tei Gardens** ❼ is another quiet Meiji-era retreat, though on a grander scale (daily 9am–5pm; admission charge; tel: 03-3823 8340). The mansion, once the residence of the industrialist Hisaya Iwasaki, was designed by the English architect Josiah Conder. Built in 1896, the house and estate, fine examples of fin de siecle Tokyo elegance and privilege, stand in immaculately kept landscaped gardens.

Shitamachi Museum

The **Shitamachi Museum** ❽ (Shitamachi Fuzoku Shiryokan) can be found in the bottom corner of the pond (daily 9.30am–4.30pm; admission charge; tel: 03-3823 7451). A transplanted tenement block and merchant house display everyday objects such as kitchenware and children's toys, many donated by people living in the area. Demonstrations of handicraft skills are regularly staged, along with videos and photo displays depicting the area up to the 1940s.

Tosho-gu Shrine

Back on the higher ground of Ueno Park, the **Tosho-gu Shrine** ❾ was

Map on page 148

The Benten temple overlooks the picturesque Shinobazu Pond.

LEFT: statue of Saigo Takamori. **BELOW:** Kiyomizu Kannon Hall.

Cherry Blossoms: An Excuse to Party

The identification between the Japanese and the evanescent beauty of the cherry blossom, the national flower, is keen but intangible, as one writer claims: "If someone wishes to know the essence of the Japanese spirit, it is the fragrant cherry blossom in the early morning."

The springtime appreciation of the cherry blossom expresses the Buddhist notion of impermanence and transcience. Japan's samurai warriors felt a special nostalgia for the cherry blossom, seeing in its brief and vivid spell a parallel with their own lives which might end abruptly at any moment. Few nations have extracted so much pleasure and sadness from the contemplation of a single flower.

The notion of the cherry blossom's transience is celebrated in countless poems. A haiku by the Japanese writer Ryota sums up the genre:

This is the way of the world –
three days pass,
you look up –
the blossom's out, or fallen.

Far more than just a springtime rite, the blossoms mark the beginning of the Japanese year. It is also the start of the academic year, and the time new recruits enter companies. It is a season for renewal.

A national event

The progress of the flower is a national event all over Japan. The moment the first cherry blossoms, or *sakura,* bloom in Okinawa and Kyushu at the southern tip of the country in early March, television and newspaper reports follow. Until the last blossoms are blown off from the trees in the northern island of Hokkaido in early May, the media monitors the progress of the *sakura zensen*, or "cherry blossom front", as it advances up the map.

In Tokyo, newspapers report that the flower is *sanbu zaki* (30 percent open) or *gobu zaki* (50 percent open). The most exquisite moment is when the flower is at *shichibu zaki* (70 percent open), a time for a *hanami* (cherry-viewing party).

Ueno Park, the best-known venue in Tokyo for *hanami*, has over 1,000 trees and attracts as many as a quarter million celebrants a day at its busiest. This is when the Japanese are at their most exuberant mood. Blue tarpaulins are laid on the open spaces of the park, gargantuan quantities of food are consumed, women in kimono dance, cameras pop, and portable karaoke sets appear from nowhere, producing a deafening beer- and *sake*-lubricated rowdiness among competing groups. Despite the towering heaps of garbage, the sludge of discarded meat skewers, corn husks and half-eaten fruit, no one dreams of picking a sprig of blossom, much less climbing a tree.

Parties last a week, but purists insist the blossoms are at their best for no longer than three days. Connoisseurs seek out Tokyo's rarer species of tree, such as the wild cherries in the Hama Rikyu Garden *(see page 190)*, or the twin-blossom cherries in the Shinjuku Imperial Gardens *(see page 106)*. The perfect end to a *hanami* occurs when a breeze releases a flurry of blossoms, a *hanafubuki* (petal storm), dusting the ground with pink and white flowers as pure as snow. ❑

LEFT: viewing cherry blossoms in Ueno Park.

established in 1627 (the present buildings date from a 1651 renovation) by a warlord wishing to honour the first Tokugawa shogun, Tokugawa Ieyasu (daily 9am–5pm; admission charge). The walkway to Tosho-gu ("Illuminator of the East") is lined with dozens of large symbolic stone or copper freestanding lanterns – the tallest is 6 metres (20 ft) – donated by warlords to cultivate merit with the shogun.

The main shrine building is a magnificent structure; its outer hall features murals by the famous Edo artist, Kano Tanyu. Also interesting is the Chinese-style **Kara-mon**, a gate decorated with dragons that are meant to be ascending to heaven. According to local folklore, the dragons slither over to nearby Shinobazu Pond under cover of night to drink.

The 36-metre (120-ft) high **Five-Storey Pagoda** ⑩ (Gojuno-to), clearly visible from the grounds of the shrine, was originally a part of the Kan'ei-ji complex, much of which was burned down. You have to be within the precincts of the Ueno Zoo for a close-up look.

Ueno Zoo

Not one of the most attractive or best maintained of its kind, the **Ueno Zoo** ⑪ (Ueno Dobutsuen), north of the Five-Storey Pagoda, has over 900 species of wildlife with some 1,200 animals on view, including a "monkey mountain", where dozens of simians roam in semi-freedom (Tues–Sun 9.30am–5pm; admission charge; tel: 03-3828 5157). Children will especially like the enclosure where they can pet small animals like goats, sheep and ducks.

Metropolitan Festival Hall

On the east side of Ueno Park is the first in a row of institutional-style buildings – the **Tokyo Metropolitan Festival Hall** ⑫ (Tokyo Bunka Kaikan). Designed in 1961 by Kunio Maekawa, its main attraction is a classical music concert hall. The Ueno area also happens to be home to prestigious music schools and colleges.

Museum of Western Art

Ahead to the right is the **National Museum of Western Art** ⑬ (Kokuritsu Seiyo Bijutsukan), con-

Map on page 148

TIP

Ueno Zoo is famous for its giant pandas. If you are interested in watching these creatures eat, 3pm is their feeding time. On Fridays, they take a day off from the prying eyes of the public.

LEFT: deer at Ueno Zoo. **BELOW:** elaborately carved doors at the Tosho-gu Shrine.

A Rodin sculpture outside Ueno's National Museum of Western Art.

BELOW: sculpture outside the Tokyo Metropolitan Art Museum.

sisting of two quite different buildings (Tues–Sun 9.30am–5pm, Fri till 8pm; admission charge; tel: 03-3828 5131; www.nmwa.go.jp). The original, completed in 1959, is the work of Le Corbusier, while the newer additional building housing temporary exhibitions is another design by Kunio Maekawa. The permanent collection includes many works by French Impressionists such as Renoir, Degas, Tintoretto, Rubens, as well as more contemporary artists like Miro, Picasso and Jackson Pollock. The outside courtyard has a display of 57 sculptures by Rodin.

National Science Museum

The next building on the right, the **National Science Museum** ⓮ (Kokuritsu Kahaku Hakubutsukan), is devoted to science and technology, engineering, natural history and aerospace research (Tues–Sun 9am–4.30pm; admission charge; tel: 03-38220111; www.kahaku.go.jp/english). Its dinosaur displays and exhibits on oceanography and botany are popular with children. Two newer halls have interactive displays and simulated videos.

Tokyo Metropolitan Art Museum

On the other side of the park, the 1975 redbrick **Tokyo Metropolitan Art Museum** ⓯ (Tokyo-to Bijutsukan) completes the set of Kunio Maekawa designs in Ueno Park (daily 9am–4.30pm; admission charge; tel: 03-3823 6921; www.tobikan.jp). Over half the building is sunken to prevent the structure from intruding on the park surroundings.

The museum's three floors are set aside for its own collection of Japanese artists, temporary exhibitions, studio space and an art school. Exhibitions range from works by established painters and calligraphers to those of promising new artists.

Tokyo National Museum

For the colossal **Tokyo National Museum** ⓰ (Tokyo Kokuritsu Hakubutsukan), the centrepiece of the park, you will need to allow at least half a day (Tues–Sun 9.30am–8pm, Dec–Mar till 5pm; admission charge; tel: 03-3822 1111; www.tnm.go.jp).

Said to house the world's largest collection of Japanese art and archeology, the complex is divided into four main galleries. A permanent collection of paintings, textiles, calligraphy, ceramics and lacquerware are housed in the main **Honkan Gallery**; archeological relics from the Jomon Period right to the early 19th century can be found in the **Heiseikan Gallery**; while the **Toyokan Gallery** has an eclectic mix of Chinese, Central Asian and Korean art treasures. The **Gallery of Horyu-ji Treasures** houses masks, scrolls, sculpture and treasures from the Horyu-ji Temple in Nara.

Kan'ei-ji Temple

Northwest of Tokyo National Museum, running parallel to a small cemetery, the modest **Kan'ei-ji Temple** ⓱ is all that remains of an extensive complex established in 1625 as the Tokugawa family temple. Ueno was at the northeast entrance to the shogun's city; northeast being a less than auspicious compass point, a temple was needed to metaphysically guard this approach.

Yanaka

The backstreets around Kan'ei-ji provide a backdoor into **Yanaka**, one of the best preserved older quarters of Tokyo, a veritable time capsule of old wooden houses, private galleries, traditional shops, temples, bathhouses and back alleys chock-a-block with potted plants and trellises – all easily explored on foot.

The town was one of the few old quarters of Tokyo to have come through both the Kanto Earthquake and the fire bombing of 1945 relatively unscathed. As temple lands were reduced, Yanaka became a fashionable, though pleasantly reclusive district for artists, writers, professors and intellectuals.

Yanaka Cemetery

Wind through the streets west of Kan'ei-ji Temple and you will soon reach Kototoi-dori, one of the main roads. Bear right and, walking past the traffic lights, you eventually reach the **Jomyo-in Temple** ⓲, well known for its Buddha statuary, its 14,000 figures of Jizo, the god of health and healing, and protector of children. Jizo statues bear distinctive red and white bibs and caps.

Walk back down the slope and take the third turning on the right to **Yanaka Cemetery** ⓳ (Yanaka Reien), its grounds spread over a small, raised plateau overlooking the JR Yamanote Line's Nippori Station. The graveyard, with its moss-covered tombs, leafy paths and time-eroded Buddha and Jizo *bodhisattva* statues, has an almost Gothic feel about it. Among the famous who have chosen Yanaka as their resting place are well-known Edo and Tokyo figures, including the great novelist Mori Ogai (1862–1922), and Japan's last shogun, Yoshinobu (1837–1913).

Tenno-ji Temple ⓴ sits in the

Map on page 148

No two "rakan" (Buddhist disciple images) are alike. If you see people placing a hand, one by one on the heads of each rakan, this is a search to find the warmest head, the belief being that this will be the image that most resembles you.

BELOW: Jizo statues at Yanaka Cemetery.

Yanaka Cemetery, with its Buddha and Bodhisattva statues and leafy paths, is a resting place for many well-known Tokyo figures.

northern corner of the graveyard, its manicured grounds filled with magnolia trees and hydrangeas, which bloom in the June rainy season. The Great Buddha of Yanaka, a seated bronze figure dating from 1691, is the temple's pride and joy.

Sculpture Museum

In this district of grave-makers and stonemasons, it seems natural to come across a gallery dedicated to sculpture. The **Asakura Choso Sculpture Museum** ㉑ (Asakura Chosokan), a gallery exhibiting the work of Fumio Asakura, is close to the borders of the cemetery, on the left of the road that bears right after exiting Nippori Station's west exit (Tues–Thur and Sat–Sun 9.30am–4.30pm; admission charge; tel: 03-3821 4549). The artist's studio-house and courtyard garden are open to the public. The water garden is just as interesting as the sculptures.

Return to the road that runs from the station, turn left and continue until you see a flight of steps leading to a narrow but lively shopping street. This is **Yanaka Ginza**, a lane full of small restaurants, tea shops and traditional crafts stores.

Yanaka's small temples

Following the southern periphery of Yanaka Cemetery brings you to the narrow main road that runs down to the Sendagi Station. **Zensho-en Temple** ㉒ sits back from the slope on the right, the resting place of more Edo and Meiji luminaries like the calligrapher and swordsman Tetsutaro Yamaoka, but also to the much-visited grave of Encho, a legendary *rakugo* comedian.

A little farther to the west is the **Daien-ji Temple** ㉓, which contains a monument to the charms of Osen, a teashop girl who was chosen by the artist Harunobu for one of his famous woodblock prints. A huge gilded statue of Kannon, the Goddess of Mercy, stands next to the monument to Osen.

Isetatsu paper shop

Just across the road from Daien-ji is one of Tokyo's best known paper art shops, **Isetatsu** ㉔ (daily 10am–6pm). This tiny, well-preserved

BELOW: bamboo flautist in Yanaka.
RIGHT: Kannon statue at Yanaka's Daien-ji temple.

shop has two floors with combs, dolls, crafted fans and colourful chests of paper drawers, made from thick *washi* paper. A hallmark of Isetatsu are its *chiyogami* designs reproduced from original samurai textiles.

Daimyo Clock Museum

Time at the **Daimyo Clock Museum** ㉕ (Daimyo Tokei Hakubutsukan), a little south of here, seems to stand still (Tues–Sun 10am–4pm, closed Aug–Sept; admission charge; tel: 03-3821 6913). Here, a fascinating collection of timepieces – from alarm clocks to watches made for the the wealthy *daimyo*, or feudal lords, are on display. Some clock faces are interesting because the hours are marked by ideograms which indicate the 12 animals of the Chinese zodiac.

Nezu-jinja Shrine

Rejoin the main road and continue down the slope for a minute or two until you reach Shinobazu-dori. Just to the right of the traffic lights is **Nezu-jinja Shrine** ㉖. This popular shrine is known for its azalea festival in late April when more than 3,000 bushes bloom. The shrine was rebuilt by Japan's fifth shogun, Tsunayoshi, in 1706. Look out for the Inari fox shrine with a row of red *torri* gates lining the approach and a stage for religious dances.

Hongo district

Return to Nezu Station for the short, uphill walk to **Hongo**. Like Yanaka, the district remains stubbornly unfashionable and rather proud of the fact. Hongo's claim to have supported human settlement predating Edo is impressive. When earthen pots and other implements were found in a prehistoric mound on the high ground towards the northern section of Hongo in 1828, their design was considered sufficiently different from the preceding Jumon era to designate a new one, the Yayoi period. The slope running down the hill from the excavation site to Nezu Station is, not surprisingly, called Yayoizaka.

Hongo was one of 15 wards created in 1878 for the new capital. By

Map on page 148

Hongo is also associated with the highly gifted writer Higuchi Ichiyo, featured on the Japanese ¥5,000 note. A long-time habitué of Hongo, Higuchi, who succumbed to tuberculosis at the age of 24, chronicled the struggles of ordinary people and the city's vanishing Meiji-era districts with a rare maturity for one so young.

Yanaka's Craft Shops

One of the most rewarding aspects of exploring Yanaka on foot are the number of crafts shops and tiny studios along its streets and back lanes. **Taguchi Ningyo-ten** specialises in Japanese dolls, many of them miniature masterpieces. Descending Goten-zaka, the road that leads from Nippori Station, the shop is on the left as you take the left lane where the road forks. Less well-known crafts such as basket weaving are also found in Yanaka. In **Miyogi Buseki**'s flower shop, just off Yanaka Ginza shopping street, watch craftsmen weaving *hanakago*, or "flower baskets" made from bamboo smoked over wood and charcoal pits.

BELOW: papercraft on display at Isetatsu.

Map on page 148

TIP

Travellers looking for cheap accommodation should bear in mind that in February, legions of young hopefuls descend from the provinces to take university entrance examinations. In many cases, budget rooms will have been booked weeks in advance.

1947, many of these old core wards, now grown to 35, were combined. Hongo and the contiguous district of Koishikawa became Bunkyo (Culture) Ward, the name reflecting perhaps its reputation as an enclave of academia and home to artists and writers.

There are still a few old homes left in the two main writer and artist quarters of **Hongo 4-chome**, but the developers are moving quickly to replace these buildings. Some, whether from nostalgia or fiscal prudence, have shown great resilience in defying Tokyo's rapacious land speculators.

Old buildings and slopes

One such building in this district of winding lanes is the **Hongokan** ㉗, an imposing three-storey wooden apartment building whose demolition has been predicted for a good decade or more. Built in 1905 to accommodate students and down-at-heel writers, it is Tokyo's largest three-storey, Meiji-era tenement building still standing. To find the building, return to the crossroad where Yayoi-zaka and Hongo-dori intersect. Turn left and take the first lane on the left (the building is on your right).

Slopes such as **Honmyoji-zaka** and **Kiku-zaka** (Chrysanthemum Slope) add interest to the Hongo district, creating a dipping and rising urban geography.

Tokyo University

An area of cheap eateries, student lodging houses and second-hand bookstores, Hongo is a residential area and an intellectual centre personified by the presence of the **University of Tokyo** ㉘ (Tokyo Daigaku) campus, a pleasant place to stroll under the shade of its massive gingko trees. Founded by Imperial decree in the 1870s, the campus, more popularly known as Todai, was built on the estate of the powerful Maeda feudal lords after being transplanted from Kanda in the 1880s. Entrance to the campus is through the original **Aka-mon** (Red Gate). The gate, a symbol for the university itself, lends an aristocratic touch to the rather shabby and vaguely pre-war art deco-style buildings. ❑

BELOW: Tokyo University students at archery practice.

RESTAURANTS

American

Hard Rock Café Ueno-Eki
Atre Ueno, 1F, 7-1-1 Ueno, Taito-ku. Tel: 03-5826 5821. Open: daily 11am–11pm. ¥¥
www.hardrockjapan.com
This American rock 'n roll café serves the usual burgers, brownies and ice cream to a familiar atmosphere of loud music and gregarious wait staff. Rock memorabilia add colour to the dining room.

Indian

Samrat
Oak Bldg, 2F, 4-8-9 Ueno, Taito-ku. Tel: 03-5688 3226. Open: daily 11am–10pm. ¥¥
www.samrat.co.jp
One of the first Indian chains to open in Tokyo, Samrat has kept up its high standards since the early 1980s with some of the most affordable curries and meal sets in town. Set lunches from ¥950; dinner *thali* mixed plate from ¥2,200, plus lots of authentic, spicy à la carte curries.

Japanese

Echikatsu
2-31-23 Yushima, Bunkyo-ku. Tel: 03-3811 5293. Open: Mon–Sat 5–9.30pm (closed Sat in August) ¥¥¥–¥¥¥¥
The setting itself is beautiful – a large, atmospheric old Japanese house that has somehow survived in the city. The food is delectable – *shabu-shabu* (beef dipped in broth) and *sukiyaki* (one-pot dish), prepared with Matsuzaka beef, the best in Japan. Several of the rooms have garden views. Reservations advised.

Hantei
2-12-15 Nezu, Bunkyo-ku. Tel: 03-3828 1440. Open: Tues–Sun L and D. ¥¥
Kushiage (deep-fried skewers of fish, meat and vegetables) is served in a wonderful old wooden building in one of Tokyo's best-preserved downtown areas. Although there is an English menu, there is no need to order as the dishes just keep coming till you ask for them to stop.

Honke Ponta
3-23-3 Ueno, Taito-ku. Tel: 03-3831 2351. Open: Tues–Sun L and D. ¥¥¥
Opened in 1905, this eatery serves *yoshoku*, a Japanised version of Western food introduced to Tokyo a century ago. Besides *tonkatsu* and other deep-fried breaded food (chicken, meat and seafood), there are also croquettes, stews and sautéed shellfish. Most dishes come with rice and miso (savoury soybean) soup.

Ikenohata Yabu Soba
3-44-7 Yushima, Bunkyo-ku. Tel: 03-3831 8977. Open: daily L and D. ¥¥
This traditional *soba* (buckwheat noodles) shop was set up by a veteran chef previously at Kanda Yabu Soba, the most illustrious soba shop in the city. Prices are very reasonable. English menu available.

Izu-ei Honten
2-12-22 Ueno, Taito-ku. Tel: 03-3831 0954. Open: daily 11am–10pm. ¥¥
A picture menu will help you to negotiate the choices of eel dishes in this smart Japanese restaurant, which comes complete with a pine tree and waterfall outside the building to help you spot it. The upper floors have lovely views over the nearby park and pond.

Nezu Club
2-30-2 Nezu, Bunkyo-ku. Tel: 03-3828 4004. Open: Thur–Sun 6–10pm. ¥¥¥
This delightful little restaurant, in one of Tokyo's traditional neighbourhoods, serves excellent Japanese cuisine that is neither casual nor formal but halfway in between. The easiest strategy is to order the ¥7,000 set dinner, but you can nibble substantially for considerably less than that.

Sasanoyuki
2-15-10 Negishi, Taito-ku. Tel: 03-3873 1145. Open: Tues–Sun 11am–9pm. ¥¥¥
Considering that this is arguably Tokyo's most famous tofu restaurant, the prices are reasonable and the atmosphere relaxed – despite its connections as suppliers to the royal family. The set courses here are quite filling even though tofu is generally light.

Takokyuu
2-11-8 Ueno, Taito-ku. Tel: 03-3831 5088. Open: daily 6pm–midnight. ¥¥
Almost a century old and run by the same family for that entire period, this is one of Tokyo's best-loved traditional purveyors of *oden* – tofu, eggs, fish cakes, vegetables, *konnyaku* (a jelly made from the "devil's tongue" tuber) and tofu served in a rich, soy-flavoured broth. Washed down with *sake*, it's the perfect winter dish.

Toriei
1-2-1 Ikenohata, Taito-ku. Tel: 03-3831 5009. Open: Mon– Sat 5–9pm. ¥¥¥
This restaurant, run for generations by the friendly Nakazawa family, occupies a traditional wooden building of great charm. It specialises in simple *nabe* hot pot dishes made with premium gamecock from the Saitama prefecture.

PRICE CATEGORIES

Prices for three-course dinner per person without drinks and taxes:
¥ = under ¥2,000
¥¥ = ¥2,000–¥3,000
¥¥¥ = ¥3,000–¥5,000
¥¥¥¥ = over ¥5,000

松下電器

ASAKUSA

This earthy downtown area, where you'll find Tokyo's most visited temple complex, is the heart of old Tokyo; to its west is a creaky old amusement park, a drum museum, and shops which sell the kitschy plastic food models seen in restaurants all over the city

From the mid-1800s until World War II, Asakusa was the centre of all fine things in Tokyo, a nucleus of theatre and literature, of cuisine and other sensual delights. Its flowering, however, began with exile; first, with the banishment of the Yoshiwara, the licensed prostitution district, to Asakusa in the 1600s, and later with theatre, especially *kabuki*, in the 1800s. In the 1930s, Asakusa was the largest entertainment district in Japan, a role that was later handed to Shinjuku.

Located to the northeast of Edo, along the Sumida River (Sumida-gawa), Asakusa soon became a vigorous port. Asakusa had two prized qualities: *iki*, a sense of style and urbane polish, and *inase*, meaning chivalry or bravado, making Asakusa, until its peak in the 1800s, *the* place to be seen in Edo Tokyo. Even samurai, banned from mixing with the lower classes, and priests, escaping strict vows of celibacy, would enter the district in disguise.

The heart of old Tokyo is still here in this quintessentially working-class district. Asakusa is a vital part of the *shitamachi* – a word that translates, literally, as "downtown", but stands more precisely for "home of the common people" – a plebeian area synonymous in Japanese minds with hard work and equally hard play, a bustling mercantile mentality, libertine pleasures, Bohemianism, and a strong sense of community. Fortunately, all these characteristics are still very much alive today.

Sumida River side

As you exit the Ginza Line subway's Asakusa Station, the district's temple area lies in one direction, and the **Sumida River** *(see page 177)* and **Azuma Bridge** (Azuma-bashi) in another. On the Asakusa side of the river, just north of Azuma

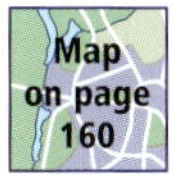

Map on page 160

LEFT: Kaminarimon Gate, the main entrance to the Asakusa Kannon Temple. **BELOW:** geisha decked out in their finery at Asakusa Kannon.

In the old days, geisha used a chalky paste made from nightingale's droppings to beautify their faces. Hyakusuke, on a side street parallel to Naka-mise, has been supplying geisha and kabuki actors with cosmetics for over a century.

Bridge, is **Sumida Park** (Sumida-koen). The park makes for a pleasant stroll, especially in spring when cherry trees are in bloom. Sadly, many of the park benches are draped with the laundry of the homeless.

Kaminarimon Gate

For a good map of the area and an update on current or forthcoming Asakusa events, drop in at the **Asakusa Tourist Information Centre** (daily 9am–5pm). The main temple compound is just across the road, approached after passing beneath the **Kaminarimon** ❶ (Thunder Gate), a weathered wooden entrance flanked by statues of meteorological gods (Fujin, the wind god, is on the right; Raijin, the thunder god, to the left) and a huge red paper lantern with the character for "thunder".

Naka-mise's shops

From Thunder Gate, move straight ahead along an avenue called the **Naka-mise** ❷, lined with tiny souvenir shops. Either explore the stores along Naka-mise or venture into the back streets, where older, more specialised shops, some run by the same family for several generations, can be found.

In Naka-mise itself, just to the left of the gate, **Tokiwada** specialises in *kaminari okoshi*, "thunder rice crackers". **Kurodaya**, which sells handmade *washi* paper and woodblock prints is just on the right as you enter the avenue. **Busendo**, on the left, has one of the best selections of Japanese fans in the area, while **Yonaya**, farther up on a side street to the left, is known for its ornamental hairpieces and combs made from boxwood.

To the right, along **Denboin-dori**, the narrow lane that transects Naka-mise, **Fujiya** is a store whose single product is *tenugui* – small hand-printed towels used in public baths or at hot springs. At the far end of

BELOW: fan shop along Naka-mise.

the avenue, **Sukeroku** is as tiny as its products: miniature handmade dolls in Edo Period costumes.

Hozomon Gate

Pass through the last grand gate, the **Hozomon** ❸ (Treasury Gate), with its ensemble of protective statues, to enter the main temple grounds. The upper storey of the gate contains Chinese sutras dating from the 14th century. A large bronze incense burner stands in front of the Hozomon where a steady stream of visitors place lighted incense sticks in the burner before offering a brief prayer. Japanese also consider it good luck to waft the incense smoke over their clothing with their hands.

Asakusa became an important pilgrimage site after three fishermen discovered a tiny image, a golden Kannon (the Buddhist Goddess of Mercy) statue in their nets in the nearby Sumida River. According to legend, when the statue appeared, a golden dragon descended to earth from the heavens. The story helped to popularise the temple, which soon became a favourite with samurai and shogun, and prospered both economically and politically.

Asakusa Kannon Temple

Founded in AD 628, the **Asakusa Kannon Temple** ❹ is still the spiritual centre of the area, the core of the old quarter. Also known as the **Senso-ji Temple**, the great pilgrimage site was also, as Ryosuke Kami points out in his book *Tokyo Sights and Insights*, a place where worshippers came "not just for religious purposes but for the entertainment that abounded in the temple's backyard, ranging from theatres, archery galleries, and circuses to brothels." The current building is a ferro-concrete replica of an earlier building from 1692, which was destroyed in an air raid during the last war.

The temple's *hondo*, or main hall sells souvenirs and fortunes. On busy days, the temple resounds to the clank of money as coins are tossed into the offertory box, hands are clapped and bells, attached to thick ropes, are rung. The statue of Kannon, a mere 6 cm (2 inches) high, is believed to be housed in a

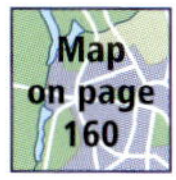
Map on page 160

Victorian-era traveller Isabella Bird, visiting Asakusa Kannon in 1878, noted the different approaches to faith, both the intellectual and intuitive. In her book "Unbeaten Tracks in Japan", she observed that the temple's main hall was "full of all the mysterious symbols of a faith which is a system of morals and metaphysics to the educated and initiated, and an idolatrous superstition to the masses."

BELOW: shop selling rice crackers along Naka-mise.

TIP

You can board water-buses at the pier beside the Azuma Bridge in Asakusa for tours of the Sumida River. It is also possible to go beyond Hinoda Pier to Rainbow Bridge, Odaiba and the bay. Departures are usually every 35 minutes from 9.50am–3pm for Hama Rikyu Detached Garden; 9am to 7.55pm to Hinode Pier and Odaiba.

fireproof box in the inner sanctum of the large *hondo*, behind the golden altar. It has never been seen by the public. Three times a day, the temple's monks gather to chant sutras in its honour. The hall contains an important collection of votive paintings dating from the 18th and 19th centuries, while the altar, the centrepiece of the main hall, is jam-packed with religious objects.

Asakusa Shrine

Dedicated to the fishermen who found the Kannon image, the 17th-century **Asakusa-jinja Shrine ❺**, just to the right of the main temple, is one of the few buildings in the complex to have remained more or less intact. The shrine is also known as the Sanja Sanma (Shrine of the Three Guardians). Just behind the shrine is the **Niten-mon**. The gate, built in 1618 and a designated Important Cultural Treasure, is usually covered with votive papers left by pilgrims.

Five-Storey Pagoda

The western section of the Asakusa complex is dominated by the **Five-Storey Pagoda ❻** (Gojuno-to), an impressive reconstruction of the original. In the early 1890s, an even taller structure than the pagoda – the tallest in Tokyo at the time – was erected nearby, rising 60 metres (200 ft). Properly called Ryounkaku (Cloud-Surpassing Pavilion) but commonly known as Junikai (Twelve Stories), the octagonal tower of red bricks around a wooden frame was designed by an Englishman. Privately owned, it sported the first public elevator in Japan and offered a view from the top, as well as shopping. Later reinforced with steel, most of it survived the 1923 earthquake, only to be torn down.

Denbo-in Monastery

The vermilion outline of the Five-Storey Pagoda stands beside one of the temple's best kept secrets, the **Denbo-in Monastery ❼**. The building itself is closed to the public but its garden, created in the 17th century by the Zen landscape gardener Kobori Enshu, can be visited.

Few people seem to know of its existence or its superb view of the

BELOW: wafting incense from the burner outside Asakusa Kannon's main hall supposedly cures ailments. **RIGHT:** the Five-Storey Pagoda.

Five-Storey Pagoda reflected in the garden's pond. A pass can be obtained on request from the booth left of the pagoda. Tea ceremonies are occasionally held on Mondays in a small pavilion beside the pond. In spring, its wisteria trellises are in blossom.

Sanja Matsuri Festival

Every year in May, Asakusa is the setting for one of Tokyo's most dynamic street events – the **Sanja Matsuri** (Three Shrines Festival). The Senso-ji, and the roads and sinuous lanes that run around it provide the epicentre for this mammoth four-day spectacle, an important spring event for many Tokyo families.

Dozens of intricate portable shrines are carried through the streets by young men and women, with much rough jostling and caterwauling. It is said the shrine gods enjoy being tossed around in this manner, something they get plenty of from the seething, swaying and chanting crowds at Asakusa. Picture opportunities abound as you will spot geisha and men sporting full-bodied tattoos, both rare sights in Tokyo these days.

Here, among the temples and busy merchant streets of Asakusa are echoes of old Edo. Aside from Asakusa's religious rituals, the seasons are not allowed to pass by without some festival or event of purely secular invention taking place: flowers in January, bean throwing in February, golden dragon dancing in March and again in October, a white crane parade in November, a kite market in December, traditional horseback archery in April and, a relatively new innovation, a Brazilian-style carnival in August.

Hanayashiki Park

West of the temple grounds, in the direction of Kokusai-dori and the Asakusa View Hotel, is Asakusa's main entertainment district. This is where the endearingly old-fashioned **Hanayashiki Amusement Park** ❽ is located (daily except Tues 10am–6pm; admission charge). There is a vintage quality to many of the attractions in the park, including an eerie, and rather run-down *obakiyashiki* – ghost house – dating from the 1950s. Visitors to the toilet at the Hana-

Map on page 160

White Heron dance at Asakusa Kannon temple – to herald the onset of Spring.

BELOW: the heaving crowds at Asakusa's Sanja Matsuri festival.

Map on page 160

Plastic food – displayed at windows of many Japanese restaurants – on sale at Kappabashi make for kitschy souvenirs.

BELOW: Nimi Building in Kappabashi Dogugai. **RIGHT:** displays outside Drum Museum.

yashiki – echoes of an old Parisian *pissoir* with a dented roof – will be amused, perhaps momentarily paralysed in the vitals, by a sudden, hurtling vibration as the one-minute roller coaster, squeezed into the confines of the park, thunders a metre (3 ft) or so overhead.

Rokku Broadway

Across the street from the Hanayashiki lie the back streets of Asakusa's sprawling entertainment district, centring on **Rokku Broadway**. Lurid posters and touts outside cinemas and fleapit clubs advertise porn and *yakuza* movies, re-runs of sentimental films and sex cabarets. This area is also known for *taishu engeki*, an enduring *shitamachi* brand of popular theatre. Tickets are cheap for these low-brow dramas, which are full of the verve and earthy humour associated with this area. Strong plots are the order of the day and audiences, equipped with boxed lunches and cans of beer, attend performances that re-enact the destinies of star-crossed lovers, double suicides and tales of vengeance.

Drum Museum

South of Rokku, at the junction of Kaminarimon-dori and Kokusai-dori, is the **Drum Museum** ❾ (Taiko-kan), on the second floor above a shop that sells drums and large items like portable shrines used in Shinto festivals (Wed–Sun 9am–5pm; admission charge; tel: 03-3842 5622). Drums from all over the world are displayed here, and visitors are encouraged to try them out. Look out for a one-metre (3-ft) diameter Japanese *taiko* (drum), which is popular with children.

Kitchenware Town

A few blocks west of the museum takes you to **Kappabashi Kitchenware Town** (Kappabashi Dogugai), where wholesale merchants sell restaurant and kitchen equipment.

The intersection where the main shops start is difficult to miss: look out for the **Nimi Building**, topped with a giant chef's head and replete with a white, pleated hat. One corner of the building is decorated with several tiers of coffee cups. Among the kitchen knives, saucepans and waiters' outfits are over 200 shops selling plastic food models of the type you will see in restaurant display windows all over the city. These *sanpuru* (food models) can be seen at the **Sato Sample** and **Biken** shops, opposite the Nimi Building.

At the northern end of Kapabashi-dori, turn right into Kototoi-dori and right again down Sushiya-dori. The **Takumi Craft Gallery** ❿ on the right, also known as Edo Shitamachi Dento Kogeikan, is the best place in Asakusa to view and buy original handmade craft objects (daily 10am–8pm; free; tel: 03-3842 1990). Skills in lacquerware, fan, glass and lantern making are clearly alive and well. Weekends often feature demonstrations of craft making. A gallery on the second floor showcases the work of local artists. ❑

RESTAURANTS

Japanese

Bon
1-2-11 Ryusen, Taito-ku. Tel: 03-3872 0375. Open: daily L and D. ¥¥¥¥
An absolutely memorable multi-course *kaiseki ryori* meal featuring exquisitely prepared seasonal foods is the attraction here. The restaurant is set in serene, Zen-like surroundings in the traditional district of Iriya (famous for its morning glory fairs in July). Although there is only one set menu here, dishes change with the seasons.

Daikokuya
1-38-10 Asakusa, Taito-ku. Tel: 03-3844 1111. Open: Tues–Sun 11am–8.30pm. ¥
Daikokuya really only serves one main dish upon which its reputation is founded. Dig into traditional Edo period-style *tendon* (tempura rice bowl) with authentic *shitamachi* – or downtown atmosphere and surroundings – to go with it. Cheap and cheerful; especially good value for a light lunch.

Hatsuogawa
2-8-4 Kaminarimon, Taito-ku. Tel: 03-3844 2723. Open: daily L and D. ¥¥
An *unagi* (grilled eel) restaurant that captures the old downtown mood of Asakusa's pre-war heyday. The old wooden building has all the usual design trimmings, down to the paper screens and stands of bamboo. Boxed sets of broiled fish are the best value, though the skewered eel is also very good.

Ichimon
3-12-6 Asakusa, Taito-ku. Tel: 03-3875 6800. Open: Mon–Fri 6–11pm, Sat–Sun noon–2pm, 5–10pm. ¥¥
A beautiful old-world setting a short walk from Senso-ji Temple in Asakusa, Ichimon is a fine place to rest your feet after a day's sightseeing. A good all-round selection of Japanese dishes and excellent *sake*. You pay for each dish as it arrives, using wooden coupons (called *mon*), which you buy on arrival.

Kamiya Bar
1-1-1 Asakusa, Taito-ku. Tel: 03-3841 5400. Open: daily 11.30am–10pm. ¥
Old bar dating from 1800. Japanese and European food can be had on the second and third floors, but the main reason that people flock to the Kamiya is the cognac-based cocktail called *denki-bran* (electric brandy). A favourite with the great Tokyo writer Nagai Kafu.

Kawakaze
3-34-11 Asakusa, Taito-ku. Tel: 03-3876 7711. Open: Tues–Sun L and D. ¥¥
Strictly traditional and located in one of Tokyo's most loved entertainment districts, Kawakaze has an interior that is decidedly more classy than the feisty, downtown streets of Asakusa that you have to walk to get here. Exquisite array of tofu dishes served with aplomb on tatami mats to the accompaniment of fine Japanese *sake* and the barely audible swish of kimono hems.

Komagata Dojo
1-7-12 Komagata, Taito-ku. Tel: 03-3842-4001. Open: daily 11am–7.30pm. ¥¥
This 200-year-old restaurant specialises in loach, a small freshwater fish similar to eel. There are only two dishes here: *yanagawa* (loach omelette) and *dojo nabe* (loach stew). Dishes are served on a wooden board laid on tatami mats.

Namiki Yabu Soba
2-11-9 Kaminarimon, Taito-ku. Tel: 03-3841 1340. Open: Mon–Sat 11am–8pm. ¥
This small *soba* (buckwheat noodles) shop is always popular, both among the local residents and the numerous visitors to the nearby Senso-ji temple. Cheap, friendly and authentic, the food and service here somehow seem very apropos Asakusa with its gritty, unpretentious folk.

Sometaro
2-2-2 Nishi-Asakusa, Taito-ku. Tel: 03-3844 9502. Open: daily noon–10.30pm. ¥¥
This rustic-looking eatery near Tawaramachi subway serves *okonomiyaki*, a flour and egg-based pancake stuffed with vegetables, shrimp and other ingredients covered with lashings of soy sauce and mayonnaise. It is sometimes called Japanese pizza, but the only resemblance to the Italian fare is its flatness. Great atmosphere.

Vin Chou
2-2-13 Nishi-Asakusa, Taito-ku. Tel: 03-3845 4430. Open: daily 5pm–midnight. ¥¥¥
Though the speciality here is upmarket *yakitori* (charcoal-grilled chicken), there is an interesting overlay of French bistro cuisine. Apart from *date-jidori*, an absolutely delicious variety of Japanese fowl, look out also for the ucculent quail and Bresse chicken. An excellent selection of French wines and a very decent cheese board complements your meal.

PRICE CATEGORIES

Prices for three-course dinner per person without drinks and taxes:
¥ = under ¥2,000
¥¥ = ¥2,000–¥3,000
¥¥¥ = ¥3,000–¥5,000
¥¥¥¥ = over ¥5,000

SUIDOBASHI, OCHANOMIZU, KANDA AND AKIHABARA

Apart from isolated gardens and obscure temples – including one supposedly haunted by the spirits of foxes – there are areas for specialist shopping: rare books in Kanda and electronic goods in Akihabara

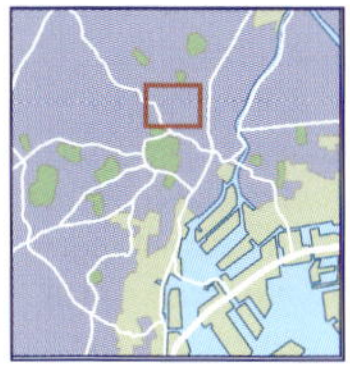

The east-west line of the **Kanda River** (Kanda-gawa) passes across a drained marshland from the districts of Iidabashi and Suidabashi and across to Kanda, Ochanomizu and Akihabara. This area of expanded flatlands cutting from the southern bluff of the Yamanote hills extending south of Yushima defines the contours of this chapter.

Yushima, which means "Island of Hot Water", an allusion to a prehistoric age when hot water bubbled up from the hills, is situated in the Soto-Kanda (Outer Kanda) district. Things have cooled down since then, but even in the late Edo and early Meiji periods, streams of clear water trickled down from the Yushima and Yamanote hills to the marshes and meadow land of the old riverine lower city. The incidental function of these *sakamichi* (areas of sloping roads), to provide drafts of fresh air and the occasional unimpeded view beyond the city, has largely been lost to high-rises and power lines, but the basic configuration remains.

Historically, the area not only marked the physical transition from the high city to the low, it was also the point where the residences, shops and trade districts of the townspeople mingled with zones set aside for the military class, the samurai and their households.

Koishikawa Korakuen

Easily approached by following directions in English from the Tozai Line's Iidabashi Station, or the Marunouchi Line's Korakuen Station, **Koishikawa Korakuen Garden ❶**, one of the city's finest Edo Period stroll gardens, is all that remains of the estate of Yorifusa Tokugawa, patriarch of the powerful Mito Tokugawa clan (daily 9am–5pm; admission charge). Work began on the garden in 1629 and was finally completed

Map on page 168

LEFT AND BELOW: lush ricefield and cherry blossoms at Koishikawa Korakuen Garden.

TIP

Although the number of cherry trees in bloom during spring at Koishikawa Korakuen garden cannot compare with other sites like Ueno Park, the tranquil setting and absence of crowds all seem somehow more appropriate to the occasion.

by his heir. Stroll gardens were intended for amusement as much as aesthetic contemplation. The designers of such gardens tried to incorporate scenes from the Chinese classics as well as miniaturised Japanese landscapes.

A small stream passing through the garden, the Oikawa River, symbolises a river of the same name in Arashiyama, near Kyoto, while two small hills, each covered in dwarf bamboo, are said to represent Mount Lu, a Buddhist pilgrimage site in China. The north end of the garden provides a completely different perspective as paddy, irises and plum trees come into view. Paddy is a rare feature within the walls of a formal Japanese garden. Schoolchildren from the neighborhood come here each May and September to plant and harvest the rice. The garden also features a large lotus pond best viewed in August when the plants are in blossom, and a section with a small pond, once a place of study for the Mito family. Apart from a Chinese gate that once graced the entrance to this inner garden, all else remains unchanged, including its original stone-paved path.

Botanical Garden

Another attractive expanse of green in this developed city, the **Koishikawa Botanical Garden** ❷ (Koishikawa Shokubutsu-en), lies to the north, easily accessed from Hakusan Station on the Mita Line and within the same Bunkyo Ward area (Tues–Sun 9am–4.30pm; admission charge). Behind a canopy of trees and the domes of the old greenhouses, one of the first things one notices is a tree with the odd name "Newton no Ringo". Grown from a cutting from the actual tree Isaac Newton sat under when the apocryphal apple fell, it is a main attraction, even if, really, it is just an apple tree, and an ordinary one at that. A

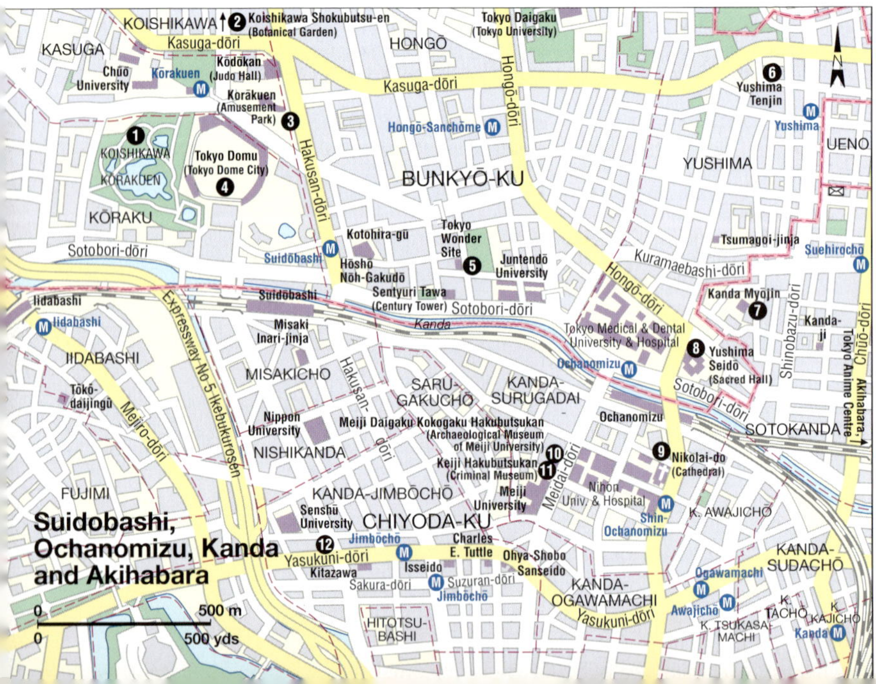

later shogun, Yoshimune, established a hospital for the destitute here in 1722. One of the few places with potable water in the days after the great 1923 earthquake, the site earned the nickname, Saviour Well.

The gardens passed into the hands of the Tokyo University faculty in 1877. Botanical studies are still conducted and over 100 species of herbs are grown here. Although you are not allowed to enter, the main building of the old Tokyo Medical School is clearly visible from the outside. Dating back to 1876, it stands at a slightly lower elevation near the pond. The building is an immaculately preserved European-style structure and, with its pink and white plaster facade and red portico, looks more like an Italian musical academy than a medical institute.

Three obscure temples

Exit the garden and turn left, following the narrow lane until you see **Nensoku-ji Temple** on your right. In an area associated with botany, herbs and medicine, it is no surprise to find in this temple the grave of a woman called Mikiko (her family name appears to have been lost in time), the first person in Japan to voluntarily donate her body to medical science.

Compounding the silence and serenity of the area are several more temples and shrines. A few minutes southwest of here, compact **Shinju-in Temple** has a tidy frontage of gravel and stone, and a cluster of well-polished Kannon and Jizo statues. Nearby **Denzu-in Temple** has a number of Tokugawa clan tombs and, in the far corner of its crowded cemetery, jumbles of what appear to be auction lots of old stone Jizo and *Bodhisattva* statuary, tendrils of plants adding to the effect.

Near the entrance to the grounds, you'll find a sculpture mounted on a plinth, called *Yubizuku* (Finger Mound). Shaped like two strong-looking hands, it was commissioned by the Japan Shiatsu Association as a tribute to the long departed masters who taught and practised this particular style of massage at the school and treatment centre here.

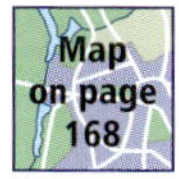

An azalea bush at Koishikawa Botanical Garden.

BELOW: an Edo period bridge at the Koishikawa Korakuen Garden.

Foxes figure prominently in Japanese folklore. Skilful at taking human form, hunting and possessing men, "kitsune" have a dual character: as Inari, messenger of the gods and a rice deity in its own right, and as meddling spirits.

BELOW: LaQua's Thunder Dolphin rollercoaster pierces the middle of the spokeless ferris wheel.

Takuzosu-Inari Shrine

Down the hill from here, in the middle of a narrow backstreet just five minutes from Kasuga Station on the Toei Mita Line, is an old tree said to be visited by an Inari fox deity. Somehow, locals have kept town planners away from this sacred spot. Overlooking it is the former house of the well-known Taisho-era author, Rohan Koda. The tree is a signpost indicating the presence a few steps away of the **Takuzosu-Inari Shrine**, one of the spookiest spots in the city. Shoehorned into the pinched precincts of the shrine are rows of *torii* gates, Jizo and Kannon statues, and fierce-looking fox messengers. This is not a place to venture into after twilight.

Stone steps descend under blackened trees (that seem permanently wet) to an eerie cave called the Oana, its dank rock-face the home, it is believed, of the resident white fox. Credence of this comes from author Nagai Kafu who, in his short story *Kitsune* ("The Fox"), relates how his father spotted the bushy-tailed messenger here one afternoon.

Korakuen Park/LaQua

Back in the Suidobashi area is **Tokyo Dome City** (www.tokyodome.co.jp) better known to locals as **Korakuen Amusement Park** ❸ ("Garden of Last Pleasure"), one of the best known sights in the Suidobashi-Kanda area (daily 10am–10pm; admission charge). The huge theme park has rides and attractions of all kinds – including the Skyflower, a free-fall parachute ride that combines a bird's-eye view of Tokyo with an exhilirating ride.

On the same grounds is **LaQua**, with equally thrilling rides – including the world's first spokeless ferris wheel, Thunder Dolphin, a dramatic roller coaster that loops through the ferris wheel and climbs over and between the rooftops of buildings, and the popular haunted Edo-Period house called 13 Doors. The **Spa LaQua** is a bathhouse that uses water pumped up from natural hot springs bubbling beneath (daily 11am–9am; admission charge).

Adjacent to Korakuen is the **Tokyo Dome City** ❹ (Tokyo Domu), also called the "Big Egg", a venue for major rock concerts – Madonna and Britney Spears have performed here – as well as professional baseball games (www.tokyo-dome.co.jp/e). This is where Tokyo's popular Yomiuri Giants team is based.

You can enjoy a comprehensive, mostly visual history of Japanese baseball at the dome's **Baseball Hall of Fame and Museum** (Tues–Sun 10am–5pm; admission charge; tel: 03-3811 3600). There are very good English-language pamphlets at hand to steer you through almost 140 years of the game in Japan.

Tokyo Wonder Site

For a more cultural experience, head east from Suidobashi Station along Sotobori-dori, then bear left when you see the signs for **Tokyo Wonder Site** ❺ (Tues–Sun 11am–7pm; free;

tel: 03-5689 5531; www.tokyo-ws.org). Set up by the Tokyo Metropolitan Government to encourage and promote exciting new works by young and up-and-coming artists, the building contains three floors of whatever is current, from paintings to video installations.

Yushima Tenjin Shrine

The populous slopes that fall from the plateau of the High City stretches into the flat riverine lands of the *shitamachi*, the Low City. Modern buildings obscure the original outline of the area, but the sensation of descent is strong as the roads fall away on either side from the heights of **Yushima Tenjin Shrine** ❻, the city's great shrine of learning. The Chiyoda Line subway's eponymously named Yushima Station is the easiest place to start from for the descent.

Yushima's "Shrine of Literature", as it is known, is dedicated to the 9th-century statesman and poet Sugawara no Michizane, deified here in the form of Tenjin, patron of learning and the arts. A steady flow of students come here to pay homage throughout the year, but spring, the traditional time for entrance exams, sees inordinate numbers flocking to the shrine to seek Tenjin's intercession on their behalf.

The shrine holds its annual Plum Festival in February (its tiny garden is said to be one of the premier spots in Tokyo for plum viewing). This is also a good time of the year to observe open-air performances of the tea ceremony. In late October, admirers of the imperial chrysanthemum throng to the shrine to see clever tableaus made from petals: arrangements of Heian-period courtiers, musicians and court ladies.

Kanda Myojin Shrine

One stop east of Suidobashi Station on the Yamanote or Chuo lines is the district **Ochanomizu**, which means "Honourable Tea Water". Water for the shogun's tea is said to have been drawn from the area's deep, and reportedly sweet, wells – an unthinkable idea today given the condition of the Kanda River.

In the Soto-Kanda 2 district to the

Map on page 168

The pachinko (Japanese pinball) arcade, with blaring sound and glitzy walls, is an industry in its own right. The 15,000 halls in Japan gross over 17 trillion yen per annum – spinning more profits than either the steel or auto industries.

LEFT: Shinto priest at Yushima Tenjin Shrine. **BELOW:** column detail at Yushima Tenjin Shrine.

Roof detail from the Yushima Seido Shrine.

north of the station is one of Tokyo's most important places of worship, the **Kanda Myojin Shrine** ❼. It is dedicated to rebel general Taira no Masakado, who fought for the oppressed Kantoites against Imperial forces. There is a *taiko* (drum) troupe attached to Kanda Myojin called Masakado Taiko. The troupe's main themes celebrate the life of Masakado, but its fame comes from being one of the few all-women *taiko* groups in Japan.

The temple, a concrete reconstruction of a 1616 original, enshrines two other deities besides Masakado: Ebisu, the god of commerce, family prosperity and good marriages; and Daikoku, entrusted with the care of farmers and fishermen. Side stores sell *mikoshi* (portable shrines) used during the Kanda Matsuri, one of the city's three great festivals marked by a magnificent street procession.

Yushima Seido Shrine

Just across the street from the Kanda Myojin is the **Yushima Seido Shrine** ❽. It is a fascinating building and one of the few Confucian centres left in Tokyo (daily except Thur 9.30am–5pm; free). Founded in 1632 by a scholar in the Tokugawa government, the centre moved to Soto-Kanda in 1691 when the hall became an academy for Edo's ruling elite. Drawn to Confucian teachings with their regard for hierarchy and obedience, the Tokugawa government happily set about adopting its more authoritarian aspects as a kind of unofficial state philosophy; this became known as neo-Confucianism.

A few steps south of Yushima Seido, cross Hijiri Bridge over the Kanda River, look right along Sotobori-dori and you will see the striking **Century Tower**. The work of British architect Norman Foster, the the building's twin towers are covered in a massive steel frame, obviating the need for interior columns.

BELOW: the bell tower of the Nikolai Cathedral.

Nikolai Cathedral

Ochanomizu's association with academia and faith, obscured now by a prevalence of ski shops and stores selling electric guitars, goes back to the Meiji Period when many of today's learning facilities – leading universities, the first official library, exhibition hall and museum – were set up there.

Two blocks south of Hijiri Bridge, the **Nikolai Cathedral** ❾ (Nikolai-do), named after its founder St Nikolai Kassatkin, a Russian missionary who spent much of his life promoting the teachings of the Russian Orthodox Church, is an unlikely presence in this part of Tokyo (Tues–Fri 1–4pm; free). The cathedral, designed by British architect Josiah Conder, was completed in 1891. The building lost the top of its dome in the 1923 earthquake, but this has been replaced with a smaller one. Sometime after the disaster, an anonymous donor left a bag full of money on one of the church's pews, with a message instructing the priest to use it to replace the cathedral's beautiful stained glass windows.

Meiji University museums

Meiji University has several buildings and departments along Ochanomizu's main street, Meidai-dori. An area of cafés and musical instrument shops, the excellent **Archaeological Museum of Meiji University** ❿ (Meiji Daigaku Kokogaku Hakubutsukan) is located in the institute's University Hall, on the right as you descend the slope (Mon–Fri 10am–4.30pm, Sat till 12.30pm; admission charge; tel: 03-3296 4432). The fourth-floor museum houses an extensive collection of objects found on digs around Japan sponsored by the university's archeological faculty, as well as items from China and Korea. Well labelled in English and Japanese, the museum has over 10,000 exhibits, ranging from stone tools of the Pleistocene Age to Kofun tomb (AD 250–538) clay *haniwa* figures.

Located one floor down is the fascinating **Criminal Museum** ⓫ (Keiji Hakubutsukan), with exhibits relating to the investigation, capture and punishment of criminals during the Edo and Meiji periods (Mon– Fri 10am–4.30pm, Sat till 12.30pm; admission charge; tel: 03-3296 4432). The university, founded in 1881 as the Meiji Judicial School, draws its exhibits from a collection exceeding 250,000 objects. Woodblock prints depicting the kind of punishments given to criminals at the time hang alongside vividly real instruments of torture and execution.

Yasukuni-dori street

Continuing down Meidai-dori will lead to the intersection of one of Kanda-Jimbocho's main streets, **Yasukuni-dori** ⓬. A concentration of shops selling sporting goods is found mostly to the left, while the right section, marked by **Sanseido**, a bookstore with a large stock of titles in foreign languages, is set aside for bookworms. Book distributors, wholesalers and some of the country's oldest publishing houses have made their home in the Kanda-Jimbocho district. There are stores specialising in art books, second-

Map on page 168

TIP

There is a flea market on the first Saturday of every month at the Iidabashi Central Plaza Ramla shopping centre next to Iidabashi JR Sobu and Tozai subway stations. From 6am to sunset.

BELOW: Meiji University students.

Map on page 168

hand books, comic books in English, French, German, Russian and more. Kanda has books that even major universities have difficulty finding.

Jimbocho's many English book shops, such as **Kitazawa**, a musty, vault-like shop bulging with out-of-print titles, are a must for book lovers. The little-known **Isseido**, an exquisite art deco building designed in 1913, is a gem of a bookstore for orientalists and collectors of rare books and maps. Several shops in this area, like **Ohya Shobo**, sell antiquarian books as well as genuine and reproduction *ukiyo-e* woodblock prints. It is still possible to find rare woodblock-printed books, typeset editions and original prints by the likes of writers such as Kunisada, Hokusai and Kiyonaga. All of these shops are easily found on your left as you walk west of Sanseido.

East along Yasukuni-dori from Jimbocho are stores specialising in sporting equipment – especially ski gear and clothing. A better pastime in Ochanomizu is to hang out in the numerous coffee and pastry shops, listening to students from nearby Hosei, Meiji or other universities practice their English or French.

Sales promoter at Akihabara showing off a new mobile phone.

Akihabara

The next stop on the Yamanote Line from either Ochanomizu or Kanda stations is **Akihabara**. The name means "Field of Autumn Leaves". Place names in Tokyo are delightful poetic abstractions that often turn out to be utterly misleading, or to have little connection to current reality. Akihabara, or Electric Town, as the English station signs refer to it, is an exception: it is the country's foremost showcase for Japanese technology.

Finding itself at the intersection between the Yamanote and Sobu lines, Akihabara's post-war black market developed into an area of stalls under the railway tracks selling radio spare parts. Akihabara is one of the few places in Tokyo where one can ask for a discount.

Despite its nouveau-tech pretensions, Akihabara remains endearingly close to its low-life roots, with its strident shop assistants, all going hoarse hawking their goods to passersby. Hundreds of tax-free shops and discount stores, ranging from multi-storey affairs to hole-in-the-wall businesses, are shoehorned into just a few blocks. At night, the multinational throng of shoppers, smoky food stalls and giant, neon billboards, evoke street scenes from the 1982 movie *Blade Runner*.

BELOW: colourful shop signages in Akihabara.

Tokyo Anime Centre

Manga-inspired buildings and sci-fi lit streets are the perfect setting for the **Tokyo Anime Centre** (daily 11am–7pm; free; tel: 03-5298 1188; www.animecenter.jp), located in the Akihabara UDX building. A showroom for the newest and best-known *anime* (animation) work done in Japan, the facilities include a screening room, exhibition galleries, a shop, and a studio where visitors can listen to voice actors recording dialogue. ❑

RESTAURANTS

Brazilian

Muito Bom
Iwanami Bldg, Annex 2F, 2-1 Kanda Jimbocho, Chiyoda-ku. Tel: 03-3238 7946. Open: Mon–Sat D. ¥¥
A tiny Brazilian restaurant in the heart of Tokyo's bookstore district, serving grilled meat dishes and an excellent, hearty muqueca fish stew. It's a relaxed place with a pleasant ambience. On the ground floor is a reliable Thai restaurant, **Muang Thai Nabe**, run by the same company.

Italian

Canal Café
1-9 Kagurazaka, Shinjuku-ku. Tel: 03-3260 8068. Open: Tues–Mon 11am–10:30pm. ¥¥¥
The outer café section serves light snacks, while the main restaurant offers capable Italian-based meals. Just the place to relax with a nice bottle of wine, next to the old castle moat, watching water fowl and rowing boats. Reservations are essential in summer.

Stefano
6-47 Kagurazaka, Shinjuku-ku. Tel: 03-5228 7575. Open: Tues–Sun L and D. ¥¥¥
For the price range, this is some of the best Italian food in the city. Chef Stefano Fastro serves the food of his native Veneto in north-eastern Italy, including homemade pasta, tasty antipasti and satisfying main dishes.

Japanese

Botan
1-15 Kanda-Sudacho, Chiyoda-ku. Tel: 03-3251 0577. Open: Mon–Sat 11.30am– 9pm. ¥¥
Sukiyaki (one-pot dish) made with chicken (not the more usual beef) is the sole dish here, but it's the location that's the real draw: a rambling wooden building in a traditional neighbourhood. Matrons in kimono bring a charcoal brazier and a small iron pan, on which you cook chicken, vegetables and tofu in a sweet-savoury sauce.

Isegen
1-11-1 Kanda-Sudacho, Chiyoda-ku. Tel: 03-3251 1229. Open: Mon–Sat L and D. (May–Aug Mon–Fri only). ¥¥¥
www.isegen.com
The current structure dates from the 1930s, but this historic restaurant has been in business for 150 years serving the same dish: *anko nabe*, monkfish casserole cooked at the table. This hearty fare is served from September to April. In the off-season, trout and other river fish are served. Cash only; reservations only for 6 people or more.

Kandagawa-honten
2-5-11 Soto-Kanda, Chiyoda-ku. Tel: 03-3251 5031. Open: Mon–Sat L and D, closed 3rd Sat of the month). ¥¥¥¥
Located near Akihabara Electric Town, this 200-year-old establishment serves broiled eel. Refined and traditional in atmosphere, the restaurant prepares and cooks to order, so allow plenty of time. Reservations essential.

Kanda Yabu Soba
2-10 Kanda-Awajicho, Chiyoda-ku. Tel: 03-3251 0287. Open: daily 11.30am–8pm. ¥
The most illustrious noodle shop in the city, Yabu serves classic Edo-style handmade *soba* (buckwheat noodles) in a classic, tranquil setting complete with a small garden. Besides the noodles, it also has a small range of simple, tasty side dishes.

Konakara
1-9-6 Yushima, Bunkyo-ku. Tel: 03-3816 0997. Open: Mon–Sat 6–10pm. ¥¥
A short walk from Ochanomizu Station, this small restaurant specialises in *oden* – tofu, eggs, fish cake and vegetables simmered in a savoury broth flavoured with premium *shiitake* mushrooms. This warm and nourishing food is served in a wooden building designed like a Japanese country house.

Seigetsu
Kamuya Bldg, 2F, 6-77-1 Kagurazaka, Shinjuku-ku. Tel: 03-3269 4320. Open: daily 5–11pm. ¥¥¥
This casual, friendly modern *izakaya* (tavern) serves a great selection of Japanese food, but the main draw here is the great *sake* list (in English), covering brews from all over Japan. Sit at the counter and watch the chefs around the charcoal grill, or at individual tables in Japanese style.

Turkish

Sofra
Hilltop Bldg, 2F, 3-6-3 Kagurazaka, Shinjuku-ku. Tel: 03-5261 3880. Open: Mon–Sat L and D. ¥¥¥
Authentic Turkish delicacies, such as *shish kebab*, marinated octopus, spicy tomato *ezme*, mussel *dolma*, grape-leaf *salma*, and much more – with a belly-dance show every evening. Set dinner menus start from ¥3,675; lunch is great value at ¥1,000.

PRICE CATEGORIES

Prices for three-course dinner per person without drinks and taxes:
¥ = under ¥2,000
¥¥ = ¥2,000–¥3,000
¥¥¥ = ¥3,000–¥5,000
¥¥¥¥ = over ¥5,000

SUMIDA RIVER, RYOGOKU AND EAST TOKYO

Along the river you can find the compact Hundred Flowers Garden and a myriad of tiny temples. Or pick from a variety of museums, showcasing ancient Edo, modern art or quirky split-toe Japanese socks

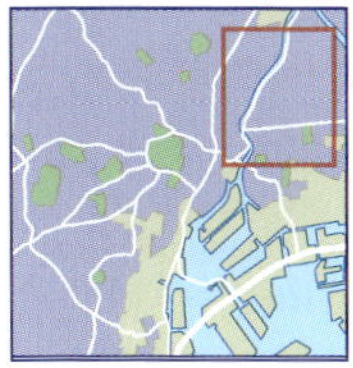

The Sumida River (Sumida-gawa) forms a strip with a number of sights, most falling within the area of the old Low City to the east of the channel. Northeast of the Asakusa district, the sprawling and crowded residential and small industry area of Mukojima was once famous for its farms and paddy fields; it was here that the shogun enjoyed the sport of falconry. Famous for its temples and pleasure quarters, its riverside teahouses were also the haunt of the literati and *demi-monde*.

The district of Tamanoi, part of what is today called the **Higashi Mukojima**, was until at least the 1940s, synonymous with prostitution in the minds of many older Tokyoites.

Today, Higashi Mukojima's backstreets are no longer the dank, ill-lit places they were during the quarter's heyday in the 1930s, but it is still possible to glimpse narrow houses of wood and mortar, some even replete with tell-tale tiles on their façades, indicating their history as brothels.

Shirahige-jinja Shrine

At the edge of this nexus of dilapidated but evocative housing zone is the **Shirahige-jinja Shrine**. Although the main buildings may have been reconstructed after the air raids, memorial stones dotting the grounds suggest an older site. A plaque tells us that Terajima village mostly comprised paddy fields between the years 1688–1704, its fertile soil carried over from the upstream Sumida River, also ideal for growing the aubergines popularly known as *terajima-nashi*. Farmers would ship their produce along the river to the daily vegetable markets at Senju, Honjo-Yotsume and Kanda.

Sumida Culture factory

Rising like an apparition amid the district's low-rise housing sprawl is

Map on page 178

LEFT: view of the Sumida River towards the city. **BELOW:** a pleasure boat on Sumida River.

architect Hasegawa Itsuko's space-age **Sumida Culture Factory ❶** (daily 9am–6.30pm; free), a community centre, library and media centre all rolled into one. Defined as a "microcosm of the greater media city", the building rises in a series of triangulated roofing, perforated screens and a large central dome that has to be seen to be believed.

Hundred Flowers Garden

Shirahige-jinja Shrine is just three minutes from the **Hundred Flowers Garden ❷** (Mukojima Hyakkaen), one of Tokyo's best known, though little visited, Edo Period gardens (Tues–Sun 9am–4.30pm; admission charge). Built during the early 19th century, the garden covers little more than a hectare (2 acres), but is intensely planted with trees, deciduous shrubs, flowering bushes and herbaceous perennials, the most notable being a beautiful, 30-metre (100-ft) tunnel of bush clover that bursts into a riot of purple-rose flowers in September.

Waterfront tea shops

Down by a row of homeless dwellings, these built directly under the roaring Shoto Expressway as it hugs the banks of the river, **Sakurabashi Bridge** (Cherry Blossom Bridge) connects two well-known viewing spots, which face each other across the river.

An old teashop called **Chomei-ji Sakuramochi** lies close to the bridge, on the opposite side of the first road to the right as you walk north (upriver) from the bridge. The shop's speciality, *sakuramochi*, is a sweetened rice-cake wrapped in cherry blossom leaves. Another popular teashop **Kototoi Dango**, just opposite, serves sweet dumplings. Mukojima once had waterways that conveniently connected it with the pleasure quarter of Yoshiwara. In days gone by, sweet

TIP

If you happen to be in Tokyo at the right time (last Saturday in July), be sure to see the spectacular fireworks display along the Sumida River. Thousands of people converge along the riverfront to see the *hanabi* ("flower fires") explode in the sky.

BELOW: the bush clover tunnel in the Hundred Flowers Garden.

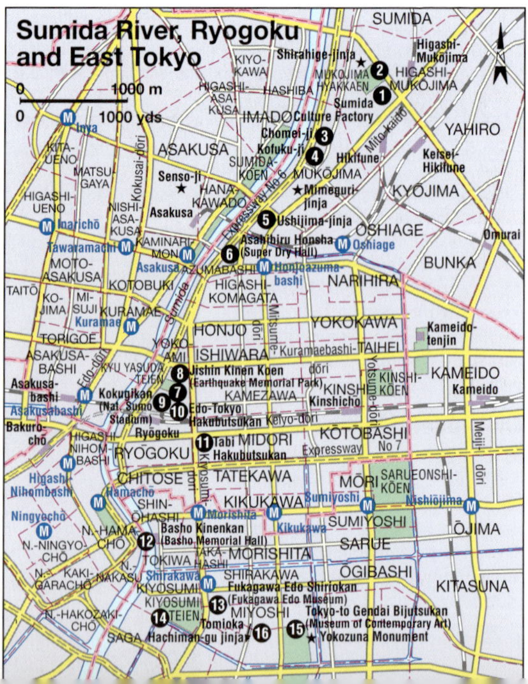

dumplings were often brought home as gifts by husbands who wished to allay their wives' worst fears.

Riverbank temples

From Sakurabashi Bridge running south, parallel with the river, are a number of temples and shrines worth investigating. The **Chomei-ji Temple** ❸ has a famous well that a shogun is supposed to have drawn water from and found pleasing. Its name means "temple of long life". Many poets, scholars and authors are buried here. A few metres on from Chomei-ji, the Zen **Kofuku-ji Temple** ❹ was founded in 1673. Look out for its distinctive Chinese gate and main hall.

Moving south, **Mimeguri-jinja Shrine** is the next structure of note. With a history that stretches back to the mid-14th century, the small shrine is identified with various fox deity stories, evidenced by a row of red *torii* gates leading to an adjacent Inari fox shrine.

The last in this batch of religious structures further south is **Ushijima-jinja Shrine** ❺, whose main deity is Susano-no-Mikoto, the younger brother of Japan's mythological sun goddess, Amaterasu. Ushijima means "Cow Island", a reference perhaps, to its main symbol, a bronze statue of a cow. Like other supernatural statues in Tokyo, the figure is said to have the power to heal – just stroke the part of the cow's body that corresponds with the area that is troubling you. As with most statues like this in stressful Tokyo, the head and stomach areas are smooth and well worn.

Asahi Beer Building

Follow the river southwards in the direction of the **Azuma Bridge** and, on the left, you will see one of the city's most striking design concepts. French designer Philippe Starck's **Asahi Super Dry Hall** ❻ (Asahibiru Honsha), built for the Asahi Beer Company, stands on this side of the river, towering above a section of the Shuto Expressway. Aggressively surrealistic, with a giant black, inverted pyramid as its base, it is topped with a sculpture resembling a gold flame. Almost as large as the building itself, the quicky structure was built using submarine construction methods. Dissonant but somehow stimulating, it could only have been built in Tokyo.

Kyu Yasuda Garden

Continue tracking the overhead expressway for a few minutes and you'll see a bank of trees on your left, squeezed up against the outer wall of **Kyu Yasuda Garden** ❼ (Kyu Yasuda Teien; daily 9am–4.30pm; free). As a screen blocking out traffic noise, it does not entirely work, but the garden does offer a degree of peace and some refreshment for the eye. This tiny, Edo Period stroll garden and the grounds of a larger estate were acquired by banker and industrialist Yasuda Zenjiro in the 1850s. Interestingly, the late Zenjiro was the grandfather of Yoko Ono, whose

Map on page 178

The Asahi Beer Company dates back to 1889, but its top-selling Super Dry only debuted in 1987. Although popular in Japan, it has received less than favourable reviews overseas.

BELOW: Philippe Starck's distinctive design is embodied in the Asahi Super Dry Hall.

claim to fame as an artist and musician was overshadowed by her marriage to John Lennon. Now owned by Sumida Ward, the garden, with its pond and orange rainbow bridge, inexplicably made of concrete and in need of a lick of paint, is popular with elderly local residents.

Earthquake Memorial Park

Across the road is the **Earthquake Memorial Park** ❽ (Jishin Kinen Koen). It is dedicated to the victims of the Great Kanto Earthquake, which struck at precisely one minute before noon on 1 September 1923, just at the exact moment charcoal and wood fires and stoves were being lit for lunch. The subsequent firestorm that engulfed and destroyed three-quarters of the city claimed some 100,000 lives.

Today, incense is burnt before the three-storey pagoda and memorial hall not only to mark the earthquake, but also in remembrance of a second catastrophe, the same number who died in bombing raids that wiped out most of this largely residential part of Tokyo in March 1945.

National Sumo Stadium

The district of **Ryogoku** is primarily known for its history of sumo wrestling. A little south, between the Super Dry Hall and Ryogoku Station, is the green roof of the enormous **National Sumo Stadium** ❾ (Kokugikan), home to Japan's national sport (open seasonally; tel: 03-3623 5111). If you are not lucky enough to be in town when one of the main sumo tournaments are held in the months of January, May and September, there is always the small but intriguing **Sumo Museum** (Sumo Hakubutsukan) to visit, located on the same premises (Mon–Fri 9.30am–4.30pm; admission charge; tel: 03-3631 2150).

There are several sumo stables in the area where wrestlers work out and live (call the International Sumo Federation for tours at 03-3360 3911). It is quite normal to see stocky wrestlers walking around Ryogoku, unmistakable with their topknots, kimono and wooden clogs. The staple diet for sumo wrestlers is a weight-inducing and nutritious stew called *chanko-nabe*.

Major earthquakes are said to effect the Tokyo area every 60 to 70 years. The last, the Great Kanto Earthquake, in which over 100,000 people perished, occurred in 1923, making the next one, if predictions are correct, long overdue.

BELOW: a sumo wrestler waits for the train at Ryogoku Station.

The dish can be sampled at several restaurants in the area – if you don't mind piling on the calories.

Edo-Tokyo Museum

Opposite the Sumo Stadium is Ryogoku's enormous **Edo-Tokyo Museum** ❿ (Edo-Tokyo Hakubutsukan), a must for anyone interested to learn how the city evolved into what it is today (Tues–Sun 9.30am–5.30pm, Sat till 7.30pm; admission charge; tel: 03-3626 9974; www.edo-tokyo-museum.or.jp).

The museum is housed in an ultra contemporary building that looks like the bridge of a space ship. The designers of the museum claim that their inspiration for the massive platform, raised on concrete stilts, came from the design of old Japanese rice storehouses elevated above ground to stop rats from destroying the crop. The museum does an excellent job in evoking the merchant life and culture of people living during the Edo Period, from the common people to samurai.

To reach the start of the permanent exhibition, visitors cross a reconstruction of Nihombashi Bridge. Exhibitions not only cover the early life of Edo, but also the years from 1868, through the post-war reconstruction years and the 1964 Tokyo Olympics. Temporary exhibitions are held in the large basement gallery. The museum shop has a good selection of traditional crafts from the *shitamachi* area.

Tabi Museum

A short stroll southeast of Ryogoku Station, just past the intersection of Kiyosumi and Keiyo-dori, takes you to the quaint **Tabi Museum** ⓫ (Tabi Hakubutsukan), one of several small, often family-run, trade and craftsmen-oriented museums that dot the Sumida Ward area (Mon–Sat 9am–5pm; admission charge; tel: 03-3631 0092).

There are only three places left in Tokyo that make *tabi*, the dainty little split-toe socks worn by women attired in kimono, sumo wrestlers and practitioners of certain traditional disciplines like archery. Few people wear them these days. The creation of *tabi* may not be an art, but as a quintessentially Japanese creation, this museum and factory, displaying the tools and equipment used in their making, has a certain curiosity value.

Basho Memorial Hall

Leaving his wattle hut on the banks of the Sumida River in 1689, the great *haiku* poet Matsuo Basho undertook his most famous literary walk, a five-month undertaking that would result in his masterpiece, *Narrow Road to a Far Province*. The hermitage is long gone, but the **Basho Memorial Hall** ⓬ (Basho Kinenkan) stands on the same spot at 1-6-3 Tokiwa (Tues–Sun 9.30am–5pm; admission charge; tel: 03-3631 1448). The museum contains original manuscripts and objects from the poet's journeys.

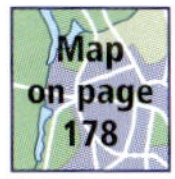
Map on page 178

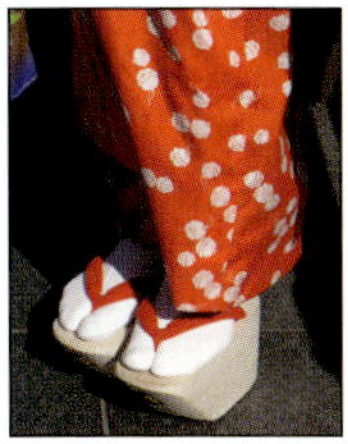

Japanese-style split-toe socks ("tabi") – on display at the Tabi Museum – are made with the "seta" (Japanese sandals) in mind.

BELOW: recreation of ancient Tokyo at the Edo-Tokyo Museum.

Dramatic entrance to the Tokyo Museum of Contemporary Art.

Fukagawa Edo Museum

A few blocks in from the river, within the Shirakawa district of Koto Ward, the **Fukagawa Edo Museum** ⓭ (Fukagawa Edo Shiri-okan) is a nice change from the colossal Tokyo-Edo Museum (daily 9.30am–5pm; admission charge; tel: 03-3630 8625). Built on a small and intimate scale, it nevertheless has 11 original buildings on site, all taken from the Fukagawa district and then reconstructed here. It gives a sense of what a working class area felt like around 1840.

Kiyosumi Garden

On leaving the Fugugawa Museum, turn onto the main north-south road, Kiyosumi-dori, and follow the walls of **Kiyosumi Garden** ⓮ (Kiyosumi Teien), until you reach its northern entrance (daily 9am–4.40; admission charge; tel: 03-3641 5892). The garden, which is fed by water from the Sumida River, was first built in 1688 by a rich lumber merchant named Kinokuniya Bunzaemon. During the Meiji era, it was bought by another wealthy businessman, Yataro Iwasaki, the founder of the Mitsubishi Group of companies, who had the grounds restored to his own liking. The Kiyosumi garden is a typical *kaiyushiki teien*, or "pond walk around garden".

Water is the focal point of the garden with a beautiful teahouse set serenely on its surface. A special feature of the garden are 55 rare stones, brought from all over Japan by Mitsubishi's steamships. Stone lanterns, miniature islands, stepping-stones and many species of flower, including Japanese quince, azaleas and hydrangeas, dot the grounds. The garden is surprisingly spacious, a fact that helped to save thousands of lives during the 1923 earthquake when people fled to its pond and green surrounds for protection.

Contemporary Art Museum

Roughly a kilometre (½ mile) east of the garden, hugging a stretch of Mitsume-dori, in the district of Kiba, the **Tokyo Museum of Contemporary Art** ⓯ (Tokyo-to Gendai Bijutsukan), is one of the latest additions to Tokyo's art scene (Tues–Sun

BELOW: Tomioka Hachiman-gu-jinja Shrine is the focus for the Fukagawa Matsuri Festival.

Ancient Art of Tattoos

Strongly identified with the *yakuza*, Japan's organised crime syndicates, tattoos were once also popular among the working class and quasi-feudal groups like firemen, carpenters and sushi chefs. The Japanese tattoo is an ancient art that is closely connected with *ukiyo-e* woodblock prints in their design and technique. The firemen of Edo were probably the first to sport the full-body tattoo, covering all but the hands, feet and head. During the Fukagawa Matsuri *(see page 183)* and Sanja Matsuri *(see page 163)* festivals, men with full-body tattoos can be seen hoisting the shrines along the streets surrounding the temples.

10am–5.30pm; admission charge; tel: 03-5245 4111; www.mot-art-museum.jp). Located on land that was once a marsh, this futuristic museum features art from a stock of over 3,500 items in its permanent collection as well as new work by both Japanese and foreign artists. The museum is great fun with plenty of experimental and interactive displays and an extensive database in both Japanese and English.

Tomioka Hachiman-gu Shrine

Situated close to Monzen-Nakacho Station, the next stop west of Kiba Station on the Tozai Line, the important **Tomioka Hachiman-gu-jinja Shrine** ⓰ can also be reached on foot from the museum by walking back towards the river along Kasaibashi-dori.

Founded in 1627, the current building, impressive with its towering copper-tiled green roof and prayer and spirit halls, was constructed from ferro-concrete in 1968. The shrine is dedicated to no less than eight deities, including the goddess Benten, Ebisu, the god of commerce, and to the spirit of the Emperor Ojin who is credited with founding the ancient city of Nara.

The shrine is strongly associated with sumo wrestling. In the Edo era, the shrine was the official venue for the sport. Some interesting stone monuments at the back of the shrine commemorate the link. One of the most important, the **Yokozuna Monument**, a 22,000-kg (22-ton) stone, is engraved with the names of sumo wrestlers who have reached the exalted rank of *ozeki*, the highest in the sumo world.

The shrine is the focus of the **Fukagawa Matsuri**, one of Tokyo's greatest festivals that is held every third year in mid-August. Portable shrines and palanquins are carried through the streets on the shoulders of some 30,000 bearers, local geisha lead a procession, and teams of chanting, hollering men heave gigantic logs through the streets. More than half a million spectators turn up for the event. If you are lucky enough to catch it, be prepared to get wet as the festival involves much splashing of water. ❑

Map on page 178

TIP

If you are shy but would like a bash at singing *karaoke* while in Japan, try a *karaoke* box. Fully licensed, often open 24 hours, and with selections in both Japanese and English, the rooms can be rented by the hour.

RESTAURANTS

Pub Grub

Beer Station Ryogoku

1-3-20 Yokoami, Sumida-ku. Tel: 03-3623 5252. Open: daily 11.30am–11pm. ¥

Located in the old station building, this is an atmospheric beer hall that serves not only good Japanese and German-style snacks, but also produces its own microbrewed lager. Because it's right next to the sumo stadium, it's very crowded whenever there's a tournament on.

Japanese

Chanko Kawasaki

2-13-1 Ryogoku, Sumida-ku. Tel: 03-3631 2529. Open: Mon–Sat 5–10pm. ¥¥

This quaint old restaurant, established in 1937, specialises in *chanko-nabe*, the hearty stew traditionally served to sumo wrestlers. You cook the hot pot yourself at your table, putting in chunks of fish, chicken and vegetables and fishing them out when they're cooked. Especially popular in the winter and during sumo tournaments, this is not a place for those on a diet. Also serves tasty *yakitori* (grilled skewers of chicken). Reservations only accepted for 4 persons or more.

Miyako-zushi

1-10-12 Yanagibashi, Taito-ku. Tel: 03-3851 7494. Open Mon–Sat L and D. ¥¥¥

Located in the old geisha quarter of Yanagibashi between the banks of the Sumida and Kanda rivers. You can trust the master chef here to serve you a great selection of sushi and sashimi. Expect only the finest and freshest cuts of fish served with homemade dip of soy sauce and fresh wasabi.

PRICE CATEGORIES

Prices for three-course dinner per person without drinks and taxes:

¥ = under ¥2,000
¥¥ = ¥2,000–¥3,000
¥¥¥ = ¥3,000–¥5,000
¥¥¥¥ = over ¥5,000

The Sport of Sumo

The training involves harsh days and a long apprenticeship, but the rewards are great for those who reach the top

In sumo, life is best at the top. Only when a *rikishi*, or wrestler, makes it to the top ranks of *ozeki* or *yokozuna* (grand champion, the highest rank and rarely achieved) does life become easier. Those in the lower ranks become the *ozeki*'s or *yokozuna*'s servants and valets, doing everything from running errands to scrubbing backs.

In most *beya* – the so-called stables in which wrestlers live a communal lifestyle with other *rikishi* – the day typically begins at 6am with practice, not breakfast. Harsh and tedious exercises work to develop the wrestlers' flexibility and strength, followed by repetitive practice matches amongst the *beya*'s wrestlers (the only time they wrestle one another, as wrestlers of the same *beya* don't compete during actual tournaments). Practice ends around noon, when the wrestlers bathe. Then the high-ranked wrestlers sit down to the day's first meal, served by the lower-ranked wrestlers. The food staple of the stable is *chanko-nabe*, a high-calorie, nutritious stew of chicken, fish or beef with *miso*. Side dishes of fried chicken, steak and bowls of rice – and even salads – fill out the meal.

Lower-ranked wrestlers, considered apprentices, receive no salary, although they earn a small tournament bonus. When a wrestler reaches the *juryo* level, he becomes a *sekitori*, or ranked wrestler, and earns at least US$7,000 a month. An *ozeki* receives about US$16,000 monthly, and a *yokozuna*, US$20,000. The winner of one of six annual tournaments receives US$100,000.

Above: sumo matches take place in a ring called a *dohyo* – made of a mixture of clay with sand spread over the top. Causing an opponent to touch the outside of the ring is one way to win a match. **Left:** the *mawashi*, or belt, is a 10-metre (30-ft) long piece of fabric; it's often used to grip and toss one's opponent out.

ABOVE: during the *dohyo-iri* (entering ceremony), wrestlers wear their *kesho-mawashi*, an ornate, embroidered silk "apron". The *rikishi* are introduced to the crowds in ascending order of rank, and they perform a number of ritual gestures to summon the gods and demonstrate they are unarmed. Afterward, they change into their fighting *mawashi*, or belt.

ABOVE: sumo wrestlers undergo years of rigorous training in the *beya*, or stable, which is run by the *oyakata* or stablemaster. All wrestlers train together, regardless of the rank they hold. Outside of the stable, though, a strict hierarchy of rules and deference applies to the respective ranks.

AN ANCIENT SHINTO SPORT

Sumo has been around for at least 2,000 years. Japanese mythology relates an episode in which the destiny of the Japanese islands was once determined by the outcome of a sumo match between two gods. The victorious god started the Yamato imperial line.

While wrestling has always existed in nearly every culture, the origins of sumo as we know it were founded on Shinto rituals. Shrines were the venue of matches dedicated to the gods of good harvests. In the Nara and Heian periods, sumo was a spectator sport for the imperial court, while during the militaristic Kamakura Period, sumo was part of a warrior's training. Professional sumo arose during the 1700s and is quite similar to the sumo practised in today's matches.

Shinto rituals punctuate the sumo match. The ritual stomping before a match (*shiko*) drives evil spirits from the ring (not to mention loosening the muscles) before a match. Salt is tossed into the ring for purification, as Shinto beliefs say that salt drives out evil spirits. Nearly 40 kg (90 lbs) of salt is thrown out in one tournament day.

LEFT: the referee of a sumo match is the *gyoji*, who shouts encouragement during the match. Like the sumo wrestlers, *gyoji* too follow a strict system of ranking. The higher ranking *gyoji*, who wear elaborate kimono and *seta* (sandals) with *tabi* (Japanese-style split-toe socks), referee matches between the higher ranking sumo wrestlers.

TOKYO BAYSIDE

First stop: a fish market at the crack of dawn. Then you can gleefully celebrate the artificial at Odaiba. There's a man-made beach, an indoor shopping "street" with simulated sunsets, and a gigantic ferris wheel

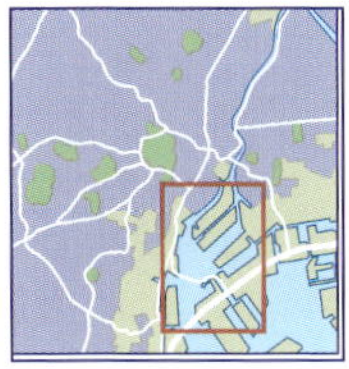

Map on page 188

If the inlets of Tokyo Bay area and the bluffs between them were the cradle of old Edo – the site for its great castle and the flatlands that accommodated the bustling merchant classes east of the Sumida River – then the shoreline was the crucible for newer developments. Even today, the area continues to expand. Landfills have been adding new dimensions to Tokyo's urban compression for over 400 years.

At the mouth of the Sumida River, a series of interlocking islands appear, the first in a number of landfills reclaimed from mudflats in the bay. The most interesting is the northern section of **Tsukudajima**. Now contiguous with two former islands, Ishikawajima to the north and Tsukishima to the south, Tsukudajima can be reached on foot by crossing Tsukuda Bridge from Tsukiji, or by walking north from Tsukishima Station on the Yurakucho Line.

The name Tsukudajima means "Island of Cultivated Rice", an allusion to the home of the island's first settlers who came in the early 17th century from villages on the rural fringes of Osaka.

Sumiyoshi-jinja Shrine

Smidgens of the past remain in the narrow back alleyways jammed with potted plants, small fish restaurants and some exquisite Meiji and Taisho periods wooden houses. If you approach this part of the island from Tsukuda Bridge, you will see a replica of an old Edo Period lighthouse on the left as you descend to the island. The structure stands above a large *torii* gate that leads to the island's main **Sumiyoshi-jinja Shrine ❶**. Protector of fishermen and sailors, Sumiyoshi is a branch of the principal shrine in Osaka. Its role as a talis-

LEFT: freshly slaughtered tuna at Tsukiji Fish Market. **BELOW:** replica of an Edo-period lighthouse at Tsukudajima.

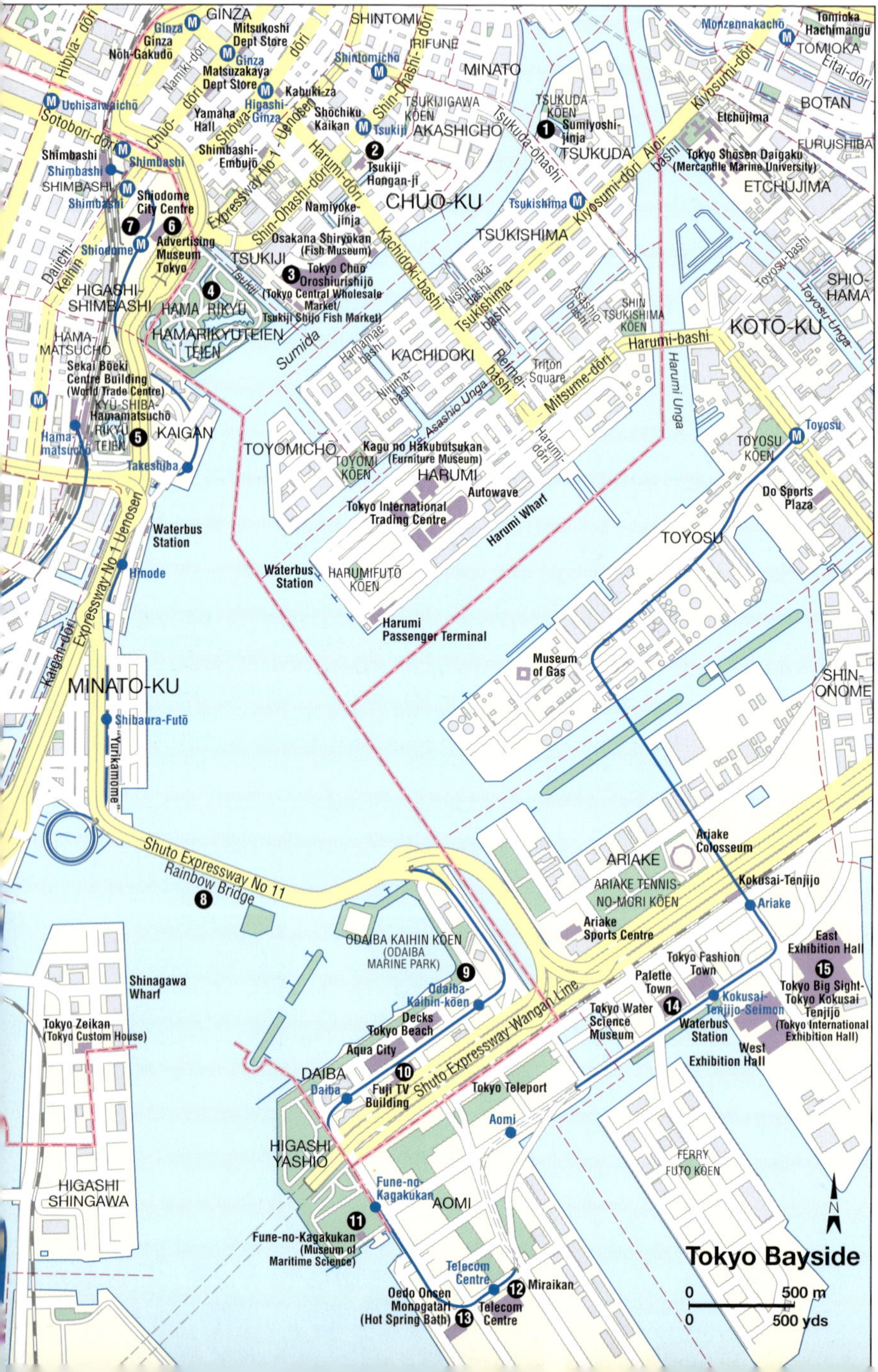
Tokyo Bayside
0 500 m
0 500 yds
N
GINZA
Ginza
Mitsukoshi Dept Store
Ginza
Noh-Gakudo
Matsuzakaya Dept Store
Kabuki-za
Yamaha Hall
Higashi-Ginza
Shōchiku Kaikan
Tsukiji
Uchisaiwaichō
Sotobori-dōri
Hibiya-dōri
Namiki-dōri
Chūō-dōri
Shōwa-dōri
Expressway No 1 - Uenosen
Harumi-dōri
Shin-Ohashi-dōri
Shimbashi
Shimbashi
SHIMBASHI
Shimbashi
Shimbashi-Embujō
Shiodome City Centre
Advertising Museum Tokyo
Shiodome
Namiyoke-jinja
Osakana Shiryōkan (Fish Museum)
TSUKIJI
Tokyo Chuo Oroshiurishijō (Tokyo Central Wholesale Market/ Tsukiji Shijo Fish Market)
Daiichi-Keihin
HIGASHI-SHIMBASHI
HAMA RIKYŪ
HAMARIKYUTEIEN TEIEN
HAMA-MATSUCHŌ
Sekai Boeki Centre Building (World Trade Centre)
KYŪ-SHIBA-RIKYŪ TEIEN
Hamamatsuchō
Hama-matsuchō
KAIGAN
Takeshiba
Waterbus Station
Hinode
Kaigan-dōri
Expressway No 1 Uenosen
MINATO-KU
Shibaura-Futō
"Yurikamome"
SHINTOMI
Shintomichō
IRIFUNE
MINATO
TSUKIJIGAWA KŌEN
AKASHICHO
Tsukiji Hongan-ji
CHŪŌ-KU
Tsukuda-ōhashi
TSUKUDA KŌEN
Sumiyoshi-jinja
TSUKUDA
Tsukishima
TSUKISHIMA
Kiyosumi-dōri
Aioi-bashi
Kachidoki-bashi
Nishinaka-bashi
Tsukishima-bashi
Asashio-bashi
SHIN TSUKISHIMA KŌEN
Sumida
Hamamae-bashi
KACHIDOKI
Niiima-bashi
Reimei-bashi
Triton Square
Mitsume-dōri
Harumi-bashi
Asashio Unga
Harumi-dōri
Harumi Unga
TOYOMICHŌ
TOYOMI KŌEN
Kagu no Hakubutsukan (Furniture Museum)
HARUMI
Autowave
Tokyo International Trading Centre
Harumi Wharf
Waterbus Station
HARUMIFUTŌ KŌEN
Harumi Passenger Terminal
Monzennakachō
Tomioka Hachimangū
TOMIOKA
Eitai-dōri
BOTAN
Kiyosumi-dōri
Etchūjima
FURUISHIBA
Tokyo Shōsen Daigaku (Mercantile Marine University)
ETCHŪJIMA
Toyosu-bashi
Toyosu Unga
SHIO-HAMA
KŌTŌ-KU
Toyosu
TOYOSU KŌEN
Do Sports Plaza
TOYOSU
Museum of Gas
SHIN-ONOME
Ariake Colosseum
ARIAKE
ARIAKE TENNIS-NO-MORI KŌEN
Kokusai-Tenjijo
Ariake
Ariake Sports Centre
Shuto Expressway No 11
Rainbow Bridge
ODAIBA KAIHIN KŌEN (ODAIBA MARINE PARK)
Odaiba-Kaihin-kōen
Decks Tokyo Beach
Aqua City
DAIBA
Daiba
Fuji TV Building
Shuto Expressway Wangan Line
Tokyo Fashion Town
Palette Town
Tokyo Water Science Museum
Kokusai-Tenjijo-Seimon
Waterbus Station
West Exhibition Hall
East Exhibition Hall
Tokyo Big Sight-Tokyo Kokusai Tenjijō (Tokyo International Exhibition Hall)
Tokyo Teleport
Aomi
Shinagawa Wharf
Tokyo Zeikan (Tokyo Custom House)
HIGASHI SHINGAWA
HIGASHI YASHIO
Fune-no-Kagakukan
AOMI
FERRY FUTO KŌEN
Fune-no-Kagakukan (Museum of Maritime Science)
Telecom Centre
Miraikan
Oedo Onsen Monogatari (Hot Spring Bath)
Telecom Centre
1
2
3
4
5
6
7
8
9
10
11
12
13
14
15

man for seafarers are visible in wood reliefs that show fishermen out in the bay, images that frequently appear in Edo Period *ukiyo-e* woodblock prints. The shrine in fact, is the putative burial place of Sharaku, an *ukiyo-e* master whose real identity has never been discovered.

Tsukiji Hongan-ji Temple

Retrace your steps over Tsukuda Bridge and bear left at the intersection where Shin Tomicho Station is located. A short stroll along this main road will take you to Tsukiji Station on the Hibiya Line, and the area's most imposing building, the **Tsukiji Hongan-ji Temple** ❷. Founded in Asakusa in 1617, the original temple was destroyed by fire.

The current structure, a stone building designed by the architect Chuta Ito, was built in 1935. Ito, a student of Tatsuno Kingo, who designed Tokyo Station *(see page 80)*, travelled extensively in the Hindu and Buddhist countries of Asia. Many of the motifs incorporated into this extraordinary building, especially its lotus-shaped main façade and domes, reflect these foreign influences.

Tsukiji Fish Market

The Tokyo Bay area has always been a vital point in the fish supply route. At the **Tokyo Central Wholesale Market** ❸ (Tokyo Chuo Oroshiurishijo), or the **Tsukiji Fish Market** as it is commonly known, more than 400 species of seafood, weighing over 2,500 tons, from all over the world arrive every day (Mon–Sat 5am–3pm).

Restaurateurs arrive to buy the day's catch between 7 and 9.30am. No thanks to over enthusiatic camera-clicking tourists, the area where the daily tuna auctions take place at 5am have been roped off. However, visitors can still enter the market.

It is wonderful to breakfast at one of its sushi and *sashimi* restaurants lining the road to the fish market, or at the dozens of makeshift stalls selling bowls of fish soup and noodles. Look out for a stone monument near the exit, placed there to appease the souls of fish that pass through Tsukiji.

Map on page 188

Frozen tuna carcasses, labelled in preparation for a morning auction at Tsukiji Fish Market.

LEFT: grilled fish in Tsukiji.
BELOW: Tsukiji Hongan-ji Temple with its Hindu-Buddhist architectural motifs.

The soaring blocks of the Shiodome City Centre complex are highly visible from the Hama Rikyu Garden.

Visit this wonderfully atmospheric market while you can, for it is slated to move to a more spacious, sanitised location in the near future.

Hama Rikyu Garden

Exiting the main entrance to the market, you will see the main offices of the *Asahi Shimbun* newspaper opposite. Turn left for the expansive **Hama Rikyu Detached Garden ❹** (Hama Rikyu Teien), just a 10-minute walk south (daily 9am–5pm; admission charge).

Developed in the 1650s as grounds for the Hama Palace (an estate owned by Matsudaira Tsunashige, a lord from Kofu Province), they passed into the hands of the sixth shogun, Ienobu, who turned the grounds into landscaped gardens and a duck shooting site. The present garden, reached by crossing the Nanmon Bridge, or by waterbus from Asakusa, were opened to the public in 1945. The highlight is a large tidal pond, with a small tea pavilion at its centre, and with islets connected by wooden bridges.

Kyu Shiba Rikyu Garden

If you have a taste for formal gardens, there is another one just a few minutes' walk south of Hama Rikyu, opposite Hamamatsucho Station on the Yamanote Line. Arranged around a large pond, the **Kyu-Shiba Rikyu Garden ❺** (Kyu-Shiba Rikyu Teien) receives fewer visitors than the Hama Rikyu (daily 9.30am–5pm; admission charge).

Advertising Museum Tokyo

In the basement of the Caretta building beside Shiodome Station is the **Advertising Museum Tokyo ❻**, with wonderful glimpses into Japanese commercial art (Tues–Fri 11am–6.30pm, Sat 11am–4.30pm; free: tel: 03-6218 2500; www.admt.jp). Starting with woodblock flyers from the Edo period, moving to art deco Meiji- and Taisho-period creations, the exhibits bring you right up to date with the best of TV advertising.

Shiodome City Centre

Highly visible from the grounds of the Hama Rikyu Garden is the **Shiodome City Centre ❼** complex,

BELOW: wooden bridge at the Hama Rikyu Garden.

a short walk away. Towering office blocks are the first thing that catch the eye, but a series of indoor malls and a brand new outdoor piazza at the rear of the complex make for a pleasant place to dine, shop or quaff a cocktail in futuristic surroundings.

Shiodome, however, is at the centre of an expanding wall of skyscrapers lining the bay that have been criticised for blocking the breezes that relieve the high summer temperatures of the city. The 31-hectare (77-acre) area, with 13 buildings reaching heights of over 100 metres (330 ft), has been blamed for increasing Tokyo's "heat island" effect.

Odaiba Island

South of the garden are the dock areas of Takeshiba, Hinode and Shibaura. **Hinode** has been redeveloped recently and new shops, restaurants, parks and galleries line this section of the waterfront.

The Hinode Station on the Yurikamome Line is a convenient spot to board the rail crossing over the bay to **Odaiba**, where some of Tokyo's newest developments are found. The Yurikamome Line runs on elevated tracks that pass the roofline of new buildings before crossing the **Rainbow Bridge** ❽. Odaiba island can best be described as an experimental pleasure zone, an urban laboratory for projects requiring more space than downtown Tokyo can conceivably spare.

Alight at Odaiba Kaihin-koen Station where **Odaiba Marine Park** ❾ (Odaiba Kaihin Koen) offers a pleasant swathe of green abutting an artificial sandy beach.

There are restaurants and cafes across the road at **Sunset Beach Restaurant Row**. The line of eateries is the exterior part of **Decks Tokyo Beach**, a themed shopping and amusement complex that has some interesting futuristic features, most notably **Joyopolis**, a virtual reality arcade. **Aqua City** next door is another centre of mass youth consumption, with boutiques, small eateries and a multiplex cinema.

Fuji TV Building

Just along from here is the highly visible **Fuji TV Building** ❿, which houses the Fuji Television and Nippon Broadcasting companies. Yet another Kenzo Tange design, its two blocks are connected by several sky corridors and girders. A landmark on the Odaiba, its 32-metre (105-ft) diameter, titanium-paneled sphere – turning the building uncannily into a giant TV set – has a viewing gallery.

Maritime Science Museum

You can either walk or take the train on to the Fune-no-Kagakukan Station for the **Museum of Maritime Science** ⓫ (Fune-no-Kagakukan), which bears the unmistakable shape of an ocean liner (Tues–Sun 10am–5pm; admission charge; tel: 03-5500 1111; www.funenokagakukan.or.jp). Exhibits here trace the history of

Map on page 188

The name Odaiba comes from the cannon emplacements placed in Tokyo Bay in 1853 to defend the city against any attack by Commodore Perry's Black Ships. The remains of two cannons can still be seen.

BELOW: Rainbow Bridge linking Tokyo city and Odaiba island.

Map on page 188

shipping and commercial transportation. Bringing the whole subject alive are two actual ships, the *Soya*, once used for expeditions to the Antarctic, and the *Yoteimaru*, one of a fleet of now almost obsolete ferries that carried passengers between Honshu and Hokkaido islands.

Pop art sculpture near Big Sight in Odaiba.

Another science museum

The next post-modernist structure on the island is the blue arch of the **Telecom Centre** at the station of the same name. Like many of the buildings on the island, this too has its own observation lounge. A robot, yes a robot, conducts tours of the Telecom Centre's cutting-edge **Miraikan** ⓬, with its displays of innovative Japanese hi-tech design and technology (daily 10am–5pm except Tues; tel: 03-3570 9151; www.miraikan.jst.go.jp).

Oedo Onsen Hot Springs

If the past has more appeal than the future, walk over to the extraordinary **Oedo Onsen Monogatari** ⓭, a traditional hot spring bath designed along theme park lines (daily 11am–9pm; admission fee; tel: 03-5500 1126; www.ooedoonsen.jp). Sample outdoor and indoor tubs, a sand bath, mixed healing sauna and a foot massage bath. Expensive but fun, the entrance fee includes towels and a *yukata* (lightweight dressing gown). Be sure to observe local bath etiquette *(see margin tip on page 91)*.

BELOW: interior of the Venus Fort indoor-street mall.

Palette Town

Follow the elevated monorail tracks in the direction of an enormous ferris wheel called the **Stream of Starlight**. Once touted as the world's largest, the wheel takes an interminably long time to complete a full circle. The ferris wheel is part of **Palette Town** ⓮, a shopping and amusement complex with several restaurants and cafés. The complex includes a shopping experience called **Venus Fort**, an indoor street whose 150 shops and cafés are lit by an artificial sky that changes throughout the day, from bright blue to sunsets to forked lightning. Enjoy the experience while it lasts. This highly original shopping venue is due to be dismantled in the near future.

Palette Town is also home to **MegaWeb**, which has the world's largest automobile showroom, the **Toyota City Showcase**, where simulated as well as real rides on the latest models can be enjoyed.

Tokyo Big Sight

Take a short walk along the track to the next chunk of futurism, the **Tokyo Big Sight** ⓯. Everything is big here. An art installation depicting a towering saw stuck into the ground – a marriage of money and bad taste – stands in front of a colossus of a building. Used as a major trade fair and exhibition space, the structure consists of four inverted pyramids standing on a narrow base. Large atriums and an eighth-floor Observation Bar Lounge provide superb views of the bay. ❑

RESTAURANTS

Indian

Khazana
Deck's Tokyo Beach, 5F, 1-6-1 Daiba, Minato-ku. Tel: 03-3599 6551. Open: daily 11am–11pm. ¥¥
www.maharaja-group.com
The attraction here is the exceptional, very affordable all-you-can-eat lunch service (until 5pm). Dinner is a bit more costly, but worth it if you can get an outside table for an evening view of the Rainbow Bridge. All the usual North Indian staples are found here. This is one of the stable of restaurants around Tokyo run by the excellent Maharaja group. Check its website for other branches and discount coupons (10–20 percent off).

Italian

La Cantinetta del Enoteca Pinchiorri
Aqua City R-501, 1-7-1 Daiba, Minato-ku. Tel: 03-5531 8081. Open: daily L and D. ¥¥¥¥
This is a very swish place specialising in meats grilled in the traditional Italian fashion over an open fire. Dishes are recreations of recipes from the 18th century. Three spacious dining areas with high ceilings impart a sophisticated, airy mood. With over 2,000 premium wines to choose from, it's difficult to know where to start.

Japanese

Edogin
4-5-1 Tsukiji, Chuo-ku. Tel: 03-3543 4401. Open: daily 11am–9.30pm. ¥¥¥
Despite the cavernous interior, this place is always busy to overflowing. Fish served here is super fresh – much of it taken from the tanks in the middle of the dining room. The portions are generous, and the restaurant's location just around the corner from Tsukiji Fish Market ensures that prices and quality are good.

Icho
Hotel Nikko Tokyo, 1-9-1 Daiba, Minato-ku. Tel: 03-5500 5500. Open: daily L and D. ¥¥¥¥
Sit back and watch as the chef prepares teppanyaki – meat, fish and vegetables cooked on a hot plate – right in front of you. The setting is quiet and romantic, overlooking an attractive landscaped garden, with the Rainbow Bridge in the background. The wine is expensive, but there's a terrific selection.

Soup Stock Tokyo
Palette Town, 3F, 1 Aomi, Koto-ku. Tel: 03-3599 2333. Open: daily 11am–11pm. ¥
One of the Soup Stock chain's soup-only cafés, this is a welcome port of call in the surreal Venus Fort shopping complex. It offers a good range of hearty soups and chowders at affordable prices and with no artificial additives. Try the *onsen tamago* (eggs boiled in a hot spring) soup, the vegetable soup, or the stronger garlic broth.

Sushi-Bun
Chuo Shijo Bldg, No.8, 5-2-1 Tsukiji, Chuo-ku. Tel: 03-3541 3860. Open: Thur–Tues 6am–2.30pm. ¥¥
www.sushibun.com
Located right in the heart of the Tsukiji Fish Market, Sushi-Bun has been operating for 150 years. Squeeze around the counter and order the sushi set platter: you won't find fresher fish or cheaper prices anywhere else in Tokyo. English menu available.

Takeno
6-21-2 Tsukiji, Chuo-ku. Tel: 03-3541 8698. Open: daily L and D. ¥¥
This simple Japanese diner used to be patronised only by workers from the Tsukiji Fish Market. But since it got discovered by the rest of Tokyo, it now stays open till dinner time. Mixed platters of sashimi and tempura are terrific value. Cash only.

Tsukiji Sushiko
4-7-1 Tsukiji, Chuo-ku. Tel: 03-3547 0505. Open: daily L and D. ¥¥
On the corner next to the Kobayashi post office, this is a spacious and elegantly designed sushi spot with all the usual choices. The restaurant is close to Shijo market, so the sushi items are always fresh and of good quality.

Wakoh
Deck's Tokyo Beach, 5F, 1-6-1 Daiba, Minato-ku. Tel: 03-3599 6555. Open: daily 11am–11pm. ¥¥
At this *tonkatsu* (deep-fried breaded pork cutlets) restaurant, the set meals (*teishoku*) are the best value. Like everywhere else in Odaiba, it can get crowded on weekends.

Mediterranean

Portofino
Omi 1, Palette Town Venus Fort 1060, Koto-ku. Tel: 03-3599 2258. Open: daily 11am–11pm. ¥¥
If you get hungry after negotiating the halls, plazas and water fountains of the weird and wonderful Venus Fort, this restaurant serving Mediterranean cuisine makes a welcome oasis. The lunchtime buffet is good value.

PRICE CATEGORIES

Prices for three-course dinner per person without drinks and taxes:
¥ = under ¥2,000
¥¥ = ¥2,000–¥3,000
¥¥¥ = ¥3,000–¥5,000
¥¥¥¥ = over ¥5,000

EXCURSIONS

An efficient rail system makes nearby getaways easily accessible if you want to escape Tokyo: choose from rambunctious Tokyo Disneyland, old-world Kawagoe, laidback Yokohama, Zen-like Kamakura, majestic Mount Fuji and temple-crammed Nikko

Map on page 198

Tokyo's congestion and big city attractions may be interesting for a short period, but after a few days, or even a month, the most seasoned traveller may find himself itching to get away. And the good news is, Japan's well-established rail system makes escaping a breeze. An hour or so by rail *(see text box on page 207)* is all you need before arriving at some of the country's most famous sights – the temple town of Nikko, the Edo-period merchant enclave of Kawagoe, cosmopolitan Yokohama, coastal Kamakura, or exploring Mount Fuji and Hakone. Most of the attractions listed in this section are day trips. However, getting out of the city can be challenging – especially on weekends, when it may seem as if all of Tokyo has the same idea.

CHIBA & DISNEYLAND

Almost every visitor to Tokyo ends up at **Tokyo Disneyland** ❶ (open daily, timings vary with season; admission charge; tel: 045-683 3333), located in a bedroom suburb of **Chiba Prefecture** to the east of the capital. Well over 100 million people have visited since it opened in 1983. A newer, contingent complex, the very popular **DisneySea**, offers attractions designed along aquatic themes.

Around Narita area

But there is much more to the prefecture than the Magic Kingdom. Most people are in a hurry to leave Chiba's **Narita** ❷ area after arriving at **Narita Airport** , which is a shame as the area has much to offer. First is the **Narita-san Temple**, a 15-minute walk from JR Narita or Keisei Narita stations. Dating back to AD 940, it is one of the most important in the entire Kanto region, drawing worshippers especially over the first three days of the New Year.

PRECEDING PAGES: Hakone Open Air Museum.
LEFT: Kamakura's Great Buddha.
BELOW: Tokyo Disneyland.

Excursions
0 20 km
0 20 miles
Tokyo
Yokohama
Kawasaki
Chiba
Funabashi
Ichikawa
Kawaguchi
Urawa
Omiya
Hachioji
Sagamihara
Tokyo-wan
Sagami-nada
PACIFIC OCEAN
Boso-hanto
Izu-hanto
Miura-hanto
Suruga-wan
Kasumi-ga-ura
Ashio-sanchi
Nikko Kokuritsu-koen
Joshin-Etsu-daichi Kokuritsu-koen
Chichibu-Tama Kokuritsu-koen
Fuji-Hakone-Izu Kokuritsu-koen
Oshima
Mihara-yama 758
Fuji-san 3776
Fuji Go-ko
Kawaguchiko
Fujiyoshida
Yamanaka-ko
Ashino-ko
Hakone-Yumoto
Odawara
Kamakura
Yokosuka
Zushi
Fujisawa
Hiratsuka
Atsugi
Yamato
Machida
Tama
Chofu
Mitaka
Tachikawa
Kodaira
Ome
Hanno
Sayama
Kawagoe
Chichibu
Kumagaya
Takasaki
Maebashi
Kiryu
Ashikaga
Oyama
Utsunomiya
Nikko
Chuzenji-ko
Mito
Tsukuba
Tsuchiura
Narita
Sakura
Kashiwa
Matsudo
Noda
Kasukabe
Haneda
Tokyo Disneyland
Kisarazu
Tateyama
Kamogawa
Atami
Ito
Shimoda
Mishima
Numazu
Fuji
Fujinomiya
Gotemba
Hadano
Isehara
Narita
Nagaoka
Koriyama
Matsumoto
Shizuoka
Chino
Hitachi
Choshi
Kashima
1 2 3 4 5 6 7 8 9 10 11 12

Map on page 198

There are several reasons for Narita-san's popularity. Foremost is its image of Fudo, the Buddhist "god of fire", said to have been carved by Kobo Daishi, the saint who founded the Shingon sect. Narita-san is also well known for its drive-in chapel at the side of the complex that welcomes drivers – and their vehicles – to be blessed by a priest and, for a fee, be adorned with lucky amulets to protect against accidents.

Sakura

An overview of the nation's history can be enjoyed in the former castle town of **Sakura** ❸, on the Narita Keisei and JR Sobu lines. Within the extensively landscaped former castle grounds is the **National Museum of Japanese History** (Kokuritsu Rekishi Minzoku Hakubutsukan), which presents Japanese history from an anthropological point of view (Tues–Sun 9.30am–4.30pm; admission charge; tel: 043-486 0123).

Other easily accessible places of interest in Chiba are the system of canals near **Sawara** and **Itako**, reached by JR trains from Tokyo or Ryogoku stations. The canals meander through thousands of hectares of marshland; tours using poled boats take visitors through them, and usually include a "traditional lunch" and even a spot of fishing.

Boso Peninsula

The hilly Boso Peninsula, shaped like a pelican's craw separating Tokyo Bay from the Pacific, is served by train lines. Farther on down this southern and western region of the Boso Peninsula is **Mount Nokogiriyama** ❹, a short walk from Hamakanaya Station on the JR Uchibo Line. A short ropeway takes visitors halfway up the mountain, which affords a fine panorama of Tokyo Bay and Mount Fuji.

Just as interesting is a 33-metre (110-ft) image of **Kannon**, the Goddess of Mercy, carved into the rockface near the top of the mountain, and a cluster of 1,553 stone statues of *rakan* (disciples of the Buddha).

Descend a long flight of steps to visit the **Yakushi Nyorai Buddha**, Japan's largest figure of the Buddha. The base to the tip of the giant lotus

With queues of up to one hour for some attractions, Disneyland can be a tiresome place. Most salaried workers in Japan get paid on the 25th of the month. Crowds at the Magic Kingdom are noticeably thinner in the week preceding that date.

BELOW: Narita-san Temple features a drive-in chapel.

The wooden bell tower of Toki no Kane is a distinctive landmark in old-world Kawagoe.

bud that stands behind the statue's head like a stone antimacassar measures an impressive 31 metres (100 ft). The Buddha image was originally built in 1783.

Easily accessed from Chiba city, the east coast of the peninsula has some of the most underrated beaches in the Tokyo area. **Onjuku**, with white sand, palm trees and beach-front cafés, is the most pleasant, though **Katsuura** and **Kamogawa**, both south of Onjuku, are also good for swimming. **Kujukuri-hama**, north of Onjuku, has over 60 km (37 miles) of almost deserted beach, but of the black, volcanic variety.

KAWAGOE

A favourite of TV directors looking for nostalgic picture bytes for historical dramas, the former castle town of **Kawagoe** ❺ prospered as a supplier of goods to Edo during the Tokugawa period. It is affectionately known as "Little Edo" on account of its main street of well-preserved, jet-black godowns and ageing temples. Visitors arriving at Kawagoe Station, northwest of Tokyo, will have to walk for another 15 minutes to reach the historical core.

BELOW: the carefully preserved old godowns of Kawagoe today house shops and restaurants.

Along Ichiban-gai

Cross over the walkway on the left in front of Kawagoe Station to the Atre Department Store, walk down the steps and across the traffic lights to Sun Road, a busy pedestrian shopping mall. Cross the next set of traffic lights until you reach a T-junction where on the right is the first *kurazukuri*, an impressive black godown, now a liquor and tea shop called **Kameya**. It specialises in *sayama-cha*, a leaf from the nearby hills of Sayama. Exiting the store turn right and walk a few steps to the next intersection. Turn right onto **Ichiban-gai**, Kawagoe's most famous street and the one with the largest concentration of *kurazukuri*.

During the Edo Period, the walls of the godowns were covered with charcoal powder mixed with plaster and its black walls were buffed to a mirror-like shine. Older women in Kawagoe still remember adjusting their kimono and hair while gazing at their reflections in the shiny surfaces.

The **Hattori Folk Museum** (Hattori Minzoku Shiryokan) along this street has pamphlets and maps in English (Tues–Sun 10am–4.30pm; admission charge; tel: 0492-22 0337). Across the street is **Yamawa**, a beautiful ceramic shop housed in a street corner godown. Its stylish café serves green tea and sweet potato delicacies.

One block up from the Hattori Folk Museum, down a lane to the right is the **Toki no Kane**, a wooden bell tower that has become synonymous with Kawagoe. The current structure was built after a fire broke out in 1893. The original bell in the three-storey tower tolls four times a day: at 6am, noon, 3pm and 6pm.

On the main street, **Osawa House**, dating from 1792, is Kawagoe's oldest *kurazukuri*. The house is now used as a handicraft shop selling traditional products like Japanese masks and Kawagoe dolls.

Two blocks up and across the street, the narrow lane on the left is **Kashi-ya Yokocho**, or Confectioners' Row. Souvenirs and trinkets have been added to shops selling old-fashioned sweets and purple sweet potato ice cream. Returning to the bell tower, a 10-minute walk east takes you to the ruins of **Kawagoe Castle**. Little remains of the original fort, but the exquisite **Honmaru-goten Palace** more than makes up for that (daily 9am–4.30pm; admission charge; tel: 0492-24 8811). Built by a local lord, one Ota Dokan and his son, the building houses beautifully painted screens and archeological artefacts from the region.

A 10-minute walk south takes you to **Kita-in Temple**, a Buddhist temple-museum with a traditional Japanese garden. Kita-in's main draw is the **Gohyaku Rakan** stones, 540 statues depicting disciples of the Buddha in different poses and expressions. One figure scratches his head, a couple get drunk on wine, others meditate, rub a sore foot, or beat drums.

YOKOHAMA

Map on page 198

West of the capital is **Yokohama** ❻. An integral part of the Greater Tokyo area, it is also a major urban centre in its own right and one of the greatest international seaports of Asia.

With a population of more than 3 million, Yokohama is second in size only to Tokyo. Easily covered on foot, it has relatively uncrowded streets (except on weekends) and laid-back atmosphere.

The bay area has been totally revamped by the massive **Minato Mirai 21** development. It includes the 73-storey **Landmark Tower**, nearby *Nippon Maru*, a majestic sailing ship, and neighbouring **Maritime Museum**, as well as **Yokohama Museum of Art** (Yokohama Bijutsukan), with its excellent collection of modernist sculpture (both museums open Tues–Sun 10am–5pm; admission charge).

A short walk from here, through the **Nippon-Maru Memorial Park** and across the Kisha-Michi Promenade, takes you to **Shinkocho**, a man-made island housing the **Akarenga Park**. The island's old

TIP

Landmark Tower has one of the fastest lifts in the world – it whisks passengers at a speed of 45km (28 miles) an hour.

BELOW: view of the Yokohama waterfront from the Landmark Tower.

Yokohama's oldest Western-style accommodation, the New Grand Hotel, was built in 1927. Its second-floor lobby is a marvellous time capsule of old Yokohama. High school students come here every year for lunch and a lesson in Western table etiquette.

red-brick custom houses have been recently renovated and now serve as shops, restaurants and boutiques.

The other side of the **Oka-gawa River** from Sakuragicho Station is an area of old government buildings, banks and other institutional structures. Farther on is a charming tree-lined street with red brick pavements called **Basha Michi-dori** (Street of Horse Carriages). The interesting **Kanagawa Prefectural Museum** (Kanagawa Kenritsu Kindai Bijutsukan) is located here (Tues–Sun 10am–5pm; admission charge; tel: 045-2001 0926). The building, erected in 1904, is one of the best surviving examples of the city's old commercial architecture.

Along the waterfront

In Yokohama's early days **Honcho-dori** became the centre of commercial activities. The wide street is still bracketed with banks and office buildings like the stately Yokohama Banker's Club and, on the right, four blocks down, the lovely red-brick **Yokohama Port Opening Memorial Hall** (Yokohama-shi Kaiko Kinen Kaikan), which miraculously survived the 1923 earthquake and World War II fire bombings (Tues–Sun 10am–5pm; admission charge).

Also in this area are numerous prefectural offices, and near the waterfront, the **Yokohama Custom House** (Yokohama Zeikan). The **Yokohama Archives of History** (Yokohama Kaiko Shiriokan), on the site of the former British consulate, houses a museum with various exhibits about Yokohama's fascinating history, and a library with related audio-visual materials (Tues–Sun 10am–5pm; admission charge; tel: 045-201 2100).

Opposite is the **Yokohama Port Opening Square**, where Japan and the United States signed the Treaty of Peace and Amity in 1854. A little bit farther down the same road is the somewhat garish 106-metre (348-ft) **Marine Tower** (open daily; admission charge for observation deck; tel: 045-641 7838) and the **Yokohama Doll Museum** (Ningyo no Ie), with almost a thousand dolls from around the world on display (Tues–Sun 10am–5pm; admission charge).

BELOW: Yokohama's Chinatown is the largest in Japan. **RIGHT:** chestnuts being roasted in Yokohama's Chinatown.

Yamashita Park (Yamashita Koen) along the waterfront is well worth a visit. The former passenger liner and hospital ship *Hikawa-Maru* is permanently moored here and can be visited.

No visit to Yokohama would be complete without a meal in **Chinatown** (Chukagai), tucked further back from the waterfront. This dozen or so blocks is the largest and best Chinatown in Japan, and is nearly as old as the port.

Yamate area

East of the waterfront is **Yamate**, where the foreign merchants used to live in palatial homes. Before exploring Yamate, pause for a spectacular view of the bay and bridge from **Harbour View Park** (Minato no Mieru Oka Koen) at the top of the hill called France Yama. In the rose garden beside the park's gate, you can visit the **British House Yokohama**, home to the city's first British legation. Cross the road opposite the gates and go straight ahead. At the **Foreigners' Cemetery** (Gaijin Bochi), around 4,200 foreigners are buried. The adjacent **Yamate Museum** (Yamate Shiriokan), with quaint displays on the life of early foreign residents, sits near where Japan's first brewery was located (Tues–Sun 10am–5pm; admission charge).

A short walk east takes you to **Sankeien Garden**, a traditional Japanese garden built in 1906 by a local silk merchant (daily 9am–4.30pm; admission charge). Its extensive grounds have a number of historical buildings, including a farmhouse and three-storey pagoda. Returning to Yamate, you can then descend to the lively shopping street of **Motomachi**.

KAMAKURA

Kamakura ❼ lies cradled in a spectacular natural amphitheatre, flanked on three sides by wooded mountains and on the fourth by the blue Pacific. For roughly 150 years from 1192, Kamakura was the de facto political and cultural capital of Japan. During those years, the warrior administration based here built impressive temples and commissioned notable works of art, a great deal of it Zen-influenced.

Kamakura's 65 Buddhist temples and 19 Shinto shrines, interspersed with walks through quiet surrounding hills resemble an open-air madhouse on weekends. Most visitors customarily begin their sightseeing from **Kita-Kamakura Station**, nearest to the great Zen temples of **Engaku-ji**, **Tokei-ji** and **Kencho-ji**.

The Great Buddha

Alternatively, take the Enoden Line and drop off at **Hase Station**, which is closest to the Daibutsu (Great Buddha). In the hills to the left on the way are **Hase-dera Temple**, with its 9-metre (30-ft) 11-headed Hase Kannon statue, along with thousands of small Jizo statues decked out in colourful bibs and bonnets, and **Kosoku-ji Temple**, known for its memorabilia associ-

Map on page 198

An offering to Daibutsu, the Great Buddha of Kamakura.

BELOW: one of numerous shrines tucked in the verdant hills of Kamakura.

The attractions of Enoshima, the wooded islet south of Kamakura, haven't changed since its heyday: fresh seafood, bracing sea breezes, spectacular views of Sagami Bay and Mount Fuji. The 600-metre long (1,970-ft) Benten Bridge (Benten-bashi) that connects Enoshima to Katase Beach and the adjacent resort town, has turned into a major causeway, providing beautiful views of the ocean.

ated with the famous priest Nichiren.

On a knoll to the right of the approach to the Great Buddha is the 1,200-year-old **Amanawa Myojin Shrine**. Dedicated to the Sun Goddess, Amaterasu Omikami, the shrine offers a majestic view of the area and the sea beyond.

At 11 metres (40 ft) in height and weighing 94,000 kg (93 tons), the **Daibutsu** (Great Buddha) is unlikely to get lost in the crowd. Stand a few metres in front of the statue to get the full impact of this artwork cast in 1252. Astonishingly, the statue has survived some massive typhoons and tsunami – one in 1495 ripped away the wooden building enclosing it – as well as earthquakes.

Enoshima

The tiny island of **Enoshima** is offshore, easily accessed on the Enoden rail, which will take you to the bridge to the island. Narrow lanes, or an escalator if you prefer, lead to **Enoshima-jinga**, a shrine housing the famous statue of *hadaka-benzaiten*, the nude goddess of the arts and beauty. Sacred caves, craggy cliffs and a pleasant **Tropical Garden** (Shokubutsu-en) are some of Enoshima's other sights.

Wakamiya-dori

On the east side of the **Kamakura Station** is the broad boulevard of **Wakamiya-dori**. Parallel is pedestrian-only Kamachi-dori, a lane full of trendy shops and eating places.

Kamakura is also known for Kamakura-*bori* (lacquerware), originated here in the 13th century as utensils used in religious ceremonies. Learn more about this art at the **Kamakura-bori Kaikan** on the right along Wakamiya-dori.

Tsurugaoka Hachiman-gu

The approach to the Tsurugaoka Hachiman-gu Shrine at the end of Wakamiya-dori crosses a steep, half-moon bridge. Behind the Heike Pond is the **Kanagawa Prefectural Museum of Modern Art** (Kanagawa Keritsu Kindai Bijutsukan), with changing exhibitions by contemporary Japanese and foreign artists (Tues–Sun 9.30am–5pm; admission charge; tel: 0467-22 5000).

BELOW: entrance to the Wakamiya-dori boulevard.

A little past the Genji Pond is the **National Treasure Hall** (Kamakura Kokuhokan) where the 2,000 treasures from the various temples of Kamakura are displayed (daily 10am–3pm; admission charge).

Continuing up the avenue, cross a 25-metre (82-ft) dirt track, along which every September 16 mounted archers gallop and unloosen their arrows at targets in an ancient samurai ritual. Then you reach an open area below the steps to the Main Hall of the **Tsurugaoka Hachiman-gu Shrine**.

On the left of the steps is a huge gingko tree measuring around 8 metres (26 ft) and reputed to be 1,000 years old. The Tsurugaoka Hachiman-gu Shrine might well be considered the physical and spiritual centre of Kamakura.

Most of the present shrine buildings are reconstructions, but the red-painted halls, lively souvenir stalls and ebullient flow of visitors make it one of Kamakura's most earthy pilgrimage spots.

MOUNT FUJI & HAKONE

It would be hard to find a mountain more highly praised for its beauty than Fuji, or a lake more often photographed than Hakone's Lake Ashi. Most of the region is designated a "national park", but due to Japan's rather weak laws at protecting and restricting commercial exploitation of such assets, national parks are considered "nature" amusement parks.

Sweeping up from the Pacific to form a nearly perfect cone, 3,776 metres (12,388 ft) above sea level, **Mount Fuji** ❽ (Fuji-san) is said to watch over Japan and her people. Like many natural monuments held to be sacred and imbued with a living spirit, Fuji was off limits to women until 1867, when an English woman scaled the mountain.

The "official" climbing season for Mount Fuji begins on 1 July and ends on 31 August. The mountain huts along the trails to Fuji's peak are open only then, and casual hikers are advised, despite the crowds, to pick this period to make the ascent.

For those who wish to see the rising sun from Fuji's peak, start in the afternoon, stay overnight at one of the cabins near the top, and complete the climb while it is still dark. Or start at about 9pm and climb all the way. The mountain air can be cold and rain is not uncommon, so bring along a sweater, gloves and a waterproof jacket, plenty of water and a torch.

Fuji Five Lakes

The **Fuji Go-ko** ❾ (Five Lakes) district skirts the northern base of Mount Fuji and provides an ideal year-round resort, offering a range of outdoor recreational activities such as camping and water sports during the summer months, and skiing and skating in the winter.

From east to west, the lakes are Yamanaka, Kawaguchi, Sai, Shoji and Motosu. **Yamanaka Lake**, which is the largest in the group, and the picturesque **Kawaguchi Lake**,

Map on page 198

TIP

The ascent to Mount Fuji's summit can take anything from 5–7 hours so don't attempt the climb unless you are reasonably fit. According to a Japanese saying, there are two kinds of fools: the ones who never climb Mount Fuji and the ones who climb it twice in a lifetime.

BELOW: Lake Ashino with the snow-capped Mt Fuji in the background.

Spectacularly positioned in the foothills of Mount Fuji, the Hakone Open Air Museum's lush grounds contain an extensive array of modern outdoor sculpture. Even non-art enthusiasts should not miss this "forest of sculptures".

BELOW: heavily gilded rooftop of the Toshogu-jinja Shrine in Nikko.

are the most frequented of the five, but some of the best spots are hidden near the smaller and more secluded three other lakes.

Hakone

Hakone, set against the backdrop of Mount Fuji, has long been a popular place for rest and recreation. Tours usually start at **Odawara Station**, where the **Hakone Tozan Railway** begins its 9-km (6-mile) zigzag route up all the way to the terminus at **Gora**. The first stop on the line and the gateway to Hakone's 16 hot springs, **Hakone-Yumoto ⑩**, nestles in a shallow ravine where the Hayakawa and Sukumo rivers flow together. If on a day trip, the **Tenzan** public bath provides an exquisite hot spring treat.

Some 20 minutes from Hakone-Yumoto lies **Miyanoshita**, the oldest and most thriving of the spa towns. Miyanoshita is home to the famous **Fujiya Hotel**. Opened in 1878, it is a veritable time capsule, with a 1930s-style wood-panelled dining room, a library full of old books and waitresses in Agatha Christie-period uniforms. Look out for the guest book with comments from personalities like Margaret Thatcher, John Lennon and Yoko Ono, among others.

The Hakone Tozan train also stops at **Hakone Open Air Museum** (Chokoku no Mori Bijutsukan) an outdoor sculpture garden that has few parallels elsewhere in the world. The works of Picasso, Rodin, Leger, Takamura Kotaro and many others are on display at this stunning location (daily 9am–5pm, Nov–Feb until 4pm; admission charge; tel: 00460-21161).

At the Gora terminal, change over to the funicular to **Mount Sounzan** and transfer to the cable car headed for **Togendai**, which lies on the shore of **Lake Ashino**, a beautiful caldera lake crisscrossed by pleasure boats. On the way up is **Owakudani** ("Valley of the Greater Boiling") in the old crater of Mount Kami. It is an interesting place but the sulphurous fumes can be overwhelming.

NIKKO

No visit to Japan would be complete without a trip to the delightful temple town of **Nikko ⑪**, a treasure house of religious art and architecture produced during the Tokugawa era, housed in temples set among cedar forests. Nikko's fortunes improved when it was chosen in 1617 by the Tokugawa as the burial place of their first shogun, Ieyasu. The clan built an astonishingly elaborate memorial, the Toshogu-jinja Shrine, which was completed in 1636.

The ideal way to approach the complex is via the steps opposite the vermillion **Shinkyo** (Sacred Bridge), spanning the Daiya River at the top of the main street. From there, follow the cedar avenue to **Rinno-ji Temple**, where you can buy a combination ticket that also includes Futarasan Shrine and Nikko's main sight, the Toshogu-jinja Shrine and mausoleum complex (all daily 8am–5pm).

Rinno-ji's **Sanbutsudo Hall** houses three gigantic images: Bato Kannon (protector of horses), Amida, and the thousand-armed Kannon, the Goddess of Mercy.

Continue along the main **Omotesando** path towards the **Five Storey Pagoda** (Gojuno-to). Just before the main entrance to the **Toshogu-jinja Shrine**, the Buddhist-style gate **Omote-mon** is guarded by two mythical kings. The adjacent **Sacred Horse Stable** is carved with scenes illustrating the life cycle of humanity. Past the *torii* gate at the top of the stone steps is Toshogu's most famous feature, the **Yomei-mon**, beyond which only the highest-ranking samurai could once pass. Standing 11 metres (35 ft) high, this gate is covered with hundreds of intricate carvings – children at play, clouds, pine trees, bamboo, and animals – all painted in a riot of brilliant colours.

More treasures await inside: the east and west corridors surrounding the main building are also covered with carvings, among them the celebrated but difficult to find **Nemuri-Neko**, or Sleeping Cat, on the side of the **Sakashita-mon** gate. Beyond this gate are the 200-odd steps to the mausoleum of Tokugawa Ieyasu. The next point of interest is the **Toshogu Treasure House**, which houses an interesting collection of Tokugawa portraits, samurai armour and swords.

Taking the second path to the left takes you to the **Futarasan-jinja Shrine**, the oldest of the buildings in the complex, dating back to 1617.

Lake Chuzenji

If you have had enough of temples and shrines, takethe half-hour bus ride up the winding mountain road to **Lake Chuzenji** ⓬. From there, savour the altitude at 1,270 metres, (4,170 ft), clear air and lakeside scenery. A sightseeing boat leaves the pier, just across the road from the bus stop, for a one-hour tour of the lake.

Five minutes' walk in the opposite direction is the observatory of the 100-metre (320-ft) high **Kegon Falls** (Kegon no Taki); a lift descends right to the bottom of the gorge (open daily; free) where a platform allows views of the thundering falls. ❑

Map on page 198

"You ask yourself whether it is a joke, or a nightmare, or a huge wedding cake, a masterpiece of sugar icing made for some extravagant prince with a perverse rococo taste, who wished to alarm and entertain his guests." – Fosco Mariani on the Toshogu-jinja in "Meeting with Japan".

BELOW: *torii* gate and Five-Storey Pagoda at Nikko.

Getting there from Tokyo

Disneyland: 15-minute train ride from Tokyo Station on the JR Keiyo Line to Maihama Station, or take the Tozai Line (subway) to Urayasu, and then catch a shuttle bus.
Nikko: A two-hour train ride to the north of Tokyo – by direct local or Tobu Line express train from Asakusa station to Tobu Nikko Station.
Kawagoe: The Tobu Tojo Line express from Ikebukuro takes 30 minutes to JR Kawagoe. The Yurakucho Line runs on the same route, but takes slightly longer.
Yokohama: Take the new Mirato Mirai Line train (35 minutes) from Shibuya, or the JR Keihin Tohoku Line (40 minutes) from Tokyo Station to Sakuragi-cho.
Kamakura: An hour from Tokyo Station (or 30 minutes from Yokohama) on the JR Yokosuka Line to Kita-Kamakura or Kamakura stations.
Mount Fuji and Hakone: The Odakyu line from Shinjuku serves Hakone. JR Pass holders can access the area from Odawara station on the *shinkansen* line. The weekday Hakone Free Pass, available from Shinjuku Station, provides unlimited two-day travel.

TRANSPORT

GETTING THERE AND GETTING AROUND

GETTING THERE

By Air

Tokyo is served by two main airports: **New Tokyo International Airport** (Narita) about 66 km (41 miles) east of the city; and the **Tokyo International Airport** (Haneda), 15 km (9 miles) to the south of the city centre. The airports are usually simply referred to as Narita and Haneda.

All international flights to Tokyo arrive at Narita, except those on China Airlines (from Taiwan), which flies into Haneda.

Narita Airport

Although rather inconveniently located, the efficiency of services at Narita have vastly improved with the recent renewal and extension of the airport. It now has two terminals and two runways. Both terminals have currency exchange counters, restaurants and cafés, Internet facilities, post offices and health clinics, and a range of shops including duty free. Terminal 2 has a children's play room, day rooms for taking a nap, and showers.
General and Flight Info: 0476-348 000; www.narita-airport.jp/en/index.html
Tourist Info: 0476-34 6251 (Terminal 2); 0476-30 3383 (Terminal 1)

Haneda Airport

Haneda airport is Tokyo's main hub for domestic flights. Both domestic airlines – Japan Air Lines (JAL) and All Nippon Airways (ANA) – operate flights throughout Japan from Haneda.

The only international flights using Haneda are those to and from Taiwan. However, the addition of a new runway will increase the number of international flights operating at Haneda. The international terminal is located well away from the main domestic terminal and is connected by a regular shuttle bus service.

Haneda does not have international facilities like business centres, but its two terminals are comfortable and well designed, with Japanese, Western and Chinese restaurants, cafés, shops, post office, information desks and a book store.
Airport Info: 03-5757 8111

Flying from UK and US

The four big name airlines serving Tokyo from the UK are British Airways, JAL, ANA and Virgin Atlantic. Flying time direct from London is between 11–13 hours.

Coming from the US or Canada, you are spoiled for choice. Besides JAL and ANA, among the better known airlines that fly the Tokyo route are Northwest, American Airlines, Delta, Continental and United Airlines. Flying time from the US west coast is 12–13 hours; from the east coast it's 18–20 hours, including stopovers.

Tokyo is an increasingly important transportation hub for direct flights to major destinations like Beijing, Shanghai, Hong Kong, Bangkok and farther afield to Singapore, Bali and Sydney.

While fares vary from airline to

KEY AIRLINES

Air China
2-5-2 Toranomon, Minato-ku
Tel: 03-5251 0711
www.airchina.com.cn
American Airlines
Tel: 03-4550 2111
www.americanairlines.jp
British Airways
Tel: 03-3570 8657
www.british-airways.com
Qantas Airways
1-16-4 Toranomon, Minato-ku
Tel: 03-3593 7000
www.qantas.com.au
Singapore Airlines
1-10-1 Yurakucho, Chiyoda-ku
Tel: 03-3213 3431
www.singaporeair.com
United Airlines
Tel: 0120-114 466, www.ual.com
Virgin Atlantic Airways
5-2-1 Minami-Aoyama, Minato-ku, Tel: 03-3499 8811
www.virgin-atlantic.com

airline, April, August and December tend to be the most expensive times to fly to Japan from the UK or US as they coincide with the country's Golden Week, O-bon and Christmas-New Year holidays. Flying even a few days on either side of these peak periods can result in huge savings.

By Sea

Although few people arrive by sea, Japan's ferry services are quite extensive, at least in their connections with South Korea, China and Taiwan.

There is a regular boat service between South Korea's port of Pusan and Shimonoseki in Japan. A hydrofoil also plies between Pusan and Hakata in Japan.

Ferries from China (Shanghai and Tanggu) arrive in Osaka and Kobe respectively, from where passengers travel either by rail or air to Tokyo.

The weekly ferries that ply between Keelung and Kaohsiung in Taiwan stop off in the Okinawan islands of Ishigaki and Miyako before arriving in Nara.

By Road

The expressways that connect major cities throughout Japan are of extraordinarily high quality. Like the British, the Japanese drive on the left, and the signs are generally self-explanatory. All major expressways charge a toll fee, so apart from traffic-congested roads, the option of using a train or bus is much more appealing. See "Driving" *(page 211)* for details on car-hire.

Japan has an excellent system of inter-city buses. They are rarely cheaper than trains, but offer a comfortable alternative. Buses often include destinations not covered by trains, and many operate direct services, unlike trains. Night buses are cheaper than trains, but leave late and arrive in the early hours. These are operated by Japan Railway; buy tickets at the Green Window offices at JR stations.

The main **JR bus office** is located on the south side of Tokyo Station (tel: 03-3215 0498). The **Tokyo Bus Association** (tel: 03-5360 7111) has information on buses arriving and departing from the city.

By Train

The majority of train lines entering Tokyo from major Japanese cities whether JR or *shinkansen* (bullet train), terminate or make a stop at Tokyo Station on the JR Yamanote Line. Going out on day trips to places like Hakone and Kawagoe usually involves taking a private line. Most of these, like the Toku Nikko line which starts in Asakusa, also connect with the indispensable Yamanote Line. Other major non-JR line terminals are Shibuya and Shinjuku stations – both on the Yamanote Line.

Information on train connections to the places of interest outside Tokyo are found on page 207.

GETTING AROUND

From Narita Airport

Because of its distance from Tokyo, you should allow at least 1½–2 hours to reach the city centre, depending on the time of day and your mode of transport.

There are basically four ways to get into Tokyo: taxi; limousine bus; Japan Railways Narita Express; or the Skyliner train on the private Keisei Railway.

By Taxi

This is most expensive option, and usually the slowest. The fare to or from downtown Tokyo is ¥20,000–30,000 and one is often sitting in a jam, watching the meter spin inexorably higher. The rides are strictly metered, and have no extra surcharges.

Expect the 66-km (41-mile) ride to central Tokyo to take anywhere between two and four hours depending on traffic density. Signs indicating taxi ranks are clearly indicated at exit points throughout the terminals.

By Limousine Bus

Convenient, frequent and comfortable airport "limousine" buses are much cheaper than taxis. However, they are also subject to traffic jams. These connect Narita Airport with most parts of the city, including major hotels, railway stations and T-CAT (Tokyo City Air Terminal), as well as Haneda Airport, Tokyo Disneyland and Y-CAT (Yokohama City Air Terminal). Tickets (around ¥3,000, depending upon destination) can be bought in the arrival lobby after clearing immigration and customs. Buses are boarded outside the terminal at the curb, and will carry any amount of luggage at no extra charge. Estimated travel time to central Tokyo: 1 hr and 15 minutes, barring major traffic jams.

For enquiries, call 03-3665 7220 (www.limousinebus.co.jp).

By Train

This is the fastest way to reach Tokyo. There are two services: the **JR Narita Express** and the **Keisei Skyliner**. The stations for both lines are found on the basement level of each of the two terminal buildings.

Narita Express connects with the JR railway network at Tokyo, Shinagawa, Shinjuku, Ikebukuro, Omiya, Yokohama and Ofuna stations. It takes one hour to travel to Tokyo Station, and costs ¥2,940 (¥4,980 for first class).

For JR train information (in English), call 03-3423 0111; www.jreast.co.jp/e/index.html.

The Keisei Skyliner runs to Tokyo's Ueno Station, stopping first at nearby Nippori. The connection to JR lines or the subway at Ueno is not as convenient as the Narita Express, but the Skyliner is more comfortable and usually less crowded. It takes one hour to Ueno and costs ¥1,920. Contact Keisei Ueno Information Centre at tel: 03-3831 0131.

Note: Using the train and subway can involve long walks. If you have more baggage than you can carry, make use of baggage delivery services at the airport which are fast and reliable. Look for counters in the arrival lobby. **ABC** service is recommended (tel: 03-3545 1131). For about ¥1,500 to ¥2,500 per piece, they deliver your baggage by the following day to anywhere in Japan. Similarly, they pick up bags from anywhere and deliver to Narita.

T-Cat Departures

Passengers of selected airlines taking the airport limousine bus to Narita can complete check-in and passport control procedures at **Tokyo City Air Terminal (T-CAT)** in downtown Tokyo. To find out if your airline offers this service, call T-CAT at 03-3665 7111. T-CAT can be accessed by taxi (most taxi drivers know it just as Hakozaki) or by subway from Suitengumae Station on the Hanzomon Line.

From Haneda Airport

By Taxi

By taxi, it should take about 30 minutes to central Tokyo, and cost around ¥5,000, but beware of traffic congestion.

By Train

Most people opt for the cheaper trains. Frequent services run from the Keihin Kyuko Railway Station in the airport basement. The train takes about 20 minutes to Shinagawa Station, and costs ¥400.

By Monorail

If travelling light, another alternative is the Tokyo Monorail, which connects Haneda with Hamamatsucho Station on the JR Yamanote line. It takes only 17 minutes and costs ¥470, but can be very crowded during rush hour.

By Limousine Bus

An airport limousine bus service connects Haneda with central Tokyo. Fares range from ¥1,000, depending on which part of the city you're heading to. There is also a service from Haneda to Narita that takes about 75 minutes and costs ¥3,000.

Orientation

Tokyo Prefecture covers 2,168 sq km (837 sq miles). Besides the 23 central wards of the inner city (616 sq km/238 sq miles), it also incorporates 27 smaller cities, plus 14 towns and villages. The Tokyo Metropolitan Government also administers various islands in the Pacific Ocean. It is, indisputably, the largest megalopolis in the world.

Tokyo is divided into 23 *ku* (wards), which are sub-divided into *cho* (districts), then numbered *chome* (blocks) – *see also page 230*. Japanese people tend to think in terms of city blocks, often finding their way from one block to the next by using landmarks such as shops, restaurants and architectural features as markers. Even taxi drivers get confused once they depart from the main thoroughfares and sights. Maps are essential for navigating the city (*see page 235*).

Exits at train stations are usually clearly marked overhead. Landmarks like museums, department stores and government offices are marked in English on yellow boards, which should be visible as you exit the ticket barriers. Train stations usually have maps near their exits. Though often in Japanese, they provide some sense of orientation.

ASKING FOR HELP

Japanese people are generally very helpful when quizzed about addresses and, if nearby, may even on occasion escort you to your destination. When in doubt, ask at the local *koban* (police box). The police are generally very helpful and will consult maps on your behalf and even phone to confirm an address.

Public Transport

The public transport system in Tokyo is unrivalled anywhere in the world. The city is served by a sophisticated and highly efficient network of railway lines, subways and bus routes. During rush hour, services run every 1–2 minutes on some lines, at a degree of reliability inconceivable elsewhere.

Both trains and subways are notoriously crowded during the morning and evening rush hour, and sometimes run at 300 percent of the seating capacity.

The roads are even more congested. For that reason, taxis are only useful if you are travelling routes not served by a subway.

Good English-language city maps which show major landmarks along with railway and subway lines can be picked up for free from major hotels or Tourist Information Centre (TIC) offices *(see page 237)*.

Subway (Metro)

The subway system (re-named Tokyo Metro in April 2004, although people continue to use the term "subway") is clean, safe and convenient. It is also the fastest and most economical means of getting across town. There are 13 lines crisscrossing central Tokyo, nine operated by the **Rapid Transportation Authority (Teito)** and four by the **Tokyo Municipal Authority (Toei)**.

Subways run to precise schedules, indicated on timetables posted at each station. Services run from 5am to 12.30am at intervals of 2–3 minutes during rush hours, with frequencies dropping to around every 5–10 minutes at off-peak periods. The frequency is slightly reduced on weekends.

All subway and train stations have a route map indicating fares for each stop near the ticket machines, usually in English.

The fares for both subways and trains are regulated on a station-to-station basis, so if you cannot determine the fare required, just purchase the cheapest ticket available (¥160 for Teito lines,

TRAVEL PASSES

Active sightseers can save by buying a **Tokyo Combination Ticket**, a one-day pass that entitles you to use all JR, subway and bus lines in the Tokyo region. Pass offices (look out for a triangle symbol on subway maps) at major stations sell the tickets for ¥1580.

¥180 for Toei lines) at the ticket machine. If you have not paid the correct fare, simply top up the difference on arrival – either at designated fare adjustment machines or at the station office.

Prepaid cards called **SF Metrocards** can be bought at subway stations for ¥1,000, ¥3,000 or ¥5,000. These can be inserted directly into the automated ticket gates as you enter, with the fare deducted at your destination. Like telephone cards, they are valid for as long as you have credit remaining.

Anyone making regular use of the subway will want to get a **Passnet Card**. In denominations of ¥1,000, ¥3,000 and ¥5,000, the cards, sold at automated ticket machines, are only for use on the subway system. Turnstiles deduct the amount for each trip. When there's only ¥160 remaining on your card, any extra fare will be shown on the screen. Insert the amount and use the new ticket issued to exit the station.

Train

Above ground, **Japan Railways** (JR) operates an equally efficient service, with equivalent frequency and operating hours (5am–1am) on commuter lines. Like the subways, the lines are colour coded.

The **Yamanote Line** (green) makes a long, 35-km (21-mile) oval loop around central Tokyo, with other lines branching out to the suburbs. These are either JR lines or several private train lines, like Keio and Tobu, radiating out to the suburbs from hubs situated around the Yamanote Line.

JR fares start at ¥150. Prepaid **Orange Cards** can be used instead of cash at ticket machines. There are also automated **IO Cards** (short for "In-Out") that can be inserted directly into the ticket slots as you enter and exit the stations. Both cards are available in ¥1,000, ¥3,000 and ¥5,000 denominations. A one-day ticket for unlimited train travel in central Tokyo sells for ¥730.

Station arrivals are announced in Japanese on the trains but are often difficult to make out. There is usually a map above the train doors indicating the stops on the line and the connecting lines. The names of stations are often conveyed in Japanese and English.

Taxis

Taxis are a convenient but pricey way of getting around town. The standard flagfall in Tokyo is ¥660, although deregulation has led to a variation in prices. Anything other than short trips can run from ¥3,000 to ¥5,000. No tipping is expected.

Taxis are readily available on almost every street corner, and at every major hotel and railway station. A red light in the front window signifies that the taxi is available. Roads are narrow and traffic congestion is appalling at rush hour – especially on Fridays or before a holiday.

Most taxi drivers speak only Japanese, so it can be helpful to have your destination written out in Japanese. Many drivers are not native Tokyoites, and are only familiar with central Tokyo and the main landmarks. Do not be surprised if taxis fail to stop when you hail them, particularly at night. Drivers will be looking for profitable long runs out to the suburbs rather than stranded foreigners wanting to return to their hotels. Recommended taxi operators are:
Hinomaru: tel: 03-3814 1111
Nihon Kotsu: tel: 03-5755 2151

TAXIS' AUTO DOORS

There is no need to touch the doors at all when getting in or out of a taxi. The doors are opened and closed by the driver, who operates a lever at the front. After hailing a taxi, wait for the door to open; on arrival, the door will be opened again for you.

Buses

Buses are plentiful in Tokyo, and are often packed well beyond their seating capacities. Buses are not as easy to use as the trains as their routes and destinations are often written only in Japanese *kanji* characters. It is best to ride the buses with someone who knows the system.

River Buses

For river cruises, enquire at **Tokyo River Buses**, tel: 03-5733 4812; www.suijobus.co.jp/english. The most popular itinerary is the trip up the Sumida River to Asakusa (40 minutes). Other routes include a 45-minute cruise around Tokyo Harbour, past the Rainbow Bridge and the Odaiba area to Kasai Sealife Park (55 minutes); and to the Shinagawa Aquarium (35 minutes). All boats depart from the Hinode Pier, located near the Takeshiba Station of the Yurikamome New Transit System (five minutes from Shimbashi). The Sumidagawa River Bus can also be boarded at the Hama Rikyu Garden (near Shimbashi Station).

Look out for *Himiko*, the latest cruise boat on the river. Designed by cartoonist Matsumoto Reiji, this manga-esque vessel is sleek and striking.

Driving

Tokyo is not an easy place to drive in, even when you know the city layout. Except on the crowded expressways, there are few road signs in Romanised Japanese. For getting out of town, it is usually faster to take public transport.
Avis : tel: 03-5550 1011
Hertz: tel: 03-5401 7651

ACCOMMODATION

WHAT'S AVAILABLE, WHERE TO LOOK AND WHAT YOU'LL HAVE TO PAY

Choosing a Hotel

There is never a shortage of places to stay in Tokyo. Accommodation ranges from deluxe Western-style hotels and no-frills business lodgings to budget "capsule hotels". Tokyo's top hotels are among the finest in the world in terms of facilities and service. The older establishments especially exude a distinctive Japanese ambience. Business hotels target Japanese salarymen rather than foreign businessmen, providing bedrooms that are clean and functional, but barely big enough to contain the bed.

Traditional Japanese inns, or *ryokan*, provide a very different experience. At their best (and most expensive), they epitomise the essence of Japanese hospitality. You sleep on *futon* mattresses on *tatami* mats, bathe in a traditional bath, and are served exquisite *kaiseki ryori* meals in your room by attendants in kimono.

On an altogether different level, there are budget Japanese-style inns that give a taste of the traditional, but at a fraction of the cost of a top *ryokan*. These simple family-run lodgings offer personalised service and simple accommodation, and give a close-up view of how many Japanese live.

Capsule hotels offer basic bunk-style accommodations in enclosed cabins just big enough to sit up in. They are not an option for long-term stay (you can't store luggage), but good in an emergency. There are capsule hotels in most areas where salarymen go carousing. Most are for men only, but a few have floors reserved for women.

Hotel Areas

For the sake of simplicity, many visitors choose to stay at places close to the circular Yamanote Line, where many of the main sights are located. Many of the bigger Yamanote stations like Shinjuku, Ikebukuro and Tokyo Station are transportation hubs linked to overground and subway lines that will take you to other sights within or outside the city.

Stations like these are mini-cities in their own right, offering a vibrant package of activities that include shopping, restaurants and nightlife. Each has its own distinctive character. While you may choose an area for a notable feature that interests you (Ueno for museums, Shibuya for fashion, Roppongi for nightlife), these micro-cities work hard at providing something for everyone.

Wherever you decide to stay, you won't be far from a station that is part of Tokyo's massive and efficient transport system.

Prices & Bookings

A complicated sliding tax scale applies with hotels. While most top-grade hotels apply a standard service charge of 10 to 15 percent, there may be other additions. The basic rate on all hotels, however, is a 5 percent purchase tax, plus a ¥100 per night surcharge on rooms costing over ¥10,000 per night; rooms above ¥15,000 are subject to a ¥200 per night surcharge.

Hotel Finder (www.japanhotelfinder.com) and **Japan City Hotel Association** (www.jcha.or.jp/english) allow direct bookings at top and mid-range hotels respectively. The TIC offices at Narita Airport *(see page 237)* can also help with on-the-spot bookings. For more modest lodgings, the **Japan Minshuku Centre** (tel: 03-5858 0103; www.minshuku.jp) can help.

Note: budget travellers should book in advance for February, when thousands of students descend on the city for university entrance exams.

PRICE CATEGORIES

Price categories are for a double room without breakfast and taxes:

Luxury = over ¥30,000
Expensive = ¥20–30,000
Moderate = ¥10–20,000
Budget = under ¥10,000

ACCOMMODATION LISTINGS

IMPERIAL PALACE AREA, YURAKUCHO AND GINZA

HOTELS

Luxury

Conrad Hotel
1-9-1 Higashi-Shimbashi, Minato-ku
Tel: 03-6388 8000
www.conradtokyo.co.jp
Shiodome's high-end accommodation doesn't come more luxurious than this 37-floor marvel. Immaculate service from a multilingual staff, designer rooms with hardwood finishing, private cedar baths, and views across the Hama-Rikyu Garden, Odaiba and the bay are just part of the pampering environment this new hotel provides. (290 rooms)

The Peninsula Tokyo
1-8-1 Yurakucho, Chiyoda-ku
Tel: 03-6270 2888
tokyo.peninsula.com
A branch of the Hong Kong flagship, the Peninsula began receiving bookings a full year before it opened its doors to business at the end of 2007, a measure of the esteem this hotel is held in. Its Yurakucho location, equidistant from the palace and the shopping and restaurant streets of Ginza and served by JR and subway lines, is hard to match. Try to get one of the middle- or upper-level rooms, from where the views are outstanding. (314 rooms)

Hotel Seiyo Ginza
1 Ginza, Chuo-ku
Tel: 03-3535 1111
www.seiyo-ginza.com
More like a private club than a hotel, this 77-room oasis in the heart of Ginza, and within walking distance of the newly developed entertainment and shopping options of the Marunouchi commercial district is intimate and elegant as well as discreet. Expect impeccable service, though the well-equipped rooms are not particularly spacious considering the astronomical rates. A three-minute walk from Ginza-Itchome subway station. (77 rooms)

Imperial Hotel
1-1-1 Uchisaiwai-cho, Chiyoda-ku
Tel: 03-3504 1111
www.imperialhotel.co.jp
Japan's first Western-style hotel (1890) is now in its third incarnation, with top service and restful rooms in the new tower. Its central location near Hibiya Park and subway station, the palace and the chic Ginza shopping area makes it a favourite of both travellers and business people. Though the hotel is showing signs of wear and tear, it remains a prestige site. (1,058 rooms)

Expensive

Mitsui Garden Hotel
13-1 Ginza, Chuo-ku
Tel: 03-3543 1131
www.gardenhotels.co.jp/ginza
Located between Shimbashi with its new Shiodome development and traditional Ginza is one of the area's best-value accommodation options. Managed by worldwide hotel group Novotel, Mitsui Garden Hotel's rooms may be shoebox-size, but with sleek, modern interiors created by Italian designer Piero Lissoni and dazzling views, you're sure to nestle in. (361 rooms)

Palace Hotel
1-1-1 Marunouchi, Chiyoda-ku
Tel: 03-3211 5211
www.palacehotelstokyo.com
Well-established hotel with spacious guest rooms and calmer ambience than at other top hotels. Upper levels allow prime views of the Imperial Palace grounds. So does the Crown Bar on the top floor, a popular place to spend an evening. Convenient for Otemachi subway and Tokyo Station. The interior, despite the sweeping views, can seem a little gloomy at times. (389 rooms)

Moderate

Diamond Hotel
25 Ichibancho, Chiyoda-ku
Tel: 03-3263 2211
www.diamond-hotel.co.jp
Just minutes from the Imperial Palace, the British Embassy and Hanzomon Station. Nice quiet area. The hotel's Chinese restaurant serves authentic favourites like Peking duck. (204 rooms)

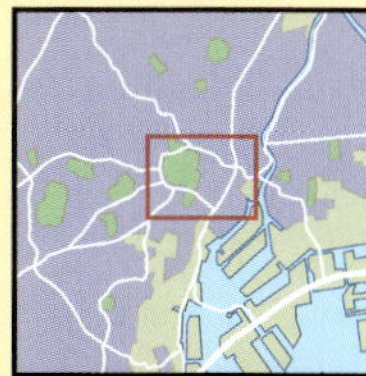
See map pages 74 & 86

Mitsui Urban Hotel
8-6-15 Ginza, Chuo-ku
Tel: 03-3572 4131
www.granvista.co.jp/urban
One of the best of this business hotel chain, right in the backstreets of Ginza. Quite comfortable if you don't mind foregoing some of the frills. Nearest station: Shimbashi. (265 rooms)

Yaesu Fujiya Hotel
2-9-1 Yaesu, Chuo-ku
Tel: 03-3273 2111
www.yaesufujiya.com
A short walk from Tokyo Station, this two–decade old hotel has some elegant touches like its majestic, red-carpeted staircase descending into the lobby. Rooms are relatively small, but each has cable TV with CNN access. (377 rooms)

Yaesu Terminal Hotel
1-5-14 Yaesu, Chuo-ku
Tel: 03-3281 3771
www.yth.jp/english
The rooms in this business hotel may be on the small side, but they are tasteful, cheerful and great value. Excellent amenities, including flat-screen TV. The location, close to Tokyo Station, is a big plus. (117 rooms)

IKEBUKURO, MEIJIRODAI AND SHINJUKU

HOTELS

Luxury

Four Seasons Hotel Chinzan-so
2-10-8 Sekiguchi, Bunkyo-ku
Tel: 03-3943 2222
www.fourseasons.com/tokyo
A superlative low-rise hotel in an unparalleled setting, overlooking the woodlands of the Chinzan-so garden with its pagoda, waterfall and Buddhist statuary. Western luxury is combined with Japanese attention to detail. A drawback is the rather remote location, a 10-minute walk from Edogawabashi station. (283 rooms)

Hyatt Regency Tokyo
2-7-2 Nishi-Shinjuku, Shinjuku-ku
Tel: 03-3348 1234
tokyo.regency.hyatt.com
In the heart of West Shinjuku, a short walk from the main Shinjuku station or the Oedo line's Tochomae station, this is one of Tokyo's most praised hotels, though you wouldn't realise it from the outside. The interior, with its soaring atrium lobby, is a different story. The posh executive floors are exclusive, with separate facilities and king-sized beds. Famed for its superlative service, its a good place to spoil yourself. (766 rooms)

Park Hyatt Hotel
3-7-1-2 Nishi-Shinjuku, Shinjuku-ku
Tel: 03-5322 1234
www.tokyo.park.hyatt.com
Fantastic setting on the top 14 floors of the 52-storey Park Tower with sky walks through glass atriums. Expect top-class facilities and very efficient service. The spacious, well-appointed rooms all have DVDs and videos, but you'll probably spend most of the time staring out the windows. Incidentally, this is where the award-winning film *Lost in Translation* was shot. Home to the excellent New York Grill restaurant. A short stroll from the Oedo line's Tochomae or JR Shinjuku stations. (178 rooms)

Expensive

Hilton Tokyo
6-6-2 Nishi-Shinjuku, Shinjuku-ku
Tel: 03-3344 5111
www.hilton.com
Set among the skyscrapers of west Shinjuku, this is said to be the largest Hilton in Asia. The rooms are Western in style, but with Japanese accents, all with modem lines and cable TV. Just five minutes' walk from JR Shinjuku, Marunouchi line's Nishi-Shinjuku station and the Oedo line's Tochomae station. (806 rooms)

Keio Plaza Hotel
2-2-1 Nishi-Shinjuku, Shinjuku-ku
Tel: 03-3344 0111
www.keioplaza.co.jp
Right next to Tochomae station on the Oedo line, this large, 45-storey skyscraper on the west side of Shinjuku has a good location. This older, established property is well maintained. Health club and business facilities, outdoor swimming pool and an arrray of fine restaurants and bars. (1,450 rooms)

Moderate

Shinjuku Prince Hotel
1-30-1 Kabuki-cho, Shinjuku-ku
Tel: 03-3205 1111
www.princejapan.com
Look down from your room at the goings-on in Kabuki-cho, the heart of Shinjuku nightlife. Right next to JR Shinjuku station, the location may not be picturesque, but there is never a dull moment in this part of town. Adequate rooms, good facilities. The 25th floor restaurant has the best views this side of Shinjuku. (571 rooms)

Sunshine City Prince Hotel
3-1-5 Higashi-Ikebukuro, Toshima-ku
Tel: 03-3988 1111
www.princejapan.com
Efficient, well-run and well-equipped with business facilities. Conveniently located in the Sunshine City complex, which is a hive of activity with its array of shops and restaurants. JR Ikebukuro station is an eight-minute walk away. (1,166 rooms)

Budget

Green Plaza Capsule Hotel
1-29-2 Kabuki-cho, Shinjuku-ku.
Tel: 03-5457 0109
Although it's just minutes from Shinjuku JR station, this hotel is designed to

See map pages 96 & 102

accommodate those who miss their last train home, a common occurrence. Located in the heart of Kabuki-cho. Surprisingly comfortable once you get used to the idea of being supine in a plastic case. (600 rooms)

Kimi Ryokan
2-36-8 Ikebukuro, Toshima-ku
Tel: 03-3971 3766
One of Tokyo's best loved budget places, the helpful English-speaking staff are a godsend. Clean communal toilets and bathrooms. This inexpensive, homely *ryokan* is very popular, so book in advance. Located in a quiet backstreet off Tokiwa-dori, and a 10-minute walk to JR Ikebukuro station. (38 rooms)

Tokyo International Youth Hostel
Central Plaza, 18F, 21-1 Kagurakashi, Shinjuku-ku
Tel: 03-3235 1107
www.tokyo-ih.jp
If the idea of a youth hostel in a skyscraper appeals, and you don't mind sharing a room, the clean, dormitory-style bunk beds here may suit. Right next to JR Iidabashi station. No access to the building between 10am and 3pm, and there is also an 11pm curfew to bear in mind. (33 rooms)

SHIBUYA

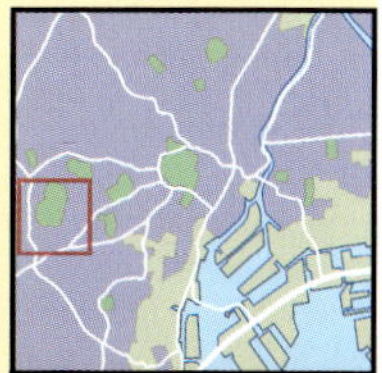

See map page 120

HOTELS

Luxury

Cerulean Tower Tokyu Hotel
26-1, Sakuragaoka-cho, Shibuya-ku
Tel: 03-3476 3000
www.ceruleantower-hotel.com
Shibuya's most upmarket hotel has the finest views in this part of town. The hotel section of the tower runs from the 19th to 37th floors. Spacious, fully-equipped and tastefully decorated rooms. On the premises are bars and several Japanese and Western eating options, including a modern *kaiseki* restaurant. There is even a Noh theatre on the premises. Expect excellent service. A three-minute walk from JR Shibuya station's south exit. (414 rooms)

Expensive

Arimax
11-15, Kamiyama-cho, Shibuya-ku
Tel: 03-5454 1122
www.arimaxhotelshibuya.co.jp
A small hotel with elite European pretensions, the atmosphere is that of a mellow cigar club: pleasantly intimate but sedative. Neo-classical and English Regency-style room interiors with full facilities. Notable in-house French restaurant called Polyantha. A quick 10-minute walk west of JR Shibuya's Hachiko exit. (23 rooms)

Moderate

Hotel Mets Shibuya
3-29-17 Shibuya, Shibuya-ku
Tel: 03-3409 0011
www.hotelmets.jp/shibuya
Besides the moderate cost, there are several advantages to staying in this roomy, mid-range business hotel: its location beside JR Shibuya station, Internet access in each unit and a price that includes breakfast. (191 rooms)

Shibuya Excel Tokyu
1-12-2 Dogenzaka, Shibuya-ku
Tel: 03-5457 0109
www.tokyuhotelsjapan.com
Well-priced accommodation for business travellers and those who want to be in the thick of Shibuya. A part of the Mark City complex attached to the JR Shibuya station. Offers two floors solely for women. Bar, restaurants and all the amenities you would expect from this chain. (408 rooms)

Budget

Capsule Land Shibuya
1-19-14 Dogenzaka, Shibuya-ku
Tel: 03-3464 1777
A 15-minute walk from JR Shibuya station, this capsule hotel might be a last resort, or a once-in-a-lifetime experience. Adequate facilities: communal showers, capsule TVs, coin lockers, a restaurant and vending machines dispensing beer and noodles. Men only. (140 capsules)

Shibuya City Hotel
1-1 Maruyamacho, Shibuya, Shibuya-ku
Tel: 03-5489 1010
A small, friendly boutique hotel seven minutes from Shibuya Station. Opposite the Bunkamura, the location is ideal for taking in the arts, shopping and nightlife of Shibuya. (57 rooms)

ROPPONGI AND AKASAKA

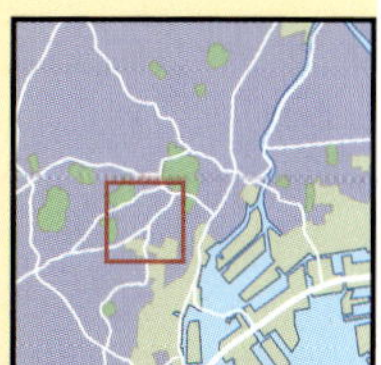

See map page 132

HOTELS

Luxury

Grand Hyatt
6-10-3 Roppongi, Minato-ku
Tel: 03-4333 1234
tokyo.grand.hyatt.com
The newest (and grandest) of the three Hyatt hotels in Tokyo, this cavernous property is truly spectacular in an understated manner. Wood, glass and marble in the public areas form clutter-free and contemporary lines. Bedrooms feature flat-screen TVs (including one in the bathroom), CD players and high-speed modem connection plus capacious bathrooms. An array of in-house restaurants and facilities means you never have to leave the premises. Roppongi station is a three-minute walk away. (389 rooms)

Grand Prince Hotel Akasaka
1-2 Kioi-cho, Chiyoda-ku
Tel: 03-3234 1111
www.princejapan.com
The showpiece of the Prince Hotel chain has an ultra-modernist design, courtesy of Kenzo Tange, and great cityscape views from every room. Elegant furnishings and decor with a decidedly contemporary touch. Complex also includes a convention centre and restaurants. (761 rooms)

Hotel New Otani
4-1 Kioi-cho, Chiyoda-ku
Tel: 03-3265 1111
www. newotani.co.jp/en
A massive complex with many restaurants and extensive Japanese gardens, one need never leave the hotel. On the borderline between Akasaka, but within a 10-minute walk of the Imperial Palace, the location is ideal for both sightseeing and nightlife. Though

beginning to show signs of wear and tear, especially on its exterior, its luxury remains subtle and understated. Former guests include diplomats, business leaders and rock stars. (1,600 rooms)

Hotel Okura
2-10-4 Toranomon, Minato-ku
Tel: 03-3582 0111
www.hotelokura.co.jp
Long held to be one of the world's great hotels, it sits in the middle of an area favoured by embassies. Also close to the Roppongi restaurant and nightlife district. An atmospheric blend of traditional Japanese decor and 21st-century facilities, the Okura is also famous for its cuisine. A five-minute walk from Roppongi-Itchome station. (858 rooms)

InterContinental ANA Tokyo
1-12-33 Akasaka, Minato-ku
Tel: 03-3505 1111
www.ichotelsgroup.com
This five-star hotel owned by All Nippon Airways is set in Ark Hills, an office and shopping complex close to the business and entertainment districts (and the interminable drone of the Shuto Expressway), just two minutes' walk from the Tameike-Sanno subway station. The huge, brightly lit lobby is a foretaste of the large rooms; those on the upper storeys have great views. (901 rooms)

Expensive

Akasaka Excel Hotel Tokyu
2-14-3 Nagatacho, Chiyoda-ku
Tel: 03-3580 2311
www.tokyuhotelsjapan.com
Reliable quality and efficient service – and very reasonable rates compared to the deluxe hotels nearby. Rooms away from the road are quieter. Good shops and restaurants in the downstairs mall, and bars up on the upper levels. The Akasaka-Mitsuke station is right in the basement. (293 rooms)

Moderate

Akasaka Yoko Hotel
6-14-12 Akasaka, Minato-ku
Tel: 03-3586 4050
www.yokohotel.co.jp
The friendly Yoko is well positioned for visits not only to Roppongi's restaurants, galleries and nighttime entertainment, but also to two famous Shinto shrines: Nogi and Hie. Though not large, the rooms are affordable, clean and comfortable, with Internet connection. (245 rooms)

Arca Torre
6-1-23 Roppongi, Minato-ku
Tel: 03-3404 5111
www.arktower.co.jp
Ideal for nightlife addicts, this is located close to the busy Roppongi Crossing, making it a little noisy at times. But the large semi-double beds in the standard single rooms perhaps make up for it. Helpful, multilingual staff. (77 rooms)

Hotel Ibis
7-14-4 Roppongi, Minato-ku
Tel: 03-3403 4411
www.ibis-hotel.com
A good, mid-range option in the heart of the Roppongi area and right above all the action. Well-designed, if smallish rooms. Good business facilities, including modem ports and multilingual staff.Good value for this part of Tokyo. (182 rooms)

Shiba Park Hotel
1-5-10 Shiba-Koen, Minato-ku
Tel: 03-3433 4141
www.shibaparkhotel.com
A little-known hotel, despite its attractive location just four minutes from the Onarimon subway and the impressive Sangedatsu Gate leading into Zojo-ji Temple. Quiet and cosy, and the staff here are helpful and attentive. (318 rooms)

Budget

Asia Center of Japan Hotel
8-10-32 Akasaka, Minato-ku
Tel: 03-3402 6111
www.asiacenter.or.jp
Popular lodging for low-budget travellers amid the lively buzz of a student dorm atmosphere. Reservations can be hard to secure. Rooms in the newer wing are a notch up from the older, cramped ones. A few minutes' walk from Nogizaka subway, the location is good for both Roppongi and Aoyoma areas. (71 rooms)

SHINAGAWA, MEGURO AND EBISU

HOTELS

Luxury

Meguro Gajoen
1-8-1 Shimo Meguro, Meguro-ku
Tel: 03-3491 4111
www.megurogajoen.co.jp
A very old and beautiful *ryokan*, the traditional lodgings here are very expensive. Lovely gardens, original art work on the walls and ceilings and a refined atmosphere add to the sublime experience. Both European and Japanese-style rooms available, but ask for the latter. Only a three-minute walk from Meguro JR station. (60 rooms)

Westin Hotel Tokyo
1-4-1 Mita, Meguro-ku
Tel: 03-5423 7000
www.starwoodhotels.com
Spacious guest rooms, sophisticated interiors, personalised service and peaceful setting opposite a fake chateau (housing a restaurant) and the soaring office blocks of Yebisu Garden Place. The Westin models itself after grand European-style hotels, with gracefully designed rooms, an elegant lobby and tastefully decorated public spaces. (445 rooms)

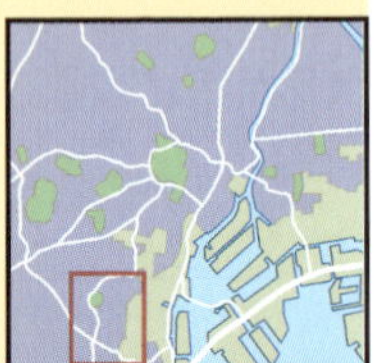
See map page 140

Expensive

Grand Prince Hotel New Takanawa
3-13-1 Takanawa, Minato-ku

Tel: 03-3442 1111
www.princejapan.com
One in a complex of three Prince hotels all occupying the same beautifully landscaped gardens. The facilities here are uniformly excellent, the rooms luxurious and spacious. The service is highly reputed. Guests at one of the Prince buildings can use all the facilities in the other two. Located in an affluent residential district, there is not much nightlife in this area. It is, however, only five minutes' walk from the JR Shinagawa station. (946 rooms)

Le Meridien Pacific Tokyo
3-13-3 Takanawa, Minato-ku
Tel: 03-3445 6711
www.starwoodhotels.com
A gleaming high-rise dominating the Shinagawa district, with 41 suites and six restaurants. Its 30th-floor Sky Lounge affords exciting night views over Tokyo Bay. A large, manicured garden adds to the sense of tranquility in an otherwise lively area just five minutes from the new Shiodome shopping and leisure complex. (954 rooms)

Sheraton Miyako Hotel Tokyo
1-1-50 Shiroganedai, Minato-ku
Tel: 03-3447 3111
www.miyakohotels.ne.jp
Affiliated with Kyoto's famous Miyako Hotel, this Tokyo version successfully attempts to replicate the prototype. Located in a pleasant, quiet neighbourhood near the Happo-en Garden and the National Park for Nature Study, this is a lovely retreat. Only 10 minutes from Shirokanedai subway station. (500 rooms)

Moderate

Haneda Excel Hotel Tokyu
3-4-2 Haneda Airport, Ota-ku
Tel: 03-5756 6000
www.panpacific.com/Haneda
Located next to Haneda Airport, this is a good option if you are planning to fly to other domestic destinations early in the day. Otherwise, the ambience is much the same as at other airport hotels around the world. Shuttle service to both terminals. (415 rooms)

Hotel Excellent
1-9-5 Ebisu-Nishi, Minato-ku
Tel: 03-5458 0087
Nothing fancy about this hotel with its plain, rather small rooms and only basic facilities, so why is it so popular? Besides its helpful staff and attractive rates, its location near the Yamanote Line, just one stop from Shibuya, with access to trendy Ebisu, seems to be the answer. Also good for exploring the western reaches of Tokyo. Close to Ebisu station's west exit. (127 rooms)

Budget

Sansuiso Ryokan
2-9-5 Higashi-Gotanda, Shinagawa-ku
Tel: 03-3441 7475
Cosy *ryokan* just a five-minute walk from the Gotanda station. Japanese-style rooms, with private or shared facilities. (19 rooms)

UENO, YANAKA AND ASAKUSA

HOTELS

Moderate

Asakusa View Hotel
3-17-1 Nishi-Asakusa, Taito-ku
Tel: 03-3842 2117
www.viewhotels.co.jp/asakusa
Nice hotel with great location for sightseeing and shopping in downtown Asakusa. Traditional Japanese rooms are also available on the 6th floor, where there are aerial gardens. The bar on the 28th floor offers an excellent river view. (338 rooms)

Hotel Sardonyx Ueno
6-6-7 Ueno, Taito-ku
Tel: 03-3833 7200
www.hotel-sardonyx.com
Adequate and comfortable rooms at this hotel, where each room is equipped with broadband Internet access and an LCD television. Conveniently located within walking distance of three JR stations in the charming Ueno district and a 10-minute walk to Ueno Park. Book online to receive a special discount.

Ueno First City Hotel
1-14-8 Ueno, Taito-ku
Tel: 03-3831 8215
www.uenocity-hotel.com
Close to the Yushima station's exit 6, this is a smart business hotel that prides itself on its comfort and efficiency. Within walking distance of both the Ueno district and the area around the Yushima Tenjin shrine. Look out for its red-brick façade. The restaurant, bar and coffee shop are as intimate as the hotel itself. (77 rooms)

Budget

Ryokan Katsutaro Annex
3-8-4 Yanaka, Taito-ku
Tel: 03-3828 2500
www.katsutaro.com
This modern *ryokan* combines the best of Japanese décor with tatami flooring and paper screen windows, private bathrooms and broadband Internet access in each room. Free Internet usage and coffee in the entrance area. Just around the corner from Yanaka Ginza, a lively street with craft and tea shops. (11 rooms)

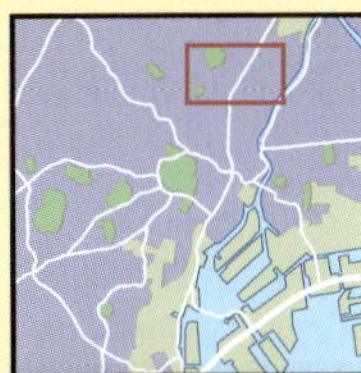
See map pages 148 & 160

Sawanoya Ryokan
2-3-11 Yanaka, Taito-ku
Tel: 03-3822 2251
www.tctv.ne.jp/members/sawanoya
Small but comfortable rooms with tatami mats in this friendly *ryokan* in a residential neighbourhood close to the old quarter of Yanaka. The ¥300 self-service breakfast is good value. A seven-minute walk from the Nezu subway station. (12 rooms)

SUIDOBASHI, OCHANOMIZU, KANDA AND AKIHABARA

HOTELS

Expensive

Hotel Metropolitan Edmont
3-10-8 Iidabashi, Chiyoda-ku
Tel: 03-3237 1111
www.edmont.co.jp
A five-minute walk southwest of JR Suidobashi station, this large hotel is efficiently run with comfortable, well-equipped rooms, but is a little impersonal. Outside the mainstream area – thus few foreign tourists – but still easy accessible to the JR and subway lines. Within walking distance of the Yasukuni Shrine and the Kanda-Jimbocho bookstore district. (450 rooms)

Moderate

Hotel My Stage Ochanomizu
2-10 Kanda, Awajicho, Chiyoda-ku
Tel: 03-3258 3911
Quiet location and yet only a five-minute walk to the frazzle of Akihabara's electronics stores. Japanese and Western restaurant on site. A three-minute walk to JR Ochanomizu station. (98 rooms)

Tokyo Green Hotel Ochanomizu
2-6 Kanda-Awajicho, Chiyoda-ku
Tel: 03-3255 4161
www.greenhotel.co.jp
Remarkably good value given its location, a stone's throw away from the teeming Ochanomizu streets, Nikolai Cathedral and the Kanda-Jimbocho used-book district. The wood and paper-screen interiors create a tranquil setting, and the friendly bilingual staff are a bonus. (207 rooms)

Yama-no-ue (Hilltop) Hotel
1-1 Surugadai, Kanda, Chiyoda-ku
Tel: 03-3293 2311
www.yamanoue-hotel.co.jp
Five minutes southwest of JR Ochanomizu station, this secluded hotel has genuine period charm. A favourite of writers and artists, including late novelist Yukio Mishima. The service is impeccable, the cuisine of a high standard. On clear days, the upper-storey rooms have good views of Mount Fuji. (75 rooms)

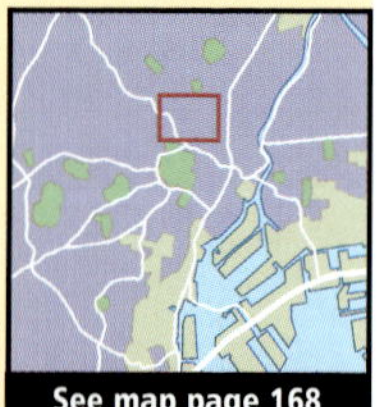

See map page 168

Budget

Sakura Hotel
2-21-4, kanda-Jimbocho, Chiyoda-ku.
Tel: 03-3264 2777
www.sakura-hotel.co.jp
Given its location, this is a surprisingly good deal. Although the rooms – all non-smoking – are tiny, it's popular with salarymen and tourists. Close to exit A6 of Jimbocho station. English-speaking staff. (41 rooms)

SUMIDA RIVER AND TOKYO BAYSIDE

HOTELS

Luxury

InterContinental Tokyo Bay
1-16-2 Kaigan, Minato-ku
Tel: 03-5404 2222
www.intercontinental.com
Overlooking the mouth of the Sumida River and Tokyo waterfront, all its rooms have panoramic views of Odaiba island and Rainbow Bridge. Rooms are spacious and stylishly appointed. The hotel is part of a complex that faces the east exit of Takeshiba station; a short walk to the Hama-Rikyu Garden. (339 rooms)

Le Meridien Grand Pacific Tokyo
2-6-1 Daiba, Minato-ku
Tel: 03-5500 6711
www.starwoodhotels.com
Right opposite Odaiba station's south exit, the five-star Meridien is another towering hotel on Odaiba with breathtaking views of the bay and waterfront skyscrapers from its middle to upper level rooms and the 30th floor Sky Lounge. Luxuriously appointed rooms and superb service. Situated between Decks Tokyo and the Museum of Maritime Science. (884 rooms)

Hotel Nikko Tokyo
1-9-1 Daiba, Minato-ku
Tel: 03-5500 5511
www.jalhotels.com
Smack bang in front of Odaiba station on the Yurikamome line, and a stroll up from the leisure complexes of Palette Town and Aquacity, the Nikko has one of the best views of the waterfront. The terrace restaurant and Captain's Bar are romantic settings popular with couples. First-rate service and food. Convenient access to all Odaiba sights. (453 rooms)

Moderate

Tokyo Bay Ariake Washington Hotel
3-1 Ariake, Koto-ku
Tel: 03-5564 0111
www.wh-rsv.com
A comfortable business hotel on Odaiba, this has the same facilities found in its other branches, but this one, at 20 storeys, is one of the larger ones. Several Western and Japanese restaurants on site. Popular with those attending exhibitions at the Tokyo Big Sight venue next door. Located a short walk away from Ariake station. (761 rooms)

See map pages 178 & 188

ACTIVITIES

THE ARTS, NIGHTLIFE, SHOPPING, SPORTS, SIGHTSEEING TOURS AND CHILDREN'S ACTIVITIES

THE ARTS

Traditional Theatre

National Theatre
4-1 Hayabusa-cho, Chiyoda-ku
Tel: 03-3265 7411 (enquiries); 03-3230 3000 (reservations)
Two auditoriums. The Large Hall stages *kabuki* for eight months of the year. *Bunraku* performances are given in the Small Hall for the remaining months. English-language summaries of the plot are included in the programmes; earphone guide available.

Kabuki Theatre (Kabuki-za)
4-12-15 Ginza, Chuo-ku
Tel: 03-3541 3131 (information); 03-5565 6000 (tickets)
The most accessible place to watch *kabuki*. Performances can last up to five hours (with intermissions). For a taste of the art form, buy a fourth-floor ticket for just one act. If you like what you see, get a seat in the main auditorium: the most expensive are those near the stage or the *hana-michi* (walkway), where the actors can be seen close up. English programme and earphone guides available. Times: about 11am–4pm and 5–9pm.

Cerulean Tower Noh Theatre
26-1 Sakuragaoka-Cho, Shibuya-ku
Tel: 03-3476 3000
This beautiful *noh* theatre hosts professional as well as amateur *noh* and *kyogen* performances (without English translations).

National Noh Theatre
4-18-1 Sendagaya, Shibuya-ku
Tel: 03-3423 1331
Noh performances are given about once a week. A short English programme is available. Times: usually during the afternoon (call for details).

Kanze No-Gakudo
1-16-4 Shoto, Shibuya-ku
Tel: 03-3469 6241
The Kanze school of *noh* is the oldest and is said to be the closest to the original form.

Other Theatres

Bunkamura Theatre Cocoon
2-24-1 Dogenzaka, Shibuya-ku
Tel: 03-3477 9999
A highly regarded dance venue, the Cocoon stages lively international acts from flamenco to modern experimental dance.

Die Pratze (Azabu)
2-12 Nishi-gokencho, Shinjuku-ku
Tel: 03-3235 7990
This black box theatre for avant-garde performances and *butoh* also hosts the annual, experimental Die Pratze Dance Festival.

Imperial Theatre
3-1-1 Marunouchi, Chiyoda-ku
Tel: 03-3213 7221
Long-established venue for everything from Ibsen to Yukio Mishima's *noh* dramas.

Kinokuniya Hall
3-17-7 Shinjuku, Shinjuku-ku
Tel: 03-3354 0141
A place for Japanese dramas. Fairly eclectic in its presentations, which run from classic dramas to contemporary works.

Meiji Theatre (Meiji-za)
2-31-1 Nihombashi-Hamacho, Chuo-ku
Tel: 03-3660 3939
Modern plays as well as samurai costume dramas staged here.

New National Theatre
1-1-1 Honmachi, Shibuya-ku
Tel: 03-5351 3011
Divided into the Opera House, Playhouse and Pit, the first is for modern dramas by both Japanese and foreign playwrights, the latter two are modern dance venues.

Shimbashi Embujo
6-12-2 Ginza, Chuo-ku
Tel: 03-3541 2600
Low-brow, swashbuckling samurai dramas, but also performances of "Super-Kabuki", by star performer Ichikawa Enosuke – a high-octane version of the original, *kabuki* drama.

Suehirotei
3-6-12 Shinjuku, Shinjuku-ku
Tel: 03-3351 2974
One of Tokyo's last remaining theatres for *rakugo*, a genre of humorous storytelling.

Takarazuka Theatre
1-1-3 Yurakucho, Chiyoda-ku
Tel: 03-5251 2001
Campy dramas and musicals from an all-women troupe who cross-dress to extraordinary effect.

Tokyo International Players
Mobile tel: 090-6009 4171
www.tokyoplayers.org
Very professional performances in English of contemporary and older plays from members of the foreign and Japanese communities. The venues change regularly. Check the website listing and city magazines like *Metropolis* and *JSelect*.

Music

Classical

Bunkamura Orchard Hall
2-24-1 Dogenzaka, Shibuya-ku 150
Tel: 03-3477 9150

Casals Hall
1-6 Kanda-Surugadai, Chiyoda-ku
Tel: 03-3294 1229

BUYING TICKETS

The major ticketing companies have outlets in all shopping areas and department stores. The two largest are **Ticket Pia** and **Ticket Saison**. Most tickets for concerts and other events can also be purchased at convenience stores (Lawsons, 7-11, Family Mart), but the transactions are in Japanese.

Ginza
Kyukyodo: tel: 03-3571 0401, open daily.
Matsuya Dept Store: tel: 03-3567 8888, closed Tues.

Shinjuku
Isetan Dept Store: tel: 03-3352 1111, closed Wed.
Keio Dept Store: tel: 03-3343 1801, open daily.

Shibuya
Seibu Dept Store: tel: 03-3462 0111, closed Wed.

Ikebukuro
Seibu Dept Store: tel: 03-3981 0052, closed Tues.
Tobu Dept Store: tel: 03-3981 2211, closed Wed.

NHK Hall
2-1 Jinan, Shibuya-ku
Tel: 03-3465 1111

Suntory Hall
1-13-1 Akasaka, Minato-ku
Tel: 03-3584 3100

Tokyo Bunka Kaikan
5-45 Ueno Park, Taito-ku
Tel: 03-3828 2111

Tokyo Metropolitan Art Space
1-8-1 Nishi-Ikebukuro, Toshima-ku
Tel: 03-5391 2111

Tokyo Opera City
3-2-2 Nishi-Shinjuku, Shinjuku-ku
Tel: 03-5353 0770

Tokyo Symphony Orchestra
www.tokyosymphony.com/e-tokyo
Arguably Tokyo's finest orchestra. Although it stages concerts of world classics, it tries to highlight recent work by contemporary Japanese composers as well.

Tea Ceremonies

Matcha, the frothy, slightly acerbic green brew served as part of the proceedings in *chanoyu*, the tea ceremony, can be sampled at several international hotels in Tokyo, or among the tea-green foliage of some of the city's Japanese gardens. One of the most elegant settings is the Gazebo in the midst of the Nezu Institute's *(see page 114)* leafy garden, where *macha* is served with a traditional bean paste sweet. Open Tues–Sun 9.30am– 4.30pm. Other places to try (advance reservations required) are:

Chado Kaikan
3-39-17 Takadanobaba, Shinjuku-ku
Tel: 03-3361 2446
Mon–Thurs 10.30am–2.30pm. Fee; one-hour session.

Imperial Hotel (Toko-an)
1-1-1 Uchisaiwai-cho, Chiyoda-ku, (4F of Main Wing)
Tel: 03-3504 1111, ext. 5858
Open Mon–Sat 10am–4pm. Fee charged for 20-minute session.

Hotel New Otani
4-1 Kioi-cho, Chiyoda-ku, (7F of Tower Bldg)
Tel: 03-3265 1111, ext. 2443
Thurs–Sat 11am–noon, 1–4pm. Fee; 15–20 minute sessions.

NIGHTLIFE

Rock & Pop

Japan, one of the world's largest music markets, has been an essential port of call for Western rock groups since the Beatles played at the Budokan back in the mid-1960s. While the best-known performers can sell out at mega-venues such as the Big Egg (Tokyo Dome) at the drop of a hat, it is often possible to catch big names playing at relatively intimate settings.

Hibiya Kokaido
1-3 Hibiya-Koen, Chiyoda-ku
Tel: 03-3591 6388

Nippon Budokan
2-3 Kitanomaru-Koen, Chiyoda-ku
Tel: 03-3216 0781

NHK Hall
2-1 Jinnan, Shibuya-ku
Tel: 03-3465 1111

O-East
2-14-9 Dogenzaka, Shibuya-ku
Tel: 03-5458 4681
The newest venue for live concerts in the youth culture mecca of Shibuya is also its best.

Shibuya Kokaido
1-1 Udagawacho, Shibuya-ku
Tel: 03-3463 5001

Tokyo Dome (Big Egg)
1-3 Koraku, Bunkyo-ku
Tel: 03-5800 9999

Tokyo International Forum
3-5-1 Marunouchi, Chiyoda-ku
Tel: 03-5221 9000

Jazz & Live Music

There is an enthusiastic and knowledgeable audience for jazz in Tokyo – and some excellent clubs to enjoy it in – like sophisticated and world-class Blue Note. At the other end of the spectrum are "live houses", where rock bands are the mainstay.

Aoyama

Blue Note Tokyo
6-3-16 Minami-Aoyama, Minato-ku
Tel: 03-5485 0088
www.bluenote.co.jp

Top international acts appear in this sophisticated venue. The ambience is much like that at the original venue in the US, and the performances are top notch. Despite the high entrance fees, the club is always full.

Body & Soul
B1, 6-13-9 Minami-Aoyama, Minato-ku
Tel: 03-5466 3348
www.bodyandsoul.co.jp
A favourite with music industry folk, the vibes here are exclusively jazz. The acts start quite late – at around 8.30pm.

Roppongi/Akasaka

B-Flat Akasaka
Akasaka 6-6-4, Minato-ku
Tel: 03-5563 2563
www.bflat.jp
A classic jazz club in the nightlife district of Akasaka. Features top local acts and the occasional international artiste.

Birdland
B2, 3-10-3 Roppongi, Minato-ku
Tel: 03-3478 3456
One of the older jazz and fusion clubs in town, Birdland may not be quite as trendy as it was a few years ago, but it manages to put on a good evening's worth of entertainment, with both live acts and DJ spots from some of Tokyo's best known acts.

Shibuya

Club Quattro
Parco Quattro, 5F, 32-13 Udagawacho, Shibuya-ku
Tel: 03-3477 8750
www.net-flyer.com
Strangely located in the Parco department store – you take the lift to reach this venue. International rock and blues bands as well as local groups play here.

Crocodile
B1, 6-18-8 Jingumae, Shibuya-ku
Tel: 03-3499 5205
One of the oldest live houses in Tokyo, Crocodile has expanded its repertoire over the years to include not just rock, but whatever happens to be hip, including rap bands, Latin combos, jazz and everything in between.

Gig-antic
Sound Forum Bldg, 2F, 3-20-15, Shibuya, Shibuya-ku
Tel: 03-5466 9339
Tiny venue popular with new and emerging bands, though some of the older established hardcore rock acts regularly perform here.

JZ Brat
Cerulean Tower Tokyu Hotel, 2F, 26-1 Sakuragaoka-cho, Shibuya-ku
Tel: 03-5728 0168
Top-name international and home-grown acts at this small but acoustically perfect venue.

La.Mama Shibuya
Premier Dogenzaka Bldg, B1F, 1-15-3, Dogenzaka, Shibuya-ku
Tel: 03-3464 0801
A longtime feature of the vibrant music scene in Shibuya, La.mama has moved away in recent years from hardcore rock and punk acts to the softer world of J-Pop.

Liquid Room
3-16-6 Higashi, Shibuya-ku
Tel: 03-5464 0800
www.liquidroom.net
Relocated from seamy Kabuki-cho to trendy Ebisu, Liquid Room is now a basement live house with a lounge bar. The location has changed, but the excellent lineup of rock concerts and DJs hasn't.

Clubs

Japanese youth are amazingly well clued in to the latest music styles, and Tokyo has developed a vibrant club scene.

Roppongi

Gas Panic Club
2F, 3-14-11 Roppongi, Minato-ku
Tel: 03-3402 7054
www.gaspanic.co.jp
A dance club and café that puts on both local and foreign DJ acts, hosts private parties and special events like tattoo nights. Second outlet at Shibuya's Centergai (tel: 03-3462 9099).

Space Lab Yellow
Cesaurus Nishi-Azabu Bldg, 1-10-11 Nishi-Azabu, Minato-ku
Tel: 03-3479 0690
A fairly large multi-purpose venue that serves as a space for parties, fashion events, disco and DJ evenings, as well as live bands. Like most of these centrally located places, it can be very crowded at the weekend. Strong on techno and Brazilian jazz.

Shibuya

Air
2-11 Sarugaku, Shibuya-ku
Tel: 03-5784 3386
www.air-tokyo.com
In between Shibuya and trendy Daikanyama, Air is a comfortable, mid-sized dance club that competes with Tokyo's leading venues for young clubbers looking to dance to house, trance, drum and bass and hip-hop.

Club Asia
1-8 Maruyama-cho, Shibuya-ku
Tel: 03-5458 5963
www.clubasia.co.jp/asia
The dance floors and bars on different levels make for an interesting design, though the music can get warped in the process. The club gets booked up for a lot of private events, so it's always best to call in advance.

Eggman
1-6-8 Jinnan, Shibuya-ku
Tel: 03-3496 1561
Talent spotters come here to see and sometimes sign up local acts. Many have gone on to greater things in the world of Japanese rock and J-Pop. Centrally located in the trendy Jinnan district.

La Fabrique
16-9 Udagawacho, Shibuya-ku
Tel: 03-5428 5100
www.lafabrique.jp
Stylish French culture outpost transforms itself from a chic restaurant into a throbbing house club on weekend nights. Lines form around the block for high-profile local and international DJs.

Milk
B1/2, 1-13-3 Ebisu-Nishi, Shibuya-ku
Tel: 03-5458 2826
www.milk-tokyo.com
Although the music these days is mostly house and techno, Milk still hosts its fair share of local and international rock live acts. Three cantilevered floors offer

good views of what's going on above and below.

Womb
2-16 Maruyama-cho, Shibuya-ku
Tel: 03-5459 0039
www.womb.co.jp
Since opening five years ago, this cavernous club has established itself as one of the serious dance culture venues in Tokyo, with DJs like Richie Hawtin and Roni Size dropping in on a regular basis. What it lacks in atmosphere it makes up for with excellent music.

Shinjuku

Club Complex Code
4F, 1-19-2 Kabuki-cho, Shinjuku-ku
Tel: 03-3209 0702
Along with Velfarre in Roppongi, this is one of the biggest clubs in Tokyo, if not Japan, with a similar 2,000-person capacity. Three dance floors and live stage for occasional band performances.

Other Areas

Ageha
2-2-10 Shin-Kiba, Koto-ku
Tel: 03-5534 1515
www.ageha.com
Ageha is the name that Studio Coast adopts on weekends, when it transforms itself into Tokyo's biggest dance club bar, with three separate dance rooms and a poolside bar. Clubbers are bussed in from Shibuya by the thousands for massive parties.

Fai
B2F, 5-10-1 Minami-Aoyama, Minato-ku
Tel: 03-3486 4910
An eclectic range of music rules here, but the emphasis is on nostalgia, with tracks from the 1970s and 80s.

Maniac Love
Tera A Omotesando Bldg, B1F, 5-10-6 Minami-Aoyama, Minato-ku
Tel: 03-3406 1166
A massive, techno-equipped dance floor that attracts a discerning crowd. Hosts a number of celebrity DJ events, including its legendary Sunday morning bashes that reach their peak around 5am. You have to be a serious party animal for this one.

Bars & Pubs

There's no shortage of watering holes in Tokyo, from local restaurant-bars called *izakaya* – the haunt of overworked Japanese salarymen – and specialist *sake* bars to sleek martini bars filled with young Japanese in their designer togs. Tokyo is also well respresented with British and Irish pubs serving draught ale and predictable but reliable pub grub.

Ginza

Mizuho
5-5-8, Ginza, Chuo-ku
Tel: 03-3571 2660
Tucked into a narrow building along Ginza's West 5th Street, close by the Chanel and Hermès stores, Mizuho specialises in only the Fukumitsuya brand of *sake*. Try the slightly cloudy variety called *ukiyo* for starters. Also serves food specially created to accompany *sake*.

Old Imperial Bar
1-1-1, Uchisaiwai-cho, Hibiya, Chiiyoda-ku
Tel: 03-3504 1111
A legendary bar in the Imperial Hotel. Part of the design has been preserved from the original Lloyd Wright design that was lost in the 1960s. Everyone from Igor Stravinsky to Tom Wolfe has patronised this bar.

Roppongi

Agave
7-15-10, Clover Bldg, B1F, Roppongi, Minato-ku
Tel: 03-3497 0229
A Mexican and Latin inclination is evident here in the decor, music and astonishing selection of tequilas. Cocktails like mojitos and daiquiris, and the other rum-based concoctions suggest strong Caribbean leanings.

Geronimo
7-14-10, 2F, Roppongi, Minato-ku
Tel: 03-3478 7449
A short stroll from Exit 4 of the Roppongi station, this is a very popular bar for both expats and local business people. Happy hours (6–8pm) are especially crowded when the drinks drop to half price.

Fiesta
7-9-3, Crest Roppongi-1, 3F, Roppongi, Minato-ku
Tel: 03-5410 3008
An "international karaoke bar" near the Roppongi Crossing, just one minute from Roppongi station. Fiesta boasts over 10,000 songs from all over the world.

Paddy Foley's
Roi Bldg B1, 5-5-1 Roppongi, Minato-ku
Tel: 03-3423 2250
Because of its Roppongi location, Paddy's can get quite congested even on weekdays. That says something though for its fine Guinness and other Irish brews, and its dependable, no-frills British food. One of the oldest British pubs in town, and one of the best places to meet locals.

Shibuya

The Aldgate
World Bldg, B1, 12-9 Udagawa-cho, Shibuya-ku
Tel: 03-3462 2983
Eastend London-style pub in the heart of trendy Shibuya. Besides the familiar French ales and stouts, the menu of pub grub includes the usual fish 'n' chips and Aldgate's vegetarian dishes. Huge collection of British rock CDs and EPL soccer matches on TV add to its appeal.

Cozmo's
1-6-3, Shibuya, Shibuya-ku
Tel: 03-3407 5166
A sleek newish bar with very plush furnishings. Extremely friendly staff serve glasses of gin and vermouth, Bass Pale Ale, and a curious line of coffee cocktails like Cappuccino Martini, a mix of Illy coffee, vodka and steamed milk.

Insomnia Lounge
26-5, Udagawa-cho, Shibuya-ku
Tel: 03-3476 2735
A basement lounge bar completely decorated in screaming crimson. If this is not your colour, stay away.

The Pink Cow
Villa Moderna, B1, 1-3-18, Shibuya, Shibuya-ku

Tel: 03-3406 5597
Beloved of the art, fashion and media crowd, this is the brainchild of artist-sculptor Traci Consoli. This café-bar offers a good range of wine, beers and cocktails as well as food. Events include poetry readings, jazz recitals, book launches and art exhibitions.

Sasagin
1-32-15, Uehara, Shibuya-ku
Tel: 03-5454 3715
Arguably, the best *sake* bar in Tokyo, although only a small cogniscenti know it. The warm, sand-coloured Zen-style interior is the setting for a very choice selection of sweet, dry, sparkling and cloudy *sake*. The master, Narita-san, speaks English.

Shinjuku

The Fiddler
B1F, 2-1-2 Takadanobaba, Shinjuku-ku
Tel: 03-3204 2698
Located in a basement and open past midnight, this establishment in run by UK expats who have managed to transplant the atmosphere of their native boozers to Tokyo. Good selection of British pub grub, and plenty of live music acts.

La Jetee
1-1-8, Kabuki-cho, Shinjuku-ku
Tel: 03-3208 9645
Cosy Golden Gai bar patronised by film buffs, including visiting luminaries like Jim Jarmusch and Francis Ford Coppola. Incidentally the second language here, spoken by the master of the establishment, is French.

New York Bar
3-7-1-2, Nishi-Shinjuku, Shinjuku-ku
Tel: 03-5323 3458
Located on the upper floors of the luxurious Park Hyatt Hotel in West Shinjuku, a popular spot because of its night views over Tokyo. The drinks list is impressive, the service impeccable.

Other Areas

Bobby's Bar
3F, 1-18-10 Ikebukuro, Toshima-ku
Tel: 03-3980 8875
A well-known bar patronised by a mix of expats, travellers and Japanese. Moderately priced and friendly.

Hotel New Otani Bar
4-1, Kioi-cho, Tower 5 40F, Chiyoda-ku
Tel: 03-3238 0020
A full range of drinks, including some excellently shaken cocktails, but the main lure here is the night view from the bar stools and tables of Akasaka and the illuminated Rainbow Bridge.

The Irish House
2-8-9 Shimbashi, Minato-ku
Tel: 03-3503 4494
A cheerful place to experience the nostalgia of Ireland. This pub tries to reconstruct that green, misty mood with its distinctive brews and pub food.

Las Meninas
3-22-7, Plaza Koenji, 2F, Koenji-Kita, Suginami-ku
Tel: 03-3338 0266
A definite Iberian flavour to this small bar that also serves, as you would expect, Spanish plonk and tapas. Run by an expat Brit and his Japanese wife.

NIGHTLIFE NEWS

The weekly free magazine *Metropolis* (www.metropolis.co.jp) has good nightlife listings. *EL Magazine*, another freebie, also has listings on club events. The monthly *JSelect* also covers the city's music scene. Handouts of club schedules are left on the counters of the 7th-floor bookshop at Tower Records in Shibuya.

CIA (Club Information Agency) has a good club data website at www.ciajapan.com. Cyber Japan (www.so-net.ne.jp) follows the club scene as well as street fashion.

Latin Music

Tokyo has not remained immune to those infectious salsa and samba rhythms that have swept the world in recent years. Propelled by the growing numbers of workers from Central and South America, the dance floors are swaying to Latin sounds.

Bodeguita
3-14-7 Roppongi, Minato-ku
Tel: 03-3796 0232
A Roppongi centre for Tokyo's ever-continuing Latin craze. A restaurant and club, the tables get cleared away once everyone has eaten. Then it's just a question of pressing up against the bar or hitting the dance floor.

Salsa Sudada
3F, 7-13-8 Roppongi, Minato-ku
Tel: 03-5474 8806
One of the biggest salsa venues in Tokyo and one of the oldest clubs around, it was completely renovated a while back, reclaiming its position as arguably the best salsa spot in town. If you don't dance, go elsewhere.

Gay & Lesbian Venues

Although gays and lesbians do not promote themselves as much as they do in other international cities, there is a very real gay scene in Tokyo – mainly centred in the Shinjuku Ni-chome district, close to Shinjuku-Sanchome station. Most of the area's 300 or more gay clubs, host bars and restaurants regularly patronised by the local gay community are difficult to seek out, and generally don't welcome foreigners who don't speak Japanese. The following places, however, are relatively easy to find and navigate.

Advocates Bar
7F, Tenka Bldg, B1F, 2-18-1, Shinjuku, Shinjuku-ku
Tel: 03-3358 8638
A well-known spot among the expat and local gay crowd. The well-stocked bar is augmented by a spacious dance floor. Sister establishment **Advocates Café** is just around the corner.

Arty Farty
2-11-7 Shinjuku, Shinjuku-ku
Tel: 03-5362 9720
A well-known, foreigner-friendly gay bar in the Shinjuku Ni-chome district. Mostly guys only, though an exception is made on Sundays when women accompa-

TRANSPORT
ACCOMMODATION
ACTIVITIES
A – Z
LANGUAGE

nied by gay male friends are allowed in.

GB
Business Hotel T Bldg, B1F, 2-12-3, Shinjuku, Shinjuku-ku
Tel: 03-3352 8972
Well known among the gay community as one of the favourite spots in Tokyo for meetings between foreigners and locals. Attached to a business hotel that offers short-stay terms. Men only.

Kinswomyn
Daiichi Tenka Bldg, 3F, 2-15-10, Shinjuku, Shinjuku-ku
Tel: 03-3354 8720
Tokyo's most popular lesbian bar. A relaxed, easy-going place that sticks to its women-only rule. Its counterpart for men, is the nearby **Kinsmen** (2F, 2-18-5, Shinjuku, tel: 03-3354 4949). Both in Shinjuku ni-chome area.

New Sazae
Ishikawa Bldg, 2F, 2-18-5, Shinjuku, Shinjuku-ku
Tel: 03-3354 1745
The gay writer Yukio Mishima, who killed himself after a failed coup attempt in 1970, is said to have frequented the former incarnation of this bar. Also popular with cross-dressers and drag queens, this is a foreigner-friendly bar with good music.

SHOPPING

Tokyo is not a cheap place to shop for anything (even cameras and electronics), but most of the products on sale are of high quality and the range is staggering. Some districts specialise in certain kinds of merchandise, and the increased competition can mean prices are kept pared down.

Almost all shops operate on a fixed-price system. The one notable exception is Akihabara, where discounts can be had on electronic goods and computers. Try to compare prices as these will vary considerably, especially for electronics, computers, watches and camera equipment.

Japan's traditional crafts are widely available in Tokyo. These include textiles, paper, lacquerware, ceramics, baskets, chopsticks and woodblock prints. So is food and drink. Premium *sake* is usually never exported.

It is highly unlikely that you will be cheated in a store in Tokyo, harassed or sold faulty goods as retailers and staff are astonishingly honest in their dealings with customers. Staff must go through a vigorous training programme in customer PR before they are allowed to work. The much eroded Western dictum, "The customer is always right" has a more closely adhered to version in Japan: "The customer is God".

In big department stores, go to the information desk if you have a complaint about service. There are often English-speaking staff operating these, especially in the bigger stores. Department stores, traditionally the ultimate in shopping, now have to compete with large shopping mall complexes with their spectacular interiors and wide range of goods.

Department stores are generally open 10am–8pm (sometimes later), and are usually closed one day (mid-week) per week. Smaller shops tend to have shorter hours, such as 9–10am till 5–6pm.

Shopping Areas

Akihabara: A high-tech bazaar of electronics and computers, with many competitively priced stores.
Aoyama: Mostly high-class fashion and designer boutiques.
Asakusa: Traditional Japanese toys, snacks and souvenirs.
Daikanyama: Upmarket fashion district for young people. Lots of small boutiques and some name designers. **Nakameguro** and **Jiyugaoka**, the next stops down on the Tokyu Den-en Toshi Line from Shibuya, continue the theme.
Ginza: The most expensive shopping district. Several major department stores are located here, such as Matsuya, Matsuzakaya, Mitsukoshi, Seibu and Wako, besides a few "fashion buildings" and many exclusive boutiques. Also some traditional Japanese goods stores. Known too for its high-quality art galleries.
Harajuku/Omotesando: Another fashion area, though mostly geared to youth/teenage tastes. Several antique shops, plus Kiddyland's four stories of toys.
Ikebukuro: Dominated by giant department stores Seibu and Tobu; also many boutiques in the Sunshine City complex; plus the Amlux Toyota showroom.
Kanda-Jimbocho: Tokyo's centre for the printed word; many new and second-hand bookstores.
Kappabashi: Restaurant/kitchen hardware supplies, especially plastic models of foods seen in restaurant window displays.
Nihombashi: A good place to pick up traditional craftwork. Two of Japan's oldest department stores, Mitsukoshi and Takashimaya are located here.
Shibuya: Has a little bit of everything: designer clothes, hiphop fashion and the most complete DIY department store in the world at Tokyu Hands. Also the Seibu, Tokyu and Marui department stores, the Parco "fashion" malls plus numerous little boutiques and record stores geared to young shoppers.
Shimo Kitazawa: A mass of small fashion, novelty and thrift shops in a district of narrow lanes near the station of the same name.

TAX REFUND

A consumption tax of 5 percent will be added to all purchases, but department stores have special tax refund programmes for foreign visitors on large purchases, usually over ¥10,000. Some stores limit this refund to clothing only. Check at the information desk – usually located on the first floor near the main entrance – before making a purchase. You will need to show your passport for a tax exemption.

Shinjuku (East): Several big camera and electronics stores, such as Yodobashi and Sakuraya. Northwest of the station are backstreets with many small shops selling CDs and rare vinyl LPs.
Shinjuku (West): Isetan, Marui and Takashimaya department stores; Kinokuniya bookstore.
Ueno: Ameyoko-cho, one of Tokyo's only open market areas, is good for cheap food, cosmetics, clothing and toys. The back streets have numerous shops selling traditional Japanese goods.

Department Stores

Isetan: 3-14-1 Shinjuku, Shinjuku-ku; tel: 03-3352 1111.
Loft: 21-1 Udagawa-cho, Shibuya-ku, tel: 03-3462 3807.
Matsuya: 3-6-1 Ginza, Chuo-ku, tel: 03-3567 1211.
Matsuzakaya: 3-29-5 Ueno, Taito-ku, tel: 03-3832 1111; branch at 6-10-1 Ginza, tel: 03-3572 1111.
Mitsukoshi: 1-7-4 Nihombashi-Muromachi, Chuo-ku, tel: 03-3241 3311; branches at 4-6-16, Ginza, tel: 03-3562 1111 and 3-29-1 Shinjuku, tel: 03-3354 1111.
Seibu: 1-28-1 Minami-Ikebukuro, Toshima-ku, tel: 03-3981-0111 and 23-1 Udagawa-cho, Shibuya-ku, tel: 03-3462 0111.
Takashimaya: 2-4-1 Nihombashi, Chuo-ku, tel: 03 3211-4111 and Times Square, 5-24-2 Sendagaya, Shibuya-ku, tel: 03-5361 1122.
Tokyu: 2-24-1 Dogenzaka, Shibuya-ku, tel: 03 3477-3111.
Wako: 4-5-11 Ginza, Chuo-ku, tel: 03 3562-2111.

Shopping Malls

Carreta Shiodome: 1-8-2, Higashi-Shinbashi, Minato-ku, tel: 03-6218 2100. Part of the Shiodome complex, this mall is strong on fashion, but also has excellent restaurants, bakeries and cafés.
Daikanyama Address: 17 Daikanyamacho, Shibuya-ku, tel: 03-3461 6492. A small but stylish retail complex that attracts those who monitor the Tokyo fashion scene. An open plaza and overhead bridges linking sections of the complex add interest.
Decks: 1-6-1 Daiba, Minato-ku, tel: 03-3599 6500. Prime beachside location on Odaiba island with two themed sections, one resembling Chinatown and the other a 1950s shopping street.
Glassarea Aoyama: 5-4-41, Minami-Aoyama, Minato-ku, tel: 03-5485 3466. Though small by comparison to the likes of Roppongi Hills, this medium-sized mall's emphasis is quality and novelty. Run by the same people as Tokyu Hands store, expect lots of intriguing household goods alongside trendy boutiques.
Mark City: 1-12-1, Dogenzaka, Shibuya-ku, tel: 03-3780 6503. The principal of all-in-one applies here. Expect boutiques, fashion accessory stores, cafés and restaurants – the works.
Marunouchi Building: 2-4-1, Marunouchi, Chiyoda-ku, tel: 03-5218 5100. A very upmarket complex even for Tokyo. Have a good look at the floor map before you enter and vanish into designer fashion stores, gourmet food hall, cafés and restaurants.
Roppongi Hills: 6-10, Roppongi, Minato-ku, www.roppongihills.com. A huge, 40-acre shopping, elite housing and entertainment centre in a part of town where most buildings are shoehorned into narrow plots. Cinemas, a contemporary art museum, restaurants, cafés and three shopping sections.
Venus Fort: Palette Town, Aomi, Koto-ku, tel: 03-3599 0700. A windowless indoor complex similar in mood to a Milanese studio set arcade. Aimed mostly at women, but there are good patisseries and cafés too.
Yebisu Garden Place: 4-20, Ebisu, Shibuya-ku, tel: 03-5423 7111. Has a major photo museum, the Westin Hotel, a beer museum, and numerous shops, restaurants and stylish cafés.

Cultural Malls

Japanese department stores, or *depato*, are cultural centres as well. Most of the large *depato* have an art gallery somewhere on a top floor, where you might find, for example, a special exhibition of masterpieces by French Impressionists.

What to Buy

Cameras & Electronics

AsoBitCity: 4-3-3 Soto-Kanda, Chiyoda-ku, tel: 03-3251 3100. Electronics, cartoon character goods, a shooting gallery and model train set. Daily 10am–9pm.
Laox: 1-2-9 Soto-Kanda, Chiyoda-ku, tel: 03-3255 9041. Massive discount chain store; staff speak English. Daily 10am–7.30pm.
Sakuraya Camera: 3-17-2 Shinjuku, Shinjuku-ku, tel: 03-3354 3636. Giant retailer with similar price range and selection to Yodobashi Camera *(see below)*. Daily 10am–8pm.
Yodobashi Camera: 1-11-1 Nishi-Shinjuku, Shinjuku-ku, tel: 03-3346 1010. Daily 9.30am–9pm. A second, newer store, along the same lines as its Shinjuku prototype, has opened in Akihabara, just to the north of the station.

Toys, Pets & Novelties

Don Quixote: 1-16-5 Kabuki-cho, Shinjuku-ku, tel: 03-5291 9211. By Shinjuku station, this chain store outlet is crammed pell-mell with character goods, toys, kitchen ware, lifestyle goods and booze. Daily 24 hours.
Hakuhinkan: 8-8-11 Ginza, Chuo-ku, tel: 03-3571 8008. Tokyo's top toy store gives kids a chance to play with the goods. Daily 11am–8pm.
Kiddyland: 6-1-9 Jingumae, Shibuya-ku, tel: 03-3409 3431. Four floors of toys, games, novelties and the latest gadgets aimed at older children (and adults too). Daily 10am–8pm.
Maidaru: 5-17 Nishi-Asakusa, Taito-ku, tel: 03-3483 1686. Specialising in highly realistic plastic food models, everything from

platters of sushi to filet mignon and French fries.

Tokyu Hands: 12-18 Udagawa-cho, Shibuya-ku, tel: 03-5489 5111. A fascinating hardware store stocking things you'd be hard pressed to find elsewhere. Many novelty goods. Daily 10am–8pm.

Tsukumo Robocon Magazine Kan: Yamaguchi Bldg, 1F, 3-2-13, Soto-Kanda, Chiyoda-ku, tel: 03-3251 0987. Robot models of insects, dogs, turtles and mutants among other models. Mon–Sat 10.45am–7.30pm, Sun 10.15am–7pm.

Japanese Fashion Stores

109: 2-29-1 Dogenzaka, Shibuya-ku, tel: 03-3477 5111. Ultra-modern, ultra-temporary fashions catering to teens and the early 20s crowd. Daily 10am–9pm.

Comme des Garçons: 5-2-1 Minami Aoyama, Minato-ku, tel: 03-3406 3951. Matt-black chic and other tones from legendery 1980s designer Rei Kawakubo. in this flagship. Daily 11am–8pm.

Hysteric Glamour: 6-23-2 Jingumae, Shibuya-ku, tel: 03-3409 7227; www.hystericglamour.jp. Nobu Kitamura's highly distinctive store has a famous line of graphic and very racy message T-shirts. Daily 11am–8pm.

Issey Miyake: 3-18-11 Minami Aoyama, Minato-ku, tel: 03-3423 1407. Miyake continues his experimentation with fabrics and curious shapes and forms. Look out for the startling window displays. Daily 11am–8pm.

Laforet Harajuku: 1-11-6 Jingumae, Shibuya-ku, tel: 03-3475 0411. A hundred or so small and innovative boutiques aimed at the more daring youth. Daily 11am–8pm.

Tsumori Chisato: 11-1 Sarugaku-cho, Shibuya-ku, tel: 03-5728 3225. The ever-youthful Ms. Tsumori's vibrant colours and designs cater to a wide age range. Daily 11am–8pm.

Jewellery & Pearls

Mikimoto: 4-5-5 Ginza, Chuo-ku, tel: 03-3535 4611. Daily 11am–7pm. Flagship branch of this famous pearl jewellery store. A newer store, the eye-catching **Mikimoto Ginza 2**, can be found in a backstreet northwest of the original.

Uyeda Jeweller: Imperial Hotel Arcade, 1-1-1, Uchisaiwai-cho, Chiyoda-ku, tel: 03-3503 2587. Mon–Fri 10am–7pm, Sat 11am–7pm, Sun 10am–6pm.

Wako: 4-5-11 Ginza, Chuo-ku, tel: 03-3562 2111. Mon–Sat 10am–5.30pm.

Antiques

Akariya: 4-8-1 Yoyogi, Shibuya-ku, tel: 03-3465 5578. Antique *tansu* chests and other furniture. Mon–Sat 11am–7pm. Second outlet called **Akariya II** at nearby 2F, 5-58-1 Yoyogi, tel: 03-3467 0580, has high-quality antique kimono and other fabrics from the Edo, Meiji and Taisho eras.

Fuji-Torii: 6-1-10 Jingumae, Shibuya-ku, tel: 03-3400 2777. Specialises in traditional screens and Imari porcelain, but also stocks simple artefacts and art souvenirs. Daily except Tues and third Mon 11am–6pm.

Hasegawa Ginza: 1-7-1 Ginza, Chuo-ku, tel: 03-5524 7576. This multi-storey emporium proffers a selection of expensive but exquisite Buddhist ceremonial objects and ornaments. In addition, the sixth floor houses a superb museum of Japanese arts and crafts. Daily 11am–7pm.

Oriental Bazaar: 5-9-13 Jingumae, Shibuya-ku, tel: 03-3400 3933. Not really an antique store, but it has some interesting pieces at reasonable prices. No bargaining, and antiques come with a certificate stating approximate age. A nice place to pick up traditional toys, *washi* paper and kimono. Daily except Thurs 9.30am–6.30pm.

Arts and Crafts

Bingoya: 69 Wakamatsucho, Shinjuku-ku, tel: 03-3202 8778. Six floors of folk crafts. Daily except Mon 10am–7pm.

Japan Traditional Crafts Centre: Metropolitan Plaza, 1F–2F, 1-11-1 Nishi-Ikebukuro, Toshima-ku, tel: 03-5954 6066. Not just a gallery but also a repository of information on Japan's traditional crafts and the people who keep them alive. Ceramics, lacquer, glass, *washi* paper and dolls. Daily 11am–7pm.

Yoshitoku: 1-9-14 Asakusabashi, Taito-ku, tel: 03-3863 4419. Doll makers since 1711; prices are moderate. Daily 9.30am–5.30pm.

Japanese Paper

Isetasu: 2-18-9 Yanaka, Taito-ku, tel: 03-3823 1453. Daily 10am–6pm. This tiny shop is worth a browse even if you don't buy anything. *(see page 154).*

Ito-ya: 2-7-15 Ginza, Chuo-ku, tel: 03-3561 8311. Nine floors of stationery and traditional Japanese paper goods. Mon–Sat 10am–7pm, Sun 10.30am–7pm.

Tsutsumo Factory: 137-15 Udagawacho, Shibuya-ku, tel: 03-5478 1330. *Tsutsumo* means "to wrap". Wide range of wrapping paper in traditional and modern designs. Daily 10.30am–8pm.

Lacquerware

Kuroeya: 2F, 1-2-6 Nihombashi, Chuo-ku, tel: 03-3272 0948. Mon–Sat 9am–5pm. A specialist store selling high-quality *makie* or lacquerware.

Ceramics

Unless you actually visit the towns where the ceramics are made, department stores are your best bet to see a wide selection of Japanese ceramics, and the prices are competitive. There are smaller ceramics shops throughout Tokyo where prices are sometimes higher.

Hasebe-ya: 1-7-7 Azabu-Juban, Minato-ku, tel: 03-3401 9998. A ceramics specialist that also carries authetic and reproduction antique furniture. Daily 10am–7pm.

Woodblock Prints

Asakusa Kuramae Shobo: 3-10-12 Kuramae, Taito-ku, tel: 03-

3866 5894. Specialist on books and prints on Edo and *sumo*. Mon–Sat 9am–7pm.
Hara Shobo: 2-3 Kanda-Jimbo-cho, Chiyoda-ku, tel: 03-3261 7444. Nice selection of prints, both old and new, with a good range of prices. English spoken.
Tolman Collection: 2-2-18 Shiba-Daimon, Minato-ku, tel: 03-3434 1300. One of the finest stocks of modern Japanese prints, with some Japanese themed work by resident foreign artists. Daily except Tues 11am–7pm.

Swords

Aoi Art: 4-22-11 Yoyogi, Shibuya-ku, tel: 03-3375 5553. Authentic pieces, some very old, from a long-established dealer. Tues–Sun 11am–7pm.
Japan Sword: 3-8-1 Toranomon, Minato-ku, tel: 03-3434 4321, www.japansword.co.jp. With a history dating back to the Meiji period, this store not only sells antique swords, but also samurai helmets and armour. Good repros are also available. Mon–Fri 9.30am–6pm; Sat 9.30am–5pm.

Books

Standing and browsing through books and magazines, with no obligation to buy, is a time-honoured practice in Tokyo. Relatively few shops specialise in English books. Foreign newspapers and magazines are also available at most major hotels.
Book 1st: 33-5 Udagawa-cho, Shibuya-ku, tel: 03-3770 1023. Also has Tokyo's largest collection of magazines on the first floor. Daily 10am–10pm.
Blue Parrot: 3F, 2-14-10 Takadanababa, Shinjuku-ku, tel: 03-3202 3671. An extensive selection of mostly used books, DVDs and magazines.
Good Day Books: 3F, 1-11-2 Ebisu, Shibuya-ku, tel: 03-5421 0957. Tokyo's best selection of used books – over 30,000 – plus several thousand new books. Great bargains. On the east side of JR Ebisu station. Wed–Mon 11am–6pm.

FLEA MARKETS

Regular Sunday flea markets are held around Tokyo, often on the grounds of shrines and temples. Expect interesting, though rarely priceless, finds. Haggling is perfectly in order, even expected.
Arai-Yakushimae Temple
Antiques, postcards, textiles and more. Held on the 1st Sunday of the month. Five minutes from Arai Yakushi-mae stop on the Seibu Shinjuku line, or a 10-minute walk from Nakano subway station.
Hanazono Shrine
Small scale but with nice items. Every Sunday from dawn to 2pm (except May and Nov). A 10-minute walk from JR Shinjuku station east exit.
Nogi Shrine Flea Market
8-11-27 Akasaka, Minato-ku
Tel: 03-3478 3001
Held on the 2nd Sunday of each month from 5am–4pm.
Setagaya Boro-Ichi
Tel: 03-3411 6663
Tokyo's best-known flea market is a huge affair dating back to the 1570s. Held Jan 15–16 and Dec 15–16.
Togo Shrine Flea Market
1-5-3 Jingumae, Shibuya-ku
Tel: 03-3403 3591
A huge market every 1st, 4th and 5th Sunday, weather permitting. Open 4am–3pm.
Tomioka Hachiman-gu Shrine
First and 2nd Sunday of the month. Four minutes' walk from Monzen-nakacho subway station.
Tokyo International Forum
The Oedo Antique Fair takes place on the 3rd Sunday of the month in the TIF courtyard. Excellent selection of Japanese ceramics. A three-minute walk from JR Yurakucho station.

Kinokuniya: 3-17-7 Shinjuku, Shinjuku-ku, tel: 03-3354 0131. Foreign books on the sixth floor. Another branch in Shinjuku's Times Square. Daily 10am–7pm.
Manga no Mori: 12-10 Udagawa-cho, Shibuya-ku, tel: 03-5489 0257. Top *manga* collection, with just about every post-war Japanese character featured. Other branches in Shinjuku and Higashi Ikebukuro. Daily 11am–9pm.
Maruzen: 1-6-4 Marunouchi, Chiyoda-ku, tel: 03-5288 8881. Located in the Oazo building next to Tokyo Station, this has Japan's largest selection of foreign books. Call to check as the store has plans to move back to their original Nihombashi location in the near future.
Sanseido: 1-1 Kanda-Jimbocho, Chiyoda-ku, tel: 03-3233 3312. Foreign books on the fifth floor. Daily except Tues 10am–7.30pm.
Tower Books: 1-22-14 Jinnan, Shibuya-ku, tel: 03-3496 3661. On the seventh floor, the most imaginative selection of English books in Tokyo. Lots of magazines as well. Daily 10am–10pm.

SPORTS

Spectator Sports

Sumo

Three 15-day tournaments a year are held in Tokyo in January, May and September. Another three tournaments are held in Osaka in March, Nagoya in July and Fukuoka in November.

Junior wrestlers begin their bouts at about 10am; senior wrestlers start at 3pm on the first and the last days, and at 3.30pm on other days.
National Sumo Stadium
1-3-28 Yokoami, Sumida-ku, near JR Ryogoku Station
Tel: 03-3623 5111
Tickets for the Tokyo tournaments are sold at the office of the Nihon Sumo Kyokai at National Sumo Stadium as well as from ticket agencies throughout Tokyo. Note: it's very difficult to obtain tickets for balcony seats (box seats are usually monopolised by corporate season ticket holders). A limited

number of unreserved seats go on sale each day of a tournament at 8am (one per person). Tickets are priced ¥2,100–10,500.

Baseball

Japan's "second national sport" maintains its appeal among the older generation; younger Japanese seem less keen these days. Tokyo has three teams: the Yomiuri Giants (in the Central League), the Nippon Ham Fighters (Pacific League) and the Yakult Swallows (Central League). The season runs April–October, culminating in the best-of-seven Japan Series between the pennant winners of the two leagues.

Tokyo Dome
1-3-61 Koraku, Bunkyo-ku
Tel: 03-5800 9999
www.tokyo-dome.co.jp
Japan's first sports dome, nicknamed the Big Egg, is home to both the Giants and the Fighters, who play there alternately.

Jingu Stadium
13 Kasumigaoka, Shinjuku-ku
Tel: 03-3404 8999
Most baseball fans prefer the atmosphere at the Jingu ballpark (built as part of the 1964 Olympic complex) to the Big Egg. It's the home ground of the Swallows, and draws big crowds for the games against the Giants and the Hanshin Tigers (from Osaka).

Horse Racing

Horse racing has become a fashionable spectator sport in recent years, one of the few chances people have to gamble. Schedules in English are available from the National Association of Racing, at www.jair.jrao.ne.jp.

Oi Racetrack
2-1-1 Katsushima, Shinagawa-ku
Tel: 03-3763 2151

Tokyo Racecourse
1-1, 1-2 Hiyoshi-cho, Fuchu City
Tel: 042-363 3141

Hydroplane Races

Popular among Tokyoites, *kyotei* as this sport is known, is usually held between six motorboats that can reach speeds of 80 kph (50 mph).This is one of the few chances people have to place bets.

Edogawa Kyotei
3-1-1 Higashi-Komatsugawa, Edogawa-ku
Tel: 03-3656 0641
www.edogawa-kyotei.co.jp

Soccer

The J-League now competes with baseball for the most popular sport slot. The season runs from March to October, with a special Emperor's Cup event in December. Regular J-League games are played at the National Stadium, as are international fixtures. The capital's two top teams, Tokyo FC and Verdy, play at the new Ajinomoto Stadium, in Chofu City, western Tokyo. Check www.j-league.or.jn for the latest info.

National Stadium
Kasumigaoka, Shinjuku-ku
Tel: 03-3403 1151

Ajinomoto Stadium
376-3, Nishimachi, Chofu City
Tel: 0424-40 0555
www.ajinomotostadium.com

Martial Arts

Judo, karate, aikido, kyudo and kendo all have championships or demonstration events on a regular basis. These are usually held at the Nippon Budokan.

All-Japan Judo Federation
1-16-30 Kasuga, Bunkyo-ku
Tel: 03-3818 4199

International Aikido Federation
17-18 Wakamatsucho, Shinjuku-ku
Tel: 03-3203 9236

Nippon Budokan
2-3 Kitanomaru-Koen, Chiyoda-ku
Tel: 03-3216 5100

World Union of Karate-do Organisation
4F, Sempaku Shinkokaikan Bldg, 1-15-16 Toranomon, Minato-ku
Tel: 03-3503 6640

Rugby

As the strongest rugby nation in Asia, Japan regularly qualifies for the Rugby World Cup. There is a keen following at the universities and a thriving corporate league.

Chichibu-no-miya Rugby Stadium
2-8-35 Kita-Aoyame, Minato-ku

Participant Sports

Golf

Though some hotels offer golf packages, it is generally prohibitively expensive for most visitors. Driving ranges can be found all over the city, even on some department store roofs. You may even occasionally see mini putting courses winding under raised expressways.

Tokyo Metropolitan Golf Course
1-15-1 Shinden, Adachi-ku
Tel: 03-3919 0111
Tokyo's cheapest public course. You will be lucky to get on this course at the weekend, but weekdays are usually better. Open daily, dawn to twilight.

Ice Skating

A popular spectator event among the Japanese, with exhibition shows and tournaments held at the National Stadium.

Meiji Jingu Ice Skating Rink
Gobanchi, Kasumigaoka, Shinjuku, Shinjuku-ku
Tel: 03-3403 3458
Mon–Fri noon–6pm, Sat– Sun 10am–6pm.

Takabanobaba Citizen Ice Skating Rink
4-29-27 Takadanababa, Shinjuku-ku
Tel: 03-3371 0910
Mon–Sat noon–7.45pm, Sun 10am–7.45pm.

Fitness Centres

Chiyoda Kuritsu Sogo Taikukan
2-1-8 Uchi-kanda, Chiyoda-ku
Tel: 03-3256 8444
A decent-sized gym and pool for local residents, which visitors can use for a small fee. Daily noon–5pm; call to confirm.

Minato-ku Sports Centre
3-1-19 Shibaura, Minato-ku
Tel: 03-3452 4151
A reasonable admission fee allows for use of a good swimming pool, gym and sauna. Daily 9am–9pm.

Yoga

International Yoga Centre
5-30-6 Ogikubo, Suginami-ku

Tel: 090-4956 7996
Specialises in Iyengar and Ashtanga yoga. Offers single sessions and classes. Daily 6am–10pm.

Sun & Moon Yoga
Meguro Eki Mae Mansion, Higashi Guchi Bldg, 3-1-5 Kami Osaki, Suite 204, Shinagawa-ku
Tel: 03-3280 6383
Beginners to advanced classes taught by American writer and yoga specialist Leza Lowitz.

SIGHTSEEING TOURS

If your time is limited, the best way to see the highlights of the city is on a tour. These vary from buses to individual taxis and even helicopters. The **Japan Guide Association** (tel: 03-3213 2706; www.jga21c.or.jp/f_introduction.html) can put you in touch with an accredited tour guide. You can then negotiate the fee and itinerary with the guide.

Bus Tours

Bus tour options include half-day, full-day and evening tours. Prices range from ¥3,300 for a morning tour to around ¥12,000 for an eight-hour trip including a river cruise. English-language tours can be booked from major hotels in downtown Tokyo or directly with the tour company.

Hato Bus Tokyo
Tel: 03-3435 6081
www.hatobus.co.jp
A long established sightseeing tour company with a variety of day and night tours. Half-day tours start from ¥4,000. All tours depart from the Hamamatsucho Bus Terminal; pick-ups from designated hotels also available.

Japan Gray Line Company
Tel: 03-3433 5745
www.jgl.co.jp/inbound
Gray Line of Japan offers a small selection of morning, afternoon and full-day tours to the main sights for between ¥4,000–9,600. Pick up from major hotels available.

Sunrise Tours
Tel: 03-5796 5454
www.jtbgmt.com/sunrisetour
This company (operated by the reputable Japan Travel Bureau) provides the widest range of tours in and around Tokyo. There are day and overnight tours to sights outside the city, like Kamakura and the Mount Fuji area, as well as "mini tours" to places farther afield like Kyoto and Osaka.

Walking Tours

Mr. Oka's Walking Tours of Tokyo
Tel: 0422-51 7673
Run by an enthusiastic retired historian, this offers a chance to see aspects of the city not covered by conventional tour companies. The highly informed Oka san's main interest is social history, a field he explains very engagingly in English. Tours run from ¥4,000, but does not include transportation costs.

River Tours

Tokyo River Bus
Tel: 03–5733 4812
www.suijobus.co.jp/english
The Sumida River Line waterbus plys the route from Asakusa, past a series of old bridges, to Hama-Rikyu Garden and Hinode Pier. In addition, there are vessels that depart regularly from Hinode Pier to Odaiba, Palette Town, Tokyo Big Sight, Kasai Sealife Park and Shinagawa Aquarium.

Taxi Tours

Taxi tours are convenient but expensive. Expect to pay between ¥26–50,000 for tours between four and eight hours. Contact the JNTO *(see page 237)* for recommendations.

CHILDREN'S ACTIVITIES

There's plenty to keep children amused in and around Tokyo. There are samurai-era relics to explore, river buses and streetcars to ride on, parks to run around in and more – plus, of course, there's always Tokyo Disneyland. Here are some possibilities:

Fukugawa-Edo Museum
1-3-8 Shirakawa, Koto-ku
Explore a 19th-century Edo neighbourhood in a wonderfully realistic reproduction complete with lighting and sound effects.

Hakuhinkan Toy Park
8-8-11 Ginza, Chuo-ku
Tokyo's top toy store gives kids a chance to play with the goods, both Japanese and imported.

Kiddyland
6-1-9 Jingumae, Shibuya-ku
Four floors of toys, games, novelties and the latest electronics gadgets aimed at older children (and many adults too).

Pokemon Centre
3-2-5 Nihonbashi, Chuo-ku
Products and merchandise from the ever popular TV programme, films and games. Has a newer branch in Odaiba.

Tama Zoo
7-1-1 Hodokubo, Hino-shi
A spacious "natural habitat" zoo, complete with safari-park rides.

Tokyo Disneyland/Disney Sea
1-1 Maihama, Urayasu-shi, Chiba Prefecture
www.tokyodisneyresort.co.jp
Tickets for both parks may be purchased on arrival or buy advance tickets from Tokyo Disneyland Ticket Centre (Hibiya Mitsui Bldg, 1-1-2 Yurakucho, Chiyoda-ku; tel: 03-3595 1777). One-day tickets restrict entry to either Disneyland or Disney Sea while multi-day tickets allow entry to both parks.

Tokyo Metropolitan Children's Hall
1-18-24, Shibuya, Shibuya-ku
Tel: 03-3409 6361
This boasts six amusement-filled floors, with art studios, fun mazes, jungle gyms and mini kitchens outfitted with rubberware items for small children.

Toshimaen
3-25-1 Koyama, Nerima-ku
Amusement park with roller coasters and other rides, plus seven swimming pools complete with convoluted water slides.

A-Z

A Handy Summary of Practical Information, Arranged Alphabetically

Addresses

Tokyo is one of the most complex cities in the world. Even the Japanese get confused, which is why businesses often print little maps out on cards, websites and advertisements.

However, with a little knowledge of how the streets are laid out and numbered, you should be able to negotiate the city without too much frustration. Apart from main roads, very few streets have names. Addresses traditionally follow a big-to-small system, with the *ku* (ward) listed first, then the *cho* or *matchi* (district) and then the *chome* (an area of a few blocks). A typical address rendered in Japanese might read like this: Minato-ku, Hamamatscho, 3-8-12, Riverfield Hotel, 4F. However, the English rendition of Japanese addresses often follows a different order, most commonly the one used throughout this guide: Riverfield Hotel, 4F, 3-8-12 Hamamatscho, Minato-ku.

Note: in Japan the ground floor equals the first; also look out for floor numbers often shown on the outside of the building.

Budgeting your Trip

Tokyo has a reputation for being one of the most expensive cities in the world, but after 15 years of economic stagnation, the cost of living index in capitals like London and Paris have caught up, and in some cases exceeded that of Tokyo. Compared to other Asian capitals though, Tokyo remains the costliest.

Accommodation can run from as little as ¥5,000 in a modest inn, to over ¥50,000 in one of its top-class hotels. Food is better value than you would think, especially lunch sets, where there is fierce competition for customers. A decent lunch set can be had for as little as ¥650. Japanese fast food restaurants have all-hours fixed sets from only ¥350. Expect to pay ¥2,000–3,500 for a 2–3 course dinner without drinks.

Taxis are expensive with a base fare of ¥660 rising quite quickly if you get stuck in a traffic jam. Subway fares are reasonable, tickets starting on average at ¥140 for the first two or three stops. Rates are slightly different for each line.

Drinks at music clubs and discos tend to be cheaper than at bars and pubs. Although some of the high-end restaurants may levy a service charge of between 10–20 percent, it is not the norm. There is no tipping system, something that offsets the cost of services in Japan.

Business Hours

Standard business hours for government offices and private sector companies are Mon–Fri, 9am–5pm. They are closed on national holidays. Banks are open 9am–3pm. Department stores and larger shops usually operate from 10am–8pm (sometimes later). Convenience stores are open 24 hours.

Business Travellers

As a foreigner, you are not expected to bow – a smile, handshake and a nod are usually quite sufficient. When you meet a Japanese person, wait to see if he or she first extends a hand. You will find that younger people are more comfortable with handshakes than their seniors. Japanese businessmen always dress smartly – suit and tie – and expect you to be similarly attired.

The Japanese love of consensus is legendary – indeed, it's the lynchpin of their society – and this can make doing business in Tokyo a frustrating experience.

Keep the following in mind. Don't expect rapid decisions. Do expect many meetings, which may seem to be leading nowhere. They are an important stage in the process of creating a long-term relationship, without which little progress is likely to be made. At meetings, expect stiff formality. Simple small talk (the weather, your flight and hotel) will suffice to break the ice. It may seem like beating around the bush, but this is an important part of the process.

The pecking order for seating is important. Don't sit first. Rather wait for someone to indicate your seat. The same applies when you are taken out to dinner – a vital part of the ritual in itself.

Exchanging business cards is an essential ritual at all first-time meetings. Since you are expected to give your card to everyone you are introduced to, be sure to bring a copious number with you. If you can, have your name printed in *katakana* script, so non-English speakers can pronounce it more easily. It is customary in Japan to place the cards you receive on the table in front of you, rather than stuffing them away in your pocket immediately. This will help you remember people's names and positions during the meeting and on future occasions. Do not jot notes or scribble on these cards.

Do not be surprised if you are asked questions regarding age, education and company service. Identity and "proper" affiliation are very important in Japan.

Interpreter Services

Japan Convention Services: Nippon Press Centre Bldg, 4F, 2-2-1 Uchisaiwaicho, Chiyoda-ku, tel: 03-3508 1211. Your hotel will be able to recommend an interpreter if you need one.

Children

Tokyo may be crowded, but with a little forward planning, travelling with children is both feasible and enjoyable, and the options, ranging from science and nature museums to amusement parks, toy shops, aquariums and zoos, are quite broad.

On trains, buses and subways, children up to age 12 travel for half-fare; those under six ride for free. When travelling with kids, try to avoid trains during rush hour, especially when using strollers.

Department stores usually have family rooms or areas set aside for mothers to nurse infants or change diapers. The malls are also good places to eat, since their restaurant floors offer a good variety of food, often with child-size portions.

Some of the larger hotels offer babysitting services. Many have outdoor swimming pools that are open to the public at specific hours during summer.

See also Children's Activities *(page 229)*.

Climate & Clothing

In Tokyo, spring is ushered in with the cherry blossoms in early April, and the temperature starts to rise. By May, the weather will become warm and pleasant, still without great humidity. June brings grey, drizzly weather, known poetically as *tsuyu* (dew), a rainy spell that lasts about a month.

Midsummer is hot and sticky, with the mercury rising to around 35°C (100°F) – up to 40°C in the especially hot summer of 2004 – and hovering overnight above 25°C (72°F). Typhoons occur between August and October (though Tokyo is affected far more rarely than Okinawa and western Japan).

From mid- to late September, there is usually a late summer, with hot days that cool when the humidity level drops at night.

During October and early November, there are many mellow autumn days – this is the Tokyoites' favourite time of the year.

After a month or so of rainy, changeable weather, winter arrives, with clear blue skies and low humidity. The harshest cold sets in January and February, although Tokyo only receives occasional snowfalls. The weather in March is usually chilly, overcast and changeable.

All this, naturally, is subject to global climate change.

Periods to Avoid

There are three times in the year when almost all of Japan is on holiday and travelling en masse. It is unwise to pass through Narita Airport or plan any train trips during these periods:
New Year Around December 25–January 4;
Golden Week April 29–May 5 (avoid weekends at either end);
Obon Seven to 10 days centring on August 15.

What to Wear

Japanese people place importance on appearance and dress accordingly. For visitors, casual clothes are acceptable in almost all situations, except on business, for which a suit is *de rigueur.*

The weather is relatively predictable, so dress for the season. In winter, bring a thick jacket or overcoat for January and February; in summer, wear light fabrics (cotton or linen); in spring and autumn, a light jacket will prove handy.

Crime & Security

For a city its size, Tokyo has a low incidence of petty theft, and personal security is far higher than in most cities in Europe and North America. Theft of luggage and money is rare, though not unheard of in Tokyo; pickpockets have begun targeting crowded trains and areas like Shinjuku's Kabuki-cho. Crime is also rising among Japanese youth. In recent years the media has been full of reports of illegalities committed by foreigners, mostly Asian immigrants.

Organised crime is another matter, and it is often violent. The police generally turn a blind eye to prostitution, gambling, ticket touting, illegal immigration and the protection rackets operated by the *yakuza* gangs, conducting sporadic crackdowns only when inter-gang warfare spills onto the streets.

However, visitors need never come into contact with the underbelly of Japanese society. If an incident occurs, report it to the nearest *koban* (police box). These are located in every neighbourhood, especially in busy areas and outside major railway stations. If possible, go with an eyewitness or a Japanese speaker. For police contact details, see "Emergency Numbers" on page 233.

Women Travellers

Tokyo is not a dangerous place for women on their own. However, instances of harassment do occasionally occur, especially on overcrowded trains. Incidents of local women being groped on crowded trains are not uncommon. Western women, while less likely to be targeted, are not completely exempt.

The idea of the independent career woman has slowly gained acceptance over the past two decades. The process has been reinforced by new legislation putting teeth into equal opportunities laws and banning sexual harassment (in Japanese, *sekuhara* – a term that men are finally becoming aware of now).

However, a deep, occasionally aggressive streak of sexism still runs through Japanese society. This is evidenced in degrading TV shows (not all late night), tabloid "sports" newspapers featuring explicit pictures, plus thinly veiled ads for prostitution services and cartoon books which glorify sexual violence towards women.

That said, it is safer to walk, travel, eat and drink anywhere in Tokyo than it is in most cities in the West. Areas like Shinjuku's Kabuki-cho are not advisable if you are alone, but two women together will generally suffer nothing more unpleasant than leering.

Customs Regulations

Non-residents entering the country are given a duty-free allowance of 200 cigarettes or 250 gm of tobacco; three 760 ml bottles of alcohol; 2 oz of perfume; and gifts and souvenirs whose total value is not more than ¥200,000. If you are carrying the equivalent of over ¥1 million, you must declare it.

Japan bans the import and use of illegal drugs, firearms and ammunition, as well as swords – and strictly punishes anyone caught with the above items.

Pornographic magazines and videos showing pubic hair are also forbidden in Japan. It is also illegal to bring in endangered species or products containing them.

For further information, contact **Tokyo Customs Headquarters**, 5-5-30 Konan, Minato-ku, tel: 03-3472 7001.

Disabled Travellers

Although Tokyo still lags behind most Western cities in wheelchair accessibility, major strides have been taken over the past decade to improve access and facilities for the disabled.

Wide doors and special toilets are being designed into new buses and trains, including the Narita Express, *shinkansen* bullet trains and some local commuter lines. Most major JR stations have elevators and/or escalators with special attachments for wheelchairs.

Similarly, consideration is given to those with visual impairments in some parts of the city, with markers built into the pavements, braille signs on new JR ticket machines and speakers emitting jingles at pedestrian crossings.

Nevertheless, it is still a struggle for the disabled to get around Tokyo, and don't contemplate using a wheelchair in trains or subways during rush hours from 7.30–10am and 5–7.30pm.

It is possible to reserve a special seat for wheelchairs on the *shinkansen*. For more information, call the **JR English InfoLine** at 03-3423 0111.

The publication *Accessible Tokyo*, is recommended. Get a copy from the **Japanese Red Cross Service Volunteers**, 1-1-3 Minato-ku, Shiba Daimon; tel: 03-3438 1311.

Club Tourism Division Barrier Free also offers help in getting around the city. Contact **Centre Kinki Nippon Tourist Co**, Shinjuku Island Wing, 10F, 6-3-1, Nishi Shinjuku, Shinjuku-ku, tel: 03-5323 6915; www.club-t.com.

Electricity

Japan's power supply is 100 volts AC. Tokyo and Eastern Japan run on 50 cycles (Western Japan uses 60 cycles). Plugs are two-pin. Most hotels have adaptors.

Embassies & Consulates

Embassies and consulates open Mon–Fri. Call ahead to find out the hours, as these vary.
Australia: 2-1-14 Mita, Minato-ku, tel: 03-5232 4111.
Canada: 7-3-38 Akasaka, Minato-ku, tel: 03-5412 6200
United Kingdom: 1 Ichiban-cho, Chiyoda-ku, tel: 03-3265 5511.
United States: 1-10-5 Akasaka, Minato-ku, tel: 03-3224 5000.

Emergency Numbers

Police: tel: 110
Fire/ambulance: tel: 119
Tokyo Police Information: tel: 03-3501 0110. A service that provides information and answers queries in English.
Tokyo English Life Line: tel: 03-3498 0231. Counselling service. Daily 9am–4pm, 7–11pm.

Entry Requirements

Visas & Passports

Visas are required only for visitors from some countries; most may stay for up to 90 days with a valid passport. A visa is necessary for foreigners living in Japan and engaged in business or study. Check with the Japanese embassy or consulate in your own country before making plans.

Extension of Stay

Foreigners wishing to extend their stay in Japan must report, in person, to the Immigration Bureau two weeks before their visa expires. Present your passport and a statement with the reasons why you want an extension. A fee of ¥3,000 will be charged. No extensions are granted to those who have entered Japan as a tourist without a visa.
Tokyo Regional Immigration Bureau: 5-5-30, Konan, Minato-ku, tel: 03-5796 7112. Mon–Fri 9am–noon, 1–4pm.
Shibuya Immigration Office: 1-3-5 Jinnan, Shibuya-ku. Mon–Fri 9–11.30am, 1–4pm.

Etiquette

There are points of etiquette for doing just about everything in Japan (blowing your nose in public for instance, especially at high volume is considered rude). Although as a visitor you may be blissfully unaware of most of them, the cardinal rule is to try to be courteous at all times.

At work and in most formal situations, the Japanese may seem reticent and lacking in spontaneity. But when drinking and having a good time, Japanese, especially the men, can become very raucous and often let out their real opinions and feelings.

It is often said that "the Japanese are only polite with their shoes off," which means that they are polite and courteous with people they know well and would be indoors with (where shoes are always removed).

Invitations

It is rare to be invited to someone's home. Most people live too far out of town or find their homes too cramped to invite guests. If you receive an invitation, take along a small gift with you: flowers, a food item or something from your own country.

Trains/Subway

On rush-hour trains you may find yourself being pushed and bumped around. You do not need to be polite here; just push along with everyone else.

Footwear

There is a strong distinction in Japan between the areas inside and outside the home. Just inside the entrance to homes (and many restaurants) is an area where you are expected to remove your shoes. From here, you step up into the living area either wearing the slippers provided or in your stockinged feet. This keeps the house clean and increases the amount of useable space, since you can sit on the floor without worrying about getting dirty. (Men sit cross-legged and women sit with their legs tucked under.) Slippers are never worn on *tatami* mats. Go barefoot instead.

Bathhouses

Whether at a hot spring resort, a local *sento* (bathhouse) or a traditional inn, the procedure is the same. Disrobe, enter the bathroom (in public you hide your modesty with a small washcloth), and wash and rinse off thoroughly under a shower before easing into the hot bath – which is for soaking, not washing yourself. Don't pull the plug after you've finished: others will use the same water.

Dining

Drinking: When having beer or *sake*, one always pours for the other party, who will hold up the glass while it is filled. It is polite to keep the glasses filled; if you have had enough, leave your glass full.

Eating: Soup is sipped directly from the bowl in which it is served. So is the broth of hot noodles, except for *ramen*, which comes with a spoon. When sipping soup, tea or other hot liquids, it is customary to draw in a good amount of air at the same time. Slurping sounds for noodles and other soup dishes are quite acceptable, but should be kept to a minimum in polite company.

Gay & Lesbian Travellers

Despite the presence of a few token transvestite personalities on prime-time television, the gay scene in Japan has a low profile and is mostly centred on Shinjuku's Nichome district, close to the Shinjuku Sanchome station.

There are hundreds of bars, clubs, bathhouses and saunas here, catering to all age groups and sexual preferences (see Gay and Lesbian Venues, page 223).

Tokyo Journal and *Metropolis* mag has gay and lesbian listings (www.metropolis.co.jp).

Gay Net Japan (www.gnj.or.jp) is a support and friendship group that also runs advertisements and discussion groups.

Utopia (www.utopia-asia.com/tipsjapn.htm) is an Asian site with Tokyo contacts and information.

Gay Scene @ Japan's site (gayscenejapan.fc2web.com) is also worth a look.

Government

Tokyo is led by a directly elected governor alongside a metropolitan assembly, which is housed in the Metropolitan Government Building in Shinjuku Ward. Each of the wards and outlying cities has its own respective elected local assembly.

Tokyo is also the seat of the national government, housed in the Diet building in Nagata-cho.

Health & Medical Care

No vaccinations are required before entering Japan, except if arriving from certain countries in Africa, Asia or South America. Hygiene levels are high, and you are unlikely to become ill as a result of eating or drinking. Tokyo's tap water is safe to drink.

Travel Insurance

Because all Japanese subscribe to national or company health insurance schemes, charges for hospitals, consultations and drugs are high. Make sure you buy a travel health insurance policy.

Hospitals/Clinics

Although some doctors speak English, it is likely the receptionist and nursing staff will not. When seeking medical aid, go with a Japanese-speaking companion.

Most hospitals and clinics do not have an appointment system for outpatient treatment, and visits usually entail a long wait. The following facilities are accustomed to dealing with foreign patients. Outpatient hours are indicated; emergency services are 24 hours.

International Catholic Hospital (Seibo Byoin): 2-5-1 Naka-Ochiai, Shinjuku-ku, tel: 03-3951 1111. Outpatients: Mon–Sat, 8–11am

Red Cross Medical Centre (Nisseki Iryo Sentaa): 4-1-22 Hiroo, Shibuya-ku, tel: 03-3400 1311. Outpatients:Mon–Fri 8–11.30am.

Tokyo British Clinic: Daikanyama Y Bldg, 2F, 2-13-7, Ebisu-Nishi, Shibuya-ku, tel: 03-5458 6099. Run by a respected British general practioner. Mon–Fri 9am–5.30pm, Sat 9am–12.30pm.

Pharmacies

American Pharmacy: 1-8-1 Yurakucho, Chiyoda-ku. Tel: 03-3271 4034. Mon–Sat 9.30–8pm; Sun 10am–6.30pm. There is a new branch in the basement of the Marunouchi Building, tel: 03-5220 7716.

The Medical Dispensary: 32 Mori Bldg, 1F, 3-4-30 Shiba-Koen, Minato-ku, tel: 03-3434 5817. Mon–Fri 9am–5.30pm; Sat 9am–1pm.

Roppongi Pharmacy: 6-8-8 Roppongi, Minato-ku, tel: 03-3403 8879. Daily 10.30–1am.

Internet

If carrying a laptop or PDA and you already have an ISP in your home country, check to see if they have a local phone number in Japan to make a connection; many do.

Internet Cafés

Telephone rates have dropped dramatically in Japan, making surfing the Internet more affordable. While 24-hour *manga* cafés are very competitive, the cheapest deal is from Yahoo! Japan who, together with Starbucks, have set up branches in Tokyo. Check http://cafe.yahoo.co.jp for locations. If not, try one of the following:

Café J Net New New: 7F, Saito Bldg, 34-5 Udagawa-cho, Shibuya-ku, tel: 03-5458 5935.

Laputa City: 1-14-14 Shibuya, Shibuya-ku, tel: 03-3407 2011.

Manga@Cafe-Gera Gera: 1-23-1 Kabuki-cho, Shinjuku-ku, tel: 03-5285 0585.

Manga Hiroba: Chuwa Roppongi Bldg, 2F, 3-14-12 Roppongi, Minato-ku, tel: 03-3497 1751.

Yahoo! Café: Garden Square, 5-11-2 Jingumae, Shibuya-ku, tel: 03-3797 6821.

Left Luggage

There are 24-hour counters offering storage facilities in both Terminals 1 and 2 at Narita Airport (tel: 0476-34 5000).

Location

Tokyo lies 35°N, 139°E, on the same latitude as the tip of the Korean peninsula, the Straits of Gibraltar and central California. The Japanese capital lies on the northwest shore of Tokyo Bay, at the eastern end of Japan's main Honshu island close to the Pacific Ocean. Mount Fuji – at 3,776 m (12,388 ft), Japan's highest – is visible on clear days from places in and around Tokyo.

Lost Property

JR trains and subways: Items left behind on trains and subways are usually kept for a few days at the station where they were handed in. After that, they are sent to one of the major stations where they are stored for another five days. Call any of the following for help: **JR** English-language infoline at tel: 03-3423 0111; **Teito** (Rapid Transportation Authority) tel: 03-3834 5577; and **Toei** (Tokyo Municipal Authority) trains and buses, tel: 03-3812 2011.

Taxis: All taxi companies in

Tokyo report unclaimed items to the **Tokyo Taxi Kindaika Centre**, tel: 03-3648 0300.

Police: The Tokyo Metropolitan Police Department maintains an efficient lost-and-found centre in Iidabashi, Chiyoda-ku, tel: 03-3814 4151.

Maps

The JNTO can provide an adequate map of Tokyo for free. For more detail, you can pick up the Shobunsha **Bilingual Map of Tokyo**, or Nippon Kokuseisha's **Map of Central Tokyo**. Visitors requiring more in-depth coverage will find the definitive 124-page Kodansha's **Tokyo City Atlas: A Bilingual Guide** very useful.

Media

Television

There are seven terrestrial TV channels. Two are from the quasi-national **Japan Broadcast Corporation** (NHK) and the other five are private-sector commercial networks. NHK also broadcasts on two satellite channels, plus a hi-definition TV channel. A small percentage of the programmes – including news bulletins – is bilingual, offering English on the sub-channel. Ask your hotel reception which button to press to see if the programme has a bilingual service.

Overseas networks CNN, ABC and BBC are available on satellite and cable TV at most large hotels.

Radio

Tokyo's main foreign language radio station is **Inter FM** (76.1 Mhz), which broadcasts news and music mainly in English. **J-Wave** (81.3 Mhz) also has some shows in English. The **Far East Network** (81.0 Mhz), broadcast by the US Armed Forces, airs music, news, US sports and some National Public Radio shows. Try also **Yokohama FM** (84.7 Mhz) and **NHK** (69.3 Mhz).

Newspapers/Magazines

There are two daily newspapers in English. *The Japan Times* (www.japantimes.co.jp) is the premier English-language paper and the oldest, followed by *The Daily Yomiuri* (www.yomiuri.co.jp). *The Asahi Shimbu/International Herald Tribune* (www.asahi.com/english/english.html) is a daily with a Japanese supplement. *The Nikkei Weekly* (www.nikkei.co.jp) is a financial digest.

For magazines, look out for the quarterly *Tokyo Journal* (www.tokyo.to), the monthly *JSelect* (www.jselect.net), and *Metropolis* (www.metropolis.co.jp), a free weekly.

The monthly *Eye-Ai* covers Japanese entertainment and culture. *Via*, a free publication, can be found in the seat pockets on the airport limousine bus.

The quarterly *J@pan.Inc*, is the foremost IT and business-related monthly magazine.

Money

The unit of currency is the yen (indicated as ¥). Coins are issued in denominations of ¥500, ¥100, ¥50, ¥10 and ¥1. There are bank notes for ¥10,000, ¥5,000 and ¥1,000. A ¥2,000 bill is under consideration. At time of press, US$1 was roughly equivalent to ¥122.

Travellers' Cheques

Travellers' cheques can be used only at a very limited number of hotels, restaurants and souvenir shops. Personal cheques are rarely used or accepted in Japan.

Credit Cards

Major credit cards (e.g. American Express, Diner's Club, Visa, MasterCard) are accepted at most establishments in and around Tokyo without surcharges. However, credit cards are sometimes not accepted in some restaurants and small bars.

Changing Money

Yen can be purchased at branches of major Japanese banks and authorised money changers on presentation of your passport. Besides the airport, authorised money changers can be found in the major hotels.

At Narita airport, bank counters remain open during airport hours. International transactions (e.g. remittances) are best conducted at major branches of Japanese banks, which have English-speaking staff. Banks are open Mon–Fri from 9am–3pm.

Emergency Cash

Credit cards issued by foreign banks cannot be used to make cash withdrawals, except at a few selected ATMs around central Tokyo. Check with your card issuer.
American Express: 0120-020 120
Diner's Club: 03-3499 1181
MasterCard: 03-5728 5200
Visa: 00531-440 022

Tipping

"No tipping" remains the rule in Japan, except for unusual or exceptional service. Most attempts to tip will elicit confusion. At more upmarket restaurants, a service charge of 10–15 percent is built into the bill.

Photography

Although there are no restrictions on what you can photograph, use your discretion in religious places.

Virtually every Japanese is an avid amateur photographer so camera stores are plentiful everywhere. Film (both 35mm and APS) is widely available at convenience stores and station kiosks. The best prices for cameras and film are found at discount chains such as Sakuraya, Laox and Yodobashi. The main stores for these are in Akihabara and Shinjuku, with outlets in the other main shopping districts.

Population

Central Tokyo's 23 wards have about 8.85 million residents, with a density of 5,300 people per sq km. The working population on weekdays is swelled by some 2.5

million commuters from outlying areas. Tokyo Prefecture, the total mass of the metropolis including its 23 wards and 27 cities, has 12 million people, while the Kanto Plain, which is the total urban area, has 27.5 million.

Postal Services

Postal services and deliveries are fast and highly efficient, but relatively expensive for both international and domestic mail. Local post offices are open Mon–Fri 9am–5pm; some open Sat mornings. Larger central post offices operate Mon–Fri 9am–7pm, and Sat 9am–noon.

The **Tokyo Central Post Office** (2-7-2 Marunouchi, Chiyoda-ku; tel: 03-3284 9539), on the Marunouchi side of Tokyo Station, accepts mail round the clock.

For 24-hour, 365-day international mail services, there is a special **Tokyo International Post Office** (Kokusai Yubin-kyoku), just north of Tokyo Station at 2-3-3 Otemachi, Chiyoda-ku.

For **Tokyo postal information**, call 03-3241 4891.

Express Mail/Courier

Larger post offices offer express mail services. International parcel post cannot exceed 20 kg per package to any international destination. For heavier packages use a commercial courier service.
Federal Express: tel: 053-298 1919; www.fedex.com
UPS Yamato Express: tel: 0120-271 040; www.ups.com

Public Holidays

January 1: Ganjitsu (New Year's Day)
January, 2nd Monday: Seijin no Hi (Coming of Age Day)
February 11: Kenkoku Kinen no Hi (National Foundation Day)
Around March 21: Shumbun no Hi (Vernal Equinox Day)
April 29: Midori no Hi (Greenery Day)
May 3: Kenpo Kinembi (Constitution Memorial Day)
May 4: Kokumin no Kyujitsu (National Holiday)
May 5: Kodomo no Hi (Children's Day)
July 20: Umi no Hi (National Maritime Day)
September 15: Keiro no Hi (Respect for the Aged Day)
Around September 23: Shubun no Hi (Autumnal Equinox Day)
October, 2nd Monday: Tai-iku no Hi (Sports Day)
November 3: Bunka no Hi (Culture Day)
November 23: Kinro Kansha no Hi (Labour Thanksgiving Day)
December 23: Tenno Tanjo Bi (Emperor's Birthday)

Public Toilets

Except in train stations, public toilets are few in Tokyo. Most people use the facilities in department stores or coffee shops. Traditional toilets are of the squatting type; these take some getting used to.

Religious Services

About 1 percent of the population is Christian (with a higher percentage in Tokyo).

Protestant

Ginza Church: 4-2-1 Ginza, Chuo-ku, tel: 03-3561 0236.
International Christian University Church: 3-10-2 Osawa, Mitaka-shi, tel: 0422-33 3323.

Catholic

Azabu Church: 3-21-6 Nishi-Azabu, Minato-ku, tel: 03-3408 1500.
Franciscan Chapel Centre: 4-2-37 Roppongi, Minato-ku, tel: 03-3401 2141.

Taxes

Consumption tax (VAT) of 5 percent is applied to all retail transactions (including at hotels and restaurants).

Telephones

The main domestic carrier is **Nippon Telegraph and Telephone** (NTT). Since deregulation, other companies such as DDI have tried to break into the market, but failed to establish a major presence.

Public phones are available throughout Tokyo, though the number is dropping because of the prevalence of mobile phones. The minimum cost of a local call is ¥10 per minute.

Telephone Cards

Telephones cards – not coins – are the primary form of payment for public phones, though you can still find machines that accept ¥10 and ¥100 coins. Each carrier issues its own prepaid cards: NTT and DDI (domestic) and KDD (international). The cards can only be used at the appropriate telephone booth.

Directory Assistance

- **NTT Information Service:** tel: 0120-505 506. A domestic telephone directory with information in English.
- **Local directory assistance:** tel: 104. Ask for an English-speaking operator.
- **International directory assistance** (English-speaking): tel: 0051.

Note: Local telephone numbers which begin with 0120, 0088 or 0053 are toll-free calls that can be dialled only within Japan.

Domestic Calls

Long-distance domestic calls (over 60 km/37 miles) are cheaper after peak hours by up to 40 percent. If calling from one province to another in Japan, be sure to dial the area code first (with the zero) before the phone number. When calling within Tokyo, don't dial the city's area code.

Area Codes

Tokyo	03
Yokohama	045
Narita	0476
Fukuoka	092
Hiroshima	082
Kagoshima	099
Kyoto	075
Nagasaki	0958
Nagoya	052

Naha	098
Osaka	06
Sapporo	011
Sendai	022

International Calls

• **International Dialling Code** for Japan is 81.
• **International operator**, dial 0051 to make a person-to-person, collect, or credit-card call from anywhere in Japan.

If calling Tokyo from overseas, dial +81-3 and then the local number. To make overseas calls from Tokyo, first dial the access code of one of the international call service providers below, then the country code and the number.
KDDI 010
NTT 0033
IDC 0061

International calls are possible from some grey and green public telephones; look for the globe logo.

Mobile Phones

Since the deregulation of the mobile phone industry about five years ago, Japan has gone from having one of the lowest rates of use to be one of the highest.

Japan uses two mobile phone systems: PDC and CDMA. If you come from a country that uses the more common GSM system found in Asia, UK, Europe, Australia and New Zealand, your phone will not work here. Check with your home service provider if unsure as you will have to rent a handset that can hook up with the local network. The largest of the several operators is **NTT Docomo** (a subsidiary of NTT), tel: 0120-680 100; www.nttdocomo.com.

Most mobile phone numbers begin with 090.

Time Zones

Tokyo (like the rest of Japan) is +9 hours GMT; +14 hours EST (New York); and +17 PST (Los Angeles). Japan does not have summer daylight savings time – although the idea is periodically mooted (and then dismissed, out of deference to the nation's farmers).

Tourism Offices

The Japan government is vigorously implementing advertising and other programmes aimed at attracting more tourists to the country. This has resulted in more information available on the Internet, and at tourism offices both within the country and overseas.

The **Tourist Information Centres** (TIC) run by the **Japan National Tourist Organisation** (JNTO), not only has massive amounts of information on Tokyo, but can also organise hotel reservations. The multilingual counterstaff found in the tourism offices are exceedingly well trained and helpful.
Japan National Tourist Organization (JNTO): 2-10-1 Yurakucho, Chiyoda-ku, tel: 03-3216 1903, fax:03-3214 7680, www.jnto.go.jp.

Local Tourism Offices

Tokyo Information Centre (TIC): 2-10-1 Kotsukaikan Bldg, 10F, Yurakucho, Chiyoda-ku, tel: 03-3201 3331, www.jnto.go.jp.
Narita Airport TIC: Arrival Floor, Passenger Terminal 2 Bldg, New Tokyo International Airport, Chiba Prefecture, tel: 0476-345 877.
Narita Airport TIC (branch): Arrival Floor, Passenger Terminal 1 Bldg, New Tokyo International Airport, Chiba Prefecture, tel: 0476-303 383.

Overseas Tourist Offices

Asia
Bangkok: 19th Floor, Ramaland Building, No. 952 Rama 4 Road. Bangrak District, Bangkok 10500, tel: 02-233 5108.
Australia
Level 18, Australia Sq Tower, 264 George Street, Sydney, NSW 2000, tel: 02-9251 3024.
United Kingdom
Heathcoat House, 20 Savile Row, London W1S 3PR, tel: 20-7734 9638.
United States
New York: One Rockefeller Plaza, Suite 1250, New York, NY 10020, tel: 212-757 5640.
Los Angeles: 515 South Figueroa St, Suite 1470, Los Angeles, CA 90017, tel: 213-623 1952.
San Francisco: One Daniel Burnham Court, Suite 250C, cnr Post Street and Van Ness Avenue, San Francisco, CA 94109, tel: 415-292 5686.

Websites

Club Information Agency (CIA): www.ciajapan.com. Excellent club events listings.
Japan Nat'l Tourist Organisation: www.jnto.go.jp/. Excellent links and travel information.
Japan Times: www.japantimes.co.jp. Oldest and most important English-language daily.
Japan Site: www.japan.com. Good general site on Tokyo and Japan travel, business and technology.
Yokoso: www.japantravelinfo.com. "The 'What's New" lifestyle section of this extensive website has useful travel articles.
Metropolis: www.metropolis.co.jp. The lowdown on Tokyo's nightlife, restaurants and events of interest.
Sumo World: www.sumo.or.jp. Site on the giant wrestlers and their upcoming bouts.
Tokyo Consumer Prices: www.pricechecktokyo.com. Guide to cost of living in Tokyo.
Tokyo Food Page: www.bento.com. Good online restaurant guide.
Tokyo Journal: www.tokyo.to. Good events site with entertainment, food and nightlife listings.
Tokyo Pop: www.tokyopop.com. Comprehensive guide to Japanese pop culture and its icons.
Tokyo Q: www.tokyoq.com. One of the better on-line guides with restaurant and nightlife postings.

Weights & Measures

Japan follows the metric system, except in cases governed by strong tradition. For example, rice and *sake* are measured in units of 1.8 litres and rooms are measured by a standard *tatami* mat size.

LANGUAGE

UNDERSTANDING THE LANGUAGE

General

Japanese is the main language and is almost exclusively spoken, but in the conduct of international business, English is used. Signs on streets, stations and public buildings are generally written in Roman letters, often with English translations. The level of spoken English is generally poor.

Japanese uses three different forms of writing (four, including Roman letters): two simple home-grown syllabaries (phonetic scripts) known as *hiragana* and *katakana*, each of which consist of 46 basic characters; plus the Chinese characters (*kanji*). Knowledge of just under 2,000 of these (plus their numerous compounds) is required to read a daily newspaper.

While it is unnecessary to memorise more than very few simple *kanji* characters (those for "man" and "woman" are useful at hot spring resorts and public toilets), it is not so daunting to learn the two *kana* scripts. This will help you read station names and some menu listings.

Hiragana is used for transliterating most *kanji* and for connectors that cannot be written with *kanji*. *Katakana* is used primarily for representing foreign names and loan words (e.g. *takushi*/taxi).

Pronunciation Tips

Apart from a few consonants, Japanese is easy to pronounce. The vowels in standard Japanese are always regular. The most important aspect is to give each syllable equal stress and to avoid the intonation patterns of English and other Western languages.

Consonants do not exist on their own, with the exception of "n" which only follows a vowel, but are always accompanied by one of the five basic vowel sounds. These are pronounced much as they would be in English, with the following notes:

chi – as in cheese
g – always hard (as in get)
ji/ju/jo – as in jeans/June/joke
n – pronounced like m before b or p (*tenpura* is read tempura; *shinbun* (newspaper) is pronounced shimbun)
tsu – like "it's" (without the i)

The basic vowel sounds are pronounced much as in Spanish.

a – like the a in about
e – like the e in egg
i – like the i in ink
o – like the o in orange
u – like the u in butcher

In combination the vowels are pronounced as follows:

ai – like "eye"
ae – almost the same as ai, but with a slight e sound at the end
ao – like the ow in cow
au – almost the same as ao, but with a more u sound at the end
ei – like the ay in way
io – like an elision "ee-yo"
iu – like an elision "ee-yu"
ue – like an elision "oo-e"
uo – like an elision "oo-oh"

When i and u occur in the middle of words, they are sometimes almost silent. For example, *shitamachi* (Tokyo's "low city") is actually pronounced "sh'ta-machi", while *sukiyaki* sounds more like "s'kiyaki". A final u is also pronounced so imperceptibly as to be unnoticeable: thus *desu* is always pronounced "dess".

Vowels are sometimes elongated (doubled), and this is indicated in Roman letters by a macron (a line over the said vowel), by an extra h (after o), or by writing a double vowel (in the case of i). The spelling in English, however, does not always reflect the double vowel.

TERMS OF ADDRESS

Japanese do not usually use first names, but the family name, followed by "-san," which can stand for Mr, Mrs, Miss or Ms. The suffix "-chan"may be used by close friends.

FURTHER READING

History & Culture

A Historical Guide to Yokohama, by Burritt Sabin (Yurindo, 2002). Meticulously researched, the definitive work on the city.

Embracing Defeat, by John Dower (Penguin Books, 2000). Pulitzer prize-winning study of Japan under the American Occupation.

Low City, High City: Tokyo From Edo to the Earthquake, by Edward Seidensticker (Knopf/Tuttle, 1983). The best history of how the city changed from shogun's capital to a modern metropolis.

My Asakusa: Coming of Age in Pre-War Tokyo, by Sadako Sawamura (Tuttle Publishing, 2000). A delightful and frank memoir of one of the city's best loved districts by the late actress-writer Sawamura.

Speed Tribes, by Karl Taro Greenfeld (HarperCollins, 1994). Profiles of Tokyo's subterranean youth culture.

The Life And Death of Yukio Mishima, by Henry Scott Stokes (Cooper Square Press, 1999). The standard work on Japan's most controversial writer by the British author and journalist who knew and understood him better than any of the other biographers.

Tokyo: A View of the City, by Donald Richie (Reaktion Books, 1999). Tokyo through the aesthetic but highly contemporary looking glass of its foremost expatriate writer.

Tokyo Now & Then, by Paul Waley (Weatherhill, 1984). A very detailed book linking the history of the city with specific locations.

Tokyo Underworld, by Robert Whiting (Vintage, 2000). Biography of an American gangster in the post-war era.

Travel

Insight Guide: Japan (Apa Publications, 2004). A companion to *Insight Guide Tokyo*, this 400-page book provides coverage of the entire country.

Insight Pocket Guide: Tokyo, by Stephen Mansfield (Apa Publications, 2003). A user-friendly itinerary-based guide to the city's major sights. Also includes excursions to places outside Tokyo.

Kids' Trips in Tokyo, by Maeda, Kobe, Ozeki & Sato (Kodansha Int'l, 1998). A host of activities for children in and around the city, written by and for parents.

Nature in Tokyo, by Kevin Short (Kodansha International, 2000). A comprehensive guide to plants and animals in and around Tokyo.

Tokyo City Atlas (Kodansha International). An essential bilingual guide with maps covering central and outlying parts of Tokyo.

Tokyo Night City, by Jude Brand (Tuttle, 1993). Jazz and salsa clubs, drinking holes, gay bars and party scenes by someone who's been there and is still doing it.

Food & Drink

A Taste of Japan, by Donald Richie (Kodansha Int'l, 1985). The finer points of Japanese cuisine explained.

The Insider's Guide to Sake, by Philip Harper (Kodansha Int'l, 1998). The only foreigner to become a full-time sake brewer explains what makes the trade so special.

The Sake Handbook, by John Gauntner (Yenbooks, 1997). Explains the intricacies of Japan's national tipple, and includes favourite Tokyo drinking holes.

What's What in Japanese Restaurants, by Robb Satterwhite (Kodansha Int'l, 1988). Invaluable for deciphering menus.

Literature

A View from the Chuo Line, by Donald Richie (Printed Matter, 2004). Minimalist stories set in Tokyo from the master observer.

Blind Willow, Sleeping Woman, by Haruki Murakami (Alfred A. Knoft, 2004). Twenty-four stories by Japan's best-known author, several of them set in Tokyo.

Green Tea to Go: Stories from Tokyo, by Leza Lowitz (Printed Matter Press, 2004). Superior stories of Tokyo life, love and cultural orientation.

Idoru, by William Gibson (Berkeley, 1998). Futurist fantasy but strangely accurate rendering of Japanese youth in the digital age. Parts of his recent *Pattern Recognition* are set in Tokyo.

Number9Dream, by David Mitchell (Sceptre, 2001). A novel set in Tokyo that was nominated for the Booker Prize.

Samurai Boogie, by Peter Tasker (Orion, 1999). Private eye Kazuo Mori investigates the underbelly of the city in Tokyo-based Tasker's *noir* novel. Check out also the more recent *Dragon Dance*, also set in Tokyo.

Scandal, by Shusaku Endo (Tuttle Publishing, 1986). An enigmatic novel of Tokyo characters and places by the late, much missed master.

Tokyo Sketches, by Peter Hamill (Kodansha, 1992). An engaging collection of short stories.

Tokyo Stories: A Literary Stroll, translated and edited by Lawrence Rogers (University of California Press, 2002). An anthology of stories by Japanese writers with Tokyo settings. Many appear for the first time in English.

Art & Photo Credits

A.M. Gross back cover right
APA 22L, 26
Arch Palais Imperial/HBL 25
Beezer 34, 51, 52, 107, 124
Blaine Harrington 6L, 10/11, 82, 201
Bunka Gakuen Costume Museum 103M
Carl Purcell 88M
Catherine Karnow 122
Click Chicago/APA 38, 49, 174, 194/195
Colin Sinclair 68, 79
Dennis Kessler/APA 50, 80, 150, 151L, 167, 179, 190, 203, 207
Figaro Magazine/HBL 32
Francis Dorai/APA 76, 81, 89R, 147, 154L, 161, 162L/R, 176, 179M, 191R
Gorazd Vilhar 27, 110, 163
Hara Museum of Contemporary Art 139
Heather Angel 169M
Japan Folk Craft Museum 127
Japan National Tourist Organization 112M, 181
Jean Kugler 199M
Jim Holmes/Axiom 58, 144M, 173, 186, 202L/R
John S. Callahan/Photo Resource Hawaii back cover bottom
Jon Burbank/Hutchison Library 35L, 123
Joseph Zanghi 16
Keyphoto 140
LaQua 170
Lee Taplinger/Photo Resource Hawaii 133R
Mark Henley/Impact Photo 126
Michael Jenner 89L
Michael Macintyre/Hutchison Library 9LT
Mitchell Coster/Axiom 87, 100, 135, 182
Nezu Institute of Fine Arts 114M
Paul Quayle/Panos Pictures back cover left, 57, 118, 180
Philip Gordon/Impact 81M
Photobank 19, 103R, 152M
R. Humphries/HBL 24
Richard Nowitz/APA 2/3, 3, 4T/B, 5L/R, 7LT, 8L, 8RT, 9LB, 9RT, 9RB, 14, 22R, 31, 35R, 45, 46, 47L/R, 48, 53, 55L, 61, 72, 73, 75, 84, 85, 86, 86M, 94, 95, 97R, 101, 102M, 103L, 104M, 105R, 107M, 113R, 115M, 116, 121, 125R, 130, 131, 132M, 134, 134M, 141, 141M, 144, 149M, 153, 156, 164M, 171L/R, 174M, 181M, 189L, 189M, 192
Robin Laurance/Impact Photo 28/29
Roppongi Hills Tokyo City View 64/65
Scott Rutherford 36, 142
Seiji Togo Art Museum 104
Shoto Museum of Art 126M
Simon Rowe 30
Stephen Mansfield/APA 1, 7LB, 7RT, 8RB, 12/13, 20, 33, 37L/R, 39, 42, 44, 55R, 60L/R, 66/67, 76M, 77, 78, 78M, 82M, 88, 90, 90M, 91, 96M, 98M, 105L, 106, 111, 115, 119, 120M, 121M, 123M, 125L, 125M, 138, 140M, 146, 149L/R, 151R, 152, 154R, 154M, 155, 158, 159, 160, 160M, 163M, 164, 166, 169, 170M, 187, 189R, 192M, 196, 203M, 204, 205, 206, 206M
Stephen Mansfield 6R, 7RB, 23, 59, 114, 116M, 143, 172, 172M, 177, 178, 190M, 200, 200M
Stuart Atkin 43
T. Bognar/Trip 199
Thierry Orban/Corbis 54
Tokyo Disneyland 197
Tokyo Museum of Contemporary Art 182M
Tokyo National Museum 17, 18
Topham Picturepoint 21
Toyota Corporation 56
Watari-um Museum 113L
Zoshigaya Missionary Museum 98

Picture Spreads

Pages 40/41: Top row from left to right: Richard Nowitz/APA, Richard Nowitz/APA. Bottom row from left to right: Stephen Mansfield, Dennis Kessler/APA, Stephen Mansfield, Francis Dorai/APA.
Pages 62/63: Top row from left to right: Stephen Mansfield, Francis Dorai/APA. Bottom row from left to right: Richard Nowitz/APA, Stephen Mansfield, C. Mccooey/ Trip (upper), Stephen Mansfield/ APA (lower), Stephen Mansfield.
Pages 184/185: Top row from left to right: Mitchell Coster/Axiom, Mitchell Coster/Axiom. Bottom row from left to right: Michael Macintyre/ Hutchison Library, Dennis Kessler/APA, Robert Holmes, Michael Macintyre/Hutchison Library.

Map Production: Dave Priestley and Stephen Ramsay

Tokyo Street Atlas

The key map shows the area of Tokyo covered by the atlas section. An index of street names and places of interest shown on the maps can be found on the following pages. For each entry there is a page number and grid reference.

Map Legend

Motorway with Junction	Airport	Motorway	Metro
Motorway (under construction)	Church (ruins)	Dual Carriageway	Bus Station
Dual Carriageway	Monastery	Main Roads	Tourist Information
Main Road	Castle (ruins)		Post Office
Secondary Road	Archaeological Site	Minor Roads	Cathedral/Church
Minor road	Cave		Mosque
Track	Place of Interest	Footpath	Synagogue
National Park/Reserve	Mansion/Stately Home	Pedestrian Area	Statue/Monument
Ferry Route	Viewpoint	Important Building	Tower
Railway	Beach	Park	Lighthouse

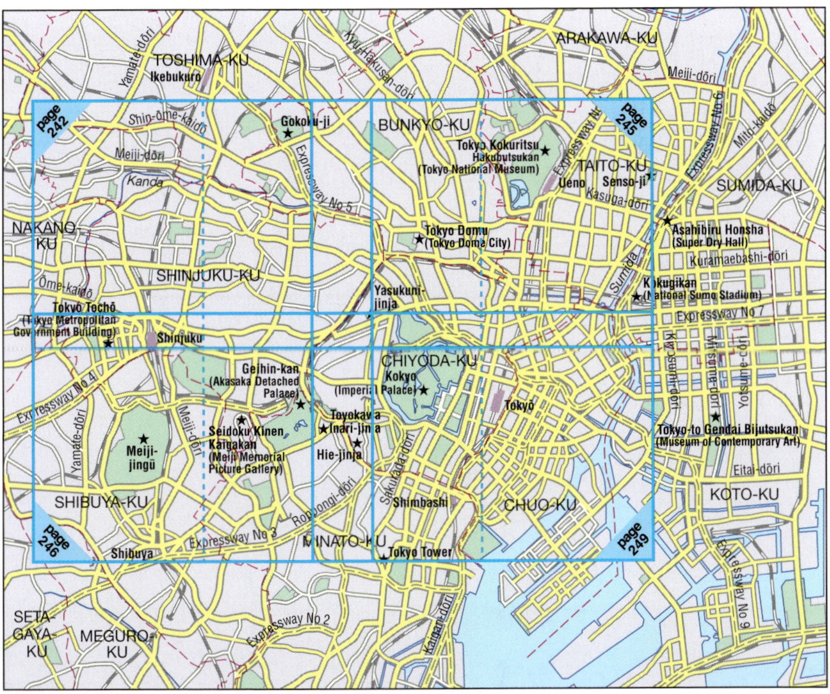

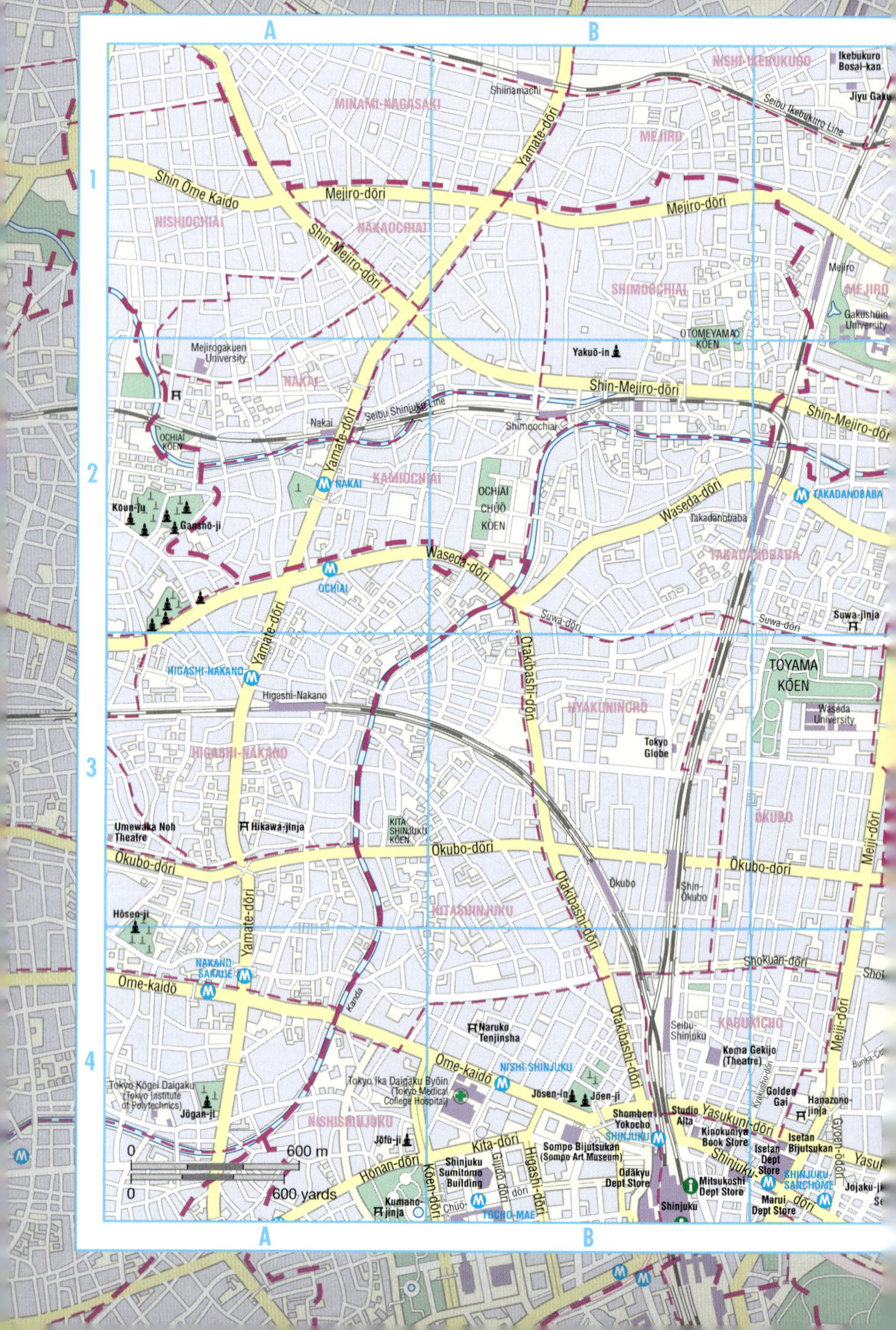
A
B
1
2
3
4
NISHI-IKEBUKURO
Ikebukuro Bosai-kan
Jiyu Gaku
Shiinamachi
Seibu Ikebukuro Line
MINAMI-NAGASAKI
MEJIRO
Yamate-dōri
Shin Ōme Kaido
Mejiro-dōri
NISHIOCHIAI
NAKAOCHIAI
Shin-Mejiro-dōri
SHIMOOCHIAI
Mejiro
Gakushūin University
OTOMEYAMA KŌEN
Yakuō-in
Mejirogakuen University
NAKAI
Seibu Shinjuku Line
Nakai
Shimoochiai
OCHIAI KŌEN
NAKAI
KAMIOCHIAI
OCHIAI CHŪŌ KŌEN
Waseda-dōri
Takadanobaba
TAKADANOBABA
Koun-ju
Ganshō-ji
OCHIAI
Suwa-dōri
Suwa-jinja
HIGASHI-NAKANO
Higashi-Nakano
Otakibashi-dōri
HYAKUNINCHŌ
TOYAMA KŌEN
Waseda University
Tokyo Globe
HIGASHI-NAKANO
Umewaka Noh Theatre
Hikawa-jinja
KITA SHINJUKU KŌEN
ŌKUBO
Ōkubo-dōri
Ōkubo
Shin-Ōkubo
Meiji-dōri
KITASHINJUKU
Hōsen-ji
NAKANO-SAKAUE
Ōme-kaidō
Shokuan-dōri
Kanda
Naruko Tenjinsha
Seibu-Shinjuku
KABUKICHŌ
Koma Gekijo (Theatre)
Bunka-Center
Tokyo Kōgei Daigaku (Tokyo Institute of Polytechnics)
Jōgan-ji
Tokyo Ika Daigaku Byōin (Tokyo Medical College Hospital)
NISHI-SHINJUKU
Jōsen-in
Jōen-ji
Golden Gai
Kyakushō-dōri
Hanazono-jinja
NISHISHINJUKU
Shomben Yokocho
Studio Alta
Yasukuni-dōri
Kinokuniya Book Store
Isetan Bijutsukan
Jōfū-ji
Kita-dōri
Sompo Bijutsukan (Sompo Art Museum)
SHINJUKU
Isetan Dept Store
Gyoen-dōri
Yasuk
0
600 m
0
600 yards
Hōnan-dōri
Kōen-dōri
Shinjuku Sumitomo Building
Gijidō dōri
Higashi-dōri
Odakyu Dept Store
Mitsukoshi Dept Store
Shinjuku-dōri
SHINJUKU-SANCHŌME
Jojaku-ji
Kumano-jinja
Chūō-dōri
TOCHŌ-MAE
Shinjuku
Marui Dept Store

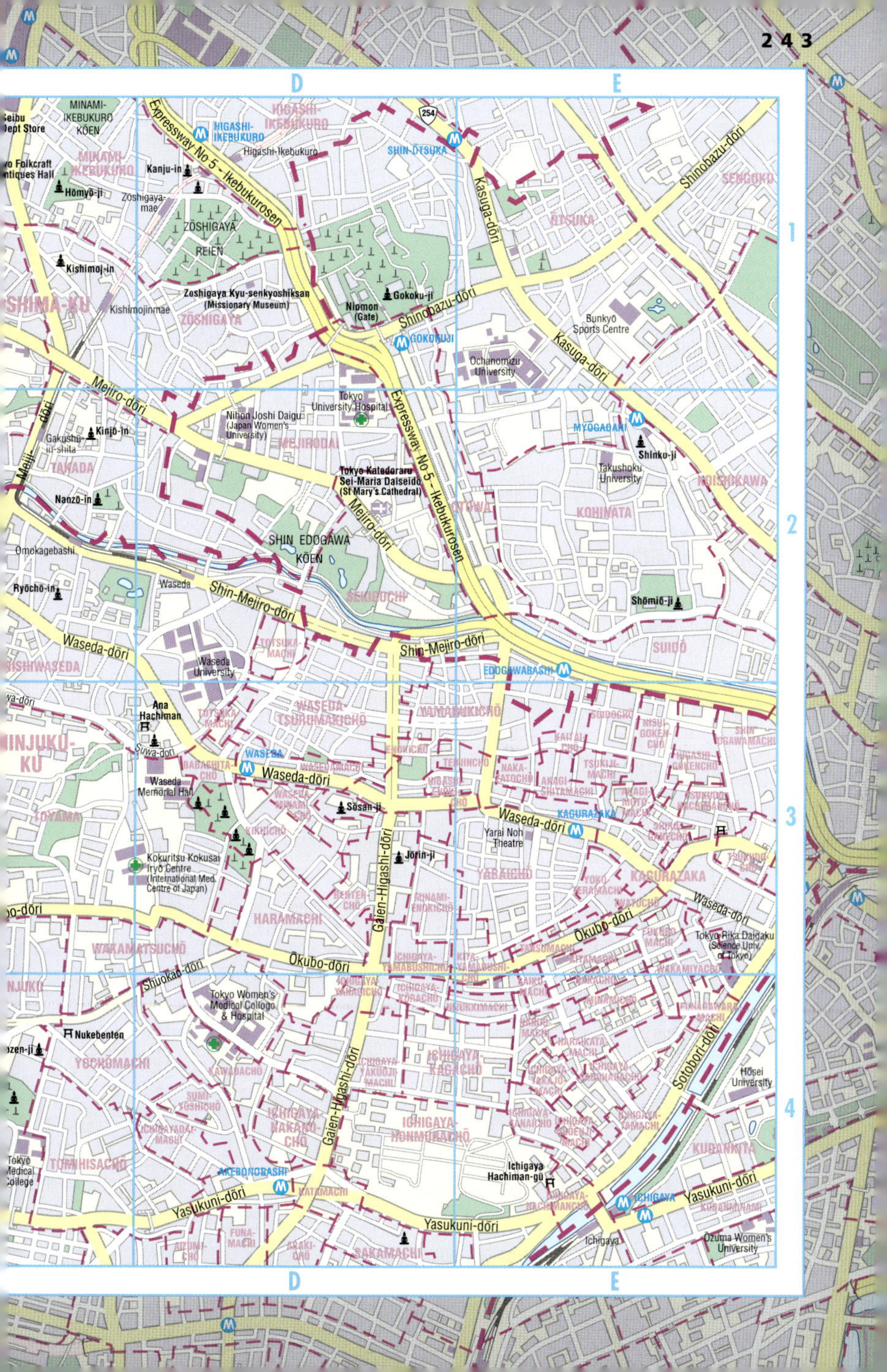
D
E
1
2
3
4
MINAMI-IKEBUKURO KŌEN
Seibu Dept Store
MINAMI-IKEBUKURO
HIGASHI-IKEBUKURO
Higashi-Ikebukuro
Expressway No 5 - Ikebukurosen
254
SHIN-ŌTSUKA
Kanju-in
Hōmyō-ji
Zōshigaya-mae
ZŌSHIGAYA REIEN
Kishimoj-in
Kishimojinmae
Zoshigaya Kyu-senkyoshiksan (Missionary Museum)
ZŌSHIGAYA
Gokoku-ji
Niomon (Gate)
Shinobazu-dōri
GOKOKUJI
Kasuga-dōri
ŌTSUKA
SENGOKU
Bunkyō Sports Centre
Ochanomizu University
Mejiro-dōri
Meiji-dōri
Kinjō-in
Gakushū-in-shita
TAKADA
Nanzō-in
Nihon Joshi Daigu (Japan Women's University)
MEJIRODAI
Tokyo University Hospital
Expressway No 5 - Ikebukurosen
MYOGADANI
Shinko-ji
Takushoku University
KOISHIKAWA
Tokyo Katedoraru Sei-Maria Daiseido (St Mary's Cathedral)
OTOWA
KOHINATA
SHIN EDOGAWA KŌEN
Omokagebashi
Ryōchō-in
Waseda
Shin-Mejiro-dōri
SEKIGUCHI
Shōmiō-ji
Waseda-dōri
Waseda University
SUIDŌ
EDOGAWABASHI
Ana Hachiman
WASEDA-TSURUMAKICHŌ
YAMABUKICHŌ
Suwa-dōri
WASEDA
Waseda-dōri
Waseda Memorial Hall
Sōsan-ji
KAGURAZAKA
Yarai Noh Theatre
TOYAMA
Jōrin-ji
YARAICHŌ
KAGURAZAKA
Kokuritsu Kokusai Iryō Centre (International Med. Centre of Japan)
Galen-Higashi-dōri
HARAMACHI
Ōkubo-dōri
Tokyo Rika Daigaku (Science Univ. of Tokyo)
WAKAMATSUCHŌ
Shuokan-dōri
Tokyo Women's Medical College & Hospital
Nukebenten
YOCHŌMACHI
Sotobori-dōri
Hosei University
ICHIGAYA-HONMURACHŌ
KUDANKITA
Tokyo Medical College
AKEBONOBASHI
Ichigaya Hachiman-gū
ICHIGAYA
Yasukuni-dōri
Ichigaya
Ōzuma Women's University
SAKAMACHI

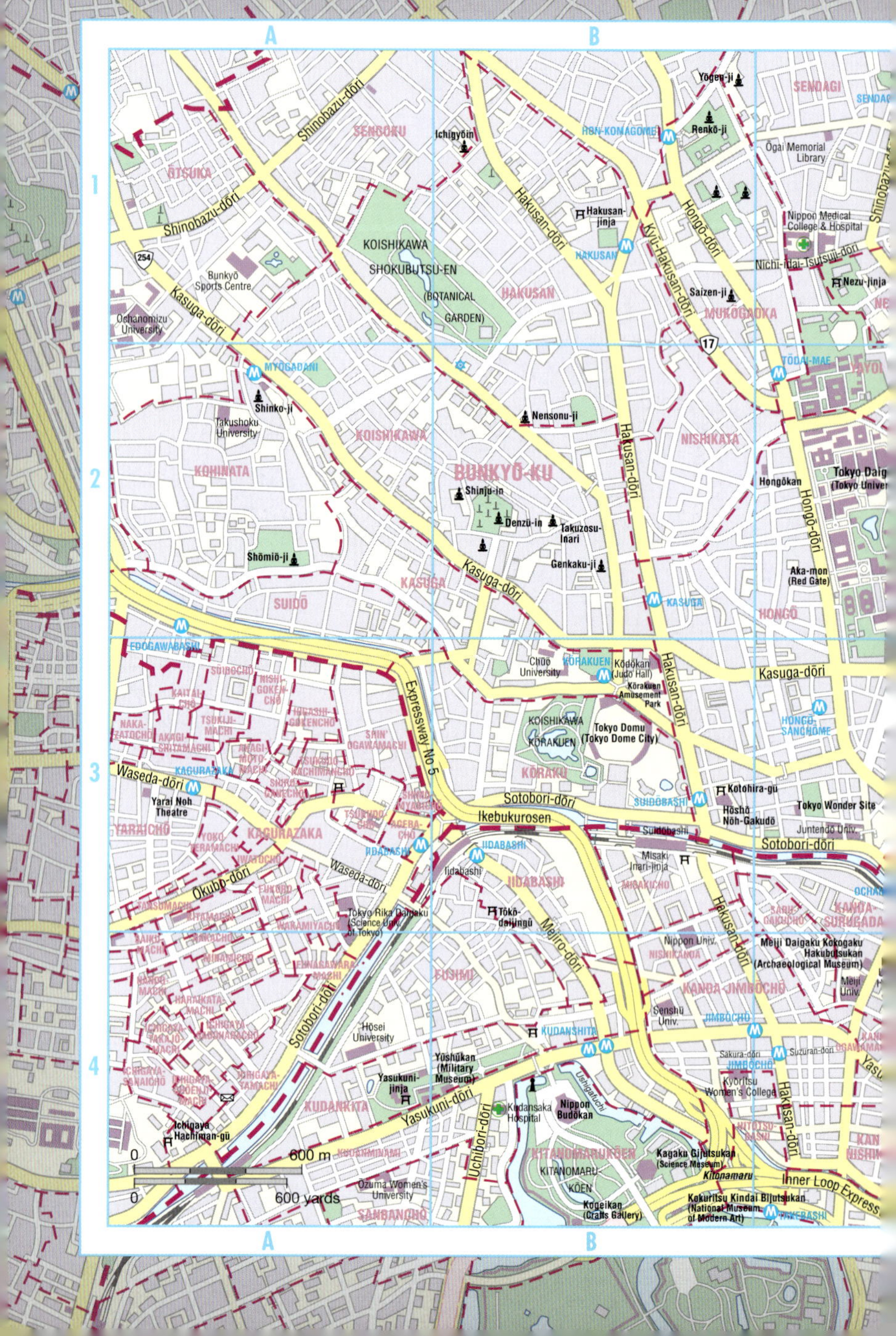
A
B
1
2
3
4
Shinobazu-dōri
SENGOKU
Ichigyōin
Yōgen-ji
SENDAGI
HON-KOMAGOME
Renkō-ji
Ōgai Memorial Library
ŌTSUKA
Hakusan-dōri
Hakusan-jinja
Hongō-dōri
Kyū-Hakusan-dōri
Nippon Medical College & Hospital
Nichi-idai-Tsutsuji-dōri
Nezu-jinja
254
Bunkyō Sports Centre
KOISHIKAWA SHOKUBUTSU-EN
(BOTANICAL GARDEN)
HAKUSAN
Saizen-ji
MUKŌGAOKA
Kasuga-dōri
Ochanomizu University
17
MYŌGADANI
TŌDAI-MAE
Shinko-ji
Takushoku University
Nensonu-ji
KOISHIKAWA
NISHIKATA
KOHINATA
BUNKYŌ-KU
Shinju-in
Denzū-in
Takuzosu-Inari
Hongōkan
Tokyo Daig
(Tokyo Univer
Shōmiō-ji
Genkaku-ji
Aka-mon
(Red Gate)
KASUGA
SUIDŌ
HONGŌ
EDOGAWABASHI
Chūō University
KŌRAKUEN
Kōdōkan
(Judo Hall)
Kōrakuen Amusement Park
Expressway No 5
KOISHIKAWA KŌRAKUEN
Tokyo Domu
(Tokyo Dome City)
HONGŌ-SANCHŌME
Waseda-dōri
KAGURAZAKA
Yarai Noh Theatre
KŌRAKU
Sotobori-dōri
Kotohira-gū
SUIDŌBASHI
Hōshō Nōh-Gakudō
Tokyo Wonder Site
Ikebukurosen
Suidōbashi
Juntendō Univ.
YARAICHŌ
IIDABASHI
Misaki Inari-jinja
Iidabashi
Ōkubo-dōri
MISAKICHŌ
Tōkō-daijingū
Mejiro-dōri
Tokyo Rika Daigaku
(Science Univ. of Tokyo)
Nippon Univ.
Meiji Daigaku Kōkogaku Hakubutsukan
(Archaeological Museum)
Meiji Univ.
FUJIMI
KANDA-JIMBŌCHŌ
Senshū Univ.
JIMBŌCHŌ
Hōsei University
KUDANSHITA
Yūshūkan
(Military Museum)
Yasukuni-jinja
Sakura-dōri
Suzuran-dōri
Kyōritsu Women's College
Ushigafuchi
Yasukuni-dōri
Uchibori-dōri
Kudansaka Hospital
Nippon Budōkan
KUDANKITA
Ichigaya Hachiman-gū
KITANOMARU KŌEN
Kagaku Gijutsukan
(Science Museum)
Kitanomaru
Inner Loop Express
0
600 m
0
600 yards
Ōzuma Women's University
SANBANCHŌ
KITANOMARU-KŌEN
Kōgeikan
(Crafts Gallery)
Kokuritsu Kindai Bijutsukan
(National Museum of Modern Art)
TAKEBASHI

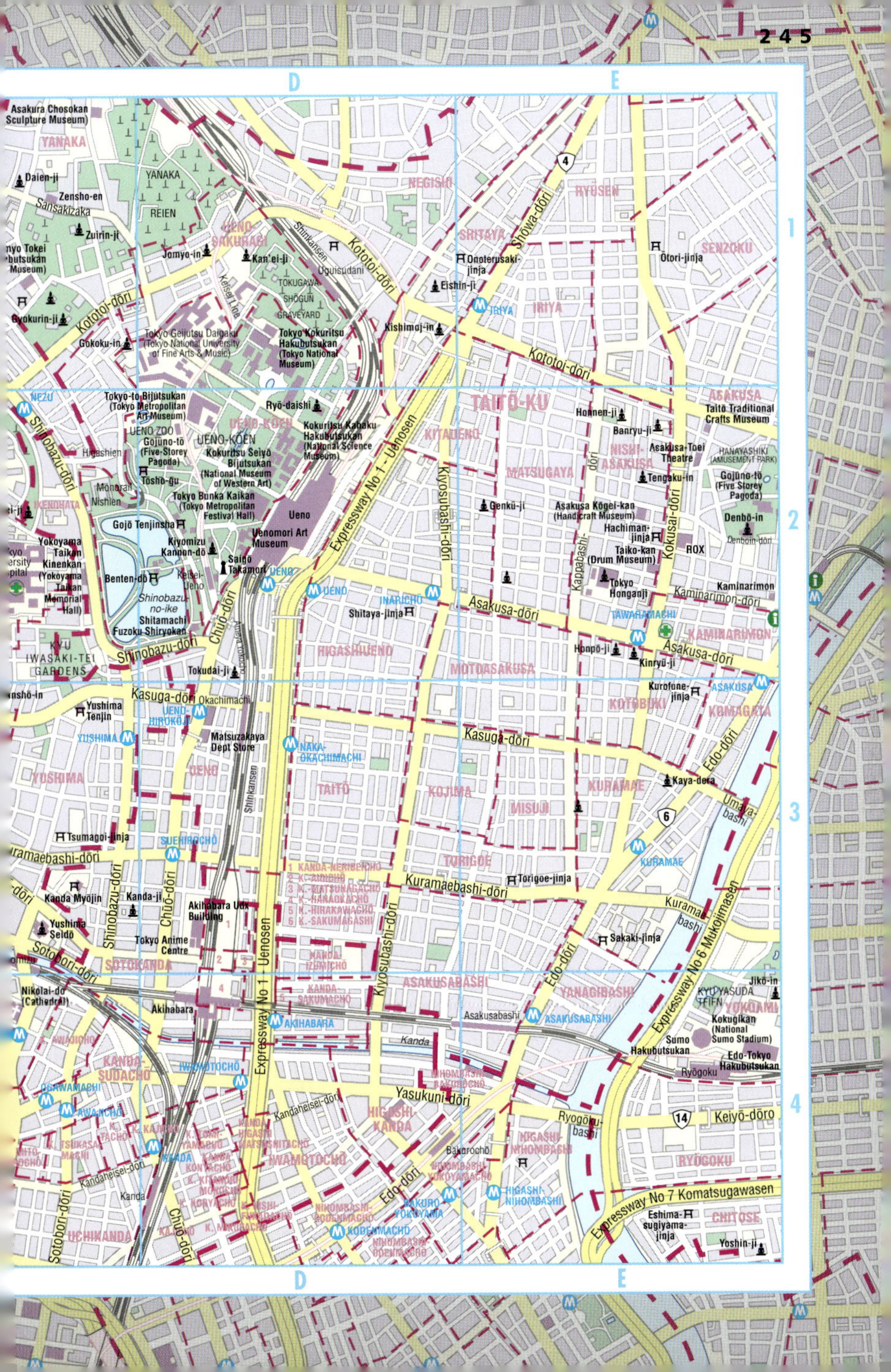
D
E
1
2
3
4
Asakura Chosokan Sculpture Museum
YANAKA
Daien-ji
Zensho-en
Sansakizaka
Zuirin-ji
YANAKA REIEN
UENO-SAKURAGI
Jomyo-in
Kan'ei-ji
TOKUGAWA SHOGUN GRAVEYARD
Shinkansen
Uguisudani
Kototoi-dōri
Gyokurin-ji
Gokoku-in
Tokyo Geijutsu Daigaku (Tokyo National University of Fine Arts & Music)
Tokyo Kokuritsu Hakubutsukan (Tokyo National Museum)
Kishimoj-in
NEGISHI
SHITAYA
Showa-dōri
Onoterusaki-jinja
Eishin-ji
IRIYA
RYUSEN
Otori-jinja
SENZOKU
NEZU
Tokyo-to Bijutsukan (Tokyo Metropolitan Art Museum)
Ryō-daishi
UENO ZOO
UENO-KŌEN
Gojūno-tō (Five-Storey Pagoda)
Tōshō-gu
Kokuritsu Seiyō Bijutsukan (National Museum of Western Art)
Kokuritsu Kahaku Hakubutsukan (National Science Museum)
Tokyo Bunka Kaikan (Tokyo Metropolitan Festival Hall)
Higashien
Nishien
Gojō Tenjinsha
Kiyomizu Kannon-dō
Benten-dō
Shinobazu-no-ike
Shitamachi Fuzoku Shiryokan
Saigo Takamori
Ueno
Uenomori Art Museum
Expressway No 1 - Uenosen
TAITŌ-KU
KITAUENO
MATSUGAYA
Kiyosubashi-dōri
Genkū-ji
Honnen-ji
Banryu-ji
NISHI-ASAKUSA
Asakusa-Toei Theatre
Tengaku-in
ASAKUSA
Taitō Traditional Crafts Museum
HANAYASHIKI (AMUSEMENT PARK)
Gojūno-tō (Five Storey Pagoda)
Denbō-in
Asakusa Kōgei-kan (Handicraft Museum)
Hachiman-jinja
Taiko-kan (Drum Museum)
Tokyo Honganji
Kappabashi-dōri
Kokusai-dōri
ROX
Kaminarimon
Kaminarimon-dōri
KAMINARIMON
Shinobazu-dōri
Yokoyama Taikan Kinenkan (Yokoyama Taikan Memorial Hall)
KYU IWASAKI-TEI GARDENS
Chuō-dōri
Tokudai-ji
UENO
INARICHO
Shitaya-jinja
Asakusa-dōri
TAWARAMACHI
HIGASHIUENO
MOTOASAKUSA
Honpō-ji
Kinryū-ji
Kurofune-jinja
KOTOBUKI
KOMAGATA
Yushima Tenjin
Kasuga-dōri
Okachimachi
UENO-HIROKOJI
YUSHIMA
Matsuzakaya Dept Store
NAKA-OKACHIMACHI
Shinkansen
TAITŌ
KOJIMA
MISUJI
KURAMAE
Kaya-dera
Edo-dōri
Umaya-bashi
Tsumagoi-jinja
SUEHIROCHO
Kuramaebashi-dōri
1 KANDA-NERIBEICHO
2 K.-AIOICHO
3 K.-MATSUNAGACHO
4 K.-HANAOKACHO
5 K.-HIRAKAWACHO
6 K.-SAKUMAGASHI
TORIGOE
Torigoe-jinja
Kanda Myōjin
Kanda-ji
Akihabara Udx Building
Yushima Seidō
Tokyo Anime Centre
Sotobori-dōri
SOTOKANDA
KANDA-IZUMICHO
Sakaki-jinja
Kuramae-bashi
Expressway No 6 Mukojimasen
Jikō-in
KYU YASUDA TEIEN
YOKOAMI
Nikolai-do (Cathedral)
Akihabara
AKIHABARA
KANDA-SAKUMACHO
ASAKUSABASHI
Asakusabashi
YANAGIBASHI
Kokugikan (National Sumo Stadium)
Sumo Hakubutsukan
Edo-Tokyo Hakubutsukan
Ryōgoku
Kanda
AWAJICHO
KANDA-SUDACHO
IWAMOTOCHO
OGAWAMACHI
AWAJICHO
Yasukuni-dōri
NIHOMBASHI-BAKUROCHO
Ryogoku-bashi
Keiyō-dōro
HIGASHI-KANDA
Kandaheisei-dōri
IWAMOTOCHO
Bakurocho
HIGASHI-NIHOMBASHI
RYŌGOKU
Edo-dōri
NIHOMBASHI-YOKOYAMACHO
HIGASHI-NIHOMBASHI
BAKURO-YOKOYAMA
Expressway No 7 Komatsugawasen
Eshima-sugiyama-jinja
CHITOSE
Yoshin-ji
NIHOMBASHI-ODENMACHO
KODENMACHO
UCHIKANDA
Chuō-dōri
KANDA
Kanda

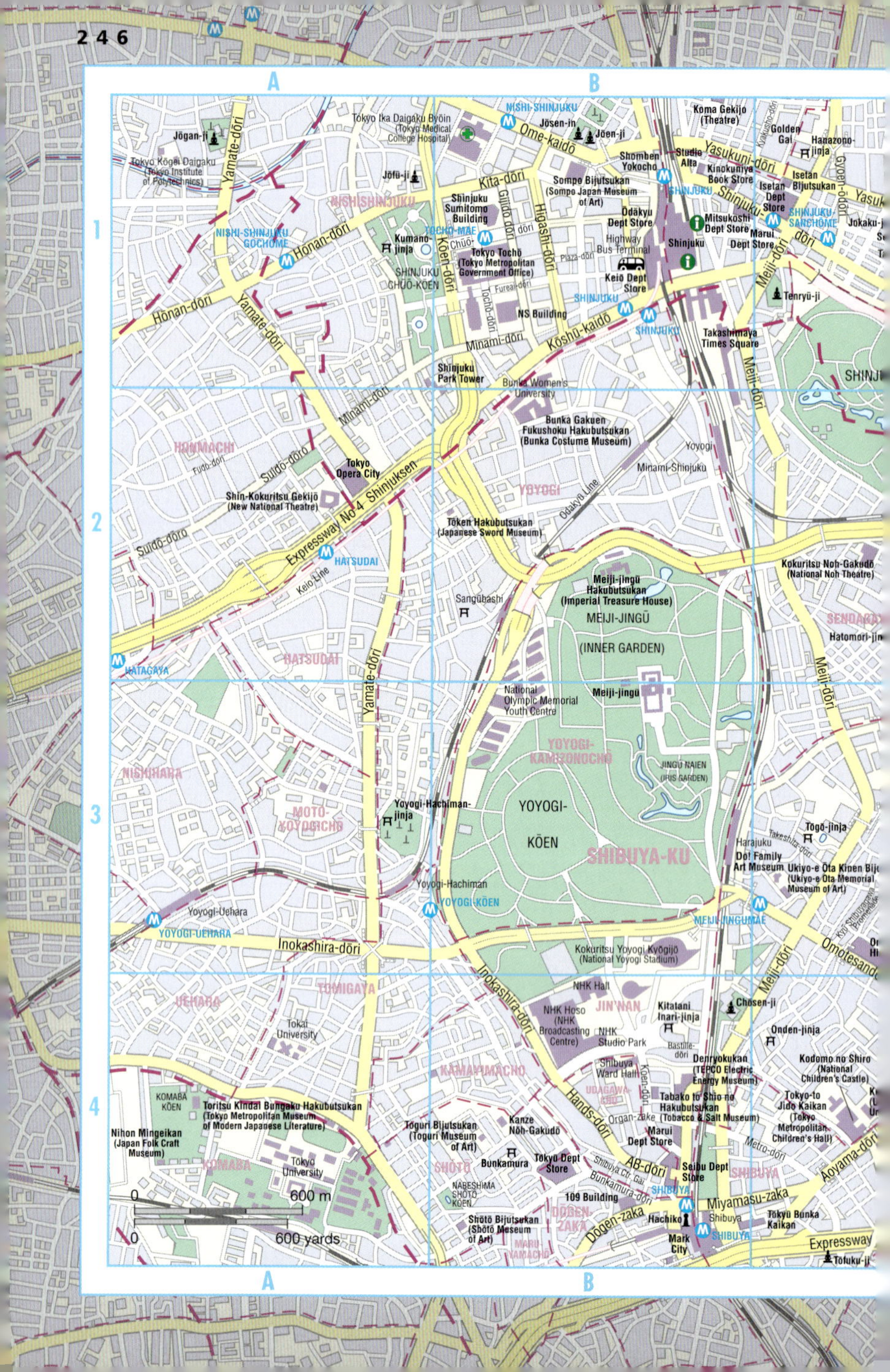
A
B
1
2
3
4
Jōgan-ji
Tokyo Kōgei Daigaku (Tokyo Institute of Polytechnics)
Yamate-dōri
Tokyo Ika Daigaku Byōin (Tokyo Medical College Hospital)
NISHI-SHINJUKU
Jōsen-in
Jōen-ji
Ōme-kaidō
Koma Gekijō (Theatre)
Golden Gai
Hanazono-jinja
Yasukuni-dōri
Studio Alta
Shomben Yokochō
Kinokuniya Book Store
Isetan Dept Store
Isetan Bijutsukan
Gyoen-dōri
Jōfū-ji
Kita-dōri
Sompo Bijutsukan (Sompo Japan Museum of Art)
SHINJUKU
Shinjuku-dōri
Shinjuku Sumitomo Building
NISHISHINJUKU
Odakyū Dept Store
Mitsukoshi Dept Store
SHINJUKU-SANCHŌME
Marui Dept Store
NISHI-SHINJUKU GOCHŌME
Honan-dōri
TOCHŌ-MAE
Kumano-jinja
Chūō-dōri
Tokyo Tochō (Tokyo Metropolitan Government Office)
Highway Bus Terminal
Shinjuku
Plaza-dōri
Keiō Dept Store
SHINJUKU CHŪŌ-KŌEN
Kōen-dōri
Giidō-dōri
Higashi-dōri
Fureai-dōri
Tochō-dōri
Tenryū-ji
Hōnan-dōri
Yamate-dōri
NS Building
Minami-dōri
Kōshū-kaidō
SHINJUKU
Takashimaya Times Square
Meiji-dōri
Shinjuku Park Tower
Bunka Women's University
Minami-dōri
Bunka Gakuen Fukushoku Hakubutsukan (Bunka Costume Museum)
HONMACHI
Fudo-dōri
Suidō-dōri
Tokyo Opera City
Yoyogi
Minami-Shinjuku
Odakyū Line
YOYOGI
Shin-Kokuritsu Gekijō (New National Theatre)
Expressway No 4 Shinjuku-sen
Tōken Hakubutsukan (Japanese Sword Museum)
Suidō-dōri
HATSUDAI
Keiō Line
Kokuritsu Nō-Gakudō (National Noh Theatre)
Meiji-jingū Hakubutsukan (Imperial Treasure House)
Sangūbashi
MEIJI-JINGŪ
(INNER GARDEN)
SENDAGAYA
Hatomori-jinja
HATAGAYA
HATSUDAI
Meiji-dōri
National Olympic Memorial Youth Centre
Meiji-jingū
Yamate-dōri
YOYOGI-KAMIZONOCHŌ
NISHIHARA
JINGŪ NAIEN (IRIS GARDEN)
YOYOGI-KŌEN
MOTO-YOYOGICHŌ
Yoyogi-Hachiman-jinja
SHIBUYA-KU
Tōgō-jinja
Harajuku
Takeshita-dōri
Dō! Family Art Museum
Ukiyo-e Ōta Kinen Bijutsukan (Ukiyo-e Ōta Memorial Museum of Art)
Yoyogi-Hachiman
YOYOGI-KŌEN
Yoyogi-Uehara
MEIJI-JINGUMAE
YOYOGI-UEHARA
Inokashira-dōri
Kokuritsu Yoyogi Kyōgijō (National Yoyogi Stadium)
Omotesandō
Inokashira-dōri
NHK Hall
UEHARA
TOMIGAYA
NHK Hōsō (NHK Broadcasting Centre)
JIN'NAN
Kitatani Inari-jinja
Chōsen-ji
Onden-jinja
Tokai University
NHK Studio Park
Bastille-dōri
Shibuya Ward Hall
Denryokukan (TEPCO Electric Energy Museum)
Kodomo no Shiro (National Children's Castle)
KAMIYAMACHŌ
UDAGAWA-CHŌ
Kōen-dōri
KOMABA KŌEN
Toritsu Kindai Bungaku Hakubutsukan (Tokyo Metropolitan Museum of Modern Japanese Literature)
Hands-dōri
Tabako to Shio no Hakubutsukan (Tobacco & Salt Museum)
Tokyo-to Jidō Kaikan (Tokyo Metropolitan Children's Hall)
Organ-zaka
Nihon Mingeikan (Japan Folk Craft Museum)
Toguri Bijutsukan (Toguri Museum of Art)
Kanze Nō-Gakudō
Marui Dept Store
Metro-dōri
Aoyama-dōri
KOMABA
Tokyo University
SHŌTŌ
Bunkamura
Tokyū Dept Store
Seibu Dept Store
SHIBUYA
Shibuya Ctr. Gai
AB-dōri
Bunkamura-dōri
NABESHIMA SHŌTŌ KŌEN
109 Building
SHIBUYA
Miyamasu-zaka
0
600 m
0
600 yards
DŌGEN-ZAKA
Dōgen-zaka
Hachikō
Shibuya
Tōkyū Bunka Kaikan
Shōtō Bijutsukan (Shōtō Museum of Art)
MARUYAMACHŌ
Mark City
SHIBUYA
Expressway
Tofuku-ji

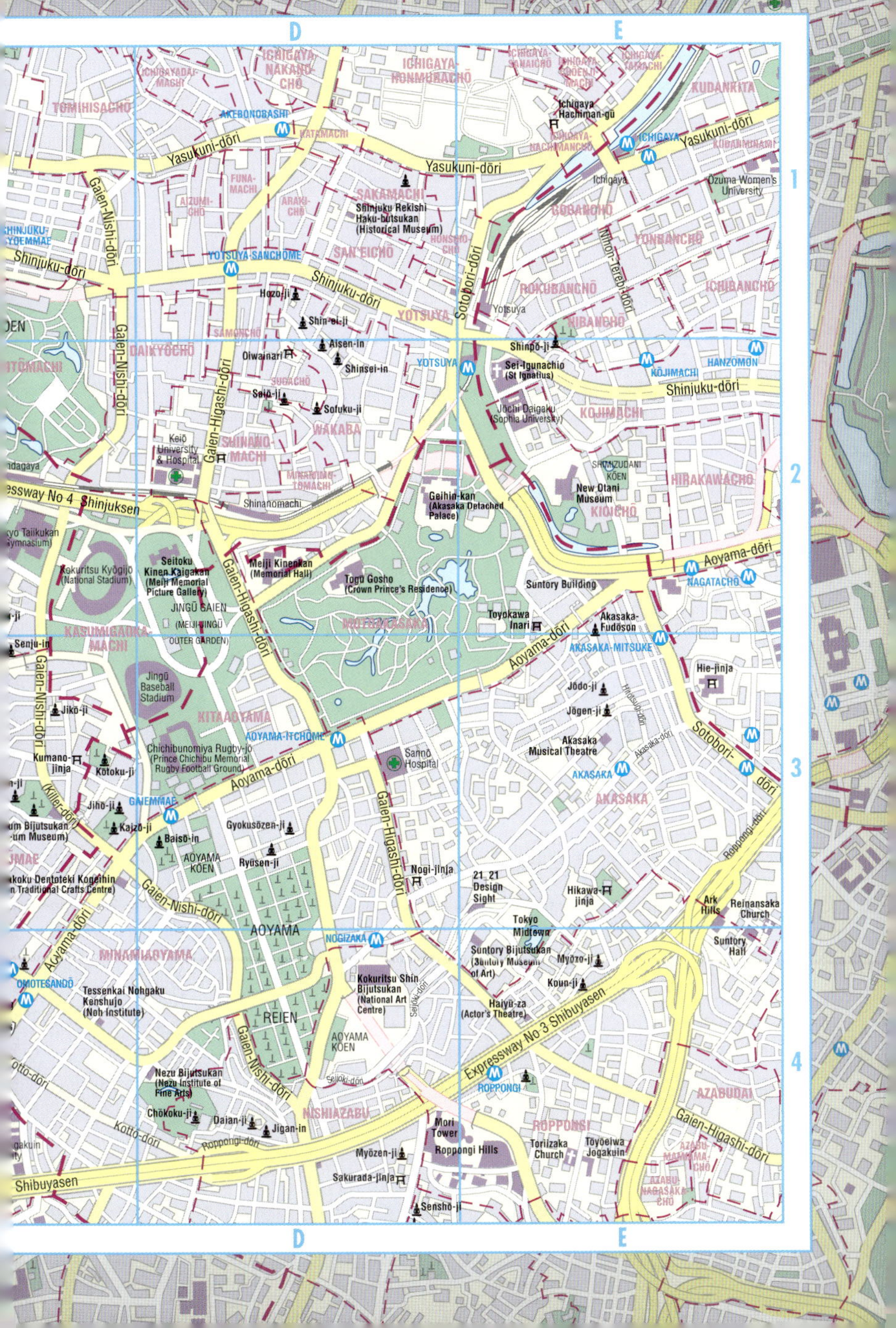
D
E
1
2
3
4
TOMIHISACHŌ
ICHIGAYA NAKANO-CHŌ
ICHIGAYA HONMURACHŌ
KUDANKITA
Ichigaya Hachiman-gū
AKEBONOBASHI
ICHIGAYA
Yasukuni-dōri
Ichigaya
Ōzuma Women's University
FUNA-MACHI
SAKAMACHI
Shinjuku Rekishi Haku-butsukan (Historical Museum)
GOBANCHŌ
YONBANCHŌ
Gaien-Nishi-dōri
SAN'EICHŌ
Shinjuku-dōri
YOTSUYA-SANCHŌME
Hozo-ji
Shin-ei-ji
YOTSUYA
Sotobori-dōri
Yotsuya
ROKUBANCHŌ
Nihon-terebi-dōri
ICHIBANCHŌ
NIBANCHŌ
DAIKYŌCHŌ
Oiwainari
Aisen-in
Shinsei-in
Shinpō-ji
YOTSUYA
Sei-Igunachio (St Ignatius)
KŌJIMACHI
HANZŌMON
Seiō-ji
Sofuku-ji
WAKABA
Jōchi Daigaku (Sophia University)
KŌJIMACHI
Keiō University & Hospital
Gaien-Higashi-dōri
SHINANO-MACHI
SHIMIZUDANI KŌEN
HIRAKAWACHŌ
Expressway No 4 Shinjuksen
Shinanomachi
Geihin-kan (Akasaka Detached Palace)
New Otani Museum
KIOICHŌ
Aoyama-dōri
Kokuritsu Kyōgijō (National Stadium)
Seitoku Kinen Kaigakan (Meiji Memorial Picture Gallery)
JINGŪ GAIEN
(MEIJI-JINGŪ OUTER GARDEN)
Meiji Kinenkan (Memorial Hall)
Tōgū Gosho (Crown Prince's Residence)
Suntory Building
NAGATACHŌ
MOTOAKASAKA
Toyokawa Inari
Akasaka-Fudōson
KASUMIGAOKA-MACHI
AKASAKA-MITSUKE
Senju-in
Jingū Baseball Stadium
Hie-jinja
Jōdo-ji
Jōgen-ji
Jikō-ji
KITAAOYAMA
AOYAMA-ITCHŌME
Kumano-jinja
Kotoku-ji
Chichibunomiya Rugby-jō (Prince Chichibu Memorial Rugby Football Ground)
Sannō Hospital
Akasaka Musical Theatre
AKASAKA
Jihō-ji
Kajzō-ji
GAIEMMAE
Gyokusōzen-ji
AKASAKA
Baisō-in
Ryūsen-ji
AOYAMA KŌEN
Nogi-jinja
21_21 Design Sight
Hikawa-jinja
Ark Hills
Reinansaka Church
Roppongi-dōri
Suntory Hall
AOYAMA
NOGIZAKA
Tokyo Midtown
MINAMIAOYAMA
OMOTESANDŌ
Tessenkai Nohgaku Kenshujo (Noh Institute)
Kokuritsu Shin Bijutsukan (National Art Centre)
Suntory Bijutsukan (Suntory Museum of Art)
Myōzo-ji
Koun-ji
Haiyū-za (Actor's Theatre)
REIEN
AOYAMA KŌEN
Expressway No 3 Shibuyasen
Nezu Bijutsukan (Nezu Institute of Fine Arts)
ROPPONGI
AZABUDAI
Chōkoku-ji
Daian-ji
Jigan-in
NISHIAZABU
Mori Tower
ROPPONGI
Roppongi Hills
Torizaka Church
Toyoeiwa Jogakuin
Gaien-Higashi-dōri
Kotto-dōri
Myōzen-ji
Sakurada-jinja
Senshō-ji
Shibuyasen
AZABU-NAGASAKA-CHŌ
D
E

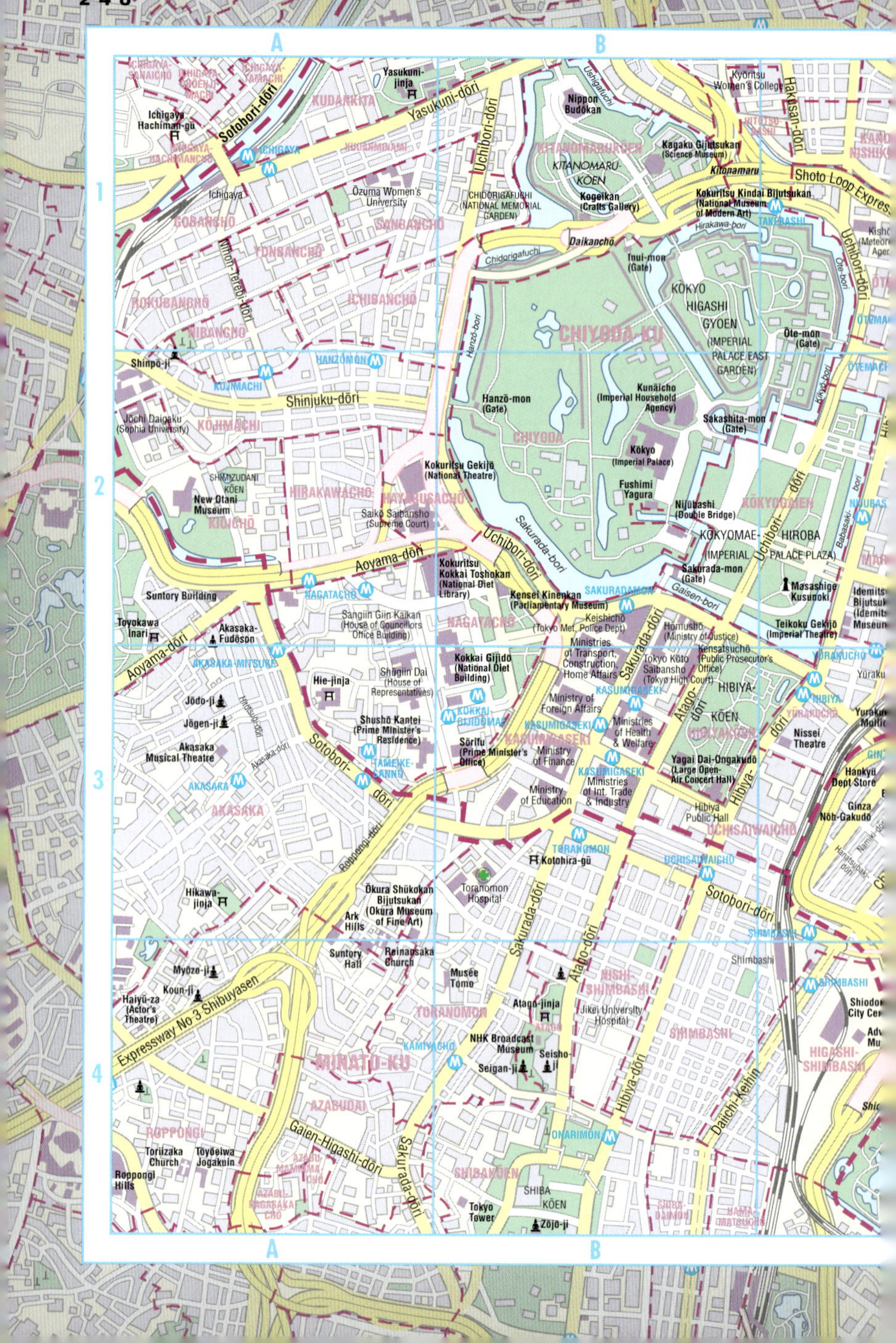

A
B
1
2
3
4
Yasukuni-jinja
Kyoritsu Women's College
Hakusan-dōri
Ichigaya Hachiman-gū
Sotobori-dōri
ICHIGAYA
KUDANKITA
Yasukuni-dōri
Uchibori-dōri
Nippon Budokan
Kagaku Gijutsukan (Science Museum)
KITANOMARUKŌEN
KITANOMARU-KŌEN
Kitanomaru
Shoto Loop Express
Kokuritsu Kindai Bijutsukan (National Museum of Modern Art)
Kogeikan (Crafts Gallery)
TAKEBASHI
Ichigaya
Ōzuma Women's University
CHIDORIGAFUCHI (NATIONAL MEMORIAL GARDEN)
GOBANCHŌ
SANBANCHŌ
Daikanchō
Hirakawa-bori
Chidorigafuchi
Inui-mon (Gate)
Uchibori-dōri
Ōte-bori
YONBANCHŌ
KŌKYO HIGASHI GYOEN (IMPERIAL PALACE EAST GARDEN)
ROKUBANCHŌ
ICHIBANCHŌ
CHIYODA-KU
Ōte-mon (Gate)
NIBANCHŌ
Hanzō-bori
Shinpō-ji
HANZŌMON
KŌJIMACHI
Shinjuku-dōri
Hanzō-mon (Gate)
Kunaichō (Imperial Household Agency)
Sakashita-mon (Gate)
Jōchi Daigaku (Sophia University)
KŌJIMACHI
CHIYODA
Kokuritsu Gekijō (National Theatre)
Kōkyo (Imperial Palace)
Fushimi Yagura
Nijūbashi (Double Bridge)
KŌKYOGAIEN
New Otani Museum
KIOICHŌ
HIRAKAWACHŌ
HAYABUSACHŌ
Saikō Saibansho (Supreme Court)
Sakurada-bori
KŌKYOMAE-HIROBA (IMPERIAL PALACE PLAZA)
Babasaki-bori
Aoyama-dōri
Kokuritsu Kokkai Toshokan (National Diet Library)
Sakurada-mon (Gate)
Masashige Kusunoki
Suntory Building
NAGATACHŌ
Kensei Kinenkan (Parliamentary Museum)
SAKURADAMON
Gaisen-bori
Sangiin Giin Kaikan (House of Councillors Office Building)
NAGATACHŌ
Keishichō (Tokyo Met. Police Dept)
Hōmushō (Ministry of Justice)
Teikoku Gekijō (Imperial Theatre)
Toyokawa Inari
Akasaka-Fudōson
Ministries of Transport, Construction, Home Affairs
Kensatsuchō (Public Prosecutor's Office)
YŪRAKUCHŌ
Aoyama-dōri
AKASAKA-MITSUKE
Kokkai Gijidō (National Diet Building)
Tokyo Kōtō Saibansho (Tokyo High Court)
Hie-jinja
Shūgiin Dai (House of Representatives)
KASUMIGASEKI
HIBIYA-KŌEN
Jōdo-ji
KOKKAI GIJIDOMAE
Ministry of Foreign Affairs
HIBIYA
YŪRAKUCHŌ
Jōgen-ji
Shushō Kantei (Prime Minister's Residence)
KASUMIGASEKI
Ministries of Health & Welfare
Nissei Theatre
Akasaka Musical Theatre
Sōrifu (Prime Minister's Office)
KASUMIGASEKI
Ministry of Finance
HIBIYAKŌEN
TAMEIKE-SANNŌ
Yagai Dai-Ongakudō (Large Open-Air Concert Hall)
Hankyu Dept Store
AKASAKA
Sotobori-dōri
KASUMIGASEKI
Ministries of Int. Trade & Industry
Ministry of Education
Hibiya Public Hall
Ginza Nōh-Gakudō
AKASAKA
UCHISAIWAICHŌ
Roppongi-dōri
TORANOMON
Kotohira-gū
UCHISAIWAICHŌ
Toranomon Hospital
Sotobori-dōri
Hikawa-jinja
Ōkura Shūkokan Bijutsukan (Okura Museum of Fine Art)
Ark Hills
SHIMBASHI
Suntory Hall
Reinanzaka Church
Sakurada-dōri
Atago-dōri
Shimbashi
Myōzo-ji
Musée Tomo
NISHI-SHIMBASHI
SHIMBASHI
Koun-ji
Haiyū-za (Actor's Theatre)
TORANOMON
Atago-jinja
Jikei University Hospital
Shiodome City Cen
Expressway No 3 Shibuyasen
NHK Broadcast Museum
SHIMBASHI
KAMIYACHŌ
Seigan-ji
Seisho-ji
HIGASHI-SHIMBASHI
MINATO-KU
AZABUDAI
Hibiya-dōri
Daiichi-Keihin
ROPPONGI
Gaien-Higashi-dōri
ONARIMON
Torilzaka Church
Tōyōeiwa Jogakuin
SHIBAKŌEN
Roppongi Hills
SHIBA KŌEN
Tokyo Tower
Zōjō-ji
Sakurada-dōri
SHIBA-DAIMON
HAMA-MATSUCHŌ

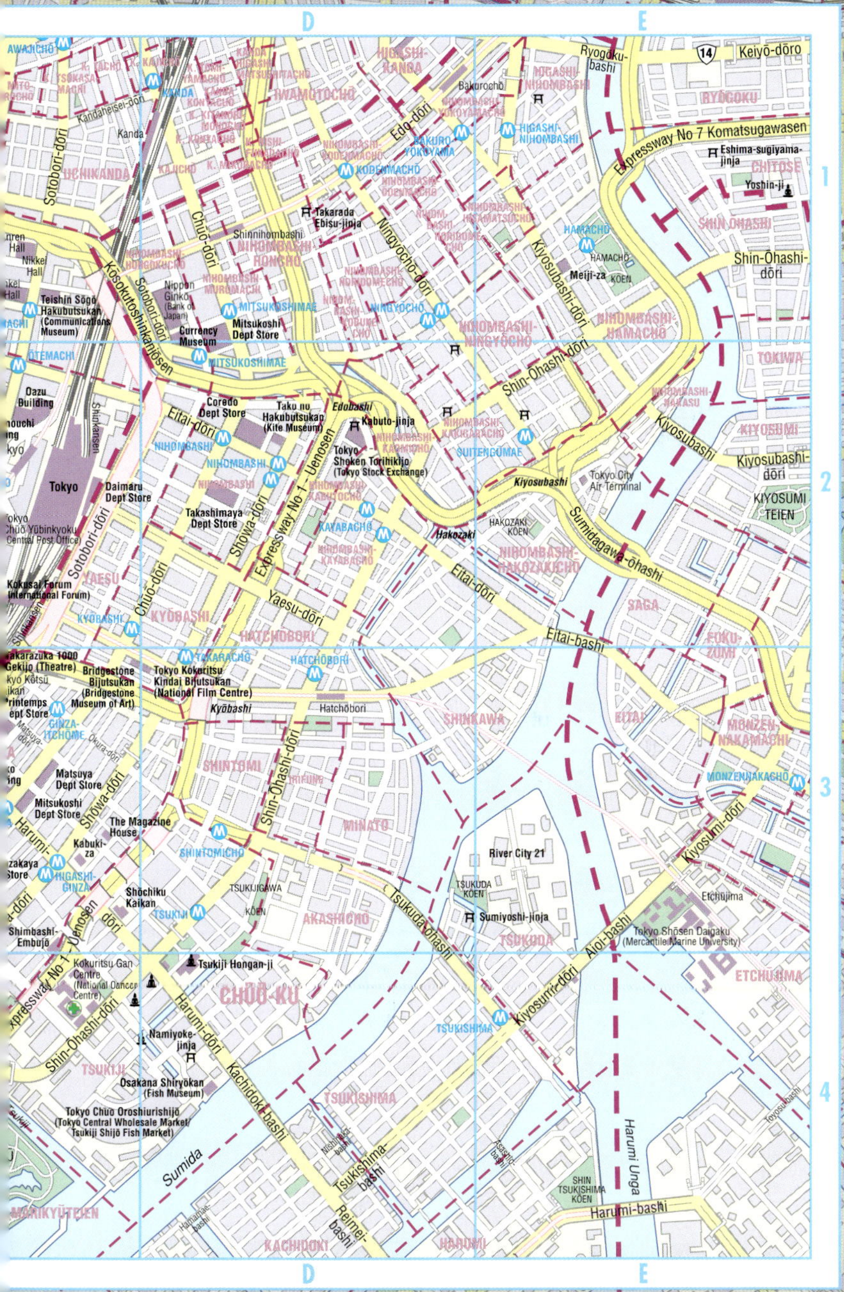
D
E
1
2
3
4
Ryogoku-bashi
Keiyō-dōro
Bakurochō
Iwamotochō
Kanda
Uchikanda
Sotobori-dōri
Chūō-dōri
Edo-dōri
Ningyōchō-dōri
Kiyosubashi-dōri
Expressway No 7 Komatsugawasen
Eshima-sugiyama-jinja
Chitose
Yoshin-ji
Ryōgoku
Shin-Ōhashi
Shin-Ōhashi-dōri
Hamachō
Meiji-za
Nihombashi-Hamachō
Tokiwa
Takarada Ebisu-jinja
Shinnihombashi
Nihombashi Honchō
Nippon Ginkō (Bank of Japan)
Currency Museum
Mitsukoshimae
Mitsukoshi Dept Store
Teishin Sōgō Hakubutsukan (Communications Museum)
Ōtemachi
Kosokutoshinkanjōsen
Nihombashi-Ningyōchō
Ningyōchō
Shin-Ōhashi-dōri
Coredo Dept Store
Taku no Hakubutsukan (Kite Museum)
Edobashi
Kabuto-jinja
Tokyo Shōken Torihikijo (Tokyo Stock Exchange)
Eitai-dōri
Nihombashi
Expressway No 1 - Uenosen
Suitengūmae
Kiyosubashi
Tokyo City Air Terminal
Kiyosumi
Kiyosubashi-dōri
Kiyosumi Teien
Oazu Building
Tokyo
Shinkansen
Daimaru Dept Store
Takashimaya Dept Store
Shōwa-dōri
Kayabachō
Hakozaki
Hakozaki Kōen
Nihombashi-Hakozakichō
Sumidagawa-Ōhashi
Saga
Fukuzumi
Tokyo Chūō Yūbinkyoku (Central Post Office)
Yaesu
Yaesu-dōri
Kokusai Forum (International Forum)
Kyōbashi
Hatchōbori
Eitai-bashi
Takarazuka 1000 Gekijō (Theatre)
Bridgestone Bijutsukan (Bridgestone Museum of Art)
Tokyo Kokuritsu Kindai Bijutsukan (National Film Centre)
Takarachō
Printemps Dept Store
Ginza-Itchōme
Shinkawa
Eitai
Monzen-Nakachō
Monzennakachō
Matsuya Dept Store
Mitsukoshi Dept Store
Shintomi
Shin-Ōhashi-dōri
Minato
The Magazine House
Kabuki-za
Shintomichō
Harumi-dōri
Higashi-Ginza
Shōchiku Kaikan
Tsukiji
Tsukijigawa Kōen
Akashichō
River City 21
Tsukuda Kōen
Sumiyoshi-jinja
Tsukuda
Kiyosumi-dōri
Etchūjima
Tokyo Shōsen Daigaku (Mercantile Marine University)
Aioi-bashi
Shimbashi Embujō
Kokuritsu Gan Centre (National Cancer Centre)
Tsukiji Hongan-ji
Chūō-ku
Namiyoke-jinja
Tsukishima
Etchūjima
Osakana Shiryōkan (Fish Museum)
Tokyo Chūō Oroshiurishijō (Tokyo Central Wholesale Market/ Tsukiji Shijō Fish Market)
Kachidoki-bashi
Tsukishima-bashi
Harumi Unga
Sumida
Hamarikyū Teien
Reimei-bashi
Shin Tsukishima Kōen
Harumi-bashi
Kachidoki
Harumi
D
E

STREET INDEX

ZONES

General Index

Tokyo Metro System

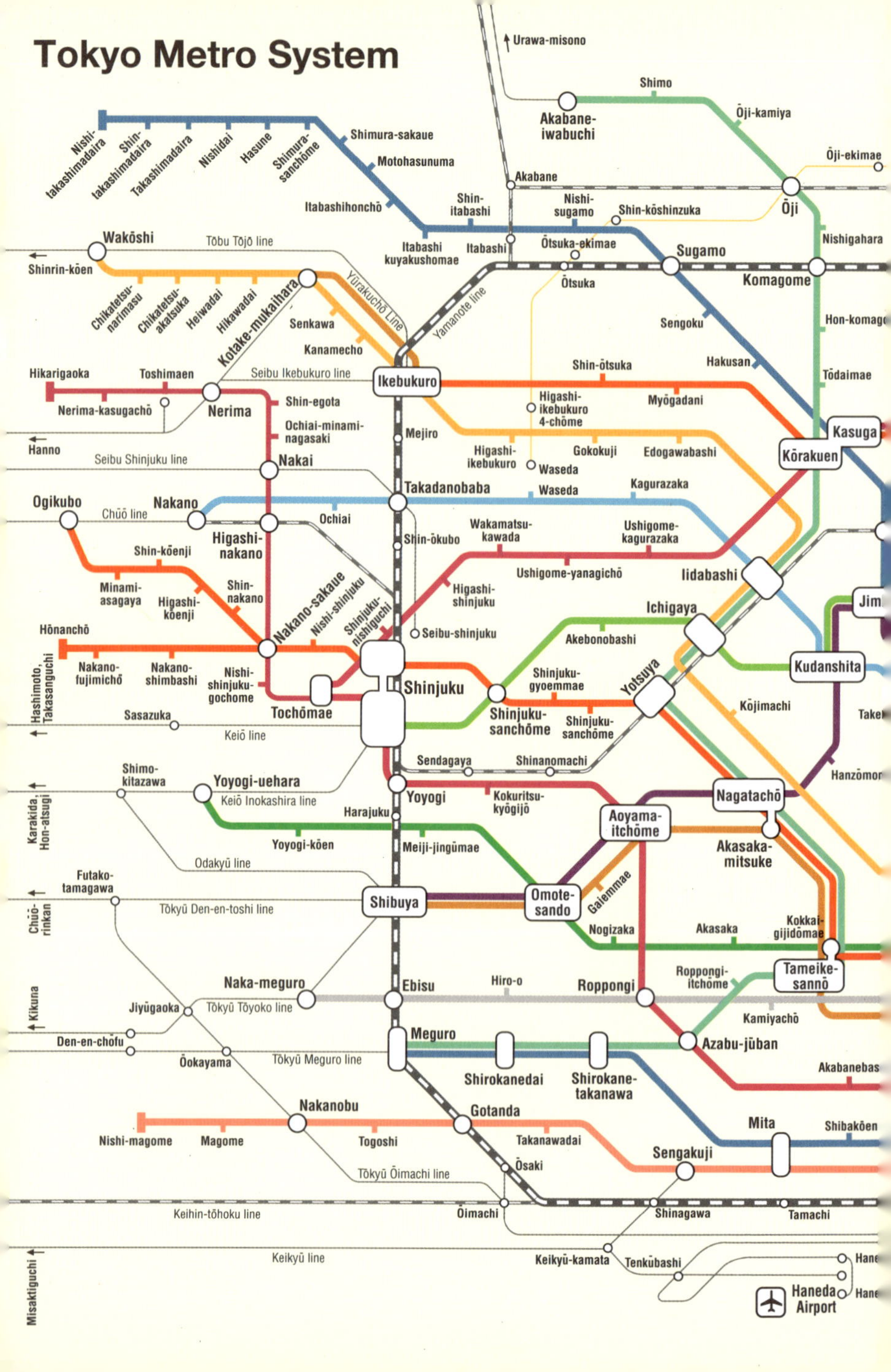